T3-BNU-303

RESTRUCTURING JAPAN'S FINANCIAL MARKETS

RESTRUCTURING JAPAN'S FINANCIAL MARKETS

Edited by
Ingo Walter
New York University
and
Takato Hiraki
International University of Japan

NEW YORK UNIVERSITY SALOMON CENTER
Leonard N. Stern School of Business

BUSINESS ONE IRWIN
Homewood, Illinois 60430

Project editor: Mary Conzachi
Production manager: Laurie Kersch
Printer: Book Press, Inc.

Library of Congress Cataloging-in-Publication Data

Restructuring Japan's financial markets / edited by Ingo Walter and Takato Hiraki.

p. cm.

"New York University Salomon Center, Leonard N. Stern School of Business."

ISBN 1-55623-636-0

1. Capital market—Japan—Congresses. 2. Money market—Japan—Congresses. 3. Finance—Japan—Congresses. I. Walter, Ingo. II. Hiraki, Takato. III. New York University. Salomon Center.

HG5772.R47 1993

332'.0952—dc20 93-11393

Printed in the United States of America

1 2 3 4 5 6 7 8 9 0 BP 0 9 8 7 6 5 4 3

CONTENTS

PART THREE

FINANCIAL MARKET DIMENSIONS OF THE COST OF CAPITAL

PART FOUR

ISSUES OF CONDUCT AND CORPORATE GOVERNANCE

PREFACE

During the late 1980s and early 1990s, a great deal of attention began to be paid to the structure and operation of financial markets in Japan. Japanese equity values seemed to be rising to exotic levels with no apparent limit. Japanese industrial companies were financing themselves, often with equity-linked bonds, at interest rates allegedly providing them with a cost of capital advantage never before seen in international competition. Japanese financial institutions, banks and securities firms alike, seemed to be mounting an onslaught on global financial markets propelling them ever higher in the rankings based on size and capital. Whatever problems remained seemed to be secondary to the stellar performance turned in by the Japanese financial sector, apparently far outstripping even that of the industrial sector of the economy.

Much of this performance now appears to have been a mirage, built upon very high Japanese savings rates and excellence in the performance of the Japanese real economy, which for many years succeeded in masking serious problems, indeed rot, that was gradually eating away at the operational integrity of the country's financial markets. These problems have now surfaced with a vengeance, and constitute the focus of this volume. It is the product of a conference in Tokyo held in May 1992, jointly sponsored by the International Management Research Institute, International University of Japan, and the New York University Salomon Center on the occasion of the tenth anniversary of IUJ's founding.

The volume contains thematic papers presented at the conference by Japanese, European and American participants. The editors are grateful to the respective authors for their contributions. They are also grateful to Raj Aggarwal, Masahiko Aoki, Ken Ariga, Bill Brown, Stephen B. Cohen, Henry James, Morihisa Kaneko, Shigekuni Kawamura, E. Han Kim, Yotaro Kobayashi, Sachio Kohjima, Fumiko Konya, Keiichi Kubota, Yoh

Kurosawa, Takeshi Nojima, Shinichiro Ohta, Toshiyuki Otsuki, Mitsuo Sato, Shigeo Uchida, John S. Wadsworth, Jr., Takaaki Wakasugi, and Richard W. Wright for helpful discussions during and after the conference.

Both Chairman Yushin Yamamuro and Honorary Chairman Sohei Nakayama of the International University of Japan did much to make the conference possible. Support for the conference was provided by the two sponsoring institutions as well as Nihon Keizai Shimbun, Japan Airlines, Bank of Tokyo, Ltd., Dai-ichi Mutual Life Insurance Co., Fuji Bank, Ltd., The Industrial Bank of Japan, Ltd., Meiji Mutual Life Insurance Co., Mitsubishi Bank, Ltd., Mitsubishi Trust & Banking Corp., Nippon Mutual Life Insurance Co., Sakura Bank, Ltd., Sanwa Bank, Ltd., and the Sumitomo Bank, Ltd. Further thanks are due the Institute for Southeast Asian Studies (ISEAS) in Singapore, where much of the editorial work was done.

Finally, we are grateful to Ms. Ann Rusolo and Ms. Gayle DeLong for capably and efficiently handling preparation of the manuscript for publication.

Ingo Walter New York City
Takato Hiraki Niigata
September 1992

OVERVIEW

JAPAN'S FINANCIAL MARKETS IN PERSPECTIVE

Ingo Walter

Much has been written in recent years about the efficiency and integrity of Japan's financial markets. The issues are as broad in scope as they are interesting and important, given the role of financial markets as allocators of capital and as determinants of performance of the economy as a whole. They have been brought into particularly sharp relief with the development of global cross-linkages among financial markets, and their integration through modern technologies into an increasingly "seamless" web.

Financial firms based in the world's major markets are engaged in vigorous competition with one-another. So are borrowers and issuers seeking pools of capital on the most favorable possible terms, as well as investors—especially institutional investment managers striving to beat the relevant indexes or benchmarks—focused on serving the ultimate assetholders through high levels of portfolio performance. And so are the world's financial centers, both by serving their domestic clients well and by capturing financial-intermediation flows from competing centers abroad. In today's world the absence in a particular market of appropriate financial instruments, lack of innovative financial products or processes, lack of liquidity or information, high costs, absence of a level playing field, and other sources of substandard performance can increasingly be avoided by simply migrating transactions to other financial centers where conditions are better.

Japan's financial markets have come under close scrutiny in this context, both domestically and internationally. Prominent among these are fixed securities commissions and other sources of high transactions costs, restrictions on market entry and operations facing domestic and foreign players, relative lack of financial innovation, and off-market arrangements between and among principals and agents that defeat the goal of equitable treatment of market participants. While difficult to observe, the actual and opportunity costs to the Japanese economy have undoubtedly been high. Yet reform has been slow and difficult in coming—despite continued domestic and international pressure—in view of the vested interests involved and the close relationships that exist between those interests and the regulators, given the unique Japanese political overlay.

Most of the structural problems that today are characteristic of Japan's financial markets have long existed. They have consistently been recognized by Japanese and foreign observers alike. Yet, they have largely been overshadowed by the superior performance of the real sector of the Japanese economy, and by the now-famous "economic bubble" of the late 1980s—involving the largest speculative run-ups in real estate and equity values in Japanese history. This made the need for structural reforms seem very remote indeed, and further strengthened the underlying vested interests.

Like a receding tide exposing dangerous rocks and shoals, more recent developments have revealed previously hidden problems of stability, efficiency and transparency in Japan's financial markets. Over a three-year period beginning in 1990 Japanese equity values dropped to less than half their previous levels. Real estate values collapsed. Undercollateralized bank lending based on equities and real property surfaced, as did capital adequacy problems of banks as the value of their large equity holdings diminished and loan losses had to be recorded—this just prior to the application of 8% risk-adjusted capital adequacy standards under the auspices of the Bank for International Settlements in January 1994. Pressures mounted on brokers to reimburse their important customers for equity market losses—a privilege not extended to others—and giving ordinary shareholders the impression of a "stacked deck" in a market they would do well to avoid. Troubling links between financial institutions and organized crime emerged, along with the usual spate of apologies and resignations among senior officials of financial firms, even as politicians and bureaucrats urged calm and confidence.

But apologies, resignations and government exhortations have little to do with the basic structural problems of the Japanese financial system. Pressures for structural market reforms have now increased significantly, and the real question is whether they stand a chance against the entrenched special interests—working in a highly politicized environment—to maintain as much of the *status quo ante* as possible.

As in the United States, one focus of reform has been removal of line-of-business restrictions that limit competition in financial markets, notably Article 65 of Japan's Securities and Exchange Law, which limits access to the securities industry on the part of credit institutions. As in the 1970s in the United States and 1980s in the United Kingdom, another focus of reform has been the abolition of fixed commissions on the Tokyo Stock Exchange. And, as in many other financial markets around the world, still another focus of reform has been the overall degree of transparency and fairness provided to all financial market participants by the rules of the game and their effective and impartial enforcement.

Periods of financial market turmoil, of course, often lead to changes in the way markets are organized. The key is to avoid the trap of creating new performance problems in the effort to remove the old ones. The U.S. experience is instructive in this regard. The 1920s covered a period of great confidence in the American economy, a time when the economies of Europe were beset by problems. Equity investments and assets under management in mutual funds soared as part of a speculative frenzy of historic proportions. Money was easy, banks were accommodative, and margin loans grew dramatically. Brokers, dealers and other participants rigged and manipulated markets shamelessly in what John Kenneth Galbraith once called an "orgy of corporate larceny."

The October 1929 New York Stock Exchange crash brought the game to an abrupt halt. Within 18 months of its all-time high in September 1929, the Dow Jones Industrials index had fallen by over 40% and two years later it had fallen by some 80%. Countless scandals emerged, including the embezzlement of customer funds by the chairman of the New York Stock Exchange. Bankruptcies, arrests and suicides predictably followed, as did massive public pressure on Congress and the new Administration of Franklin D. Roosevelt to clean up the mess and reform financial market conditions thought to have been instrumental in triggering the bank collapses and Great Depression of the 1930s.

The response—in the form of the Securities and Exchange Act of 1933 and the Banking Act of 1934—were efforts to deal with the underlying causes, rather than symptoms, of perceived problems in U.S. banking and financial markets. Federal deposit insurance, reforms in the operation of the Federal Reserve System, creation of the Securities and Exchange Commission, and imposition of the Glass-Steagall restrictions on securities activities on the part of commercial banks, among other measures, all date back to this period. Many of the reforms undoubtedly were both necessary and reasonably well executed. Others may have been overkill, or lacked the built-in flexibility that would facilitate future adaptation to changing market conditions. They also created new vested interests that would make future regulatory change vastly more difficult, and a few—notably the design of deposit insurance—sowed the seeds of future financial instability problems.

Some 60 years later, Japan now finds itself in similar circumstances under rather different economic and political conditions. The country must, as a matter of urgency, undertake structural reforms in its financial markets that:

- Promote *static* efficiency in terms of minimizing the economic resources that are absorbed in the process of financial intermediation, narrow spreads and information asymmetries, and assure adequate market liquidity.
- Promote *dynamic* efficiency by creating an environment in which new financial instruments and processes can be developed in response to evolving borrower and investor needs, in the context of rapidly changing technologies.
- Foster *transparency* and fairness in which buyers and sellers understand what is being bought and sold and the precise conditions of the transaction, with levels of disclosure appropriate to the nature of the market participants involved.
- Assure *equality of competitive opportunity* on the part of domestic and foreign-based market participants alike, the only condition that will guarantee financial market efficiency and viability in the context of globally integrated markets.
- Advance the cause of *stability* in banking and financial markets so that problems do not become systemic in nature, by means of regulation that is appropriately targeted on the financial functions being performed, whether they involve banking, insurance or securities transactions.

These are the benchmarks against which the existing structure of Japan's financial markets and their regulatory overlay must be calibrated. Even more complex is the assessment of the optimum financial linkages between financial institutions and non-financial firms. Is the German type approach involving strong bank influence within industrial groups, the Japanese *keiretsu*-type arrangement, or the Anglo-American capital-markets approach superior in terms of contributing to satisfactory economic performance? Any changes in the structure of financial regulation are bound to have an impact on this critical dimension of corporate control as well.

This volume is addressed to all of these difficult issues, and brings to bear the views of Japanese, American and European academic observers with no particular stakes in prospective regulatory changes, and therefore able to be reasonably objective on these matters. The book is divided into four substantive sections: (I) Issues relating to the structure and performance of Japan's financial markets; (II) A comparison of the regulatory issues facing Japan with those in Europe and the United States; (III) Financial market aspects of the cost of capital; and (IV) How transactions are conducted in Japan's financial markets and their implications for corporate governance. Here we shall briefly summarize the discussion of each of these issues.

I. FINANCIAL SYSTEM STRUCTURE AND PERFORMANCE

Trading activity in the Japanese stock market is characterized by a hierarchy in terms of trading volume and company size, with the Tokyo Stock Exchange at the apex. In Chapter 1, Shinji Takagi argues that the hierarchical structure of the Japanese stock market reflects a set of regulations, restrictions or practices that are highly specific to the market. The hierarchical order of stock exchanges has resulted from the microstructure of the secondary market itself, where stock trading is based on competitive auction rules with no obligatory market-making. In this type of market environment, liquidity becomes dependent on trading intensity so that, in the absence of transactions costs, there are natural economic forces to minimize total liquidity risk by concentrating trading in a central location.

Most other aspect of Japanese stock market organization are likewise shaped by government regulations or restrictions, including (1) tougher listing requirements of the larger exchanges relative to those of the regional exchanges, (2) a "market concentration" requirement that listed stocks be traded only at the exchanges, (3) a fixed brokerage commission system, (4) an effective ceiling on the number of member firms admitted to the Tokyo Stock Exchange, and (5) restrictive regulations imposed on margin transactions. Combined, these regulatory distortions—which effectively suppress the role of the regional stock exchanges—also help perpetuate their existence in the hierarchy of the Japanese stock market.

Chapter 2, by Yui Kimura and Thomas A. Pugel, provides an analysis of the economic performance of the securities industry in Japan. It focuses on the markets for two major types of securities activities or services: (1) The provision of underwriting services for new issues of corporate securities; and (2) The trading of corporate securities, in terms of both brokerage services and securities dealing. The analysis applies the classic structure-behavior-performance framework of market economics. The standard of performance used is the achievement of economic efficiency, together with minimization of exploitation of conflicts of interest.

Kimura and Pugel document that the number of securities firms in Japan fell from 1949 through the mid-1980s, and that the number has risen somewhat since then as foreign firms have entered the Japanese industry. Continued dominance of the Big 4 firms—Nomura, Yamaichi, Daiwa, and Nikko—was confirmed by estimates of four-firm seller concentration ratios. Seller concentration is high for the underwriting of corporate securities, for bond brokering, and for the provision of investment trust services. In addition, *keiretsu* links of smaller securities firms to the Big 4 firms imply that the effective concentration is higher than the direct estimates indicate.

Barriers to entry and mobility exist as well. There has been almost no entry of new Japanese firms since the late 1960s, and those foreign firms which have entered have faced substantial mobility barriers. The most severe barrier has been the legal prohibition to entry on the part of banks and insurance companies, based on the Securities and Exchange Law of 1948.

The structure of moderate-to-high seller concentration and barriers to entry interact with the regulatory approach of the Ministry of Finance to produce behavior that results in both economic inefficiencies and exploitation of conflicts of interest. Kimura and Pugel discuss inefficiencies arising from the underwriting fees and brokerage commissions that are collectively fixed by sellers. Shortcomings in economic performance include the distortions caused by inappropriate price signals to buyers, encouragement of nonprice competition for business, and limitations on the ability of new firms to compete for business using pricing. Inefficient pricing also encourages such practices as churning of accounts and investment trusts to generate commissions and the payment of secret compensation to certain investors.

The authors show that profit rates, on average, have been very high indeed for the larger securities firms since at least the mid-1970s, a finding consistent with a lack of effective competition and the resulting inefficiencies in pricing.

Kimura and Pugel conclude with the implications for reform of Japanese regulatory policy toward the securities industry. First, a new commission independent of the Ministry of Finance should be created to regulate securities firms and markets. Second, fixed brokerage commission rates should be scrapped. Third, fixed fees for underwriting should be ended. Fourth, the legal barriers to the entry of banks (and perhaps also insurance companies) into securities activities should be removed. The authors show that these four measures would go far toward altering the structure and behavior of the Japanese securities industry in ways that promote the interests of the users of financial services and Japan's national interest.

Chapter 3, by Yakov Amihud and Haim Mendelson, discusses the relationship between liquidity and asset prices in Japan, and examines some of its major implications. A theoretical framework is presented, which predicts that expected returns on capital assets depend on their liquidity in addition to risk. The authors show that—for both bonds and stocks—the greater the illiquidity of the asset, the greater its return. The effects of liquidity on asset values and returns are far larger than the one-time trading costs, because the costs of illiquidity are incurred *repeatedly* whenever the asset is traded.

Amihud and Mendelson focus their empirical analysis on increasing market liquidity as a public policy objective in Japan, where trading costs are much higher than they are in the United States. They show that increasing liquidity is expected to reduce the cost of capital and to increase asset values, and examine four strategies for accomplishing this objective: (a) Repealing the securities transfer tax; (b) Eliminating the increase in the minimum tick from 1 to 10 yen for stocks whose prices exceed 1,000 yen; (c) Reducing commission rates; and (d) Extending trading hours. The authors expect the first three measures to be liquidity-enhancing, and predict that their implementation would significantly increase the prices of assets traded in the Japanese capital markets.

In Chapter 4, Kevin Hebner and Takato Hiraki examine several characteristics of the Japanese market for initial public offerings (IPOs), the first time shares are offered to the public by companies initiating listing on stock exchanges. They apply a model that allows the firm to recapture, from informed traders with whom a contractual relationship exists, a part of the "money left on the table" and derive the prediction that, for such traders, their expected trading profits and their explicit compensation from the company should be negatively correlated. Two corollary predictions follow for these informed traders—their explicit compensation and the firm's mean initial return should be negatively correlated, and their trading profits during the IPO process as well as the firm's mean initial return should be positively correlated.

The authors find that: (1) Contrary to the U.S. evidence, mean initial returns in Japan are at least not inversely related to IPO size; (2) Again unlike the U.S. experience, the relationship between mean initial returns and the proportion of the IPO representing shares sold by existing major Japanese shareholders (rather than by the company itself) is not only statistically less significant, but also turns out to be weakly positive, for the Japanese IPOs; and (3) Mean initial returns decreased significantly following regulatory changes to the IPO market which occurred in April 1989 and introduced an element of public bidding into the determination of IPO prices. The second and third empirical results are both consistent with predictions that follow directly from adverse-selection models of IPO pricing.

In Chapter 5, Roy C. Smith examines one of the more interesting phenomena in postwar international financial markets, the raising of massive amounts of equity capital by Japanese companies outside of Japan. He addresses two questions: (1) Why so much equity? and (2) Why abroad? The answers to the first question relate to special opportunities in equity markets related to the dramatic run-up in Japanese stock prices in the 1980s, an "abnormal" period that came to an abrupt end in the early 1990s—with Japanese corporates having to redeem large amounts of equity-linked debt securities due to the worthlessness of the equity warrants. The answers to the second question relate to the regulatory structure of the Japanese financial market, which made undertaking new equity issues significantly cheaper abroad, mainly in London. Recapturing this business, which the author thinks would be highly beneficial for the Japanese economy, depends on meaningful and sustained regulatory reforms centered around removing barriers to market competition.

II. GLOBAL COMPETITIVENESS BENCHMARKS

Section II of this volume is devoted to an evaluation of efforts to come to grips with the problem of optimum financial regulation in other parts of the world, notably in Europe and the United States, and compares them with the regulatory-reform challenges that confront Japan.

Chapter 6, by Ingo Walter, considers the German experience with universal banking as an amalgam of strengths and weaknesses, with some degree of convergence likely between the universal and separate approaches to the organization of financial services firms during the 1990s. EC financial liberalization and the wider use of the securities by continental European corporations, together with increasingly performance-oriented portfolio management on the part of mutual funds, insurance companies and other institutional investors, is leading to a gradual shift away from bank finance, and the appearance of unwanted takeover attempts through acquisition of shareholdings by unaffiliated (often foreign) investors. At the same time, easing of bank activity-limits in the United Kingdom and the United States is beginning to allow them to play a larger role in industrial restructuring transactions, and to exploit some of the information and relationship advantages they possess as lenders.

Certainly in terms of international competitive performance, financial institutions that are subject to legal or regulatory barriers on the lines of business they are allowed to pursue as well as how (and where) they may pursue them could well suffer at the hands of rival institutions that are freely able to choose the optimum organization form. The fact is that regulatory environments which are totally unrestricted as to the organizational form of financial services firms are home to true universal banks. Scrapping Article 65 and other line-of-business distortions in Japan may well lead to a significant role for universal banks in that environment as well.

In Chapter 7, Jean Dermine notes that the integration of financial markets in Europe represents a very useful case-study of the international integration of financial markets in a setting where independent national central banks retain substantial regulatory and supervisory powers. Dermine presents the essential characteristics of the European banking industry, and analyzes the early effects of European financial integration. He shows that the European banking industry is undergoing a massive restructuring, caused by competitive policy changes among national regulators. He also analyzes the regulatory framework proposed by the European Commission for the integration of financial markets, and argues that far more work remains to be done to achieve open and stable markets. In particular, the prudential regulation of firms with significant risks located in foreign offices should be organized jointly by the home and host country authorities.

In Chapter 8, Bevis Longstreth, Ivan E. Mattei, and David P. Mason point out that periods of acute economic stress provide an opportune time to reassess the efficacy of regulatory policy in achieving its intended objectives. During the late 1980s and early 1990s, prompted in large part by the savings and loan crises, the United States was in the midst of a comprehensive reexamination of regulations affecting banks and S&Ls. That reexamination generated a consensus that change is necessary. However, it failed to produce a plan of action for several reasons, including a lack of strong political leadership and, by many of the policymakers involved, a misdiagnosis of the problems to be solved. With Japan in the midst of its own re-examination of financial services regulation—with particular attention to the separation between commercial banking and securities activities—developments in the Japanese securities markets, and the implications of those developments for Japanese commercial banks, have brought a new urgency to that re-examination. Participants in Japan's policy debate are advised to look to the U.S. experience and learn from its mistakes.

The authors set forth the thesis that effective regulatory reform requires (1) an understanding of the proper role of regulation in serving the public interest, and (2) an application of that understanding to the banking industry in order to derive sound regulatory policies. In the authors' view, regulatory restrictions on the banking industry are justified if, *but only if*, the individual pursuit of economic gain by market participants would lead to inefficient outcomes. That simple precept suggests six guidelines for sound banking regulation:

- Competitive forces should be harnessed wherever possible to do the bidding of policymakers.
- Regulatory medicine should be limited to just what's needed to cure the ill.
- Price controls are bad policy.
- Activity prohibitions should generally be avoided.
- Diversification is good.
- Regulation should permit, if not foster, dynamic efficiency.

The authors apply these guidelines to develop specific reform proposals regarding deposit insurance, interstate banking, industry consolidation,

Glass-Steagall and other product restrictions, universal banking and the bank regulatory structure.

III. FINANCIAL MARKET DIMENSIONS OF THE COST OF CAPITAL

Section III of this volume addresses one of the more controversial aspects of Japan's financial system—its bearing on the cost of capital facing the country's industrial firms and, in turn, their competitive performance in global markets.

In Chapter 9, Jeffrey A. Frankel recalls that a number of American businessmen in the 1980s raised the question whether the cost of capital was persistently lower in Japan than in the United States, and whether this difference has placed U.S. firms at a competitive disadvantage vis-a-vis Japanese rivals.

This issue has been examined in a large body of research into the nature of the two financial systems. The general finding has been that the cost of corporate capital, by most measures, was indeed lower in Japan than in the United States in the 1980s. This conclusion corresponded well to a conclusion of mainstream macroeconomists, namely, that a shortfall in the U.S. national saving rate in the 1980s drove the rate of return in the United States above that prevailing in Japan and elsewhere, thereby attracting the large capital inflow that was the counterpart of the infamous bilateral trade imbalance.

Frankel examines the cost of capital in Japan in the 1980s. He finds evidence for all four of the claims that, individually or in combination, have been put forward by the low-cost-of-capital school: (1) The real cost of debt was lower in Japan than the U.S.; (2) Debt-equity ratios were higher; (3) The cost of equity was lower; and (4) Japanese firms were better able to use banking relationships to avoid information problems and thereby reduce the effective cost of capital below rates prevailing in open securities markets.

In this context, it is useful to distinguish two sorts of changes in the Japanese financial system: (1) longer-run structural trends; and (2) shorter-run cyclical developments. The late 1980s covered a period of expansionary Japanese monetary policy. This pushed down interest rates and pushed up price/earnings ratios in the Japanese stock market. It was followed by a tightened monetary policy in the early 1990s, which pushed up interest rates and succeeded in "bursting the stock market bubble." The underlying structural trend of international liberalization worked to narrow the gap between rates of return in the two countries since the early 1980s. But it was not until the cyclical tightening of monetary policy in 1990 that the narrowing of the gap showed up dramatically, and observable measures show that the cost of capital in Japan thereafter was no longer below that in the United States.

Frankel discusses a number of puzzles. First, if low interest rates explain the high level of the Japanese stock market in the late 1980s, what explains the *increase* in stock market prices during the decade? Second, if banking relationships represent a more efficient way to raise capital, why have Japanese corporations been moving away from them and relying more heavily on securities markets for their funds?

Chapter 10, by Toshiaki Tachibanaki, estimates the cost of capital facing the banking industry in Japan, using a method that enables the author to take into account several features of financing or collecting funds that are different from the nonfinancial sector. Emphasis is placed on the difference not only between categories of banks but also between individual banks. An additional purpose of the chapter is to compare the cost of capital for the banking sector between Japan and the U.S., which sheds light on competition among banks in these two countries.

In Chapter 11, Timothy A. Luehrman argues that, if indeed some Japanese corporations have benefitted from a lower cost of capital than their competitors elsewhere in the world, it is mainly because their capital, ownership and governance structures made them more efficient users of capital. It is not because government restrictions on Japanese capital markets succeeded in "trapping" capital, or because Japanese investors were inherently more "patient" than other investors.

Luehrman shows that published formal comparisons of the weighted average cost of capital in the two countries suffer from four serious shortcomings: (1) They have built-in violations of the Modigliani-Miller theory; (2) They are not controlled for differences in risk; (3) Country-level measurement errors bias the estimates; and (4) Estimates of the cost "gap" have very large standard errors. In contrast, most studies that *do not* suffer from these flaws also do not find significant capital cost differences between Japan and the United States.

He then argues that internal considerations of how companies use capital affects the required expected return on that capital. A stylized comparison of Japanese and U.S. companies suggests that the traditionally strong relationships between debtors and creditors, shareholders and lenders, and among a company's many commercial affiliates help attenuate agency and information problems in Japan. This in turn makes capital less expensive. The magnitude of this organizationally-driven cost of capital difference has been small, however, and not all Japanese companies benefit from it.

Finally, Luehrman argues that the relationships which made for more efficient use of capital in Japan have been eroding, as evidenced by striking decreases in leverage, increases in issuance of securities outside Japan, and an unmistakable loosening of ties between large Japanese industrial companies and their main banks. These changes are likely to continue, suggesting an increase in conflict among stakeholders, and a concomitant increase in the marginal cost of capital.

IV. ISSUES OF CONDUCT AND CORPORATE GOVERNANCE

One of the key elements in judging the performance of any financial market is equitable treatment of all market participants. The final section of this book concerns the conduct of financial transactions in Japan, as well as linkages between financial institutions and business firms.

In Chapter 12, Clifford W. Smith provides an economic framework for the discussion of ethics in the context of the operations of financial markets. He presents evidence which indicates that markets impose substantial costs on institutions and individuals engaging in unethical behavior, so that market forces provide private incentives for ethical behavior. He identifies the nature of these market forces, how they help to enforce contracts, and those transactions where they are most likely to be effective. He uses the 1991 Salomon Brothers treasury bond bidding scandal as an example of the effectiveness of market forces in imposing costs on parties to unethical conduct.

In Chapter 13, Young S. Park considers Japan's financial scandals in the summer of 1991, beginning with an announcement by the Japan Security Dealers Association (JSDA) that the Big Four and 13 second tier brokerage companies paid ¥171.9 billion in loss compensation to 608 corporate clients and 9 individuals. These payments by brokerage companies were believed to have violated the Security and Exchange Law, which prohibits firms from attracting customers by promising compensation for possible losses on their investments or from paying compensation without promising it beforehand, and reflects long-standing ties between brokers, regulators, and favored customers. He summarizes the characteristics of the Japanese brokerage industry in terms of: (1) Strong government regulations via a licensing system and fixed brokerage commission; (2) An oligopolistic brokerage industry dominated by the Big Four; (3) A decline in the importance of individual investors in the stock market; and (4) A lack of incentives for fund managers at industrial corporations to undertake higher risk and higher return portfolios. Under these circumstances, major brokerage companies in Japan competed against each other to keep important market shares in brokerage and underwriting businesses with corporate customers. There is no clear distinction between brokerage and underwriting functions in Japan, which facilitates smooth behind-the-scenes teamwork, and makes it possible for the brokerage companies to manipulate transactions for the sake of maintaining strategic relationships.

Given excess funds raised through the security markets in the 1980s, Japanese corporations reinvested in the security market and needed a system which could enhance returns. *Tokkin* accounts were set up for that purpose. Unlike ordinary *tokkin* (specified money in trust) contracts—in which an investor or designated advisory company instructs trust banks how to invest funds—brokerage companies directly managed funds in *eigyo-tokkin* accounts. Such discretionary accounts enabled the security companies to move in and out of big clients' accounts easily. In return for guaranteeing a minimum return, brokerage companies could turn the excess returns (above the guaranteed return) from *eigyo-tokkin* accounts into brokerage commissions through unnecessary transactions.

Park presents a game-theoretic analysis which shows that providing loss compensation to fund managers from industrial corporations has been the dominant strategy for the Japanese brokerage companies under non-price competition. He argues that the liberalization of brokerage commissions alone cannot solve the loss compensation problem and that, as a preventive measure, providing incentives to fund managers at large corporations to set higher return goals should be accompanied by liberalization of brokerage commissions.

In Chapter 14, Frederick D.S. Choi focuses on the renewed interest in developing an international set of accounting standards that will serve as a universal language for international commerce and finance. This effort stems from the asymmetry between business decisions that are increasingly global in orientation versus financial information that is premised on a diverse set of national accounting standards and practices. Far from being an international language, accounting remains a babble of heterogeneous dialects. Given the differences between Japanese financial reporting standards and those employed elsewhere in the world, international accounting standards are increasingly being promoted in Japan as a promising solution to the problem of international accounting diversity. However, acceptance of international standards by Japan's financial executives and market regulators is likely to be slow in the absence of any empirical evidence as to whether or not international accounting differences are actually a problem in the sense that they in fact impact market behavior.

Choi reports on the results of a survey of capital market participants designed to assess whether and to what extent international accounting differences—i.e., accounting principles, financial disclosure and auditing differences—impact market decisions. Interviews with institutional investors, corporate issuers, market regulators and investment underwriters in the world's major capital markets suggest that the decisions of a significant number of market participants are affected by accounting differences. While all groups attempt to cope with accounting diversity, coping mechanisms varied in terms of their nature and success both within and between groups.

Choi also examines whether differences in accounting treatment for goodwill affect merger premia associated with the acquisition of U.S. target companies. The evidence suggests that merger premia are indeed associated with goodwill, and that higher premiums paid by U.K. acquirers are associated with not having to amortize goodwill to earnings. This suggests that the market for corporate control may not in fact be a level playing field due to differences in accounting standards.

In Chapter 15, Shinichi Watanabe considers two observations that seem to be particularly interesting as descriptions of changes in the sources of finance or Japanese companies since the mid-1970s: (1) The share of funds financed from their own internal resources increased significantly; and (2) Large-size firms reduced the fraction of their borrowing from banks as a source of external finance and turned to security markets to raise funds, while small and medium sized firms increased the share of bank borrowing and reduced the role of borrowing from associated companies.

The first observation has been explained by the rapid decline in the growth rate of the Japanese economy as a whole, and is plausible given the fact that external funds require extra agency costs. The second is believed to be due to the "reputation" effect, plausible because the reputation of a firm changes the structure of agency costs associated with alternative methods of external finance. Neither explanation, however, addresses one important question: Is there a relationship between the two observations, or are they a coincidence? Watanabe tries to answer this question by building a theoretical model that permits an examination of the effects of the decline of the growth rate of a firm on its external financial arrangements.

In the final chapter of the book, W. Carl Kester considers a number of highly controversial issues relating to corporate governance in Japan. As global capital and product markets become more integrated, national differences in systems of corporate governance have been thrown into sharp relief. The contrast between the Japanese and Anglo-American systems of corporate governance appears particularly sharp. This has triggered considerable debate about the merits of each. In particular, aspects of the Japanese system of corporate governance have been criticized as promoting restraint of trade and being incompatible with competitive, free-market economics. This view has gained sufficient ascendancy in the United States that the U.S. Justice Department in 1992 announced its intention to take antitrust enforcement action against foreign companies whose "exclusionary activities" in their home markets are believed to have an adverse effect on U.S. exports. Japanese *keiretsu* were identified as being primary targets of this new enforcement.

Kester analyzes the Japanese corporate governance system and compares it to the Anglo-American system. He concludes that many Japanese business practices—such as cross shareholdings, reciprocal trading arrangements, close main-bank relationships, presidents clubs (within major *keiretsu*), lifetime employment, and others viewed as offensive to Anglo-American concepts of fair trade—are in fact elements of a rational system of incentives, safeguards, and dispute resolution processes that promote genuine transactional efficiency, not primarily restraint of trade. From this perspective, the absence of a deep and active market or corporate control in Japan should be viewed as a sign of effective corporate governance, not of unhealthy managerial entrenchment or welfare-reducing barriers to investment.

The author suggests that Japanese policymakers be cautious in responding to demands by critics that the *keiretsu* system of corporate ownership and governance be dismantled. It does harbor some problems that must be addressed, but they should be assessed with a complete understanding of the economic purposes served by the various commercial, financial, ownership, and information-sharing relationships commonly found among Japanese companies. For their part, American policymakers should take the effort to understand these economic purposes and critically examine the relative efficacy of existing U.S. governance institutions in comparison to those found in other nations.

PART ONE

FINANCIAL SYSTEM STRUCTURE AND PERFORMANCE

CHAPTER 1

HIERARCHY AND COMPETITION IN THE JAPANESE STOCK MARKET

Shinji Takagi

I. INTRODUCTION

The Japanese secondary stock market is characterized by a hierarchy of component markets in terms of trading volume and company size. At the top of this hierarchy is the Tokyo Stock Exchange, with the largest trading volume and the listing of the largest corporations. In terms of trading volume, the Tokyo Stock Exchange is followed by the Osaka Stock Exchange, the over-the-counter (OTC) market, the Nagoya Stock Exchange and five regional exchanges. In terms of company size, the OTC market has the least stringent registration (or listing) requirements so that the trading of the stocks of the smallest companies tends to take place there. There is an implicit understanding that these companies will eventually be listed at the larger exchanges as they increase in size. Likewise, companies that are listed at the regional exchanges are expected to move up eventually to the Tokyo Stock Exchange as their operations expand in size and geographical scale.

This chapter discusses the characteristics of the Japanese secondary stock market in terms of hierarchy and competition. The chapter argues

The author thanks Hirotaka Kobayashi for useful comments. The opinions and interpretations expressed are the author's personal views and do not necessarily reflect those of the Ministry of Finance.

that the hierarchical structure of the Japanese stock market reflects the set of regulations, restrictions and practices that are specific to the market. The most significant of these is the microstructure of Japanese stock exchanges where stock trading is based on competitive auction rules with no obligatory market making. In this type of market environment, liquidity becomes endogenous to trading intensity so that, in the absence of transactions costs, there are natural economic forces towards market concentration. The chapter also discusses the nature of intermarket competition in this environment.

The chapter is organized as follows. Section II presents an overview of salient features of the secondary stock market in Japan. Section III briefly explains the microstructure of the Japanese secondary stock market and the pattern of successive price movement of heavily traded stocks at the Tokyo Stock Exchange and in the OTC market. Section IV discusses the hierarchy of Japanese stock exchanges in terms of trading volume and market liquidity, and Section V the nature of intermarket competition and the extent of market integration in the Japanese stock market. Section VI discusses possible reasons why several exchanges can coexist with the Tokyo Stock Exchange. Finally, Section VII presents concluding remarks.

II. SALIENT FEATURES OF THE JAPANESE STOCK MARKET

The secondary stock market in Japan consists of eight organized stock exchanges and an OTC market (Table 1–1). The Tokyo Stock Exchange is by far the largest, with over 1600 listed stocks and a value of transactions in excess of 110 trillion yen (over 80 percent of the country's total stock trading) during 1991. The second largest is the Osaka Stock Exchange, followed by the OTC market and the Nagoya Stock Exchange. The value of stock trading at the remaining five exchanges (Kyoto, Hiroshima, Fukuoka, Niigata and Sapporo) is extremely small. For convenience, the term "regional exchanges" will be used in this chapter to refer to these five exchanges.

Of the eight exchanges, the exchanges in Tokyo, Osaka and Nagoya have two sections. At these exchanges, companies are in principle first listed in the second section and are moved up to the first section when they meet the more stringent listing requirements in terms of equity capital, ownership

TABLE 1–1
Stock Exchanges and the OTC Stock Market in Japan (at the end of or during 1991)

	Number of Member Firms[a]	*Number of Listed Companies*[b]		*Trading Value (in billions of yen)*
Exchanges:				
Tokyo	124	1,641		110,897
Section I		1,223		107,108
Section II		418		3,789
Osaka	113	1,158	(300)	18,723
Section I		851	(56)	16,921
Section II[c]		307	(244)	1,802
Nagoya	47	552	(103)	3,586
Section I		435	(16)	2,970
Section II		117	(87)	616
Kyoto	29	238	(1)	300
Hiroshima	20	198	(10)	149
Fukuoka	24	252	(27)	174
Niigata	18	199	(10)	208
Sapporo	18	191	(15)	123
OTC Market:	n.a.	446		5,043
Registered		430		5,009
Managed		16		34

[a] Excluding *saitori* and special members.
[b] For the Nagoya and regional exchanges, the numbers in parentheses refer to the numbers of independently listed companies. For Osaka, they are the numbers of stocks not cross-listed at Tokyo.
[c] Including special second section stocks, to which less stringent listing requirements are applied.

Source: Ministry of Finance; Tokyo Stock Exchange.

distribution, dividend performance and trading volume. In turn, first section companies may be moved down to the second section if they cease to meet those requirements.

The exchanges are membership associations whose operating revenues come mainly from the fees charged the member firms on the value or volume of stock transactions.[1] In addition to regular members, the exchanges in Tokyo, Osaka and Nagoya have what are called *saitori* (*nakadachi* in Osaka) members who mediate trades between member firms; in the regional exchanges, this function is performed by exchange officials. There is also a special securities company, Japan Kyoei Securities, whose function is to submit unmatched orders of local member firms at regional exchanges and Nagoya to the larger exchanges of Tokyo and Osaka, of which they are not members.[2]

Stock trading is conducted in two sessions per day. The morning session is from 9:00 to 11:00; the afternoon session runs from 12:30 to 3:00 in Tokyo, Osaka, Nagoya and Kyoto, and from 1:00 to 3:00 in the other exchanges.[3] A computerized trading system has been in operation at the Tokyo Stock Exchange since January 1982 and at the Osaka Stock Exchange since March 1991. At both exchanges, almost all listed stocks are now traded on the computerized system, leaving only the 150 most active stocks to the floor.

In Japan, the stock exchanges impose on member firms a requirement that they trade listed stocks only at the exchanges (the so-called "concentration" requirement). As a result, the OTC market has been small and subordinate to the exchanges. Although any unlisted stock can in principle be traded over the counter, OTC trading has been dominated by "registered stocks" (stocks that have met the registration requirements of the Japan Association of Securities Dealers) and "managed stocks" (stocks that are so designated by the association after they have been delisted at the exchanges). At the end of 1991, there were 430 registered stocks and 16 managed stocks (Table 1–1).

The Japan Association of Securities Dealers designates at least two securities companies that are, in theory, market makers (called *toroku* dealers, or TDs) for each OTC stock. The TDs are required at least twice a week to quote prices at which they must transact with investors. In practice, however, the TDs typically set spreads so large that hardly anyone actually trades with the TDs.[4] Consequently, securities companies generally submit all buy and sell orders to Japan OTC Securities, an intermediary firm.[5] Since October 1991, the Japan Association of Securities Dealers Automated Quotations (JASDAQ) has been in operation, where orders submitted by securities companies are entered on a computer-based automated trading system and executed by Japan OTC Securities. The function of Japan OTC Securities is comparable to that of a *saitori* member (see below) at the exchanges.

III. THE MICROSTRUCTURE OF THE JAPANESE STOCK MARKET[6]

The Japanese secondary stock market is an auction market. The *saitori* members (the *nakadachi* member in Osaka, exchange officials in the smaller exchanges, or Japan OTC securities in the OTC market) do not take positions in any stock and do not trade on their own account. They simply match buy and sell orders that are submitted by regular members, according to the two auction rules: the price priority principle and the time precedence principle. The price priority principle means that (1) market orders (which do not specify execution price) take precedence over limit orders (which specify execution price); and that (2) for limit orders, selling orders with the lowest price are first matched with buying orders with the highest price. The time precedence principle means that, for two or more orders with the same price, the earlier order takes precedence over the others. In the OTC market, however, no market orders are allowed.

Two types of auction method, called *itayose* and *zaraba*, are employed to set transaction prices. The *itayose* method, which is a call auction, establishes prices at the beginning of a trading session, after an interruption in trading and, in some cases, at the end of a trading session. The *itayose* method is also used when a large amount of orders come to the market within a short period of time. For each stock, the *itayose* method places all orders received during a specified period according to the price priority principle only, and sets the price so as to clear the market. Once the opening price is established, the *zaraba* method, which is a continuous auction, set stock prices on an on-going basis until the end of the session where the *itayose* method may again be used to set the closing price.

Because there is no obligatory market making in a *zaraba* market, the Japanese stock exchanges as well as the Japan Association of Securities Dealers have established two measures that are presumably meant to prevent a sharp price fluctuation. First, under the system of daily price limits, listed stocks cannot be traded at a price higher or lower than the daily limit given by the previous day's closing price. For instance, the maximum permissible amount of daily price change is 80 yen for the previous closing price of 500 yen, 100 yen for 1000 yen, 200 yen for 1500 yen, 300 yen for 2000 yen, and so forth.

Second, under the system of special price quotations, the exchange posts a "special bid quote" or "special asked quote" to solicit counter orders when there is a major order imbalance, rather than allowing the price to move too much too fast. If no counter orders are received for some time, a new special quote may be posted within the price quotation spread specified by the exchange (e.g., a one-time upward or downward movement from the last price is 5 yen if the price is less than 500 yen, 10 yen if less than 1000 yen, 20 yen if less than 1500, and so on). Obviously, these measures only work well when price fluctuations are caused by the "temporal fragmentation" of potential market participants (Garbade and Silber 1979). When there is a fundamental change in the equilibrium prices, however, they are impediments to the smooth adjustment of stock prices.

Although there is no obligatory market making, the pattern of successive price movement of heavily traded stocks at the Tokyo Stock Exchange is similar to what is considered to be the typical pattern of successive price movement in a specialist-dealer market in the United States (Takagi 1993).[7] For example, the price movement of a major company stock (HT) on July 11, 1991 was bounded by the upper price of 1180 yen and the lower price of 1170 yen and was characterized by perfectly negative serial correlation (Figure 1–1); while the price movement of another major company stock (NS) on the same day was not as perfect, it also unmistakably showed a clear pattern of negative serial correlation (Figure 1–2).

In contrast, the pattern of successive price movement of OTC stocks is similar to that of less heavily traded stocks at the Tokyo Stock Exchange: it does not show a clear pattern of negative serial correlation. For example, the price movement of one stock (TR) on February 27, 1992 showed a sharp uni-directional movement from 5800 yen to 5680 yen (or 12 ticks) in four quotations as well as a sharp jump from 5680 yen to 5780 yen (or 10 ticks) in one quotation (Figure 1–3). To a lesser extent, the price movement of another stock (TH) on February 26, 1992 also confirmed the tendency of OTC stock price changes to be positively correlated (Figure 1–4). This pattern of price behavior in the OTC market may reflect the absence of market orders and voluntary market making.

IV. HIERARCHY OF JAPANESE STOCK EXCHANGES

During recent decades, the relative importance of the Tokyo Stock Exchange has risen at the expense of the other exchanges. Tokyo now accounts for over 80 percent of the country's total stock trading, while Osaka accounts for less than 15 percent and the rest of the exchanges for only a few percentage points. Even this small share of the Nagoya and regional ex-

FIGURE 1–1
Transaction Prices at the Tokyo Stock Exchange (HT: July 11, 1991)

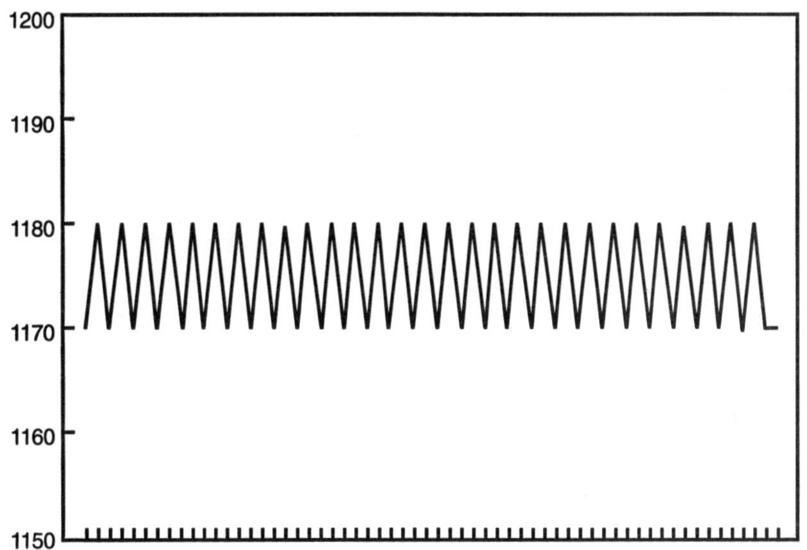

FIGURE 1–2
Transaction Prices at the Tokyo Stock Exchange (NS: July 11, 1991)

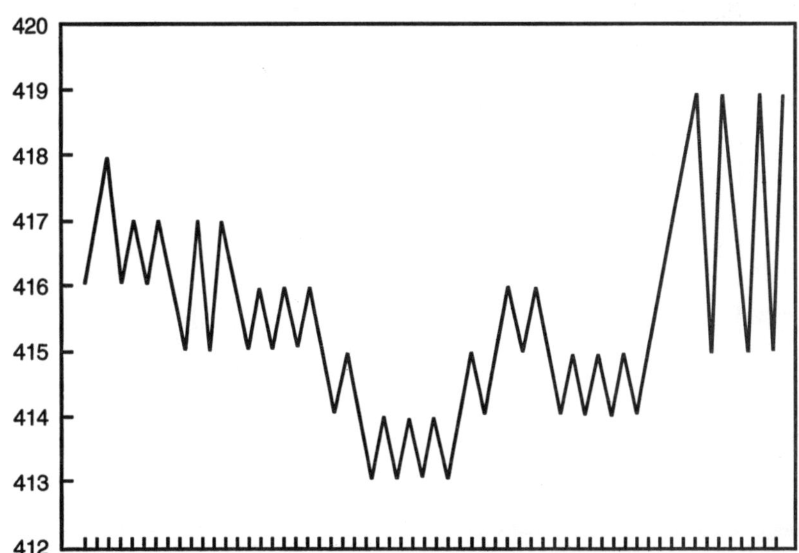

FIGURE 1–3
Transaction Prices in the OTC Market (TR: February 27, 1992)

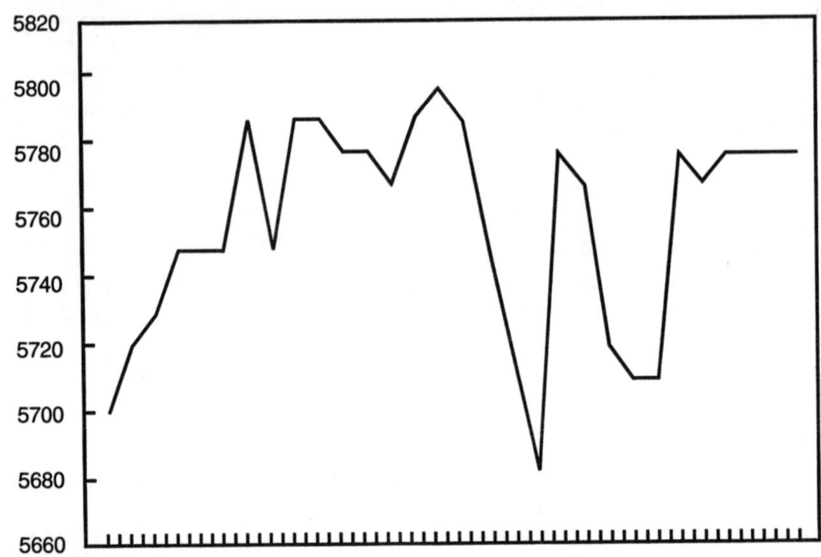

FIGURE 1–4
Transaction Prices in the OTC Market (TH: February 26, 1992)

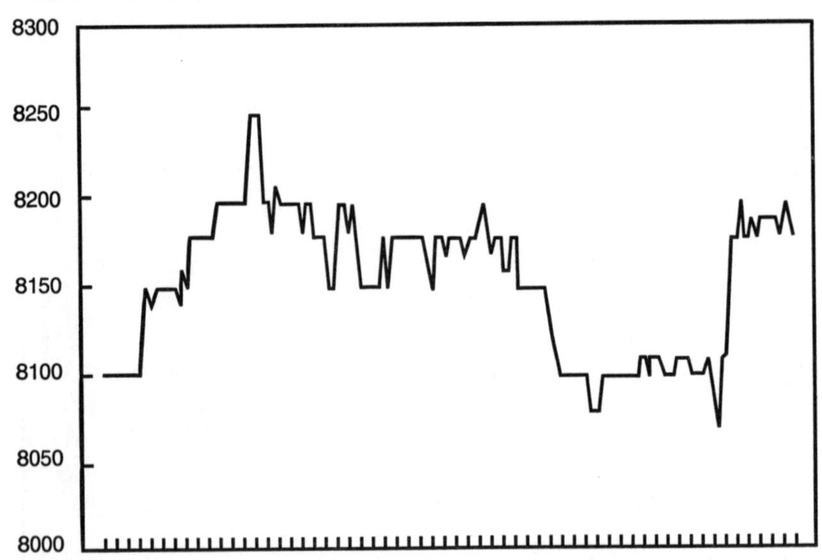

changes is likely an overstatement of their true importance because some orders placed there are in fact executed by Japan Kyoei Securities upon submission to the Tokyo and Osaka Stock Exchanges.

The limited role of the regional exchanges is indicated by the small number of companies that are independently listed at each exchange (Table 1–1). For example, the Kyoto Stock Exchange has only one company whose stock is independently listed.[8] The other regional exchanges have a somewhat greater number of companies which are independently listed, perhaps reflecting their closer ties with the local economies. For all practical purposes, the only substantive function of the regional exchanges is to serve as an exchange for a handful of local company stocks that are not listed at any other exchange.

This, however, does not necessarily mean that the independently listed local stocks are actively traded at the regional exchanges. One measure of the liquidity of an exchange can be given by its trade ratio, which is defined as the ratio of the number of stocks traded to the number of stocks listed on the exchange. According to this measure, we find that the liquidity of the regional exchanges is not very high, even if we confine our attention to the independently listed local stocks only (Table 1–2). Independently listed local companies are generally small in size and their stocks are often tightly held, so that very little trading in fact takes place.

The liquidity of the Nagoya Stock Exchange with respect to independently listed stocks is somewhat higher than that of the regional exchanges (Table 1–3). In Nagoya's first section, the trade ratio of independently listed stocks was always greater than 80 percent during 1988–1992, while the ratio of all first section stocks ranged between 11 and 28 percent.[9] During this period, the second section as a whole had a considerably higher trade ratio than the first section, although the trade ratio of independently listed second section stocks was lower than that of independently listed first section stocks. This reflects the fact that (1) proportionately more stocks (87 out of 117) are independently listed in the second section than in the first section (16 out of 435) and that (2) first section stocks are generally traded more heavily.

Although the share of Osaka in the country's stock trading has declined from almost 30 percent in 1960 to less than 15 percent currently, it is still significant relative to the other exchanges outside of Tokyo, in part reflecting the presence of some 300 Osaka-based companies whose stocks are independently listed. The overall liquidity, as measured by the trade ratio, of the Osaka Stock Exchange is also generally high (ranging on average be-

TABLE 1–2
Trade Ratios of Independently Listed Stocks in the Regional Stock Exchanges, 1988–92[a]

	Kyoto	*Hiroshima*	*Fukuoka*	*Niigata*	*Sapporo*
			(in percent of total)		
1988	0.00 (1)	0.65 (7)	0.42 (15)	0.60 (8)	0.40 (13)
1989	0.05 (1)	0.70 (7)	0.61 (17)	0.65 (9)	0.58 (13)
1990	0.00 (1)	0.77 (9)	0.80 (17)	0.81 (10)	0.72 (14)
1991	0.16 (1)	0.63 (11)	0.55 (27)	0.45 (9)	0.36 (14)
1992	0.05 (1)	0.39 (19)	0.36 (27)	0.61 (10)	0.33 (15)

[a] For each category, the trade ratio is the number of stocks traded as a percent of the total number of listed stocks. The figures are monthly averages for January only. The figures in parentheses refer to the numbers of independently listed stocks at the beginning of the month.

Source: Nihon Keizai Shinbun.

TABLE 1–3
Trade Ratios in Major Stock Exchanges and the OTC Market, 1988–92[a]

	Tokyo		*Osaka*		*Nagoya*		*OTC*
	1st	*2nd*	*1st*	*2nd*	*1st*	*2nd*	*registered*
			(in percent of total)				
1988	94.7	86.1	64.1	62.4	27.5 (83.3)	43.7 (62.6)	45
1989	96.5	87.8	68.0	67.7	26.6 (95.7)	55.7 (77.6)	61
1990	97.4	91.1	63.3	73.2	16.6 (92.1)	60.4 (80.3)	83
1991	93.5	67.5	50.3	52.1	15.0 (86.5)	40.7 (54.3)	59
1992	93.5	62.3	40.3	45.6	11.4 (84.6)	36.5 (48.5)	53

[a] For each category, the trade ratio is the number of stocks traded as a percent of the total number of listed (or registered) stocks. The figures are monthly averages for January only. For the Nagoya Stock Exchange, the figures in parentheses are for independently listed stocks only.

Source: Tokyo Stock Exchange; Osaka Stock Exchange; Nagoya Stock Exchange; and Japan Securities Dealers Association.

tween 40 and 70 percent during 1988-92),[10] although it is considerably lower than that of the Tokyo Stock Exchange (Table 1–3). The liquidity of the Osaka Stock Exchange is comparable to that of the OTC market.

Although the trade ratio of independently listed stocks is obviously greater, the Osaka Stock Exchange also has a significant role in the trading of some cross-listed stocks. It is well known that close to 300 Tokyo stocks are heavily traded in Osaka for a variety of historical, institutional or economic reasons.[11] In fact, trading in some of these stocks is so concentrated in Osaka that very little trading takes place in Tokyo. In general, their pattern of price movement in Osaka is similar to that of heavily traded stocks in Tokyo: successive price changes tend to be negatively serially correlated. The price movement of two such stocks (SH on February 14, 1992 and OP on February 7, 1992), however, seems to indicate that the range of price fluctuation is greater and the incidence of sharp changes (say, more than two ticks in one quotation) is more frequent than that of stock heavily traded in Tokyo (Figure 1–5 and Figure 1–6). It is not clear to what extent this reflects the difference in trading volume resulting from company size differences or the smaller involvement of member firms as market makers.

V. COMPETITION AND INTEGRATION IN THE JAPANESE STOCK MARKET

The "concentration" requirement means that member firms cannot trade listed stocks over the counter. For listed stocks, therefore, there is a definite segmentation in stock trading between the exchanges and the OTC market. Competition, however, exists between the exchanges and the OTC market when a corporation is deciding where to go public. The listing requirements of the exchanges are tougher than the registration requirements of the OTC market (Table 1–4), and there is some perception that registering in the OTC market is an initial step towards an eventual listing at an exchange (Table 1–5). In this sense, the OTC market may be considered to be at the bottom of the hierarchy.

With the computerization of trading, however, the OTC market has increased its status as an alternative to the exchanges. The market now offers liquidity and national recognition to prospective companies wishing to go public. As a result, the smaller exchanges now consider the OTC market as a threat to their own survival. Smaller corporations going public

FIGURE 1–5
Transaction Prices at the Osaka Stock Exchange (SH: February 14, 1992)

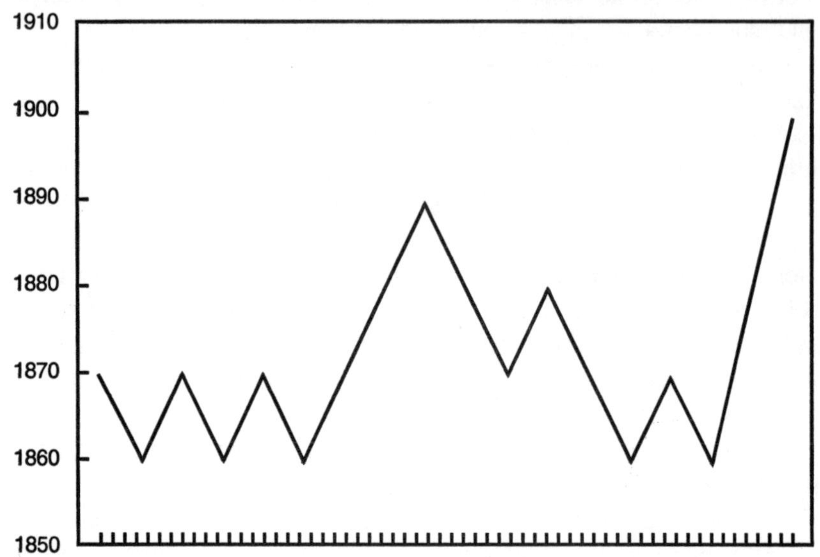

FIGURE 1–6
Transaction Prices at the Osaka Stock Exchange (OP: February 7, 1992)

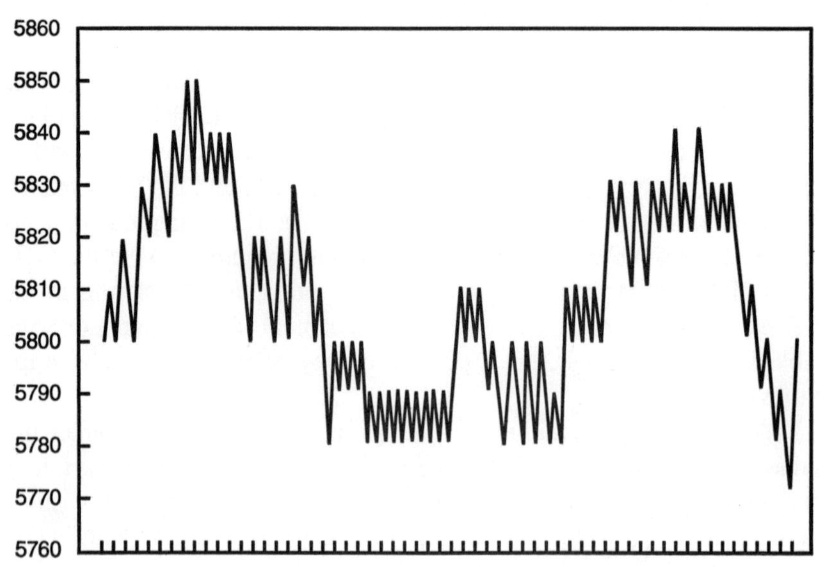

TABLE 1–4
Main Listing and Registration Requirements (as of February 1, 1992)[a]

	Tokyo	*Osaka*[b]	*Nagoya*	*Regional*	*OTC*
(1) minimum number of shares (in millions):[c]	4 (20)	4 (20)	3 (10)	2	2
(2) minimum number of shareholders:					
less than 10 million shares	800	800	500	400	—
less than 20 million shares	1,200	1,200	1,000	500	200
less than 30 million shares	2,000	2,000	2,000	600	400
(3) minimum number of years since establishment:	5	5	5	5	2
(4) minimum amount of net assets (in millions of yen):	1,000	500	500	300	200
(5) minimum profit during the last 3 years (in millions of yen):[d]					
first year	200	80	80	40	n.a.
second year	300	100	100	50	n.a.
third year	400	120	120	60	n.a.
(6) profit per share during the most recent year (in yen):	20	20	20	20	10

[a] Assuming that the par value of a share is 50 yen.
[b] Less stringent requirements are applied to specially designated second section stocks.
[c] The figures in parentheses refer to the minimum number of listed shares required for companies located outside the assigned local regions of the exchanges.
[d] For Tokyo and Nagoya, these requirements can be waived if certain other criteria are met.

may no longer consider a regional exchange as a place in which to raise equity capital, unless their operations are highly regional in nature. With the introduction of the JASDAQ system in October 1991, even larger corporations may decide to remain in the OTC market even after they can meet the listing requirements of the larger exchanges. In part responding to this competition, the Osaka Stock Exchange lowered the listing requirements of

TABLE 1–5
Listing of OTC Stocks at Stock Exchanges, 1980–91

Year	*Tokyo*	*Osaka*	*Nagoya*	*Regional*[a]
1980	1	1	1	0
1981	1	1	1	0
1982	4	2	0	0
1983	1	0	0	0
1984	3	2	0	0
1985	3	0	0	0
1986	7	1	0	0
1987	7	1	0	1[b]
1988	8	0	0	0
1989	1	2	1	1[c]
1990	6	0	0	0
1991	6	0	0	0

[a] The two OTC stocks which are shown to have been locally listed (i.e., at Hiroshima and Kyoto) reflect the Osaka Stock Exchange's "gentleman's agreement" with each regional exchange that the stocks being listed at Osaka should be cross-listed if the companies are headquartered in the immediate local region of the regional exchange.
[b] Cross-listing at Osaka and Hiroshima.
[c] Cross-listing at Osaka and Kyoto.

Source: Japan Association of Securities Dealers.

special second section stocks on February 1, 1992.[12] On the same day, the Tokyo and Nagoya Stock Exchanges lowered the general listing requirements.

While there is no intermarket competition for independently listed stocks, cross-listed stocks can in principle be traded at any of the exchanges. In order to understand why a particular exchange is chosen over the other exchanges for the trading of certain stocks, the concept of total liquidity risk, as suggested by Garbade and Silber (1979), may be useful. The total liquidity risk (*TLR*) of a particular stock is defined as some weighted sum of the variance of its equilibrium price changes [$\text{Var}(dp_e)$] and the variance of the difference between its equilibrium price and its market price [$\text{Var}(p_e - p_m)$],

$$TLR = F\,[\text{Var}(dp_e),\ \text{Var}(p_e - p_m)]. \tag{1.1}$$

The first component of (1.1) is presumably a positive function of the length of a trading interval. As the interval between transactions becomes longer, there is a greater probability that the equilibrium price will change. From the point of view of minimizing this component of total liquidity risk, therefore, a continuous auction is a reasonable market organization. However, a shorter trading interval would increase the second component of (1.1), because fewer potential market participants could then enter the market at each transaction. It can thus be argued that, from the point of view of minimizing the total liquidity cost as a whole, it is beneficial to increase trading intensity if the continuous form of trading is to be maintained.

From this standpoint, the "concentration" requirement imposed on member firms, as well as the short trading sessions, are mechanisms of increasing trading intensity, and are complementary to the nature of the Japanese exchanges as auction markets. Likewise, the hierarchical structure of the Japanese stock market can be explained as a response of the marketplace to minimize the total liquidity risk by concentrating trading activity in a central location. With the integration of the national stock market resulting from the improvement in telecommunication technology, trading in cross-listed stocks has become increasingly concentrated in Tokyo. Only in rare situations, implicit trading rules have emerged by which trading in some cross-listed stocks is concentrated in Osaka.

Given the nature of the Japanese stock market as an auction market, market integration is the key to understanding its current hierarchical structure. Whereas traders could obtain information at a considerable cost only through telephones a few decades ago, they now have instantaneous access to information on trading conditions in Tokyo and Osaka on computer terminals at little cost. When trading cross-listed stocks at the Osaka Stock Exchange, for example, all the member firms are observing what is happening at the Tokyo Stock Exchange. The extent of market integration is clearly evident by comparing the transaction prices between Tokyo and Osaka for two cross-listed stocks (OP and ND) which were heavily traded in Osaka on February 6 and 7, 1992, respectively (Figure 1–7 and Figure 1–8). For all practical purposes, arbitrage between Tokyo and Osaka is perfect.

In an integrated national market, there are direct economic forces towards market concentration, such that only one central exchange can be supported for cross-listed stocks.[13] With the concentration of economic activity in Tokyo, therefore, it is natural that the Tokyo Stock Exchange has assumed the role of the central exchange for most cross-listed stocks. In this environment, the Osaka and other exchanges can compete with the Tokyo Stock Exchange only by offering lower transactions cost.[14] If the reduction in the transactions cost is large enough to offset the reduction in the total

FIGURE 1–7
Transaction Prices in Osaka and Tokyo (OP: February 6, 1992)

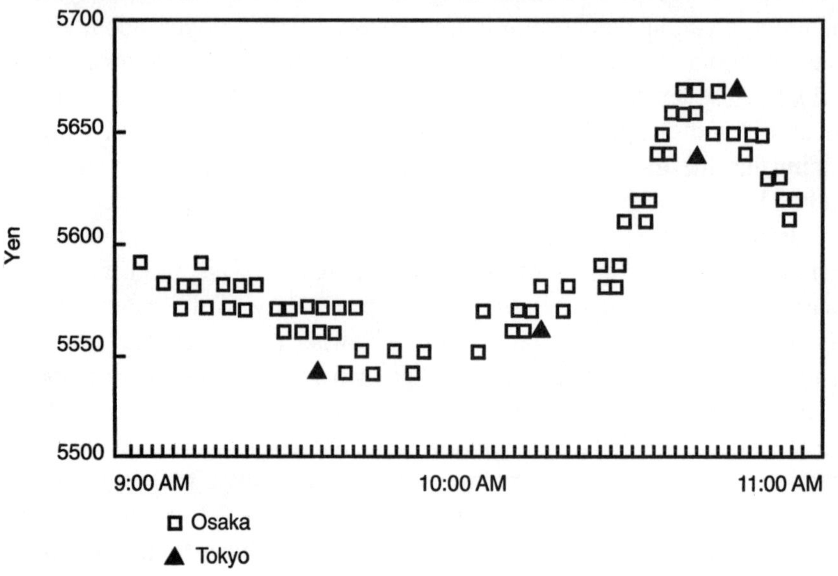

FIGURE 1–8
Transaction Prices in Osaka and Tokyo (ND: February 7, 1992)

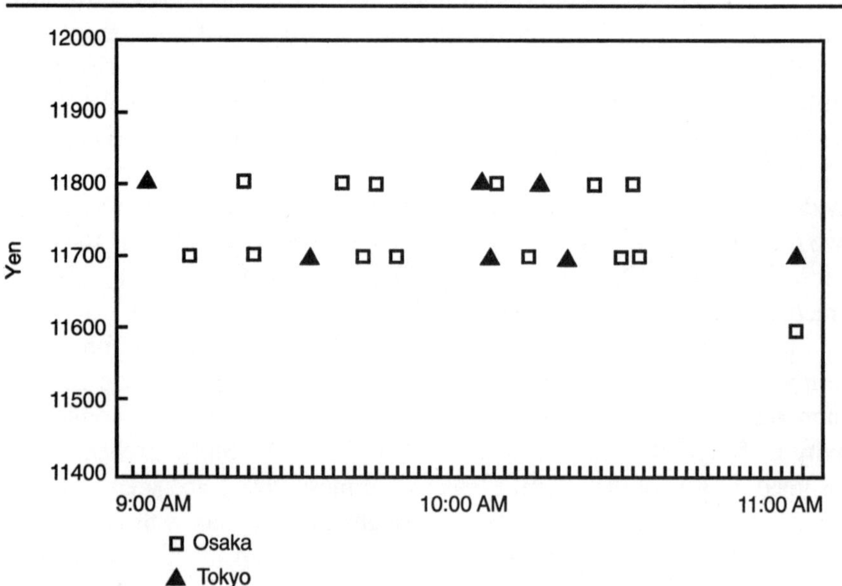

liquidity risk resulting from greater trading intensity at Tokyo, trading may begin to shift from Tokyo to Osaka and other exchanges. In this context, it is possible that the relative increase in trading activity in Osaka in recent years is in part due to the smaller fixed membership and commission fees charged by the Osaka Stock Exchange (Table 1–6).

VI. THE ROLE OF NONCENTRAL EXCHANGES

The question of why the noncentral exchanges of Osaka, Nagoya and the five regional cities can (or should) coexist with the Tokyo Stock Exchange is closely related to the role of these exchanges. First, one obvious function of these exchanges is to provide a means of trading independently listed local stocks. In this role, however, we have already seen that the regional exchanges are facing competition and a real threat to their survival from the emergence of a liquid and efficient national OTC market with less stringent registration requirements. When listing their stocks at a stock exchange, OTC companies altogether skip the regional exchanges (see Table 1–5). Moreover, in the absence of government regulation, there would be no reason for the listing requirements of the regional exchanges to be kept less stringent than those of the larger exchanges.

Second, given the restrictions on the number of member firms admitted to the major exchanges, some member firms of the regional exchanges remain nonmembers of the Tokyo or Osaka Stock Exchange. Under the fixed brokerage commissions system, the commission rates are so priced that it is cheaper for these firms to submit transaction orders to the regional exchanges of which they are members than to submit orders to the Tokyo or Osaka Stock Exchange through a major brokerage firm. The rate charged by Japan Kyoei Securities at the regional exchanges for the transmission of orders to Tokyo or Osaka is 17 percent of the fixed commission rates applicable to individual investors, while the rate charged by other brokerage firms on nonmember securities companies is 20 percent. In this respect, the existence of regional exchanges will likely be threatened if the fixed brokerage commission system or the membership at the Tokyo Stock Exchange is completely liberalized in the future.

Third, while all the listed stocks at the regional exchanges are eligible for margin transactions, not all stocks are eligible at the larger exchanges. Moreover, there is a significant number of cross-listed stocks that are eligible for loan transactions at the regional exchanges but are ineligible at the

TABLE 1–6
Fixed Membership and Commission Fees in Stock Trading in Tokyo and Osaka

	Tokyo			*Osaka*		
	Membership	*Commission*	*Total*	*Membership*	*Commission*	*Total*
			(in percent of a transaction's value)			
1988	0.0027	0.00157	0.00427	0.0040	0.00243	0.00643
1989	0.0027	0.00133	0.00403	0.0027	0.00191	0.00461
1990	0.0027	0.00147	0.00417	0.0020	0.00157	0.00357
1991	0.0024	0.00205	0.00445	0.0013	0.00179	0.00309
1992	0.0036	0.00289	0.00649	0.0013	0.00288	0.00418

larger exchanges.[15] Thus, for certain designated stocks, investors or securities companies wishing to conduct transactions with borrowed cash or stocks have an incentive to use one of the regional exchanges. According to market participants, however, trading in these stocks is so thin to begin with, that the role of the regional exchanges in this area is quite limited at best.

Fourth, perhaps most important in terms of trading volume, the noncentral exchanges provide a convenient facility for the timely execution of large-lot transactions by a single securities company, often called *cross* trades.[16] A cross trade is a simultaneous submission of large buy and sell orders at an identical price by a single securities company. Given the "concentration" requirement, which obliges securities companies to submit all transactions to an exchange, companies wishing to make a cross transaction have a better chance of instant success at one of these exchanges with less trading and fewer participants. It is believed that a significant portion of trading at these exchanges is accounted for by cross trading.[17]

More cross trading takes place at the Osaka Stock Exchange (and, to a lesser extent, the Nagoya Stock Exchange) because there are more member firms and more listed stocks there than at the regional exchanges. To understand this role of the Osaka Stock Exchange, comparing the trading activity in Tokyo and Osaka between March 24 and March 30, 1992 may be useful (Table 1–7).[18] On March 24, the volume and value of stock transactions in the Osaka first section significantly exceeded those in the Tokyo first sec-

TABLE 1–7
Trading Activity in Tokyo and Osaka (March 24 and 30, 1992)

	Tokyo		Osaka	
	1st	*2nd*	*1st*	*2nd*[a]
Trading Volume (in thousands of shares)				
March 24, 1992	310,250	7,061	613,940	6,154
March 30, 1992	154,395	2,281	8,279	729
Trading value (in millions of yen)				
March 24, 1992	316,142	11,054	676,759	6,754
March 30, 1992	165,229	2,591	14,283	1,258
Number of listed stocks[b]				
March 24, 1992	1,234	419	861 (56)	307 (244)
March 30, 1992	1,235	421	861 (56)	307 (244)
Number of stocks traded[b]				
March 24, 1992	1,174	302	459 (50)	179 (168)
March 30, 1992	1,150	255	160 (44)	127 (114)
Trade ratio (in percent)[b]				
March 24, 1992	95.1	72.1	53.3 (89.3)	58.3 (68.9)
March 30, 1992	93.1	60.6	18.6 (78.6)	41.4 (46.7)

[a] Includes special second section stocks.
[b] For Osaka only, the figures in parentheses apply to stocks which are not cross-listed at Tokyo.

Source: Nihon Keizai Shinbun; the author's calculation.

tion, which was indeed an extremely rare event. Despite this trading activity in Osaka, however, the trade ratio of first section Osaka stocks (53 percent) fell far short of the trade ratio of first section Tokyo stocks (95 percent).

On March 30, the volume and value of stock transactions fell at both exchanges. Tokyo's trading volume and value fell by about 50 percent. The decline was much sharper at the Osaka Stock Exchange: trading in Osaka was only about 5 percent of Tokyo in volume and about 10 percent in value. The differential effects of this decline in trading on market liquidity between Tokyo and Osaka are remarkable: while the trade ratio of first section Tokyo stocks changed very little (from 95 to 93 percent), that of first section Osaka stocks declined from 53 to 19 percent. At the same time, the trade ratio of independently listed first section stocks at Osaka only moderately declined from 89 to 79 percent. Because the normal trading activity of investors cannot be so variable, we can interpret the variable trade ratio of Osaka first section stocks as indicating the importance of cross trading of Tokyo stocks at the Osaka Stock Exchange.

VII. SUMMARY AND CONCLUSION

The hierarchical structure of the Japanese stock market reflects the set of regulations, restrictions or practices that are specific to the market. Most importantly, we have argued that the hierarchical order of stock exchanges is related to the microstructure of the secondary market where stock trading is based on competitive auction rules with no obligatory market making. In this type of market environment, liquidity becomes endogenous to trading intensity so that, in the absence of transactions costs, there are natural economic forces to minimize the total liquidity risk by concentrating trading in a central location. With the increasing concentration of economic activity in Tokyo, the Tokyo Stock Exchange has naturally assumed the role of the central exchange for most stocks.

Most other aspects of the stock market organization are likewise shaped by regulations or restrictions. In the absence of implicit government regulations, for example, there would be no reason for the listing requirements of the regional exchanges to be kept less stringent than those of the larger exchanges. In the absence of the "concentration" requirement, moreover, there would be no reason for securities companies to conduct large in-house transactions at a noncentral exchange.[19] Thus, the existence of the regional exchanges depends on the presence of regulations.

The existence of the regional exchanges, moreover, is enhanced by the fixed brokerage commission system as well as the ceiling on the number of member firms at the Tokyo Stock Exchange. The regulations on margin transactions also help strengthen the existence of the regional exchanges by making all the listed stocks at the regional exchanges (but not at the larger exchanges) eligible for margin or loan transactions. In this sense, we can say that noncentral stock exchanges, or the regional exchanges in particular, continue to exist in Japan for the same reasons that they rank lower in the hierarchy of the Japanese stock market.

NOTES

1. See Table 1–6 for the current schedule of fixed percentage fees in Tokyo and Osaka.
2. At the Tokyo and Osaka Stock Exchanges, Japan Kyoei Securities is a regular member. Japan Kyoei Securities no longer operates in Fukuoka because all the member firms of the Fukuoka Stock Exchange are now members of the Tokyo Stock Exchange. Orders received in Nagoya are submitted only to Tokyo.
3. In an attempt to get some business away from the Tokyo Stock Exchange, certain designated stocks begin trading at 8:50 a.m. on the Osaka Stock Exchange and end trading at 3:10 p.m. on the Nagoya Stock Exchange.
4. On February 21, 1992, for example, when the highest buying price and the lowest selling price of a particular stock were 2510 and 2530 yen, respectively, one of the TDs posted the buying price of only 2030 yen and did not even quote a selling price.
5. Japan OTC Securities was established in 1976 by a group of 187 securities companies. It is said that over 90 percent of trading in the OTC market is conducted through the mediation of Japan OTC securities.
6. For a fuller discussion of this topic, see Takagi (1993).
7. Takagi (1993) suggests the possibility that member securities companies are providing voluntary market making in the sense that they are simultaneously submitting buy and sell orders at each end of a narrow price spread.
8. The Kyoto Stock Exchange still has the largest trading volume of all the regional exchanges in part because it has the largest number (6) of member firms that are not members of either the Tokyo or the Osaka Stock Exchange. Most of the orders submitted by these local member firms are executed by Japan Kyoei Securities at either Tokyo or Osaka. See Section VI.
9. This figure does not include the amount of trading that was mediated and executed in Tokyo by Japan Kyoei Securities. When Japan Kyoei Securities' trading is included, the trade ratio of Nagoya first section stocks typically increases by some 20 or 30 percentage points. The difference between the trade ratio of independently listed stocks and that of all listed stocks in the first section presumably reflects the cross trading of major Tokyo stocks.
10. On individual days, however, the trade ratio can be quite low. See, for example, the trade ratio of first section stocks on March 30, 1992 in Table 1–7.
11. For example, when stock ownership is heavily concentrated, or the company headquarters is located in the Osaka region.
12. The system of designating some stocks as special second section stocks was instituted in November 1983 in order to promote the listing of smaller and newer companies at the Osaka Stock Exchange. Less stringent listing requirements are applied to special second section stocks. For example, companies can be listed after three years of continuous operation.
13. Although market concentration can also occur in a specialist-dealer market, it is not necessarily through market integration but rather through the price-setting behavior of the specialist-dealer. For example, a more active market allows the specialist-dealer to reduce the amount of inventories and provides him with more information, relative to a less active market. The end result is that the bid-ask spread becomes smaller in a more active market, thus further increasing market concentration.

14. The noncentral exchanges can also specialize in futures, options and other new financial products as a way of survival. In fact, the Osaka and Nagoya exchanges are moving in this direction.
15. Securities companies can borrow only the eligible stocks from securities finance companies.
16. Some cross trades are dealing transactions, and others are large transactions between two parties mediated by member securities companies.
17. According to market participants, over 80 percent of first section trading in Osaka and Nagoya is said to be cross trading. Cross trading also takes place at the Tokyo Stock Exchange in inactively traded stocks or heavily traded Osaka stocks.
18. For Nagoya, see footnote 8.
19. In fact, there would even be no reason why stock trading should be concentrated in the Tokyo Stock Exchange.

REFERENCES

Amihud, Yakov, and Haim Mendelson, "Dealership Market: Market-Making with Inventory," *Journal of Financial Economics 8*, March 1980, 31–53.

Amihud, Yakov, and Haim Mendelson, "Trading Mechanisms and Stock Returns: An Empirical Investigation," *Journal of Finance 42*, July 1987, 533–55.

Amihud, Yakov, and Haim Mendelson, "Market Microstructure and Price Discovery on the Tokyo Stock Exchange," *Japan and the World Economy 1*, 1989, 341–70.

Cohen, Kalman J., Steven F. Maier, Robert A. Schwartz, and David K. Whitcomb, "Limit Orders, Market Structure, and the Returns Generation Process," *Journal of Finance 33*, June 1978, 723–36.

Garbade, Kenneth D., and William L. Silber, "Structural Organization of Secondary Markets: Clearing Frequency, Dealer Activity and Liquidity Risk," *Journal of Finance 34*, June 1979, 577–93.

Garman, Mark B., "Market Microstructure," *Journal of Financial Economics 3*, June 1976, 257–75.

Goldman, M. Barry, and Avraham Beja, "Market Prices vs. Equilibrium Prices: Returns' Variance, Serial Correlation, and the Role of the Specialist," *Journal of Finance 34*, June 1979, 595–607.

Logue, Dennis E., "Market-Making and the Assessment of Market Efficiency," *Journal of Finance 30*, March 1975, 115–23.

Macey, Jonathan, and Hideki Kanda, "The Stock Exchange as a Firm: The Emergence of Close Substitutes for the New York and Tokyo Stock Exchanges," *Cornell Law Review 75*, July 1990, 1007–52.

Mendelson, Haim, "Market Behavior in a Clearing House," *Econometrica 50*, November 1982, 1505–24.

Ministry of Finance, *Shoken Kyoku Nenpo*, annual issues.

Niederhoffer, Victor, and M. F. M. Osborne, "Market Making and Reversal on the Stock Exchange," *Journal of the American Statistical Association 61*, December 1966, 897–916.

Smidt, Seymour, "Continuous versus Intermittent Trading," *Journal of Financial and Quantitative Analysis 14*, November 1979, 837–66.

Takagi, Shinji, "The Japanese Equity Market: Past and Present," *Journal of Banking and Finance 13*, September 1989, 537–70.

Takagi, Shinji, "The Organization and Microstructure of the Secondary Stock Market in Japan," in Shinji Takagi (ed.), *Handbook of Japanese Capital Markets* (Oxford: Basil Blackwell), 1993, pp. 302–39.

Tokyo Stock Exchange, *Monthly Statistics Report*, monthly issues.

CHAPTER 2

THE STRUCTURE AND PERFORMANCE OF THE JAPANESE SECURITIES INDUSTRY

Yui Kimura
Thomas A. Pugel

I. INTRODUCTION

In recent years a number of important questions have arisen regarding the performance of the securities industry and the securities markets in Japan. Several major financial scandals have arisen, including widespread profiting by political people from the purchase of securities whose market price then increases dramatically, rebates by securities firms to certain customers who experience losses on their securities portfolios, and legal settlements in favor of client firms who purchased overpriced securities on the promise that they would be able to sell the securities subsequently for a profit. More generally, there is concern that such practices as fixed commissions and fees indicate that the securities industry is poorly serving the interests of its customers, both investors and issuers of new securities. In addition, the role of the Ministry of Finance as the regulator of the industry has been questioned, especially given that Ministry officials often find employment positions

The authors are grateful for the research assistance of Naoya Takezawa.

after their retirement from the Ministry (amakudari) through the efforts of the securities firms that they previously regulated.

This chapter provides an examination of the economic performance of the securities industry in Japan. It focuses on the markets for two major types of securities activities or services in Japan. First, it examines the provision of underwriting services for new issues of corporate securities—both equities and bonds. Second, it examines the trading of previously issued corporate securities—both equities and bonds. The trading activities of securities firms include both the provision of brokering services—acting as the agent for buyers and sellers of securities—and dealing—buying and selling securities as a principal for the securities firm's own account.

A number of other activities of securities firms in Japan are related to the focus activity areas. One that will be prominent in the analysis is the creation and distribution of investment trusts. Investment trusts in Japan are of two types, unit trusts and open trusts, with the latter being the equivalent of mutual funds in the United States. Although the funds invested in an investment trust are nominally placed with a trust bank, the trusts are effectively managed by the investment trust management company that originated the trust. The investment trust management company is typically a subsidiary of a securities company. Another activity that will be examined is trading in government bonds. To some extent, government bonds are included because they are the major part of trading in all bonds in Japan and are often combined with trading in corporate bonds in the data that is published. In addition, structural changes based on changes in regulations affecting trading in government bonds occurred in the 1980s, and the effects of these changes will be of noticeable interest for the study.

The chapter analyzes the economic performance of each of the focus activities as a market activity in its own right. The standard of economic performance used here is the economic efficiency of the market for this activity. The approach used is the application of the structure-behavior-performance framework developed in industrial organization economics. Pugel and White (1985) represents one example of previous research that has applied this framework to the securities industry, specifically in their work to an examination of the economic efficiency of the market for the services of underwriting of publicly issued corporate securities in the United States.

This analysis of the economic performance of the securities industry in Japan presumably also has implications for the evaluation of the efficiency of the financial markets (the markets for the securities themselves, rather than the markets for the services related to the securities) in Japan. Although this issue arises in several places in our study, we do not attempt to present a full analysis of this market efficiency.

The chapter is organized in the following way. The next section presents the essentials of government regulation of the securities industry in Japan. Section III then examines the structure of the industry. The next two sections of the chapter analyze the behavior and performance of the markets for the services related to the two focus product areas, underwriting of corporate securities and trading in corporate securities. The final section of the chapter offers a summary of the findings and discusses the implications for government regulation of the securities industry in Japan.

II. BASIC REGULATION

As in most countries, the Japanese government imposes substantial regulation on securities firms and securities activities, and the nature and details of this regulation have evolved over time. In this section of the chapter, we outline some of basic characteristics of this governmental regulation, focusing on regulation that can have a major impact on market structure. The details of specific regulatory measures that have their major impacts on various types of market behavior are deferred to the subsequent sections of the paper that examine competitive conduct.

Following passage of the 1874 Securities and Exchange Law and the 1878 revised Securities and Exchange Law, securities (or stock) exchanges were opened in Tokyo and Nagoya in 1878. Prior to World War II, the securities firms that operated in Japan were relatively small, and engaged mostly in bond trading, with stock trading limited mostly to speculative positioning in stock futures.

The Banking Law of 1927 was based on the philosophy that commercial banking was a separate type of enterprise. Although no law provided for the separation of banking and securities businesses, banks were active in only a limited part of the securities business (Suzuki, 1987). Banks (and trust companies) were very important in underwriting bonds and holding them for their own account. However, even in this bond underwriting, banks used securities firms to distribute the issues. Banks were not active in securities brokering or dealing.

Thus, in the pre-War period substantial compartmentalization of financial services firms existed. Such compartmentalization is also seen in laws from this period regarding special types of banks and trust companies.

At the beginning of the Occupation after World War II, all stock exchanges were closed (although some trading continued through informal gatherings of traders). In 1948 the Securities and Exchange Law was passed, in preparation for the reopening of the exchanges in 1949. The stated objectives of this law were to manage the national economy properly and to protect securities investors. In addition, it is generally believed that another objective was to nurture the small securities companies and protect them from the large banks.

The 1948 Law created a Securities and Exchange Commission, consisting of three commissioners appointed by the Prime Minister. The Commission had its own staff and was charged with regulating stock exchanges and securities activities. In 1951 this Commission was abolished and absorbed into the Ministry of Finance (MOF).

Article 65 of the 1948 Law generally prohibits banks from engaging in securities business, with several exceptions. These exceptions include holding securities as long-term investments, acting as a broker for the private placement of corporate bonds, and securities activities related to trust contracts. In addition, exceptions were made for activities related to national government bonds, local government bonds, and government-guaranteed bonds. However, administrative guidance from the Ministry of Finance effectively prohibited banks from engaging in underwriting, distribution, and trading activities for government bonds until the 1980s, when these prohibitions were reversed following the passage of the Banking Law of 1981.

The 1948 Law also prohibits securities firms from engaging in any form of banking business—taking deposits or making loans. In addition, the Law separates the insurance business from the securities business, with insurance companies retaining powers for real estate investment and real estate investment trusts. Thus, the 1948 Law is a major part of a broader set of laws and regulatory actions that created the substantially compartmentalized structure for financial services firms in post-War Japan.

As noted above, since 1951 the Ministry of Finance has been responsible for regulating securities companies in Japan. Activities that are subject to the supervision and guidance of the Ministry include entry into and exit from specific securities activities, mergers and sales of businesses, and creation and relocation of branch offices. The Ministry also relies to a noticeable extent on self-regulation by various industry associations and by the stock exchanges. This reliance on self-regulation is related to the fact that the Ministry has a relatively small number of personnel, including an investigative staff of only 140 people, less than one quarter that of the U.S. Securities and Exchange Commission (Moran, 1991).

A major change in regulation occurred with the revision of the Securities and Exchange Law in 1965. The revision required licensing of all securities firms rather than simple registration. Four different types of licenses can be obtained—a license for dealing in securities, a license for brokering securities, a license for underwriting and distribution of new securities issues, and a license for acting as the agent for the distribution of new issues. The shift to the licensing system, completed in 1968, also effectively increased the minimum level of capital required for each type of activity. In addition to these four types of licenses, the Ministry has created another category, with a high capital requirement, for acting as the lead manager in the underwriting of a new securities issue. Firms that have all four licenses and can act as lead manager are called "sogo," comprehensive, or integrated securities firms.

A number of other regulatory actions have occurred as international activities have increased in recent years. These regulatory actions have responded both to efforts by foreign financial institutions to enter into securities activities in Japan and to the foreign securities activities of Japanese financial institutions. Further discussion of these types of regulatory actions and changes is deferred to the conclusions section of the chapter.

III. MARKET STRUCTURE

The structure of a market is comprised of those features that are relatively stable and largely beyond the control of any firm in the market. The features of most interest are those that have implications for market behavior and thus for the economic performance of the market. This section provides information on three major aspects of the structure of the markets in Japan for underwriting services and for securities trading services. The section begins by discussing the number of securities firms and different ways in which these firms can be divided into various types. Measures of the concentration in the provision of the various securities services are then presented and discussed. The section concludes with some observations on barriers to entry into the industry and barriers to mobility within the industry.

A. Number and Types of Firms

An examination of the number and types of firms in the securities industry in Japan provides information on the development of the industry and on the different businesses pursued by various firms in the industry. Table 2–1 provides an overview.

As shown in Table 2–1, the number of firms in the Japanese securities industry was 1,127 in 1949, when the exchanges were reopened. This number fell dramatically in the 1950s and 1960s, and it continued to fall more slowly into the mid-1980s. Less than half of the securities firms in 1965 were members of at least one of the stock exchanges in Japan, but more than half are now members of at least one exchange. The Tokyo Stock Exchange (TSE) is by far the largest exchange in Japan, accounting for over 80 percent of total equity trading in Japan. The number of member firms of the Tokyo Stock Exchange fell from 129 in 1949 to 83, where it remained stable through the 1970s and the first half of the 1980s. Membership has recently been expanded, and reached 124 firms in 1990.

In the mid-1970s, all but two of the total number of securities firms in Japan were Japanese firms, and the only foreign firm with a noticeable presence in Japan was Merrill Lynch. Beginning in the late 1970s, additional foreign firms began to obtain licenses. The number of foreign firms reached 14 in 1985 and 52 in 1990. Thus, the recent increase in the total number of securities firms in Japan has been due to the entry of foreign firms—the number of Japanese securities firms continues to decline slowly. In addition, by 1992 the number of foreign firms declined to 45, as several foreign firms exited from Japan.

The recent increase in the number of members on the Tokyo Stock Exchange has permitted foreign firms to become members. In 1986 six foreign firms obtained seats, and by 1990 24 foreign firms were members. Foreign members accounted for 6 percent of turnover on the TSE in 1989 (Zielinski and Holloway, 1991). It may also be noted that more than 100 other foreign securities firms maintain representative entities in Japan (Viner, 1988).

Another way of distinguishing types of securities firms is by the types of licenses that each has. Table 2–2 provides the numbers of securities firms holding different combinations of licenses. The number of firms holding all four licenses has risen from 55 in 1970 to 165 in 1990. In contrast, the numbers of firms holding only three of the four licenses has decreased during this period, as has the number of firms holding only a brokering

TABLE 2–1
Number of Securities Firms, 1949–1990

Years	*Total Firms*	*Exchange Members*	*TSE Members*[a]	*Japanese Firms*	*Foreign Firms*
1949	1,127	NA	129	NA	NA
1955	700	NA	105	NA	NA
1960	552	NA	99	NA	NA
1965	425	197	91	NA	NA
1970	271	169	83	NA	NA
1975	260	161	83	258	2
1980	255	154	83	251	4
1985	240	138	83	226	14
1990	272	159	124	220	52

NA=Not available.

[a] Excluding Saitori members.

Source: Adapted from information from the Japan Securities Dealers Association, the Ministry of Finance, and the Tokyo Stock Exchange.

TABLE 2–2
Number of Securities Firms, By Types of Licenses, 1970–1990

	1970	*1980*	*1990*
All four licenses	55	69	165
Dealing, brokering, and selling licenses	185	158	94
Dealing, underwriting, and selling licences	4	1	0
Dealing and brokering licenses	2	1	4
Brokering license	22	22	9
Total firms	270[a]	251	272

[a] In addition to the categories shown, one firm had dealing and selling licenses, and one firm had only a dealing license, in 1970.

Source: Adapted from Tokyo Stock Exchange, *Annual Securities Statistics 1990*, Table 66, p. 270.

license. Thus, as the number of firms has generally decreased, the breadth of licenses held by the typical firm has increased.

Within the category of firms that hold a license to underwrite and distribute new issues, only firms with capitalization of 3 billion yen or more are permitted to be the lead underwriter, giving rise to the category of "sogo" firm. In 1968 there were 7 sogo firms, and this number rose to 8 in

1971, 12 in 1977, 14 in 1982, 16 in 1984, 20 in 1985, and 25 in 1986 (Sudo, 1987).

Within the category of sogo firms, and generally viewed as being dominant in most securities activities, are the "Big 4"—Nomura Securities, Daiwa Securities, Nikko Securities, and Yamaichi Securities. Each of the Big 4 firms was a government and corporate bond specialist before World War II. They were thus outside of the regulation on branches imposed on firms that participated in securities exchange trading, and were able to develop a network of branches in Japan. These firms were well-positioned in the early 1950s to obtain the business of the increasing numbers of individual investors, and the reintroduction of investment trusts in 1951 provided the products that could be sold to these small investors (Sudo, 1987).

Entering the 1960s Yamaichi and Nikko were the largest and second largest securities firms in Japan. However, both were particularly badly affected by the securities market downturn and depression of the early 1960s, and both came close to bankruptcy. With the market recovery, Nomura became the largest Japanese firm, and it remains so today.

Each of the Big 4 has a set of subsidiary companies that include an investment trust management company, a research institute, and an international capital management company, as well as real estate, venture capital, computer, and credit card companies. Some observers suggest that these subsidiaries are so closely managed as to be more like departments of the Big 4 rather than separate companies (e.g., Viner, 1988). The investment management and international capital management subsidiaries are major sources of brokerage commissions for the parent company.

An important feature of the structure of the Japanese securities industry is the keiretsu linkages that exist among various financial institutions. One linkage is that between each of the Big 4 and banks—Nomura with Daiwa Bank, Yamaichi with Fuji Bank and International Bank of Japan, Daiwa with Sumitomo Bank, and Nikko with Mitsubishi Bank. Probably of more importance, many of the other sogo firms and other securities firms have keiretsu links to the Big 4 firms and to banks. These links have developed for various reasons. For the larger securities firms, keiretsu links have been forged with smaller securities firms in order to work around restrictions on branch expansion imposed by industry-association self-regulation or by MOF regulatory guidance. Sudo (1987) argues that this was particularly important in the 1950s (and also explains some of the consolidation of numbers during this period, as the larger firms acquired some of the smaller firms). She notes that in 1949 most members of the TSE operated independently of each other, while by 1956 most were linked to other securities firms or to banks. Since the early 1970s the further emergence of keiretsu links among large and small securities firms is explained in part by the desire by the smaller firms to gain access to the computer and information systems of the larger firms, and by the desire of smaller non-Tokyo firms to gain access to the Tokyo market.

The keiretsu links between banks and securities firms have been driven since the early 1970s by the needs for banks to meet the requirements of their clients for financial services that increasingly cut across the boundary set by Section 65. Banks use their keiretsu links to build resources and expertise in securities activities. Banks provide their securities firms with financial support, including additional capital to meet licensing requirements, as well as personnel and introductions to corporate clients.

Sudo (1987) provides one careful effort to document these keiretsu links. She concludes that, as of 1978, 31 securities firms were linked to Nomura, 38 were linked to Yamaichi, 21 were linked to Daiwa, and 35 were linked to Nikko. In addition, 24 other securities firms were linked to other sogo firms, and 12 were linked to banks or other non-securities firms. Thus, she concludes that well over half of the firms in the industry were involved in keiretsu links by 1978. Sudo (1987) also carefully examines the keiretsu links for the sogo firms, as of 1986. She finds that 17 of the 21 sogo firms (excluding the Big 4) had keiretsu links with the Big 4 or with banks, including 4 each with Nomura and Nikko, 3 with the International Bank of Japan, and one each with Daiwa and Yamaichi. Only four of the sogo firms could not clearly be placed in keiretsu links.

B. Seller Concentration

The number and size distribution of sellers in a market is considered a key element of a market's structure, with major implications for behavior and performance. Various measures can be used to summarize the information on the number and size distribution of sellers. We will here utilize the most common summary measure, the concentration ratio, defined as the share of the total market activity held by the largest firms. Given the importance of the Big 4 securities firms, it is natural to focus on the four-firm concentration ratio.

Tables 2–3, 2–4, and 2–5 present information on seller concentration in the various securities activities that are the focus of this chapter. Table 2–3 provides information on the four-firm concentration ratio for the underwrit-

TABLE 2–3
Four-firm Concentration Ratios for the Underwriting of New Issues of Equity, 1970–1989

	Four-firm Concentration Ratio	
Year	*By Number of Shares*	*By Value of Issues*
1970	82.4	NA
1975	90.5	89.7
1980	90.8	88.9
1985	82.2	81.3
1989	80.0	61.6

NA=Not available

Source: Computed from Ministry of Finance, *Securities Bureau Annual Report*, various years.

TABLE 2–4
Four-firm Concentration Ratios for Trading in Equity, 1953–1990

	Four-firm Concentration Ratio		
Year	*All Trading*	*Brokering*	*Dealing*
1953	33.2	NA	NA
1955	49.7	NA	NA
1960	64.9	NA	NA
1965	57.9	NA	NA
1970	50.8	44.2	63.6
1975	42.0	44.4	33.5
1980	45.1	46.0	43.0
1985	45.1	43.8	48.5
1990	40.0	41.9	34.3

NA=Not available.

Sources:For 1953-1965, Sudo (1987), Table 1-5. For 1970-1990, adapted from Tokyo Stock Exchange, *Annual Securities Statistics*, 1990, Table 71(1), pp. 276–77.

TABLE 2–5
Four-firm Concentration Ratios for Trading in Bonds, 1970–1990

	Four-firm Concentration Ratio		
Year	*All Trading*	*Brokering*	*Dealing*
1970	65.5	85.8	64.4
1975	64.5	94.8	61.4
1980	77.5	94.4	75.5
1985	60.9	74.4	60.5
1990	71.9	71.9	71.9

Source: Adapted from Tokyo Stock Exchange, *Annual Securities Statistics 1990*, Table 71 (2), pp. 278–79.

ing of new issues of equity. Provision of underwriting services for equity issues is a highly concentrated activity in Japan, with the Big 4 firms typically accounting for 80 percent or more.[1] The exception appears to be a decrease in the concentration ratio measured by value of issues for 1989 (and 1988 as well). However, there is no decline if the ratio is measured by the number of shares underwritten for these years. We are not sure of the basis for or meaning of this apparent divergence.

Underwriting of corporate bonds is also highly concentrated. Honjo and Turbessi (in Fabozzi, 1990) report that the Big 4 firms account for about 80 percent of the underwriting of corporate bonds in Japan, and charts in Sudo (1987) indicate that the four-firm concentration ratio for bond underwriting varied between 70 and 80 percent during 1974–1984.

Table 2–4 reports seller concentration for trading in equities. For all trading in equities, the activity was moderately concentrated in the early 1950s, but rapidly became more concentrated during this decade. Concentration then declined into the 1970s, before rising again in the late 1970s, and peaking at 52.9 percent in 1981. The concentration ratio has declined since then, to 40 percent in 1990. Table 2–4 also shows concentration in the two trading activities of brokering and dealing separately, for the years 1970-1990. Brokering, which is the larger of the two activities for equities trading in Japan, shows a pattern similar to total trading, while dealing is somewhat more variable.

Table 2–5 reports seller concentration for trading in bonds. It should be noted that the data for this table include trading in all bonds, both government and corporate bonds. Trading in government bonds is the larger of the two. For overall trading, concentration is moderate to high, with concentration rising in the late 1970s, and peaking in 1981 at 79.5 percent. The impact of the entry of banks into trading activities for government bonds, based on the 1981 banking law, is apparently seen in the decline in the four-firm concentration ratio for bond trading from 74.7 percent in 1984 to 60.9 percent in 1985. However, the ratio then increased in the latter 1980s, reaching 75.0 percent in 1988.

Dealing is the larger of the two types of bond trading activities. As shown in Table 2–5, the pattern for concentration in bond dealing is similar to that for total bond trading. The concentration of bond brokering, the activity that involves provision of services to outside investors, is shown to be very high into the early 1980s, but then to have fallen somewhat, perhaps again reflecting the entry of banks into this business.

Concentration in two other securities activities is of interest. First, concentration in the provision of investment trusts is high. Sudo (1987) reports that the Big 4 firms accounted for 95.9 percent of investment trusts in 1953, and 85.4 percent in 1960. Zielinski and Holloway (1991) estimate that investment trust management firms owned by the Big 4 firms accounted for about three-quarters of investment trusts in the 1980s. Second, brokerage services for foreign securities is also highly concentrated in Japan, with data from the Ministry of Finance indicating that the four-firm concentration ratio has been above 90 percent since 1985.

It is important to note that the estimates presented so far in this section reflect the direct activities of the Big 4 firms but do not include any activities of their keiretsu-linked smaller securities firms. Because the Big 4 firms may have a noticeable ability to influence or control the activities of their keiretsu-linked firms, the picture thus may be incomplete. For instance, it is believed that the Big 4 firms often send stock orders through their keiretsu firms to obscure their trading activities or to reward the smaller firms for other business activities that have benefited the Big 4 (such as selling their investment trusts).

Unfortunately, it is a difficult and tedious process to attempt to account for these keiretsu links. Sudo (1987) reports that including keiretsu-linked firms would increase the four-firm seller concentration ratios for the period 1972-1977 by varying amounts according to the activity measure used. For total commission revenues, the keiretsu links add 10 to 13 percentage points to the concentration ratio. For brokerage commissions, the addition is 11 to 15.5 percentage points, and for total dealing the addition is 15 to 17.6

percentage points. For commissions for underwriting and distribution, which is highly concentrated even without considering keiretsu links, the addition is only 2.5 to 4.4 percentage points. For total commissions, brokerage commissions, and total dealing, the inclusion of keiretsu links generally increases the four-firm concentration ratios into the range of 60-65 percent. Zielinski and Holloway (1991) report that the inclusion of 34 smaller firms affiliated with the Big 4 increases the four-firm concentration ratio for equity trading from 36 percent to 54 percent, although they do not indicate the method of their calculations or the precise year examined.

Overall, the picture of seller concentration that emerges is that concentration rose dramatically during the 1950s, fell somewhat in the 1960s and into the 1970s, before rising in the late 1970s and early 1980s, and then apparently declining somewhat in the 1980s. Seller concentration is high for such activities as the underwriting of equities and corporate bonds, and at least moderately high for trading in bonds and the provision of investment trusts. Concentration is in the moderate range for trading in equities.

As discussed to some extent in the previous sub-section, the rise of concentration in the 1950s appears to be based on the ability of the Big 4 firms to use their network of branches and the distribution of products such as investment trusts to individual investors to build a dominance of the industry. Since the early 1970s, according to Sudo (1987), the increasing importance of large-scale trades and institutional investors has favored the securities firms with the larger capital bases and the capabilities to manage risks involved in such trading. These trends, plus the growing importance of the abilities to invest in and utilize computer and information systems, have tended to reinforce the dominance of the Big 4 firms.

The appearance of some decline in concentration during the 1980s is open to question. The rising concentration in trading up to 1981 apparently was of concern to the MOF in its role as regulator, and the MOF was encouraging the emergence of additional sogo firms. The MOF generally favored mergers if they would result in stronger firms outside of the Big 4. Nomura apparently responded to this encouragement and merged three of its affiliated firms to form Kokusai Securities in 1981 (Alletzhauser, 1990). Nikko merged three of its affiliates to form Tokyo Securities in 1982. Daiwa and Yamaichi followed in 1984, merging two and three affiliates to form Universal Securities and Pacific Securities, respectively. Thus, the apparent decline in some measures of concentration in the 1980s may reflect a greater use of keiretsu-linked firms by the Big 4. The efficacy of the MOF policy may then be questioned, as the change in structure may be more apparent than real. It is also interesting to note that this episode also appears to be one of oligopolistic reaction, in which the leader, Nomura, takes a strategic action, and then the other three firms follow by imitating Nomura's action.

C. Barriers to Entry and Barriers to Mobility

The height of barriers to entry, indicating how difficult it would be for a new firm to enter successfully into competition with firms already established in the industry, is of interest because this height suggests the degree to which the established firms may feel insulated from potential competition. Barriers to mobility are similar to barriers to entry, but tend to protect firms in one competitive group (or of one type) in the industry from shifts into this group (or type) by firms of other groups (or types).

The height of entry barriers (as well as mobility barriers) appears to vary by type of security activity. Unfortunately, there is little rigorous research on barriers to entry or mobility for the Japanese securities industry. There appears to be a number of sources of entry barriers that are of some importance, including the established retail distribution networks of the larger firms, the need for investments in computer and information systems and networks, and the need for expertise and know-how of employees. These factors are important for brokering, dealing, and underwriting activities. In addition, for underwriting, capitalization (to be able to hold unsold securities if necessary or to affect market prices through own-account transactions if necessary) and established corporate relationships, reputation, and credibility are also important.

These factors suggest that barriers to entry and mobility could be moderate to high. The only rigorous research, however, is by Sudo (1987). She examines two possible sources of entry barriers, established underwriter relationships with issuer clients and economies of scale and scope.

Sudo (1987) examines changes in underwriter-issuer pairings between 1975-1984. Using a sample of 948 issuing companies, she finds that the relationships are highly persistent, with only 5 percent of firms changing underwriters during this period. For the largest 500 firms only 23 changed underwriters and all changed from one Big 4 firm to another Big 4 firm. For the smaller firms in the sample, 24 firms changed underwriters, and only one firm shifted to a sogo firm outside of the Big 4 firms.

Sudo (1987) also tests for the existence of economies of scale and scope. Her estimates for economies of scale using data for the mid-1970s suggest that economies of scale do exist, at least within the size range that includes the smaller firms that are mainly engaged in brokerage activities. Unfortunately, her estimates of economies of scope between brokerage and underwriting activities do not appear to be reliable because of problems in her methodology.

The other sources of barriers to entry and mobility in the industry are the various governmentally imposed laws and regulations. The clearest barrier is the prohibition on entry by banks into securities activities based on Section 65, as well as a comparable prohibition for insurance firms. The licensing system also provides a barrier to entry and mobility, and the ability of the MOF to use administrative guidance may also do so. In addition, the licensing system tends to raise the barrier created by capital requirements, because the licensing system is based on the paid-in capital of the firm.

The importance of entry barriers may be seen in the very small numbers of outside entry into the industry, at least until the early 1980s. We could identify only four cases of de novo entry of Japanese firms into the industry from 1969 through 1985. These were small firms that entered in the mid-1970s. Since about 1980 there has been substantial entry of foreign firms into the industry. However, these foreign firms still apparently face substantial barriers to mobility in the industry, based on such factors as the established corporate relationships and the established retail branch distribution networks of the larger Japanese firms in the industry.

IV. BEHAVIOR AND PERFORMANCE: UNDERWRITING SERVICES FOR CORPORATE SECURITIES

Behavior refers to the activities of the firms in a market, and especially to decisions about pricing and nonprice aspects of competition. Performance represents the evaluation of outcomes in the market, judged against some normative standard. The principal standard used in this chapter is economic efficiency. The major features of economic efficiency are that firms are operating with the lowest costs possible, that prices closely reflect costs, and that consumers have available sufficient and accurate information. If these conditions are met, then buying decisions by consumers are guided by prices and other information in such a way that economic surplus for the national economy is maximized, indicating that resources in the economy are allocated to their most efficient uses. In addition, issues of dynamic efficiency can arise, with respect to the pace of innovation in the industry, and, particularly for the financial services industries, with respect to efficient access by firms to the financial capital necessary for the growth of the general economy. A related standard of performance that will also be applied in this chapter is the minimization of the exploitation of potential conflicts of interest that can arise across the various activities of financial institutions.

Although behavior and performance are analytically distinct, they are closely related. In this chapter we will present a unified discussion of behavior and performance for each of the two activity areas that are the focus of the chapter. This section examines behavior and performance in the provision of underwriting services for new issues of corporate equity and debt. For each, a brief review of the history of such new issues in Japan is followed by analysis. For equities the analysis focuses on the choice of underwriting firm, the pricing of underwriting services, and the underpricing of new issues, a major issue regarding "quality of service." For bonds, the analysis focuses on the process of bringing issues to market, the pricing of underwriting services, and indications of distortions caused by this process and pricing.

A. Underwriting of New Issues of Equity

Prior to World War II, and reflecting the zaibatsu form of corporate organization, most new issues of equity were made directly by the issuing company, at face value, and sold to a few specific investors. After World War II, this system was modified somewhat, but until 1969 most new issues of equity were rights offerings to current shareholders at par value. In 1969 Nihon Gakki made the first completely public issue of new equity at a market price. Market-price issues increased in importance, and by 1986 about 90 percent of paid-in capital increases in Japan were made at market prices (Viner 1988).

Nearly all underwriting of new equity issues in Japan is done on a firm-commitment basis, in which the underwriter buys the entire issue from the issuer and then endeavors to distribute it to investors. The underwriter thus bears some risk that the entire issue cannot be sold at the offering price.

The method by which an issuer chooses a lead underwriter for its equity issue appears to raise major questions for performance. Because of the rigid fee system discussed below, the choice does not appear to be related to the pricing of the underwriting services themselves. Rather, many observers believe that the issuer choice of an underwriter is based in large part on the ability of the underwriter to increase the market price of the issuer's previously issued stock (at least for new issues of seasoned equity), in the time period prior to the new issue. Such support for the stock price can be accomplished in a number of ways, including purchases by the securities firm for its own account, purchases by the firm's investment trusts, purchases by other trusts or accounts that are effectively controlled by the securities firm, or dissemination of favorable information about the issuer company, in order to encourage others to purchase the stock. In some cases the simple news that one of the Big 4 firms will be managing an issue is enough to increase demand and the stock price. At the same time, such support for the share price must be discreet and not too large. The MOF generally does not permit a new issue if the share price exhibits unusual movements or rises by more than 30 percent in the six weeks before the application for a new issue is filed, although this rule was relaxed somewhat in 1988 (Zielinski and Holloway, 1991).

Such linkage of share price enhancement with the underwriting of a new issue appears to create or exploit inefficiencies in the equity market itself. In addition, the securities firm appears to be exploiting a conflict of interest, by requiring its trading, brokerage, and research areas to support its underwriting area. Until 1988 no Chinese walls separated these different areas. Since 1988 the major securities firms have established such walls between the underwriting and trading areas (Nihon Keizai Shimbunsha, 1989), but it is not clear that they have been effective in eliminating the exploitation of the conflict of interest.

The pricing of underwriting services also raises major performance issues. The underwriting fee is set within the narrow range of 3.5 to 4.0 percent of the value of the new issue, with 1.0 percent of this fee reserved as special remuneration for the lead underwriter. This narrow range is apparently set collectively by the group of securities firms licensed to underwrite new issues. Omae and Maruyama (1991) suggest that this fee is fixed to be high enough to provide an umbrella for the less cost-efficient underwriters, and that MOF guidance has condoned or encouraged this approach.

Kunimura and Iihara (1985) analyze this fee and the extent to which its size is related to the fair return to the risk-bearing of the firm-commitment underwriting. They conclude, using an options-pricing approach, that on average only about one-half percentage point of fee is needed to compensate for risk-bearing, and that the underwriters are earning a "large excess return."

Thus, the pricing of underwriting services for new issues of equity raises several performance issues. First, the narrow range may not permit the fees to vary adequately with respect to differences in the costs of underwriting for different issues. In the absence of adequately varying pricing, underwriters should tend to favor low-cost underwriting, and to avoid high-cost underwriting. Second, the pricing appears to be substantially above costs on average. Issuers are charged too high a price for underwriting services, and this may distort some decisions about whether or not to make new issues. Third, the system prevents newer or aggressive firms from competing on a price basis to gain business. It thus can reinforce entry and mobility barriers.

The pricing of the issue itself, in comparison to the market price at or shortly after the issue, is a major performance question regarding the quality of service provided by the underwriter. Kunimura and Iihara (1985) also examine the underpricing of new issues of seasoned stock—for which the underwriter could observe the market price when pricing the new issue. They found that underpricing of the new issues was substantial in the early 1970s, but then declined in the late 1970s and early 1980s. The underpricing averaged about 5 percent in 1980.

The pricing of initial public offerings (IPOs) is more difficult, because the underwriter has no market price for the issuing company's stock to act as a guide. The underwriter in Japan uses a formula to determine the offering price, which is based on the market price of a comparable firm's (or firms') seasoned shares, adjusted for various differences between the IPO firm and the comparison firm, and then discounted to create a small amount of underpricing. While apparently objective, this formula approach does not obviously limit underpricing of the IPO. In addition to the discounting factor, the IPO price can be manipulated by the selection of the comparison firm.

A number of studies show substantial underpricing of IPOs. Fukuda (1984) examines 104 new issues listed for the first time on the second section of the TSE during 1970-1979, and finds an average of 35 percent underpricing by comparing the offering price to the market price at the end of the first month of trading. Hiraki (1985) examines 108 unseasoned new issues during 1979-1984, and finds an average of 53 percent underpricing (or a median of 30 percent), by comparing the offering price to the initial market price (typically two days after issue). Sakakibara et al (1988) examine a sample of 147 IPOs listed on the second section of the TSE during 1970–1986. In comparing the offering price with the initial market price, they find an average of 41.5 percent underpricing. Using a more sophisticated approach that includes a zero-beta version of the capital asset pricing model, they find average underpricing (excess returns) of 40.5 percent.

Since 1988, MOF guidance has apparently instituted changes that have reduced the average amount of underpricing.

This underpricing, for both seasoned issues and IPOs, can be used to benefit specific groups who are able to purchase at the offering price. Managers of the issuing company may be able to reserve the right to allocate a large number of shares, including allocation to themselves. The underwriters can allocate shares to preferred customers or can use tie-ins to sell less attractive securities with the underpriced new-issue shares. In addition to questions regarding conflicts of interest and fairness, this underpricing suggests the existence of economic inefficiency. For instance, such large underpricing raises less financial capital for the same number of shares issued, and this can deter firms from making new issues in order to raise capital. This effect may be particularly onerous for smaller growth-oriented companies that are considering IPOs in order to finance their further growth.

In concluding this section, we note a practice that indicates an unwillingness to allow competition to guide behavior. During the stock market depression of 1961–1964, a committee composed of representatives of the Central Bank, the financial industries, and nonfinancial corporations limited new stock issues (Zielinski and Holloway, 1991), and in 1965 new stock issues were stopped completely for a period of time (Sudo, 1987). In 1990, during another severe bear market, the securities firms declared a moratorium on all new equity or equity-linked issues. Such collusive efforts are inherently suspect as being inefficient. Although few firms may decide to bring new issues to market under depressed conditions, some may still believe that a new equity issue is the best available method to raise funds. A moratorium is inefficient because it distorts their decision and forces them to use less desirable methods of funding.[2]

B. Underwriting of New Issues of Corporate Bonds

The first issue of a corporate bond in Japan was made in 1890 by the Osaka Railway Company. Corporate bonds were first listed on the securities exchanges in 1912, and in 1920 the government eased regulations on bond dealings. Corporate bonds increased substantially with the issuance of reconstruction bonds following the 1923 earthquake, but bondholders suffered large losses on uncollateralized bonds in the panic of 1927. Until this panic, collateralized bonds were rare, but the banks then launched a "clean up the bond market" effort. An agreement in 1933 among the important banks, insurance companies, and trust companies created the principle that all corporate bond issues must have collateral and provisions for sinking funds.

This principle of collateralized bonds continued after World War II. In addition, the Bond Issue Arrangement Committee (Kisaikai), which includes the banks that act as commissioned banks for bond issues and the major underwriters, determines the issuing conditions for straight corporate bonds. This committee meets monthly and decides the volume of new issues in total, the position of various potential issuers in the queue to issue, the issuing terms and amounts, and the coupon rates on the bonds.

The bonds are issued on a firm-commitment basis and distributed through syndicates of securities companies. In this process of bond issuance, the primary bank of the issuing company typically acts as the lead commissioned bank. As the lead commissioned bank, it may be active in designing the terms of the issue, and it negotiates the deal with the securities company that is the lead manager for the issue. The commissioned bank also handles paperwork and administers any bond collateral.

This relatively rigid process of issuing corporate bonds has resulted in the increasing use by potential issuers of alternative approaches to the issuance of bonds in order to raise funds. This apparent distortion of issuer behavior suggests inefficiency in the process of issuing straight bonds.

One alternative that has been increasingly used is the issuance of convertible bonds. In 1983 the size of issues of convertible corporate bonds surpassed the size of issues of straight corporate bonds in Japan. Convertible bonds have a number of process advantages. Issues of convertible bonds are not controlled by the Kisaikai. In addition, convertible bonds shifted away from the requirement for collateral much faster than did straight bonds. In 1973 convertible bonds could be issued using reserved assets rather than collateral, and in 1979 convertible bonds could be issued without any reserved assets or collateral. In 1979 Matsushita issued a convertible bond with no asset or collateral backing. By 1987 85 percent of convertible bonds were issued with no backing (Kaneko and Battaglini, in Fabozzi, 1990).

A second major alternative is the issuance of Euroyen bonds (yen bonds sold outside of Japan). In 1985 80 percent of all issues of straight bonds by Japanese corporations (excluding bonds issued by electric power companies) were Euroyen bonds (Viner 1988). Again, Euroyen issues appear to avoid some of the inefficiencies of the domestic process. Although the MOF does impose certain requirements on issuers, Euroyen bonds do not require collateral and offer a range of contract features that can be chosen by the issuer.

In 1984 conditions permitting some issuance of uncollateralized straight bonds (still through the Kisaikai process) were instituted, and these conditions have been liberalized since then. In 1985 TDK floated the first issue of an uncollateralized straight corporate bond by a Japanese company in Japan since 1932. In addition, the conditions imposed on unsecured issues of convertible bonds and Eurobonds have also been liberalized over time.

Fees for the services of underwriting corporate bonds are set collectively by the major securities firms, and, in a manner similar to equity, may involve an umbrella for the less cost-efficient underwriters. The fees for underwriting straight corporate bonds are 1.3 percent of the issue value for bonds of 4 year maturity, 1.5 percent for a 6–7 year maturity, and 1.6 percent for bonds with a maturity of 7–15 years. In addition, the commissioned bank fee is 0.2 percent if the bond is not collateralized, and 0.25 percent if it is. Fees for underwriting convertible bonds are 2.3 percent for 6 year bonds and 2.5 percent for 10 year bonds. In a way similar to fees for equity underwriting, these collusively fixed fees are very unlikely to represent economically efficient pricing. Instead, the presumption is that pricing inefficiencies exist. We might also note that a similar fixed fee system applies to the underwriting of local government bonds. Lee and Sakagami (in Fabozzi, 1990) discuss the price penalty that is apparently paid under this system by the larger cities and by the higher-rated prefectures.

V. BEHAVIOR AND PERFORMANCE: TRADING CORPORATE SECURITIES

This section analyzes behavior and performance for the second major activity area examined in the chapter—trading of corporate securities. It begins with a discussion of commission rates for brokerage services. It then examines the management of investment trusts. It concludes with an exploration of various practices that appear to involve manipulation of stock prices, insider trading, and related issues.

A. Commission Rates on Brokerage

Brokerage commissions are a major source of revenue for securities firms. The Big 4 firms typically earn about half of their revenues from brokerage commissions. For many smaller securities firms brokerage commissions are typically three-quarters or more of revenues.

Brokerage commissions in Japan are fixed by schedules determined by the stock exchanges and the brokers. These commission rates vary by type of security and by size of trade.

Discounts from these fixed rates may be obtained by specific customers in several ways (Viner, 1988). First, discounts of up to 20 percent have been negotiable for large transactions, and some block transactions may be done on a net price basis. Second, hidden discounts can also be obtained. For instance, the securities firm offering the brokerage service may purchase something else (e.g., research) from the client and pay a relatively high price for it. Also, billing errors can effectively offer discounts to specific clients.

Based on fixed commission rates, and even allowing for these effective discounts, the price of brokerage services generally appears substantially to exceed the cost of providing the services. That is, the pricing of brokerage services is inefficient. This can lead to or encourage several types of distortions. First, the relatively high price can result in the standard distortion of under-purchase. The buyer (investor) that has control over individual transactions will tend to make fewer transactions because of the high price of brokerage services. Second, the high profit margin increases the incentive for churning of accounts that the securities firms effectively control. Churning of accounts is illegal, but appears to be fairly common. The legal definition of churning is vague, and the investor who suspects churning has little legal redress possible, except to negotiate for a settlement of partial compensation. Third, the fixed commission rates enhance barriers to entry by making it difficult to compete for business on a price basis (Wright and Pauli, 1987).

In addition, the high profit rate encourages competing for business on a non-price basis. This is presumably a major part of the incentive for securities firms to suggest that returns on investments are guaranteed, and to provide compensation to some large investors for losses that they subsequently incur. In 1991 it was revealed that the Big 4 as well as 17 other securities firms had paid compensation to major customers that totaled about $1.5 billion dollars. The MOF had known of this compensation practice for many years but only moved clearly to bar it is 1990, and then with little effect. Late in 1991, following an investigation, the Japan Fair Trade Commission (FTC) issued a decree against each of the Big 4 firms, indicating that each had paid secret compensation to make up for losses or to produce guaranteed returns, and mandating each to promise not to do so in the future. Each firm admitted guilt and signed the decree. The concern of the FTC was that such practices are unfair to brokers that do not compensate clients. The FTC documented that such compensation was paid not only to maintain the brokerage business of important clients and to ensure informally guaranteed returns, but also to maintain or to attract underwriting business. As noted in the previous section, profit margins on underwriting also appear to be maintained at high levels by a system of fixed fees.

B. Management of Investment Trusts

Investment trusts were initially offered in Japan in 1937, and were reactivated in 1951, when the Big 4 firms and three others registered to offer them under the 1951 Securities Investment Trust Law. Prior to 1962 the management of investment trusts occurred in a department of the securities firm, and the investment trusts were subject to frequent manipulation and abuses. In 1962 the MOF required a separation of the management of investment trusts. Each major securities firm then created a subsidiary for the management of investment trusts, by divesting the relevant portion of its investment trust department. It is generally believed that this reorganization may have reduced the levels of abuses, but that it did not end them. In addition, the industry structure of the business may not be consistent with strong competition. Up to 1990 only 15 firms had licenses to offer investment trusts.

Three types of abuses of investment trusts appear to exist. First, the investment trusts are a major source of brokerage revenue for the parent securities firm, and it appears that the trusts are churned to generate additional commission revenues. Zielinski and Holloway (1991) report that equity investment trusts that they examined had an average turnover of 2.5 times per year. Essentially, this churning represents an exploitation of a conflict of interest, between producing returns for the investors in the trusts and producing brokerage commissions. Second, the securities firms appear to place poorly performing securities in their trusts, including parts of underwritten issues that the parent cannot sell. Again, this represents an exploitation of a conflict of interest. Third, the securities purchasing of the investment trusts can be used to affect the prices of specific securities, including the prices of the securities of underwriting clients of the securities firm.

These practices would tend to lower the rates of return achieved by investment trusts, and the returns have been poor. Zielinski and Holloway (1991) report that in the 1980s the prices of Japanese stocks increased on average by 21 percent per year, while the average return on equity investment trusts was less than 4 percent per year. In addition, it would appear that unit investment trusts would be less subject to abuses, and Robins (1987) reports that unit trusts have generally achieved much higher rates of return than have open-ended trusts. In 1990 several foreign investment-trust managers were permitted to begin selling domestic funds. These foreign managers lack a domestic distribution system, so that it is unclear whether they will have much impact.

C. Stock Price Manipulation, Insider Trading, and Related Issues

The practices of Japanese securities firms may also contribute to inefficient movements in stock prices. One example has already been discussed—the enhancement of a company's equity price in the period prior to a new issue of its stock. This previous discussion also noted the effort beginning in 1988 to form Chinese walls to prevent this practice. This sub-section focuses on other practices that represent stock price manipulation, as well as on insider trading and tobashi.

It is generally believed that other episodes of stock-price ramping occur, in addition to support directed toward a new issue. The larger securities firms may obtain some profit in such stocks from early purchases for their own accounts, but their major function appears to be to inform others, including corporate leaders, politicians, and important clients, that gains may be available (Viner, 1988). "Political stocks" appear to create profits that can be used as campaign funds, and "ambulance stocks" create profits for clients that have recently incurred major losses on other securities activities (Zielinski and Holloway, 1991). Ramping may also be instigated by stockbrokers from smaller securities companies and by "market experts," acting alone or in groups that pool funds.

Share price manipulation is illegal in Japan, but the laws and regulations have been somewhat vague and appear to be weakly enforced. The TSE and other exchanges also provide self-regulation. However, if the TSE discovers abuses, it reprimands the guilty parties but does not publicly release information about the manipulation.

In response to charges that the Big 4 firms manipulate share prices, the MOF in 1989 offered a guideline that a major broker should not account for more than 30 percent of trading in a stock in a month. Following the collapse of stock prices and trading volumes in 1990, it appears that the MOF has not been enforcing this guideline.

A noticeable amount of insider trading also appears to occur in Japan, although this does not obviously derive from the structure of the securities industry or the activities of the securities firms themselves. Prior to recent changes in the laws, financial information on firms circulated in draft form to selected recipients several weeks prior to its public release. Sakakibara et al (1988) find that significant stock price changes corresponding to the financial information occurred 11–15 trading days before the financial statements were publicly released. They believe that this creates a strong presumption of the use by insiders privy to the drafts or the leakage of this information to others by these insiders.

In September 1987 some stockholders and correspondent banks sold the stock of Tateho Chemical Industries before the public announcement of its severe financial problems. Although insider trading was suspected, regulators could not obtain sufficient evidence, in part because of the vague legal definition of insider trading. With amendment of the law in 1988, rules and regulations on insider trading have been tightened. Nonetheless, in this area as well as in share price manipulation, it is questionable whether the MOF, with its relatively small staff and its mixed objectives, can be a strong enforcer.

Another recent scandal involves the practice of tobashi, an activity that does directly involve the securities firms. In tobashi a client firm agrees to purchase securities from a securities firm, with the understanding that the securities firm will buy back the securities at a slightly higher price (to cover interest costs). If the market price of the securities declines, the client firm must sell the securities before the end of its accounting period, in order to avoid posting a loss on the investment. The securities firm is forced to repurchase the securities at the higher price, but it also does not want to record a loss. Thus, it sells the securities to another client firm (whose accounting period is different from the first firm's period) at a price that is above the market price, with the same understanding that the securities firm will buy back the securities. The investments thus are shifted from one investor to another before the end of the current investor's accounting period. The underlying hope is that the market price will eventually rise to or above the inflated price, which itself tends to rise with each transfer. This practice is itself not illegal. It has, however, created major problems for the securities firms involved, when the market turned down in 1990. New investors could not be found. Many cases of unfulfilled pledges existed, and many of these are being settled by arbitration or litigation, with large financial losses for the securities companies.

In concluding this sub-section, we note that these sorts of practices, although often not illegal, can cause effects similar to inefficiency. As a result of observing these practices, individual investors may distort their behavior by refraining from purchasing corporate equities, in the belief that the market is manipulated in favor of certain large investors.

VI. SUMMARY, CONCLUSIONS, AND POLICY IMPLICATIONS

This chapter has focused on two major activity areas of the securities industry in Japan—the provision of underwriting services to issuers of new corporate securities, and the trading of corporate securities, including both the provision of brokering services and dealing for the securities firms' own accounts. It has used the structure-behavior-performance framework to provide an evaluation of the economic performance of the industry in these product areas. The evaluation of performance has been based on the standard of economic efficiency, as well as the minimization of exploitation of conflicts of interest. This section provides a summary of the major findings of the study and discusses the implications for the reform of government regulatory policy toward the securities industry in Japan.

A. Summary

The chapter has endeavored to discuss the key features of the industry's structure. The number of Japanese securities firms has been falling since 1949, although the total number of securities firms in Japan has been rising since the mid-1980s as a result of the entry of foreign firms. The Big 4 firms are considered dominant, and this was generally confirmed by four-firm seller concentration ratios. Seller concentration is moderate to high for the activity areas examined in this chapter, with high levels of concentration for underwriting of corporate securities, for bond brokering, and for the provision of investment trusts. In addition, effective seller concentration is higher than the numbers on direct shares indicate, because of substantial keiretsu links of smaller securities firms to the Big 4 firms. Barriers to entry and to mobility exist, but it is not possible to calculate the height of these barriers. There has been almost no entry by Japanese firms into the industry since the late 1960s, suggesting substantial barriers. The clearest barrier is the legal barrier to the entry of banks and insurance firms. Foreign firms have entered since the late 1970s, but they appear to face substantial barriers to mobility based on the retail distribution networks and the corporate relationships of the established Japanese firms.

This structure of moderate to high seller concentration and barriers to entry and mobility interact with the regulatory approach of the MOF to produce behavior that results in economic inefficiencies and exploitation of conflicts of interest. Fixed fee schedules for the provision of underwriting services for corporate securities are collectively set. Although a rationale for this collective setting of fees may be self-regulation by the underwriters, it appears to serve mainly as a basis for collusion, and it produces pricing that appears to be well above the costs of providing the underwriting services.

Several other aspects of the provision of underwriting services raise performance questions. Rather than competing on price, underwriters of equity appear to compete for business through their ability to enhance share prices in the months leading up to an issue, potentially creating inefficient movements in share prices and exploiting conflicts of interest across underwriting, trading, and informational activities. In addition, there is some amount of underpricing of seasoned issues of new equity, and substantial underpricing of IPO equity issues. For the underwriting of bonds, the collective control imposed by the Kisaikai committee has resulted in a rigid process for the issuance of straight corporate bonds. Some distortion of issuer behavior results, and this has contributed to the increased use in the 1980s of issues of convertible corporate bonds in Japan and of corporate Eurobonds.

Fixed brokerage commissions are set collectively for each type of asset and size of trade. Again, self-regulation appears to be the basis for collusion that raises prices well above the costs of providing brokerage services. This results in the inefficiency of distorted purchasing decisions by investors. In addition, the relatively high brokerage commissions enhance the incentives for the churning of accounts and investment trusts. The provision of compensation to major clients to ensure guaranteed returns or to compensate them for losses also is related to the high brokerage commission rates, as this compensation is a form of nonprice competition for business.

Several other aspects of securities trading activities raise performance questions. In addition to churning, investment trusts sometimes are used as a place to dump poorly performing securities, and sometimes are used to affect stock prices through their market purchases. On average these investment trusts have produced very poor rates of return to their investors. The securities firms are also apparently involved in the ramping of the prices of specific stocks, and often provide information on these efforts to outsiders, including politicians, who can then secure substantial profits. This ramping of stock prices is one of a number of practices, also including insider trading and tobashi, that may deter individuals from investing in the stock market.

Thus, this study of the securities industry in Japan has produced evidence that suggests substantial shortcomings in the economic performance of the industry, including evidence of economic inefficiencies and of exploitation of conflicts of interest by securities firms. With respect to pricing inefficiency, profit rates are often examined to provide evidence about the relationship of prices to costs. Ideally, we would like to have information on profit margins for each activity, but such information is not available. We can examine the overall profit rates of securities companies. Table 2–6 reports averages by year from 1976 through 1990, for the Big 4 firms and for 18 medium-sized firms for which data are available throughout this period. The long period is used to examine profitability through several business cycles. For comparison the average profit rates for all manufacturing industries and for all (nonfinancial) industries is also shown in the table. The profit rate reported measures the after-tax rate of return on equity or net worth. The table indicates that the profit rates achieved by the securities firms generally are higher than the the profit rates of manufacturing or nonfinancial firms. The profit rates of the securities firms thus appear to be higher than the cost of capital for these firms during most years in this period. This high profit rate and its persistence is consistent with a lack of adequate competition that would drive prices down to the level of costs. It is thus consistent with other evidence presented in this chapter that a substantial amount of economic inefficiency exists.

In part, this poor economic performance is related to the structure of the industry, but it also reflects substantial shortcomings in the regulation of the industry. Indeed, some aspects of the industry's structure are the result of the government's regulatory approach and actions.

The regulatory approach of the MOF is affected by the mixed objectives pursued. Although protection of investors is one of its mandates, the MOF has often been more concerned with the support and fostering of the securities firms that form the industry. This has led the MOF at times to be protective of the industry and lax in its oversight. In addition, the Ministry has a relatively small staff with which to attempt to regulate the industry. The Ministry's reliance on self-regulation has not been effective in serving the interests of the users of securities services. In some activities self-regulation has interacted with the relatively concentrated structure to form the basis for collusion by the securities firms.

TABLE 2–6
After-Tax Returns on Equity,[a] 1976–1990

	Securities Firms[b]			
Year	*Average for Big 4 Firms*	*Average for 18 Medium-Sized Firms*	*Manufacturing Industries Average*	*All Industries Average*[c]
1976	11.7	8.0	8.1	8.2
1977	16.0	12.7	8.2	8.4
1978	15.6	15.6	9.3	9.1
1979	11.8	9.3	12.1	9.7
1980	9.6	6.6	11.8	11.6
1981	11.2	6.5	9.0	8.9
1982	7.5	2.8	8.6	8.6
1983	9.7	17.3	8.0	8.1
1984	12.9	13.1	9.1	8.9
1985	15.1	16.5	8.1	8.0
1986	21.4	22.0	5.5	6.4
1987	23.6	21.4	6.5	7.0
1988	14.9	16.2	7.9	7.8
1989	8.4	8.2	8.0	7.7
1990	14.2	12.6	7.4	7.1
Average	13.6	12.6	8.5	8.4

[a] After-tax return on equity calculated as the ratio of after-tax income to net worth.
[b] For securities firms, the data for years through 1988 are for the fiscal year ended on September 30 of that year. For 1989 and 1990, the data are for the fiscal year ended on March 31 of that year.
[c] Excluding financial and insurance firms.

Source: For securities firms, computed from financial statements of individual securities firms reported in the Ministry of Finance, *Securities Bureau Annual Report*, various years. For manufacturing industries and all industries, adapted from Daiwa Institute of Research, *Analyst Guide 1991*.

MOF efforts to add competition by encouraging the development of additional sogo firms have been countered by the development of keiretsu relationships that link many of these firms to the Big 4 firms.

A number of observers also conclude that the MOF has been resistant to financial innovations, resulting in lagging dynamic performance for the Japanese securities industry (e.g., Omae and Maruyama, 1991). The MOF sometimes discourages innovations through informal guidance in consultations that occur prior to a formal application for approval (Onuma, 1991).

B. Implications for the Reform of Regulatory Policy

Major reforms of the regulation of the securities industry in Japan are currently underway. Important implications for such reforms follow from the findings of this study. We believe that the findings offer support for the cases for four major reforms. First, the regulatory structure should be amended, with the creation of a commission independent of the MOF to oversee the securities firms and securities exchanges. This commission should have investigative and enforcement powers. While we recognize that this structure may not be perfect, we believe that it should be a major improvement on the current structure, in which the MOF is often protective of the industry's interests rather than of the broader interests of the users of financial services.

Second, the regulatory authorities should move to end fixed brokerage commissions and promote competitive pricing of brokerage services. It is possible that such a shift could drive some smaller securities firms out of the industry. Indeed, this may be required to achieve economic efficiency, if these firms have high costs relative to the business that they can obtain.

Third, the regulatory authorities should move to end fixed fees for underwriting and promote competitive pricing of underwriting services. The FTC should be at the lead of both of these reform efforts to end price-fixing. Its efforts with respect to secret compensation are laudable, and it should now take a position with respect to these fundamental practices that restrain competition. At the same time, we are unsure of the actual effects of ending fixed brokerage commission rates and underwriting fees, because of the relatively concentrated structure of the industry. If the industry maintains its current structure, it is not clear that sufficient competition will exist that can reduce prices to the users of these services.

Thus, our fourth recommendation is important—to remove the Article-65 barriers to the entry of banks into securities activities (both underwriting and trading), and perhaps also to remove similar restrictions on the entry of insurance companies. We believe that this is the most direct way to address the current concentrated structure of the securities industry. The lifting of this entry barrier will result in the entry by some banks into securities activities, and these banks can become major players that to a noticeable extent will be free of keiretsu links to the Big 4 securities firms. We believe that it is important to permit the entry of banks in ways that allow the banks to circumvent barriers to mobility, especially with respect to retail distribution and corporate relationships. We believe that the approach of allowing banks to enter securities activities through securities subsidiaries can be acceptable, as long as it does not restrict the ability of the banks to use their existing branch networks and their existing relationships with corporate customers.

C. Bank Entry Into Securities Activities

This proposed removal of the barrier between banking and securities activities can be viewed as the culmination of trends that are already strong. Since about 1980 banks and securities firm have been offering certain products that are close substitutes for some products of the other industry. For instance, the medium-term government bond funds first offered by securities firms in 1980 function much like savings accounts, and funds in these accounts can even be accessed through automated teller machines. In addition, banks and securities firms compete directly in such securities products as brokering and dealing in government bonds and acting as the intermediary for the issuance of commercial paper.

Furthermore, Japanese banks and securities firms also confront each other as direct competitors in their activities outside of Japan. Both are very active in the Eurobond markets. Nonetheless, the MOF has imposed some restrictions on the overseas securities activities of Japanese banks through the 1975 "Three Bureaus Agreement" involving the Ministry's banking, securities, and international finance bureaus. Under this agreement, the foreign branches and joint ventures of Japanese banks are prohibited from acting as the lead manager for bonds issued overseas by Japanese companies. In addition, Rosenbluth (1989) reports that the agreement indicates that the Japanese banks should have lower market shares, so as not to upstage the Japanese securities firms. Some Japanese banks have used their keiretsu-linked securities firms to circumvent the restrictions of this agreement. In addition, the MOF has permitted the foreign securities affiliates of Japanese banks to open representative offices in Japan to market Eurobonds.

The trend toward the convergence of banking and securities activities is also seen in the activities of foreign financial firms in Japan. In 1983 Citicorp, which had banking activity in Japan, purchased a majority share in the East Asian operations of Vickers da Costa, including its licensed securities firm in Japan. The MOF decided not to revoke any licenses, which resulted in a bank in Japan having a majority ownership of a securities firm in Japan. In 1985 the MOF issued a securities license to DB Capital Markets, 50 percent owned by Deutsche Bank. Subsequent licenses have been approved for securities firms owned by foreign banks, as long as the foreign bank's ownership share is 50 percent or less.

We believe that entry of banks into securities activities can have a major impact on the structure and behavior of the securities industry in Japan, and we expect that major improvements in economic performance can result. Two studies of previous entry of Japanese banks into specific securities activities are supportive of these propositions.

Maru and Takahashi (1985) examine bid-ask spreads on secondary market trading of government bonds as a measure of transactional efficiency in this activity. The Big 4 securities firms accounted for about two-thirds of this trading activity in 1983. The Banking Law of 1981 permitted banks to begin over-the-counter sales of government bonds in 1983, and to begin dealing activities in outstanding bonds in 1984. Maru and Takahashi analyze the determinants of the average bid-ask spreads for a representative basket of bonds for the time period 1978-1984. After controlling for such influences as the cost of financing bond inventories, transactions volume, yield to maturity, and the introduction of an improved information system in 1981, a dummy variable representing the period of bank entry into selling government bonds is negative and highly significant. They conclude that transactional inefficiency existed before the entry of banks, and that removal of the entry barrier reduced the spread and improved market efficiency.

Marr et al (1989) examine the impact of Japanese (and U.S.) bank participation in the management of the underwriting of Eurodollar bonds. They note that this activity was initially a cartel of European merchant and investment banks, but that the entry of non-European investment and commercial banks increased competition. In their analysis they use a sample of 242 straight-debt Eurodollar bond issues by U.S. firms during 1982-1986. They examine the determinants of the interest cost to the issuer and the reoffering yield (each relative to a comparable-maturity U.S. Treasury bond yield), as well as the underwriting fee measured as a spread per $1000 of proceeds. Controlling for a large number of other potential determinants, they find that the presence of a Japanese bank as the manager or co-manager of the issue significantly reduces both the interest cost to the issuer and the reoffering yield, while having an insignificant effect on the underwriting spread. Thus, the competitive presence of Japanese banks produces benefits for issuers by providing a lower cost of funds (an estimated 32.4 basis points lower), without an increase in the fee for the underwriting services provided.

The results of both of these studies support the proposition that entry of Japanese banks into securities activities can have a major impact on competition and result in significantly improved pricing efficiency for securities activities. There appears to be a substantial degree of economic inefficiency resulting from securities activities in Japan as they are currently conducted. The four proposed reforms suggested in this concluding section—creation of a regulatory commission independent of the MOF, an end to fixed brokerage commission rates, an end to fixed underwriting fees, and removal of barriers to the entry of banks (and perhaps also insurance firms)—are intended to alter the structure and behavior of the Japanese securities industry in ways that promote the interests of the users of financial services and promote the national interest in enhancing economic efficiency.

NOTES

1. Underwriting of the initial public offerings of a company's stock is also highly concentrated, with the four largest underwriters accounting for 87 percent of such offerings in 1987 (Suzuta, 1989).
2. A related issue is the existence of a set of requirements imposed on firms in order to issue various types of bonds. These requirements specify minimum values for such items as the size of net assets, the debt-equity ratio, the return on assets, and so forth. Generally, these may be termed barriers on the demand side of the market for underwriting services. They tend to limit the range of options available to nonqualifying firms by rule, rather than allowing the financial markets to determine what firms can make issues (at what prices).

REFERENCES

Alletzhauser, Albert J. *House of Nomura.* New York: Arcade Publishing, 1990.

Fabozzi, Frank, ed. *The Japanese Bond Markets: An Overview & Analysis.* Chicago: Probus Publishing Company, 1990.

Fukuda, S., "Shinki-Jojo-Kabushiki no Kakaku Performance," *Shogaku-Kenkyu,* Kansei-Gakuin University, Vol. 32, No. 1, 1984.

Hiraki, Takato. "Pricing Problems of Unseasoned Equity Issues in Japan: An Empirical Test for Primary and Secondary Market Efficiency," *Finance Kinkyu* [Financial Research], No. 4, December 1985.

Kunimura, Michio, and Yoshio Iihara. "Valuation of Underwriting Agreements for Raising Capital in the Japanese Capital Market," *Journal of Financial and Quantitative Analysis,* Vol. 20, No. 2, June 1985.

Marr, M. Wayne, Robert W. Rogowski, and John L. Trimble. "The Competitive Effects of U.S. and Japanese Commercial Bank Participation in Eurobond Underwriting," *Financial Management,* Winter 1989.

Maru, Junko, and Toshiharu Takahashi. "Recent Developments of Interdealer Brokerage in the Japanese Secondary Bond Markets", *Journal of Financial and Quantitative Analysis*, Vol. 20, No. 2, June 1985.

Moran, Michael. *The Politics of the Financial Services Revolution: The USA, UK and Japan.* New York: St. Martin's Press, 1991.

Nihon Keizai Shimbunsha, ed., *Insider Tengoku: Kensho Nihon no Kabushiki Shijo* (Insiders' Heaven: An Examination of the Japanese Stock Markets). Tokyo: Nihon Keizai Shimbunsha, 1989.

Omae, Ken'ichi, and Yoshihiro Maruyama, *Shoken Kin'yu Shijo Kaikaku* (A Market-Oriented Reform of the Japanese Financial System). Tokyo: President-sha, 1991.

Onuma, Keiji, *Shoken no Haiboku, Shoken no Saisei* (Fall and Rebirth of the Securities Markets). Tokyo: President-sha, 1991.

Pugel, Thomas A., and Lawrence J. White, "An Analysis of the Competitive Effects of Allowing Commercial Bank Affiliates to Underwrite Corporate Securities," in Ingo Walter, ed., *Deregulating Wall Street: Commercial Bank Penetration of the Corporate Securities Market.* New York: John Wiley & Sons, 1985.

Robins, Brian. *Tokyo: A World Financial Centre.* London: Euromoney Publications, 1987.

Rosenbluth, Frances McCall. *Financial Politics in Contemporary Japan.* Ithaca: Cornell University Press, 1989.

Sakakibara, Shigeki, Hidetoshi Yamaji, Hisakatsu Sakurai, Kengo Shiroshita, and Shimon Fukuda. *The Japanese Stock Market: Pricing Systems and Accounting Information.* New York: Praeger Publishers, 1988.

Sudo, Megumi. *Nihon no Shoken-gyo: Soshiki to Kyoso* (Japanese Securities Industry: Structure and Competition). Tokyo: Toyo Keizai Shimposha, 1987.

Suzuki, Yoshio, ed. *The Japanese Financial System.* Oxford: Clarendon Press, 1987.

Suzuta, Atsuyuki. *Yondai Shoken* (Top Four Securities Companies). Tokyo: Daimond-sha, 1989.

Viner, Aron. *Inside Japanese Financial Markets.* Homewood, Illinois: Dow Jones-Irwin, 1988.

Wright, Richard W. and Gunter A. Pauli. *The Second Wave: Japan's Global Assault on Financial Services.* New York: St. Martin's Press, 1987.

Zielinski, Robert and Nigel Holloway. *Unequal Equities: Power and Risk in Japan's Stock Market.* New York: Kodansha International, 1991.

CHAPTER 3

LIQUIDITY, TRADING COSTS, AND ASSETS PRICES: IMPLICATIONS FOR JAPAN

Yakov Amihud
Haim Mendelson

An asset is liquid if it can be traded at the prevailing market price quickly and at low cost. Our research shows that liquidity is an important factor affecting the pricing of capital assets. Traditional theories of asset pricing suggest that the expected return on a capital asset is an increasing function of its risk, because investors require a compensation for the risks they bear. We demonstrate that, in addition, asset returns increase in illiquidity, because investors want to be compensated for the direct and indirect costs associated with trading. Thus, capital asset prices depend on two key characteristics: risk and liquidity.

We first survey our research which finds that liquidity has a strong effect on asset prices and returns. This suggests that portfolio managers should explicitly consider the liquidity effect in their investment decisions, and that public policy should be designed to increase market liquidity. We then examine the implications of these results for the Japanese capital market. In particular, we examine the effects of repealing the securities transfer tax and reducing the bid-ask spreads and commission rates in the Tokyo Stock Exchange.

1. ILLIQUIDITY: WHAT IS IT?

Illiquidity reflects the costs of executing a transaction. These costs depend on the traded asset as well as on additional investor and market characteristics. Consider, for example, a transaction in a stock which is listed on the Tokyo Stock Exchange (TSE). The costs of trading the stock may be classified as follows (Amihud and Mendelson (1991d)):

(1) *Bid-ask spread,* which is the difference between the buying and selling prices (respectively) currently quoted for the stock by the *Saitori.* The *Saitori* book contains limit orders that specify the prices and quantities at which the various securities companies are currently willing to buy or sell the stock. These securities companies (or their clients) play the role of market-makers, providing liquidity to the market by standing ready to buy and sell the stock at these quoted prices. They are the ones who enable the continuous market to function.

At any given point in time, the best bid is the highest price at which anybody is willing to buy the stock, and the best offer (or ask price) is the lowest available sale price. The highest bid is always lower than the lowest ask price, resulting in a "bid-ask spread." The bid-ask spread represents a compensation to dealers for providing liquidity to the market. It also represents a cost to investors, who are the consumers of liquidity, because a pair of simultaneous "round trip" buy and sell transactions incurs the full cost of the bid-ask spread.

(2) *Market-impact costs* reflect the price discount of a large sell order or the price premium paid for a large buy order, both beyond the currently quoted bid-ask spread. The best bid and ask prices apply only to the limited quantity quoted by the market-maker. If an investor wants to buy or sell a larger quantity, he will necessarily exhaust the limited quantity given the best quotes and will have to continue to the second-best quotes and so on, resulting in a sequence of increasingly unfavorable prices. Thus, whenever a trader wants to buy or sell a large quantity of stock, the very execution of his transaction will move the market price against him (i.e., up for a buying transaction or down for a sale transaction). The market impact thus represents an additional cost to investors.

(3) *Search and delay costs* are incurred when a trader looks for better prices than those quoted by the *Saitori* or searches for, say, buyers when selling a large block in order to reduce the market impact costs of the sale. This often happens when a member firm puts together a block transaction and "crosses" the block on the floor of the TSE. While saving on the two

cost components discussed above, traders bear instead additional search and delay costs. These costs include direct costs as well as the risk borne while the orders wait to be executed.

Another example of a delay cost is the cost of executing a transaction at the *Itayose,* i.e., at the opening of the morning or afternoon trading session. On that transaction, the bid-ask spread is expected to be minimal due to the pooling of many orders, however this type of transaction takes place only twice a day. Against the potential gain from the narrower spread, the trader has to forego immediate execution in the continuous market and he bears the risk that the price of the security will move against him by the time his order is executed.[1]

(4) *Direct trading costs*, including the securities transfer tax (0.3% for individual traders or 0.12% for securities companies) and brokerage commissions.

These four components of transaction costs are highly correlated: assets with high bid-ask spreads often suffer from large brokerage commissions, large market impact and high search and delay costs. Further, as discussed above, the four attributes of illiquidity can often be substituted for one another.

2. LIQUIDITY AND ASSET PRICES

We have developed[2] a model that shows how liquidity affects asset prices. In our model, assets are characterized by their transaction costs, and investors—by their investment horizons. Investors maximize the expected present value of the cash flows generated by the assets they invest in, taking into account the negative cash flows associated with the costs of transacting.

In equilibrium, the return on an asset is an increasing function of its transaction cost. This is because investors require a compensation for bearing trading costs. Further, the equilibrium return-illiquidity relationship reflects investor *clienteles* based on their holding periods: The more liquid assets are allocated in equilibrium to short-term investors, whereas the long-term investors hold the less-liquid assets. As a result, the illiquidity effect is stronger for more liquid assets, because they are traded more frequently and hence are more sensitive to transaction costs. This results in a *concave* relationship between excess return and the bid-ask spread (i.e., the slope of the return-spread curve declines as we move to less liquid securities).

We present below empirical evidence on the liquidity effect. First, we demonstrate that the cross-sectional variation of stock returns in explained by liquidity and systematic (β) risk differentials. Then, we examine the effects of liquidity on bond yields. We finally examine evidence on the impact of trading restrictions on stock prices and present evidence on the impact of changes in liquidity during the stock market crash of 1987.

2.1 Liquidity and Stock Returns

Our theory on the liquidity effect suggests a positive relation between the bid-ask spread and risk-adjusted average returns. We tested this relation using 20 years of data on NYSE stocks [Amihud and Mendelson (1986, 1989)]. We formed 49 stock portfolios grouped by their bid-ask spread and by their β (systematic risk) coefficient, seven groups for each ($7 \times 7 = 49$). Then, we estimated the relation between the bid-ask spread and the portfolios' average returns (in excess of the 90-day T-bill rate), controlling for β.

The empirical results were consistent with the theoretical predictions: average returns were increasing in the bid-ask spread, and the rate of increase was lower for portfolios with higher spreads. Table 3–1 (based on Amihud and Mendelson (1986b)) summarizes empirical results for our seven spread groups (group 1 has the lowest bid-ask spread and group 7 has the highest spread). The table shows that required returns increase with the illiquidity of the stock groups. For example, the average monthly return on stocks in group 1 (that had an average spread of 0.486%) was 0.322% lower than the average monthly return on stocks in group 5 (whose average bid-ask spread was 1.4%). On average, each 1% increase in the spread was associated with a 0.175% higher monthly average return.

The increase in required return compensating for a given increase in the bid-ask spread is smaller for more illiquid assets. Comparing groups 1 and 2 in Table 3–1, an increase of approximately 0.26% in the spread was associated with an increase of 0.16% in the required return. However, comparing groups 4 and 5, we see that an increase of approximately 0.25% in the spread was associated with an increase of only 0.08% in the required return. These results are consistent with the clientele effect discussed above.

The last column of Table 3–1 shows the effects of liquidity on asset *values*. Assume that the required monthly return on the lowest-spread group (group 1) is 1%. Then, the value of $1 invested in group 1 is $100.

TABLE 3–1
The Relation Between the Bid-Ask Spread and Required Monthly Risk-Adjusted Return for Seven Spread Groups (in percentage)

Spread Group	*Average Spread (%)*	*Excess Required Return*[a]	*Relative Value*[b]
1	0.486	0.000	100.00
2	0.745	0.164	85.01
3	0.939	0.082	92.42
4	1.145	0.242	80.52
5	1.396	0.322	75.64
6	1.774	0.509	66.27
7	3.208	0.681	59.49

[a] The excess required return in this column is relative to the required return on spread group 1 (normalized to 0). For example, the average required monthly risk-adjusted return on stocks in spread-group 2 is 0.164% higher than for stocks on spread-group 1.
[b] The relative values were calculated assuming that the required monthly return on stocks in spread-group 1 is 1% (leading to a benchmark value of 100).

Source: The data are from Amihud and Mendelson (1986a).

Using this number as a benchmark, the last column of Table 3–1 shows the corresponding value for each of our seven spread groups. Clearly, liquidity has a paramount effect on asset values. For example, if the cash flows generated by an asset give rise to a market value of $100 in group 1, changing its liquidity to that of group 7 will cut its value down to $59! This large difference shows that illiquidity costs play a significant role in determining asset values.

The effect of illiquidity on asset values is large because its costs are incurred *repeatedly*, whenever the stock is traded, and then the stock price reflects the full present value of the costs associated with trading it over its lifetime. Consider for example a stock whose trading costs are 3% of its value and its turnover rate is 75%, *i.e.*, the stock trades on average once every 16 months.[3] If the discount rate is 8% over the investment horizon and the illiquidity costs associated with each trade are 3%, the present value of the illiquidity cost stream is

$$0.03 \cdot \Sigma_{t=0}^{\infty} \frac{1}{1.08^{4/3 \cdot t}} = 0.308.$$

Thus, over a long horizon we find that about *thirty percent* of the value of the stock is lost due to illiquidity costs. This total illiquidity cost is significantly higher than the one-time cost of 3%.

2.2 Liquidity and Bond Yields

Bond prices should also reflect the costs of illiquidity. By our theory, the yield to maturity should be higher on bonds with lower liquidity. We tested this theory by examining the differences in liquidity and in yields of U.S. treasury bills and notes with less than 6 months to maturity [Amihud and Mendelson (1991a)]. Both are then discount instruments having identical cash flows for the same maturities. However, Treasury-bills are much more liquid than notes. For example, the average bid-ask spread on bills in our sample was 0.00775%, whereas the average bid-ask spread on notes was 0.0303%. The brokerage fees exhibit the same pattern: they are \$12.5 to \$25 per \$1,000,000 value for bills and \$39.0625 to \$78.125 per \$1,000,000 for notes.

Because notes are less liquid than bills, our theory predicts that their yields should be higher than those of bills *with the same maturity*. We tested the predicted liquidity effect using data from the quote-sheets of First Boston Securities for 37 randomly-selected days between April and November of 1987. We matched each note with two bills whose maturities straddled the note's, giving rise to 489 triplets of matched notes and bills with essentially the same maturity. Then, we calculated the (annualized) yield to maturity on the notes and on the bills.

The results are presented in Table 3–2. The average yield differential between notes and bills was 0.43% per annum with a standard error of 0.021%, highly significant. This strongly supports the liquidity effect: the notes, which had lower liquidity, compensated for their higher transaction costs by higher yields.[4]

Our findings are that liquidity differences strongly affect the pricing of bonds: the lower the liquidity, the higher the yield to maturity. We expect to find a similar relationship in other segments of the bond market. For example, government bonds which are just issued—"on the run"—are most liquid and have a slightly lower yield than seasoned bonds that were issued earlier and are less liquid ("off the run").

TABLE 3–2
Estimated Means and Standard Deviations for the Relative Bid-Ask Spread and Annualized Yield to Maturity for 489 Triplets of Notes and Bills[a]

		Spread (%)	*Yield (%)*
Notes (N)			
	Mean	0.0303	6.523
	StDev	0.0004	0.606
Bill 1 (B1)			
	Mean	0.00761	6.039
	StDev	0.00547	0.756
Bill 2 (B2)			
	Mean	0.00801	6.137
	StDev	0.00664	0.677

[a] Each note is matched with two bills whose maturity dates straddle the note's: Bill 1 just precedes it (i.e., has less days to maturity) and Bill 2 just follows. The data consist of 37 days during April–November 1987.

Source: Amihud and Mendelson (1991a)

2.3 Restricted Stock

That illiquidity exacts a toll in terms of price discounts is clearly seen from the evidence on restricted stock. Some U.S. companies whose stock is publicly traded issue stock which is identical in all rights to the publicly traded one except that it cannot be traded in public markets, and its sale is subject to restrictions.[5] Thus, we observe two securities—the publicly traded stock and the restricted stock issued by the same company—with the only difference between them being in their liquidity.

Naturally, the restricted stock, whose liquidity is lower, has a lower price. Silber (1991) recently found that the price of restricted stock is on average 33.75% lower than the contemporaneous price of the publicly traded stock of the same companies. The median difference was 35%. This price discount is about the same as that found twenty years earlier in the SEC's Institutional Investors Study (1971), and is also often observed in court cases which determine the values of restricted stock. There are large differences in discounts between the restricted stocks of various companies. Silber found that the discount is decreasing in the revenues and earnings of the company (which indicate good creditworthiness). Also, the discount depends on the existence of a special relation between the restricted stockholders and the company, implying better monitoring.

The conclusion is that lower asset liquidity, even if temporary, leads to considerably lower asset prices.

2.4 Liquidity and the 1987 Stock Market Crash

We have shown that differences in liquidity between assets affect their prices. It is also expected that *changes* in liquidity should change asset prices over time. We have shown this in the context of the October 1987 stock market crash. In general, market liquidity deteriorated during the Crash to levels not hitherto experienced in the U.S. securities markets. Orders could not be promptly executed, which means lack of liquidity, and information on execution and other market data were available with a considerable time lag. There were even expectations of closing the markets—the ultimate in illiquidity. Thus, the crash taught investors that the markets are not as liquid as they originally thought. By our theory, this should lead to lower asset values.

In our study of the Crash on a sample of NYSE stocks included in the S&P 500 list [Amihud, Mendelson and Wood (1990)], we found that on October 19th the dollar bid-ask spread increased by more than 63% compared to its pre-Crash level, and the quote size (the amount which dealers are willing to execute at the quoted prices) also showed a dramatic decline. A similar decline in liquidity was also found in London, where the bid-ask spread of the most liquid stocks increased From 1.2% prior to the crash to 3.4% on the Crash day and remained at about 3% through November. The sharp decline in market liquidity came after a period when investors had believed that the market had the capacity to process arbitrarily large order flows with a small effect on prices. This was reflected, for example, in the belief that portfolio insurance transactions and program trading will not adversely affect market prices (i.e., that their market impact is negligible). This belief was, however, dented in the sharp price declines on the week before the Crash, which made investors realize that the market is not as liquid as had been previously thought. The downward revision in investors' expectations regarding the liquidity of the market was reflected in the price declines that followed.

By our theory, stocks that suffered a relatively greater decline in liquidity should have experienced greater price declines. We tested this on our sample by relating the price decline of each stock (relative to the market) to the increase in its bid-ask spread. The results support our theory: The stocks whose bid-ask spread increased relatively more on the day of the Crash suffered greater price declines. Adding the quote size as a measure of liquidity, we also found that the price declines were greater for stocks whose quote size shrunk more than the average.

We also examined how the recovery in stock prices by the end of October 1987 was related to the recovery in liquidity. The average market bid-ask spread somewhat narrowed during the period following the crash, but it was still almost 40% higher than its pre-Crash level. We found that the price recovery was greater for stocks whose bid-ask spreads became narrower. This provides further support to our liquidity-effect theory. We also found that in the wake of the Crash, the market grew to appreciate liquidity more so than before. More liquid stocks were in greater demand after the Crash and enjoyed a relatively larger price recovery.

The conclusion from our evidence on the 1987 Crash is that changes in asset liquidity over time result in value changes. This means that security analysis should incorporate liquidity considerations. Just as expected increases in profitability or a decline in risk should lead to an increase in the price of a stock, so should an increase in its liquidity.

3. LIQUIDITY-INCREASING POLICIES IN JAPAN

The private benefits of higher liquidity in the form of reduced cost of capital create incentives to undertake private investments to enhance it. These private incentives, however, are insufficient, because there are positive externalities from increased liquidity [Amihud and Mendelson (1991c)]. Because of these externalities, we should expect an underinvestment in liquidity compared to the social optimum. Further, economic agents can take actions which are self serving but generate negative externalities by reducing market liquidity. These "public good" aspects of liquidity call for public policies to complement private liquidity-enhancing actions [Amihud and Mendelson (1991d)].

This role of public policy is one of the key reasons for government intervention in the form of securities market regulation. In fact, many of the policies implemented by regulatory agencies can be properly understood only in light of the notion of increasing market liquidity as a public policy objective. For example, the implementation of consolidated quotation and transaction-reporting systems reflects the objective of making information available market-wide and reducing search and delay costs through the use of information technology. Opening up the capital markets to foreign securities companies clearly increases liquidity (in addition to facilitating capital flows). In the U.S., regulatory efforts to foster competition between market centers, both in the equity markets and then in the markets for derivative instruments, also reflect the policy objective of increasing liquidity.

In Japan, an important area where public policy can affect liquidity is the area of transaction costs. In particular, we consider here three components of transaction costs: securities transaction taxes, commission rates and bid-ask spreads. We examine the effects of changing these costs, as well as extending the Exchange's trading hours, on the Tokyo Stock Exchange.

3.1 Transaction Taxes

The securities transfer tax in Japan is 0.12% for securities companies and 0.30% for others. This tax represents a direct cost of illiquidity and by our foregoing results, its repeal should have a positive effect on the Japanese capital market and on the prices of capital assets. The question that arises is whether a tax of the order of a fraction of a percentage point can have a meaningful effect on asset values. Our research on U.S. data is informative on this question.

Public policy initiatives led to the reduction or elimination of taxes on securities transactions in a number of countries (e.g., in Germany, Ireland, the Netherlands, and Sweden). In mid-1987, the European Commission proposed the harmonization of securities transaction taxes throughout the European Community, with a strong recommendation to eliminate them altogether, as has already been done by a number of countries. In the U.S., the imposition of a Securities Transaction Excise Tax (STET) was proposed as part of the discussions leading to the budget accord of September 1990. Our results were used to analyze the effect of such a transaction tax, and our estimates enabled policy makers to quantify their effect on the U.S. capital markets.

Securities transaction taxes make capital markets less liquid by increasing the direct trading costs (component (4) in Section 1). In addition to the immediate increase in cost due to the actual tax being paid, the tax makes the provision of liquidity more costly and reduces the supply of market-making services. The resulting decline in trading volume reduces market depth and increases the price impact of large orders, and the decline in available quotes increases search costs and brokerage fees. Therefore, the effect of the tax on the total cost of illiquidity is greater than that directly implied by the tax rate because of its detrimental secondary effects on market liquidity. On the other hand, some of the incidence of transaction taxes may be borne by the suppliers of liquidity, thereby reducing their impact on the public at large.

Our foregoing results show that the effect of securities transaction taxes on stock returns is a function of the stock's liquidity: the higher the liquidity, the greater the effect of a given tax rate due to the clientele effect. Because liquid stocks have greater market value, and because these stocks are more sensitive to declines in liquidity, the effect of the tax on the market is heavily weighted by its effect on the large, liquid stocks.

We analyzed the effect on stocks' expected returns of the 1990 proposal to impose a 0.5% tax on stock transactions in the U.S. [Amihud and Mendelson (1990b)]. We calculated the effect for a large sample of NYSE stocks assuming that the tax will not increase any other illiquidity cost component.[6] We found that a 0.5% tax would cause an increase of 1.3% in the value-weighted expected annual return on NYSE stocks (adjusted for risk). This represents a considerable increase in the cost of capital. The effect on stock prices depends on the stocks' required returns and growth rates; for a set of representative values, the expected decline in the value-weighted price of NYSE stocks was 13.8%. Thus, an apparently small 0.5% tax can have a sizable effect on stock values and returns.

A similar analysis can provide an order of magnitude for the expected impact of *repealing* the Securities Transfer Tax in Japan. Because we do not have data from Japan, we estimated what would be the expected impact of repealing a 0.3% transaction tax if it were imposed on U.S. stocks and then repealed. Table 3–3 shows the expected impact on asset returns as well as on their values (assuming a perpetuity paying 8% per annum). Clearly, the impact is most pronounced for the more liquid securities.

For the Dow stocks, which have a median spread of about 0.35%, this corresponds to a decline of 1.23% in the required return and to a 15% increase in price. For the NYSE as a whole, the market value would increase by about 10% as a result of the repeal.

Note the difference between the impact of the repeal on the value of the "average stock" and its impact on the market as a whole. Because market capitalization is heavily concentrated in large firms' stocks which have low bid-ask spreads, the impact of the repeal on these stocks is particularly large.

TABLE 3–3
Effects of Repealing a 0.3% Transaction Tax on Annual Return and Price

For a stock with spread of	*The annual return declines by*	*The price increases by*
0.5%	0.91%	11.44%
1.0%	0.50%	6.22%
1.5%	0.34%	4.28%

For example, 80% of the total market value of the NYSE is concentrated in firms with bid-ask spreads below 1%, and about 40% of total market value comes from stocks with spreads of 0.5% or less. For these stocks, turnover is high and consequently their sensitivity to the tax is also high. The result is that the impact of the tax is well above what one would naively expect.

Because of the lack of data, we "simulated" the impact of the repeal using U.S. data. We expect similar orders of magnitude to hold for the case of Japan.

3.2 Cutting Down the Minimum Spread

The minimum "tick" or price-change in the NYSE is $1/8, which is also the bid-ask spread for heavily-traded stocks. On a stock with a price of $40, this means a bid-ask spread of 0.31% of value.

In the Tokyo Stock Exchange, the minimum tick is one yen on stocks with prices below 1,000 yen and it jumps to 10 yen on stocks whose prices are above 1,000 yen. The result of this structure is that a stock with a price of 999 yen could have a minimum spread of 0.1%, but if its price goes up and crosses the 1,000 mark, its bid-ask spread grows ten-fold, increasing to 1%. In the U.S., for example, an increase in stock price is usually accompanied by a narrower bid-ask spread and greater liquidity, whereas in the Tokyo Stock Exchange, an increase in the price could make the stock less liquid.

Figure 3–1 shows the relationship between the price and the percentage bid-ask spread on a random sample of 43 stocks traded on the first section of the Tokyo Stock Exchange, recorded on the afternoon trading session of December 20, 1991. For the group of stocks whose price is below 1,000, the median bid-ask spread was about 0.35% (similar to the spread on the Dow Jones Industrial Index stocks). However, for stocks whose prices are just

FIGURE 3–1
Bid-Ask Spreads on the Tokyo Stock Exchange—Selected First-Section Stock, December 20, 1991

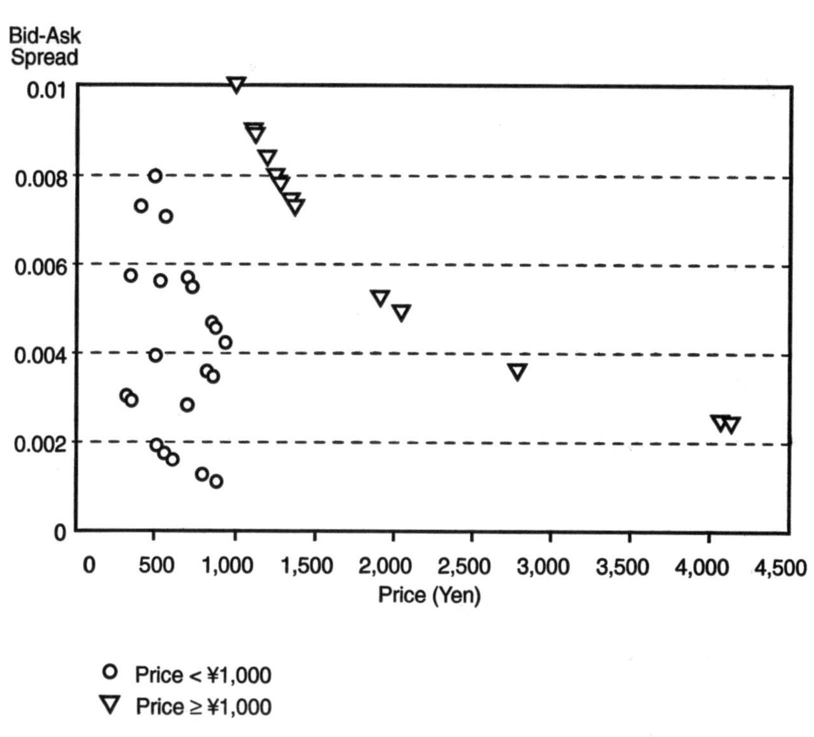

above 1,000, the bid-ask spread jumped to 1%. Thus, for example, Hitachi had a bid price 891 yen and a bid-ask spread of 0.11% (= 1/891), whereas Bridgeston Corp. and Sumitomo Shioji had a bid price of 1,000 and a bid-ask spread of 1%. Above the 1,000 yen price level, the spread declined steadily as the stock price increased. The bid-ask spread on the two stocks in our sample with prices of 4,000 yen, Sony and Fanuc, was only 0.25% (= 10/4000). It follows that the minimum tick of 10 yen creates a bid-ask spread which is many times higher than the spread that would prevail without such a restriction. This imposes a burden on the market and reduces stock prices. By our theory on the liquidity effect and using the evidence from the U.S., stock prices on the TSE could increase significantly if the minimum tick of 10 yen were reduced.

It is worth noting that the minimum tick on TOPIX futures is 1 yen. In December 1991, TOPIX was at 1,700. The minimum tick then implies a bid-ask spread of 0.06%. This is far smaller than the percentage spread on stocks. This may be one important reason for the shifting of trading in Japan from the cash market to the index futures market.

3.3 Brokerage Commissions

Brokerage commissions are an important component of trading costs. These commissions are considerably higher on the Tokyo Stock Exchange than they are in the U.S. For example, on a transaction whose value is $40,000, the commission on the TSE is about $376, whereas the commission in the U.S. on a transaction of the same size executed, for example, by Charles Schwab, is $188, practically half the cost. The marginal commission rate charged in the TSE for transactions of, say, $200,00 is 0.575%, whereas the marginal commission for the same size transaction in the U.S., executed by Charles Schwab, is 0.11% (possibly less if the stock has a high price)—five times lower!

Higher commission rates in the TSE prevail also in trading of index futures and options. Trading 100 million yen of TOPIX Futures contracts costs 80,000 yen in commissions, about $615. Trading the same value of S&P500 futures contracts (about 4 contracts) costs $100 to individual investors and $44 to institutions. It is worth noting that the commissions on trading futures and options on futures were recently doubled on the TSE.

Trading in corporate bonds is also much more costly in Japan compared to the U.S. A transaction of $50,000 worth of bonds will cost in commissions $325 in Japan and $200 in the U.S. (Charles Schwab). Institutional investors enjoy much lower costs in the U.S., while in Japan they are bound by minimum commissions.

Brokerage commissions constitute an important part of the total trading costs in securities. Our theory predicts that if commission costs were reduced, the value of the stocks and bonds in the Japanese markets would increase.

3.4 Extending the Trading-Hours

Liquidity is associated with the ability to trade. Thus, one might expect that extending the trading hours should improve market liquidity. However, the relation between liquidity and trading hours is not as simple: if the current trading hours do not impose a binding constraint on traders in the market, the increased cost of the longer hours and the diluting effect of spreading a fixed volume of liquidity-motivated trading over longer hours may actually *reduce* liquidity [see Amihud and Mendelson (1992)].

We studied the effects of extending the trading hours on market performance by examining the impact of the extension of the afternoon trading session on the TSE that took place as of April 30, 1991, for a sample of 59 heavily-traded stocks.[7] Specifically, the TSE moved the opening of its afternoon trading session from 1:00 PM to 12:30 PM.

Figure 3–2 shows the behavior of the average daily share trading volume in the 59 sampled stocks on the days surrounding the change.[8] Clearly, volumes went down on average after the trading-hour extension. While this does not indicate a causal relationship between the extension and the decline in trading volume, the extension certainly did not increase trading volume, as some might have expected.

To study the effect of the trading-hour extension on liquidity, we first examined the behavior of the first-order autocorrelations of the individual security returns before and after the extension.[9] The average autocorrelation of the opening returns declined from –0.0368 before the extension to –0.0818 afterwards (the difference is statistically significant). The effect was larger for the lower-volume stocks. A similar effect occurred for the closing return autocorrelations, although the decline there was smaller. However, for the subsample of 29 lower-volume stocks, the mean closing return autocorrelation turned from 0.0313 before the extension to –0.0064 afterwards, a statistically significant change. Thus, the results indicate that on average, the market became *less* liquid following the extension of trading hours, particularly for the less-liquid stocks.

We tested the same effect more accurately by calculating the return autocorrelations conditional on the return on an appropriate portfolio.[10] The results strengthened and reconfirmed those obtained for the autocorrelations: both for the opening and for the closing, the period after the extension of trading hours is characterized by significantly lower liquidity, as measured by a more negative conditional autocorrelation coefficient.

Thus, in contrast to one's intuitive expectations, the trading-hour extension seems to have *reduced* liquidity (or at least not improve it) as measured by trading volume as well as by the conditional and unconditional autocorrelations of returns.

FIGURE 3–2
Average Daily Volume—Tokyo Stock Exchange

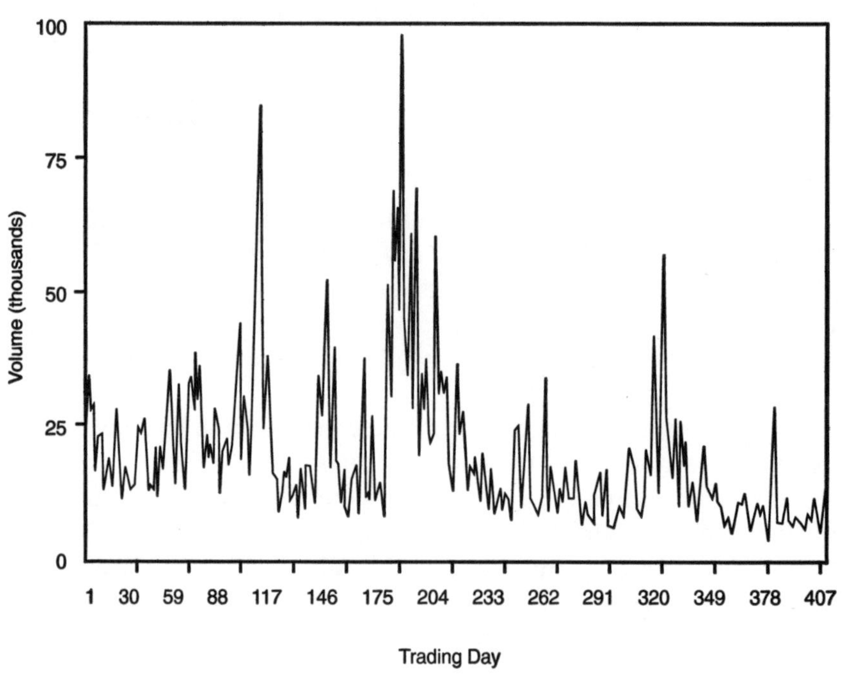

4. CONCLUSION

Our theory predicts that the expected returns on capital assets depend on their liquidity (or marketability) in addition to risk. For both bonds and stocks, *the greater the illiquidity of an asset, the greater its return,* after controlling for risk. The effects of liquidity on asset values and returns are far larger than the one-time trading costs, because the costs of illiquidity are incurred *repeatedly* whenever the asset is traded.

These results have important implications for investments, corporate financial decisions and public policy. Securities analysis should incorporate, in addition to cash-flow and risk considerations, the liquidity of the security and possible changes in it. In selling new securities, attention should be given to their liquidity in order to increase their price. And companies should employ strategies[11] to make their publicly-traded securities more liquid.

Increasing market liquidity could be an objective of public policy, because this would reduce corporate cost of capital. A liquidity-increasing public policy is particularly valuable for Japan, where trading costs are much higher than they are in the U.S. We examined here four strategies for increasing the liquidity of the Tokyo market: repealing the securities transfer tax, eliminating the increase in the minimum tick from 1 to 10 yen for stocks whose prices exceed 1,000 yen, reducing commission rates and extending the trading hours. We expect that any of the first three would result in an increase in the values of capital assets in the Japanese capital markets.

NOTES

1. In addition, the opening transaction of the day is more volatile (Amihud and Mendelson (1991b)), resulting in additional risk.
2. Amihud and Mendelson (1986b).
3. This is the average turnover rate on Tokyo Stock Exchange stocks over the period 1986–1990 (TSE Fact Book, 1991).
4. The note-bill yield differential declined recently, perhaps because of improved information systems which usually contribute the most to the liquidity of the less-liquid assets.
5. The inferior liquidity of restricted stocks is temporary, because they can usually become publicly traded within a period of two to four years.
6. In particular, we assumed no increase in brokerage fees, which effectively diminishes significantly the detrimental effect of the tax.
7. We thank Kazuhisha Saito of Nihon Keizai Shimbun for providing the data.
8. The extension of the morning trading session occurred on april 30, 1991, which is represented in Figure 2 as day 224.
9. The more negative the autocorrelation, the larger the "noise" variance, and the lower the liquidity and efficiency of the market. See Roll (1984), Amihud and Mendelson (1987, 1991b).
10. This was done separately for the 30 higher-volume stocks and for the 29 lower-volume stocks, in each case using the mean group return as the portfolio return.
11. Such strategies are detailed in Amihud and Mendelson (1988).

REFERENCES

Y. Amihud and H. Mendelson, "Liquidity and Stock returns." *Financial Analysts Journal*, Vol. 42, May-June 1986a, pp. 43–48.

Y. Amihud and H. Mendelson, "Asset Pricing and The Bid-Ask Spread." *Journal of Financial Economics*, Vol. 17, December 1986b, pp. 223–49.

Y. Amihud and H. Mendelson, "Liquidity and Asset Prices: Financial Management Implications." *Financial Management*, Vol. 17, Spring 1988, pp. 5–15.

Y. Amihud and H. Mendelson, "The Effects of Beta, Bid-Ask Spread, Residual Risk and Size on Stock Returns." *Journal of Finance*, Vol. 44, 1989, pp. 479–86.

Y. Amihud, H. Mendelson and R. A. Wood, "Liquidity and the 1987 Stock Market Crash." *Journal of Portfolio Management*, Spring 1990a, pp. 65–69.

Y. Amihud and H. Mendelson, "The Effects of a Securities Transaction Tax on Securities Values and Returns." The Mid-America Institute for Public Policy Research, 1990b.

Y. Amihud and H. Mendelson, "Liquidity, Maturity and the Yields on U.S. Government Securities." *Journal of Finance* Vol. 46, 1991a, pp. 1411–26.

Y. Amihud and H. Mendelson, "Volatility, Efficiency and Trading: Evidence from the Japanese Stock Market." *Journal of Finance* Vol. 46, 1991b, pp. 1765–89.

Y. Amihud and H. Mendelson, "How (Not) to Integrate the European Capital Markets," in A. Giovannini and C. Mayer (eds.), *European Financial Integration.* Cambridge University Press, 1991c, pp. 73–111.

Y. Amihud and H. Mendelson, "Liquidity, Asset Prices and Financial Policy." *Financial Analysts Journal*, 1991d.

R. W. Kamphuis, Jr., R. C. Kormendi and J. W. Henry Watson, *Black Monday and the Future of Financial Markets.* Homewood, Ill: Irwin, 1989.

H. Mendelson, "Consolidation, Fragmentation and Market Performance." *Journal of Financial and Quantitative Analysis,* 1987, pp. 189–207.

Roll, Richard, "A simple implicit measure of the bid/ask spread in an efficient market," *Journal of Finance* 39 (September 1984), 1127–39.

W. L. Silber, "Discounts on Restricted Stock: The Impact of Illiquidity on Stock Prices," *Financial Analysts Journal,* (July-August), 1991, pp. 60–64.

Tokyo Stock Exchange 1991 Fact Book, 1991.

CHAPTER 4

JAPANESE INITIAL PUBLIC OFFERINGS

Kevin J. Hebner
Takato Hiraki

1. INTRODUCTION

Recently a large number of studies, both empirical and theoretical, have examined the IPO process in the U.S.[1] The studies have proposed a number of explanations for the observed underpricing of IPOs, and for cross-sectional variations in the extent of underpricing.[2] Very few studies however have examined the Japanese IPO market,[3] which is similar to the U.S. market in terms of size, depth and sophistication, yet possesses a number of interesting (i.e., different from the U.S.) institutional, regulatory and market structure features.

In addition to being relatively under-researched, there are at least three reasons why examining the Japanese IPO market is interesting. First, for a number of IPO pricing issues there are inconsistencies and puzzles in the U.S. evidence. Tests undertaken using Japanese data may be able to shed some light on these issues. For example, does the Japanese and U.S. data exhibit similar patterns regarding the size effect, "hot issue" markets, offers for sale, and industry effects? If similar cross-sectional variations are observed in both the Japanese and the U.S. data, then they are more likely to

The authors acknowledge helpful comments by Clifford W. Smith, Jr.

be reflecting fundamental economic forces, rather than being idiosyncratic characteristics of a specific data set.

Second, two important regulatory changes have occurred recently in Japan. In May 1988 insider trading laws were tightened significantly and in March 1989 (following the Recruit Cosmos experience), the rules governing IPOs were changed dramatically. It is important to determine if, following these regulatory changes, there has been a significant alteration in the pattern of IPO underpricing in Japan.

Third, the Japanese data set allows us to test a modification of the Rock (1986) adverse selection model of IPO underpricing. In Rock underpricing occurs because uninformed investors require a price discount as compensation for their expected losses to informed investors. We assert that some informed investors (e.g., officers and directors, and executives) may receive valuable information as a costless by-product of providing certain contractual services to the firm. If the firm knows the statistical properties of the value of the information received by these individuals, then the firm can recapture the information's value by reducing, by the expected value of the information, the wage paid for their services.

Consequently, we predict that IPO initial returns are: inversely related to the total wage (explicit compensation) received by informed investors; and positively related to their total expected informed trading profits (implicit compensation). We test these predictions using data on firms' officers' total shareholdings and their total wage. Our modification of Rock (1986) also implies that the cost of going public may be exaggerated if one does not take into account how the firm can "recapture," from informed investors with whom it has a contractual relationship, a portion of the money "left on the table."

The remainder of the chapter proceeds as follows: Section Two presents three empirical predictions which follow directly from Rock's (1986) adverse selection model of IPO pricing. Then, a fourth empirical prediction is obtained through a slight modification, to recognize the prominent role banks perform in Japanese corporate finance, of Muscarella and Vetsuypens' (1989) test of Baron (1982). Section Three derives two additional empirical predictions by modifying Rock to allow the issuing firm to recapture part of the money "left on the table", from those informed investors with whom it has a contractual relationship. Section Four provides a description of the data set created and of the variables used to test the six empirical predictions. Section Five presents our test results, first from a set of single variable regressions and then from six multiple variable regressions. Section Six presents concluding remarks.

2. THE FIRST FOUR EMPIRICAL PREDICTIONS

A. Rock's Adverse Selection Model

In the seminal article by Rock (1986) (and the closely related studies by Ritter (1984), Beatty-Ritter (1986) and Ritter (1987)), there is uncertainty about the post-IPO equilibrium price, P_1. The issuing firm and the underwriter are uninformed (knowing only the unconditional p.d.f. $f(P; \sigma)$, with standard deviation σ, from which P_1 is drawn), as are most investors. However, some (unspecified) investors can incur certain (unspecified) costs to become "better" informed.

If the IPO offer price, P_0, is set equal to the unconditional expected post-IPO price, $\bar{P}$, then uninformed investors systematically earn below normal returns. This occurs because uninformed investors submit bids for all IPOs, while informed investors condition their bidding behaviour on their superior information. If, *ex post*, an issue is underpriced ($P_0 < P_1$) it is likely that informed investors also submitted bids and hence, the issue is likely to have been rationed. However if, *ex post*, the IPO is overpriced ($P_0 > P_1$) informed investors are less likely to have submitted bids and the issue is more likely to have been undersubscribed. Hence, uninformed investors systematically receive more overpriced issues and fewer underpriced issues.

Rock (1986) asserts that uninformed investors anticipate the above adverse selection problem and bid only if the offer price, P_0, is set below the unconditional expected post-IPO price, $\bar{P}$, by enough to compensate for their expected losses on overpriced issues. Issuing firms consequently (and reluctantly) underprice their IPOs (i.e., they set $P_0 < \bar{P}$) to keep uninformed investors in the market.[4] Note the assumption, implicit in the above discussion, that uninformed investors and the issuing firm know the statistical properties of the informed investors' expected profits.

The following two paragraphs introduce notation that allows us to be more precise regarding what generates Rock's (1986) adverse selection mechanism and hence, the mean underpricing of IPOs. This is particularly helpful for understanding Section 3, where Rock's model is modified slightly. Let $\eta(P) \in [0,1]$ denote the proportion of the total number of IPO shares that are received by informed investors (where, for simplicity and without loss of generality, we set the number of IPO shares equal to unity). Also let Ξ denote the uninformed investors' expected profit.

The three assumptions driving Rock's (1986) model can be expressed as follows: (i) $\partial\eta(P)/\partial P > 0$, the proportion of the IPO received by informed investors is an increasing function of the post-IPO price; (ii) P_0 is set $\ni \Xi = 0$, the firm sets the IPO's offer price such that uninformed investors' earn zero expected profits; and (iii) $f(P;\sigma)$ and $\eta(P)$ are public information, uninformed investors and the issuing firm know the statistical properties of the model (and hence of informed investors' profits). Then uninformed investors' expected profit, Ξ, and the total expected profit of informed investors (denoted by Π) are given by:

$$\Xi = \int_0^\infty (P - P_0)[1-\eta(P)]\, f(P;\sigma)dP = 0$$

$$\Pi = \int_0^\infty (P - P_0)\eta(P)\, f(P;\sigma)dP > 0$$

The firm determines the IPO offer price, P_0, directly from the uninformed investors expected profit equation, so that:

$$P_0 = \frac{\int_0^\infty [1-\eta(P)]\, f(P;\sigma)dP}{\int_0^\infty [1-\eta(P)]\, f(P;\sigma)dP} < \bar{P}$$

where $\bar{P} = \int P\bullet f(P;\sigma)dP$ denotes the unconditional expected value of P_1, the post-IPO price. Note that $P_0 < \bar{P}$ because, in the numerator of P_0, higher values of P receive progressively lower weightings (because $[1-\eta(\mathrm{P})]$ declines as P rises). That is, the IPO offer price, P_0, is set below the unconditional expected value, $\bar{P}$, because uninformed investors realize they receive a progressively smaller proportion of the "better" IPOs.

Two results follow immediately from the above discussion. First, $\partial\Pi/\partial\sigma > 0$ and hence, $\partial P_0/\sigma > 0$. As σ rises, uncertainty regarding P_1 increases and informed investors earn greater expected profits, which leads to increased average underpricing as uninformed investors require a lower P_0. Second, $\partial\Pi/\partial\eta' > 0$ and hence, $\partial P_0/\partial\eta' < 0$, where $\eta' = \partial\eta(P)/\partial P > 0$. As η' increases, the adverse selection problem facing uninformed investors worsens; they receive fewer shares of "good" IPOs and relatively more shares of "bad" IPOs. Consequently, informed investors earn greater expected profits, which leads to increased average underpricing as uninformed investors require a lower P_0.

The first result was initially derived by Beatty-Ritter (1986), who asserted that the inverse of an IPO's proceeds is a good proxy for *ex ante* uncertainty. Hence **Prediction 1**: Initial returns and IPO size are negatively correlated. Beatty-Ritter, and a number of others, present U.S. evidence supporting this prediction.

Uninformed investors require underpricing as compensation for their expected losses to informed investors. Hence an increase in informed trading, *ceteris paribus*, leads to increased underpricing. Let OFS denote the proportion of the total number of shares sold in the IPO that consist of "offers for sale"; i.e., shares in the IPO that are being sold by existing major shareowners, not by the issuer itself. An increase in OFS may indicate that the prevalence of information motivated trading has risen. Hence, **Prediction 2**: Initial returns are increasing in OFS. Contrary to Prediction 2, Carter and Manaster (1990) present U.S. evidence that initial returns and OFS (their "insiders" variable) are negatively related, but only significantly so in single variable regressions.

There have been several important regulatory changes affecting the Japanese IPO market in recent years. In March 1989 (following the Recruit Cosmos experience), the rules governing IPOs were changed dramatically.[5] Second, insider trading laws were tightened significantly in May 1988 (see Swan (1991)). The essence of these two regulatory changes was to decrease η'; i.e., to make it more difficult for informed investors to exploit their information advantage, thus reducing the adverse selection problem facing uninformed investors. Hence **Prediction 3**: Pre-March 1989 mean initial returns are greater than post-March 1989 returns. To the best of our knowledge, no previous study has examined whether or not these regulatory changes have had a significant impact on IPO pricing in Japan.

B. An Empirical Prediction from Baron (1982)

Baron (1982) assumes that underwriters have better information than issuers about conditions prevailing in capital markets. This results in the issuer optimally delegating the IPO price decision to the underwriter. Then the issuer's inability to perfectly monitor the underwriter, results in IPO prices being set lower than would prevail in the absence of this form of information asymmetry.

Muscarella and Vetsuypens (1989) test Baron (1982) by examining IPOs of 38 U.S. security companies that took part in the marketing of their own IPO securities. Since, in their sample, the issuer and the (not necessarily lead) underwriter are the same firm, there cannot exist an information asymmetry in Baron's sense. That is, if underpricing is caused solely by an information asymmetry (regarding conditions prevailing in capital markets) between the issuer and the underwriter, then firms who market their own IPO shares would not underprice them. More generally, if factors unrelated to this type of information asymmetry also cause IPO underpricing, then self-marketed IPOs should be less underpriced than IPOs in which the issuer and underwriter are not the same firm.

Unlike Muscarella and Vetsuypens (1989), we do not possess data on which security company IPOs were self-marketed. Also, in formulating a test of Baron (1982) for Japanese data, it is important to recognize the prominent role played by banks in Japanese corporate finance [see, for example, Aoki (1988)]. In particular, it is unlikely that Japanese banks are less well informed, on average, than security companies regarding conditions prevailing in Japanese capital markets. Consequently, a slightly modified version of Muscarella and Vetsuypens' test is presented. **Prediction 4**: Mean initial returns are lower for IPOs of security companies and banks, than for IPOs of non-financial companies. Muscarella and Vetsuypens' U.S. evidence is inconsistent with Baron. To the best of our knowledge Baron's model has not previously been tested using Japanese IPO data.

3. THE RECAPTURE THEORY MODIFICATION OF ROCK'S MODEL

Section Two presented three empirical predictions that follow directly from Rock's (1986) adverse selection model of IPO underpricing, and a fourth prediction from Baron (1982). The purpose of this section is to develop two new empirical predictions that follow from a modification of Rock's model.

Rock (1986), and several closely related studies, stress that "underpricing is merely compensation to investors for the costs of becoming informed—doing security analysis and so on" [Ritter (1984; 220)] and that "the aggregate costs of becoming informed equals the amount of money "left on the table"" [Beatty-Ritter (1986; 229)]. This section modifies their argument slightly by examining who the informed investors are likely to be, and what are their costs of becoming informed. If the firm has unbiased expectations of who the informed investors are, and knows the statistical properties of their informed trading profits, then the firm may be able to "recapture" a portion of the money "left on the table" from the informed investors with whom it has a contractual relationship.

Rock (1986) does not explicitly state who the informed investors are and what are their costs of becoming informed. To be more explicit let there exist, for each firm, a set of *S* individuals who may become informed. The S individuals at each firm can be categorized according to the following six mutually exclusive and exhaustive subsets:

i) top shareowners .... $s \in S_1$
ii) officers and directors .... $s \in S_2$
iii) executives............................. $s \in S_3$
iv) auditors, lawyers, underwriters and venture capitalists .... $s \in S_4$
v) others, who possess a fiduciary relationship with the firm[6] .... $s \in S_5$
vi) others, who do not possess a fiduciary relationship with the firm[7] .... $s \in S_6$

The *S* individuals expect to earn trading profits totaling Π, where $\Pi = \Sigma_{s \in S} \pi_s$ and π_s denotes the expected value of individual *s*'s trading profits.

Two assumptions are important to this section. First, the firm knows the statistical properties of the *S* individuals' informed trading profits Π. As demonstrated by the simple model in Section Two, this is not a new assumption; it is an assumption implicit in Rock (1986). Second, the firm possesses unbiased expectations of who the *S* individuals are; e.g., its officers and directors, and executives.

The firm has a contractual or fiduciary relationship with each of the individuals in subsets one to five. In their contracts (implicitly or explicitly), each individual s agrees to provide a specified service to the firm, for which he is to receive total compensation $C(\Omega_s)$. Let Ω_s denote s's attribute vector and let $C(\Omega_s)$ be a compensation function which is exogenous to the firm, determined in a competitive (for example, labour) market.

Then, each individual *s* in subsets one to five agrees to provide a service to the firm for which he is to receive total compensation $C(\Omega_s)$.

However prior to drafting the contract, the firm and individual s agree that, as a costless by-product of providing services to the firm, individual s receives information with expected value π_s. While in some states the individual may not receive valuable information, it is the information's expected value, π_s, that is most important. Hence, individual s's (exogenous) total compensation $C(\Omega_s)$ consists of two components:[8] (i) expected insider trading profits, π_s (implicit compensation) and (ii) a wage, ω_s (explicit compensation), determined residually such that $C(\Omega_s) = \pi_s + \omega_s$ holds.[9]

If both the firm and the individuals in subsets one to five are risk neutral, then they are indifferent regarding the composition of $C(\Omega_s)$. Hence, a version of the Coase theorem may apply: the externality (informed trading profits) can be internalized (recaptured) if a contractual relationship exists between the two parties, the informed investors and the firm. However, for informed investors from the sixth subset (the "others, who do not possess a fiduciary relationship with the firm") the informed trading externality cannot be internalized (recaptured).[10] Hence, it is only their informed trading that results in inefficient IPO underpricing and the firm leaving money "on the table," net of what it can recapture.

A more accurate measure of the indirect cost of going public, the amount of money "left on the table," is then given by the net (of what the firm can recapture) value Π^N, rather than by the gross value Π. Clearly

$$\Pi^N = \sum_{s \in S_6} \pi_s < \Pi = \sum_{s \in S} \pi_s$$

where S_6 denotes members of the sixth subset, and the inequality holds provided the first five subsets are not all empty. An important question concerns the prevalence of informed trading by members of the sixth subset. For example, there exists a large body of evidence suggesting that, while corporate insiders consistently earn informed trading profits, security analysts and portfolio managers do not and hence, should not typically be considered as informed investors (see, for example, Fama (1991) and references cited therein).

Two empirical predictions follow directly from the above discussion. As the total wage paid to members of subset i (i can be any one of the first five subsets) rises, one can infer that, *ceteris paribus,* their total expected insider trading profits have declined and consequently, less IPO underpricing is expected. Hence, for the members of any one of the first five subsets, **Prediction 5**: Initial returns and the total wage received are negatively correlated, and **Prediction 6**: Initial returns and total expected informed trading profits are positively correlated. In Section 5 we test these predictions using data on officers' (subset 2) total shareholdings and their total wage.

4. DESCRIPTION OF THE DATA SET

A. Basic Features of the Data Set

An IPO issue can be either listed on an organized exchange or registered for OTC (over-the-counter) trading. Our tests focus on the 350 exchange-listed IPOs that occurred in Japan from January 1981 to July 1991. We also possess a sample of 307 OTC-registered IPOs that occurred from January 1984 to July 1991. Further, if we include the 46 exchange-listed IPOs that previously traded in the OTC market, the number of observations in the exchange-listed sample increases to 396. However, since such ("indirect") issues are typically not defined as IPOs we generally either explicitly exclude them from the sample or employ a dummy variable, ID, to distinguish exchange-listed IPOs that previously traded in the OTC market from those that did not.

Price and attribute data for IPOs listed on the three major Japanese exchanges (Tokyo, Osaka and Nagoya) was obtained from the exchanges' monthly publications. Data for IPOs listed on regional exchanges and the OTC market was obtained from Nikko Securities. Additional (accounting) data required for the eleven explanatory variables [defined in Table 4–3(a)] used in our cross-sectional analysis was obtained from the NIKKEI NEEDS Financial Data File.

Figure 4–1(a) presents arithmetic initial returns (i.e., from the IPO offer price, P_0, to the post-IPO first market price, P_1) for the total sample of 396 exchange-listed issues, while Figure 4–1(b) displays the corresponding logarithmic initial returns. Table 4–1 provides evidence on the arithmetic initial returns for various subsamples of exchange-listed IPOs. From Panel A of Table 4–1, the total sample of 396 IPOs possesses a mean initial return of 32.49% and a standard deviation of 48.76%. Panel B excludes the 46 "indirect" issues which previously traded in the OTC market and obtains results similar to Panel A's; a mean of 32.24% and a standard deviation of 51.50%. Panel C demonstrates that, as intuition suggests, the 46 "indirect" listings

TABLE 4–1
Exchange-listed IPO Initial Returns: January 1981-July 1991 (unless otherwise noted)[a]

	Mean	Std. Dev.	N	No. of (–) Returns	Max.	(Quartile Values) 75%	Mid.	25%	Min.
A. Total Sample: W: Normal 0.56 (Prob. (<W) = 0.0001) [b]	32.49%	48.76%	396	3	650.00%	34.53%	21.41%	10.00%	-9.18%
B. Direct Exchange Listing (IPO): W: Normal 0.57 (Prob. (<W) = 0.0001) [b]	32.24%	51.50%	350	3	650.00%	38.25%	21.73%	9.93%	-9.18%
C. Indirect Listing through OTC: W: Normal 0.96 (Prob. (<W) = 0.2215) [b]	19.15%	9.87%	46	0	39.53%	25.00%	20.78%	10.19%	0.00%
D. "Ordinary" Market Periods: Excluding November 1982-October 1984 and January 1988-March 1988 W: Normal 0.89 (Prob. (<W) = 0.0001) [b]	21.86%	19.04%	291	3	100.00%	31.10%	17.65%	6.80%	-9.18%
E. "Hot" Market Periods: November 1982-October 1984 and January 1988-March 1988 W: Normal 0.69 (Prob. (<W) = 0.0001) [b]	95.32%	97.88%	59	0	650.00%	116.67%	79.28%	37.04%	0.00%
F. Subperiod I: January 1981-March 1989 (before the regulatory change) W: Normal 0.56 (Prob. (<W) = 0.0001) [b]	43.14%	57.60%	248	1	650.00%	49.39%	27.39%	16.34%	-5.04%
G. Subperiod II: April 1989-July 1991 (after the regulatory change) W: Normal 0.67 (Prob. (<W) = 0.0001) [b]	12.62%	19.58%	102	2	100.00%	14.16%	4.61%	2.40%	-9.18%

H. Manufacturing Companies: W: Normal 0.69 (Prob. (<W) = 0.0001)[b]	40.24%	51.78%	139	1	340.52%	53.85%	23.24%	12.50%	-5.04%
I. Service Companies (other than financial): W: Normal 0.46 (Prob. (<W) = 0.0001)[b]	33.19%	54.11%	182	2	650.00%	36.63%	23.10%	10.43%	-9.18%
J. Financial Service Companies: W: Normal 0.71 (Prob. (<W) = 0.0001)[b]	12.16%	14.82%	29	0	61.54%	12.20%	5.52%	2.99%	0.34%
K. Listing on Major Exchanges: W: Normal 0.57 (Prob. (<W) = 0.0001)[b]	37.57%	55.84%	278	2	650.00%	43.10%	11.76%	10.00%	-9.18%
L. Listing on Regional Exchanges: W: Normal 0.56 (Prob. (<W) = 0.0001)[b]	21.42%	48.76%	72	1	151.32%	28.97%	12.65%	4.61%	-5.04%
M. IPOs without Offers for Sale: W: Normal 0.74 (Prob. (<W) = 0.0001)[b]	31.27%	35.59%	237	3	254.29%	36.36%	27.52%	10.00%	-9.18%
N. IPOs with Offers for Sale: W: Normal 0.49 (Prob. (<W) = 0.0001)[b]	40.48%	74.41%	113	0	650.00%	44.00%	21.07%	9.76%	0.00%

[a] 408 companies went public through an exchange listing from January 1981-July 1991. The three major exchanges are Tokyo, Osaka, and Nagoya, and the five regional exchanges are Fukuoka, Hiroshima, Kyoto, Niigata, and Sapporo. Of the 408 IPOs, twelve did not have initial returns since no new shares were offered and thus they are excluded from the total sample. The total sample, however, includes companies which are exchange-listed for the first time, but previously traded in the OTC market. There are 46 such companies included in the total sample, but they are excluded in all panels other than Panel A.

[b] W: Normal> shows the Shapiro-Wilk statistic for the test of normality. Prob. (<W) represents the confidence level at which the null hypothesis of normality is wrongly rejected.

possess both a smaller mean (19.15%) and a smaller standard deviation (9.87%) than the 350 IPOs which did not previously trade in the OTC market.

Note that while IPO initial return distributions are often characterized by citing their means and standard deviations, the underlying distributions are highly unlikely to be normal [as documented by Table 4–1's normality tests, and as can be seen in Figure 4–1(a)]. For example, while there exists a number of extremely large observations (the largest being 650%), the number of issues with negative initial returns is surprisingly small; only three out of 350 observations.[11]

Figures 4–1(a) and 4–1(b) reveal two interesting features of the IPO sample. First, there appear to be two "hot" market periods (in the sense of Ritter (1984)): November 1982-October 1984, and January 1988-March 1988. The first "hot" market period is longer in duration and includes more extremely large returns than does the second "hot" market period. Panels D and E of Table 4–1 demonstrate that the "hot" market periods' mean initial return (95.32%) and standard deviation (97.88%) are both much larger than the "ordinary" market periods' mean (21.86%) and standard deviation (19.04%). While the cause of "hot" market periods is not well understood, they appear to be a phenomenon that is not unique to the U.S. IPO market.

The second interesting feature revealed by Figures 4–1(a) and 4–1(b) is that pre-March 1989 and post-March 1989 (when new IPO regulations came into effect) initial return distributions appear to be different. Panels F and G of Table 4–1 demonstrate that the pre-March 1989 period's mean return (43.14%) and standard deviation (57.60%) are both much larger than the post-March 1989 period's mean (12.62%) and standard deviation (19.58%). To recognize these features of the IPO sample, two dummy variables are employed in our empirical analysis: HD, to distinguish between "hot" and "ordinary" market periods; and SD, to distinguish between the pre- and post-March 1989 periods.

Panels H, I and J of Table 4–1 partition the sample according to three industrial classifications: manufacturing, service (other than financial), and financial service. Observe that Panel J's sample of 29 financial service companies has both a relatively low mean initial return (12.16%) and a low standard deviation (14.82%). Next, Panels K and L compare IPOs listed on major exchanges with those listed on regional exchanges. Somewhat counter-intuitively, the major exchange-listed IPOs' mean (37.57%) and standard deviation (55.84%) are both larger than the regional exchanges' mean (21.42%) and standard deviation (48.76%).

FIGURE 4–1(a)
Arithmetic Initial Returns for Japanese Exchange-Listed IPOs—January 1981–July 1991 [N (total) = 396)

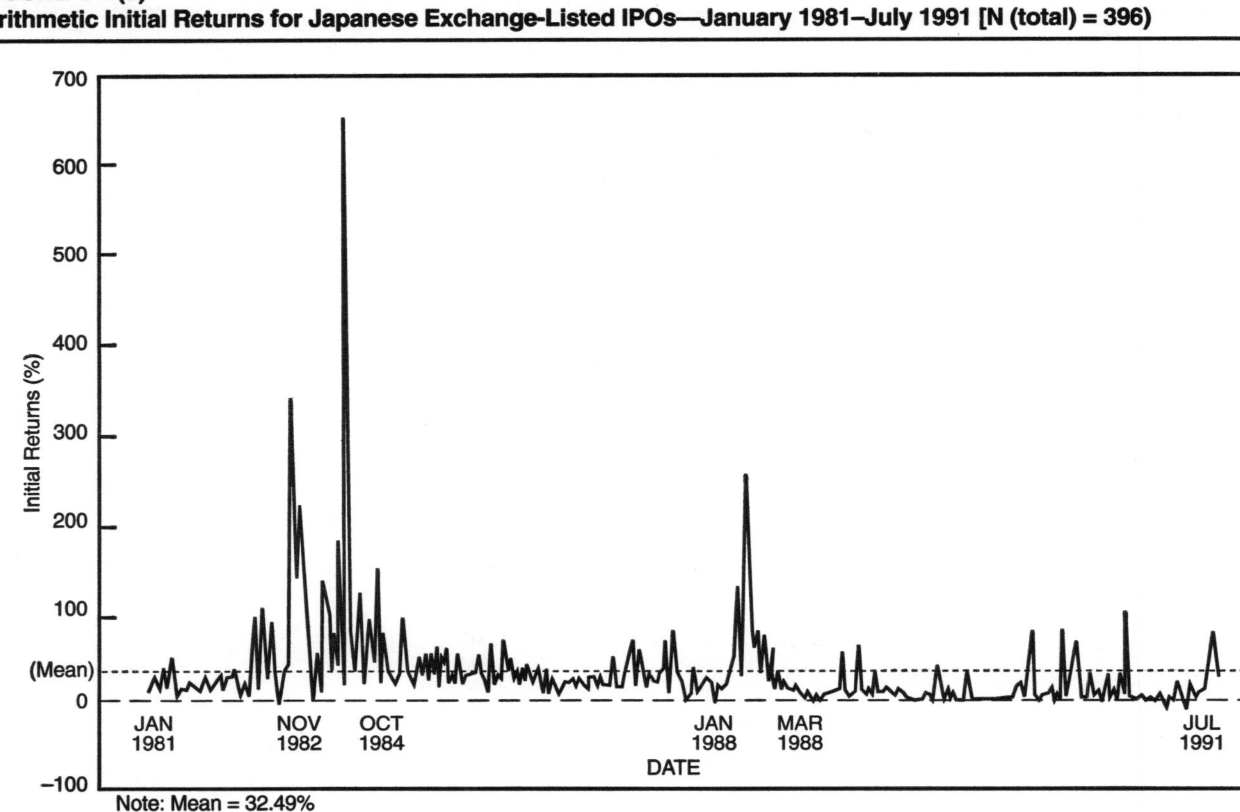

Note: Mean = 32.49%

FIGURE 4–1(b)
Logarithmic Initial Returns for Japanese Exchange-Listed IPOs—January 1981–July 1991 [N (total) = 396]

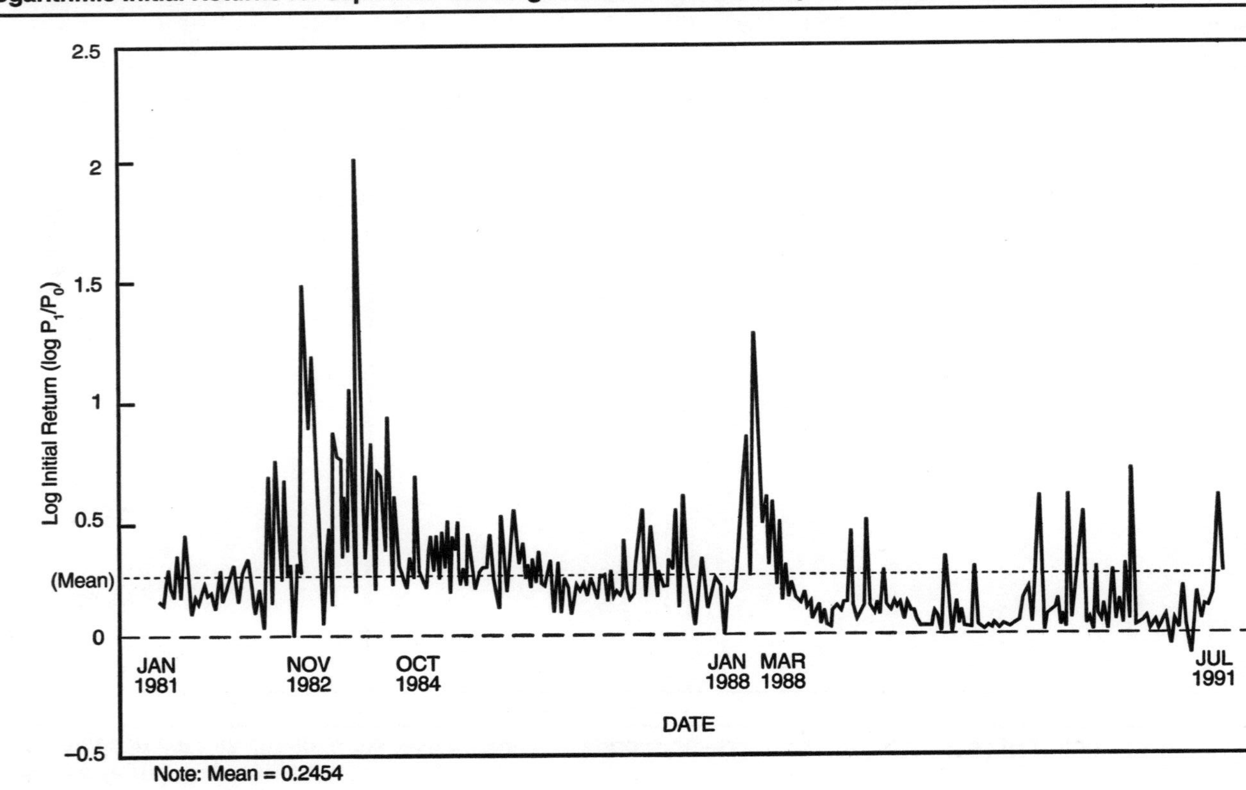

Note: Mean = 0.2454

Panels M and N partition the sample into, respectively, IPOs without OFS (offers for sale) and IPOs with OFS. Panel M's mean (31.27%) and standard deviation (35.59%) are both smaller than Panel N's mean (40.48%) and standard deviation (74.41%). However, the difference between the two means is not likely to be statistically significant, particularly since the second subsample's standard deviation is so large. To recognize these features of the IPO sample, three additional dummy variables are introduced into the empirical analysis: FD, to distinguish financial service companies from companies in other industries; ED, to differentiate between major and regional exchange listings; and UD, to distinguish IPOs without OFS from IPOs with OFS.

Table 4–2 briefly examines IPOs registered for the OTC market, and compares their mean initial return with the mean return for exchange-listed IPOs. The OTC sample consists of 307 IPOs, from January 1984 to July 1991. Panel I of Table 4–2 provides basic statistics for the OTC issues, for the total sample period as well as for the two subsample periods (pre- and post-March 1989). The pre-March 1989 period's mean return (33.93%) and standard deviation (44.89%) are both larger than the post-March 1989 period's mean (21.30%) and standard deviation (39.47%). Panel II tests whether mean returns (for the total sample period, in logarithmic form) are equal for OTC and exchange-listed IPOs. We find that the means are not significantly different from one another.

B. Basic Statistics of IPO Variables

Table 4–3(a) defines and provides some basic statistics for the dependent variable and eleven explanatory variables used in our cross-sectional analysis. The dependent variable, denoted by LINITIAL, is the logarithmic initial return. As revealed in Table 4–1, arithmetic returns exhibit significant (positive) skewness. This feature of the return distribution may reduce the reliability of t-statistics employed to test the significance of both estimated regression coefficients, and the differences between subsample means. Using logarithmic returns reduces, but does not eliminate, this problem. The eleven explanatory variables are defined in Table 4–3(a). Additional accounting data required for these variables was obtained from the NIKKEI NEEDS Financial Data File (upto the end of 1991).

Table 4–3(b) displays Pearson correlation coefficients for the twelve variables defined in Table 4–3(a). The probability that the eleven explanatory variables are not correlated with one another is typically quite small. For

TABLE 4–2
Initial Returns for OTC-registered IPOs: January 1984–July 1991[a]

	Mean	*Std. Dev.*	*N*	*No. of (–) Returns*	*Max.*	*(Quartile Values) 75%*	*Mid.*	*25%*	*Min.*
I. Return Analysis									
A. Total Period: January 1984-July 1991 W: Normal 0.56 (Prob. (<W) = 0.0001)	26.65%	42.24%	307	1	313.22%	29.31%	11.94%	4.49%	–1.10%
B. Subperiod: January 1984-March 1989 W: Normal 0.59 (Prob. (<W) = 0.0001)	33.93%	44.89%	130	0	313.22%	30.60%	20.14%	11.89%	2.50%
C. Subperiod: April 1989-July 1991 W: Normal 0.56 (Prob. (<W) = 0.0001)	21.30%	39.47%	177	1	233.33%	19.41%	5.49%	2.99%	–1.10%

II. Comparison with Exchange-listed IPOs: January 1984-July 1991

Logarithmic Mean Returns:[b]
Exchange-listed IPOs: mean = 0.2200 and std. dev. = 0.2029
OTC-registered IPOs: mean = 0.1999 and std. dev. = 0.2450

Mean Return Difference (on a log-return basis) = 0.0201 (or 2.01%)
t-statistic = 0.67
Prob. (<*t*) about 0.50

[a] The total sample period is divided into two subperiods; before and after the regulatory changes on April 1, 1989. W represents the Shapiro-Wilk statistic for the test of normality. Prob. (<W) represents the confidence level at which the null hypothesis of normality is wrongly rejected.

[b] Since the arithmetic returns are highly skewed towards the right, the t-test is not too useful. The *t*-statistic is used to test for the equality of mean initial returns between two samples of unequal size [see Snedecor and Cochran (1980)]. H_0: equal mean.

TABLE 4–3(a)
Basic Statistics and Definitions of IPO Variables

Variable	*N*	*Mean*	*Std. Dev.*	*Min.*	*Max.*
LINITIAL	396	0.2454	0.2392	–0.0862	2.0149
OFS	396	0.1047	0.1903	0.0000	1.0000
RELSIZE	396	0.2056	0.0692	0.0133	0.6706
YENSIZE	396	15.4128	0.9641	12.5054	18.1418
LMV	396	17.0728	1.0052	14.6238	20.3044
DEBT	396	0.5239	0.2061	0.0808	0.9839
LD (–1)	249	0.0989	0.2146	–0.2179	1.7306
LD(+1)	249	–0.0172	0.1588	–0.9294	0.5265
TD	249	0.0813	0.2246	–0.5034	1.6366
W/SALES (–2)	335	0.5652	0.7487	0.0048	10.0456
W/SALES (–1)	337	0.5461	0.7294	0.0038	10.3995
W/SALES (+1)	333	0.5791	1.0739	0.0096	15.6667

Definitions of Variables:

LINITIAL = $Log_e (P_1/P_0)$ = Natural logarithmic initial return (%/100);

OFS = (Offers–for–sale)/(total IPO shares). Total IPO shares consist of new shares offered by the issuer plus existing shares offered for sale by major shareholders;

RELSIZE = (Total IPO shares newly offered)/(total shares outstanding after the IPO);

YENSIZE = Natural log of the yen value of total IPO shares, measured at the offer price;

LMV = Natural log of the yen value of total shares outstanding after the IPO, measured at the offer price;

DEBT = (Total liabilities)/(total assets) at t=+1, i.e., at the end of the fiscal year that includes the IPO;

LD(–1) = $Log_{10} (S_{-1}/S_{-2})$ where S_t = officers' shareholdings at time t. t=–2 is the fiscal year-end two years prior to t=+1, and t=–1 is the fiscal year-end one year prior to t=+1;

LD(+1) = $Log_{10} (S_{+1}/S_{-1})$ where S_{+1} = officers' shareholdings at t=+1, the end of the fiscal year that includes the IPO;

TD = LD(–1) + LD(+1);

W/SALES(–2) = (Officers' total compensation/sales)(100) measured at t=–2, the fiscal year-end two years prior to t=+1;

W/SALES(–1) = (Officers' total compensation/sales)(100) measured at t=–1, the fiscal year-end one year prior to t=+1; and

W/SALES(+1) = (Officers' total compensation/sales)(100) measured at t=+1, the end of the fiscal year that includes the IPO.

TABLE 4–3(b)
Pearson Correlation Coefficients; Prob.> |R| under H_0:Rho (p) = 0; N (Number of Observations)

	LINITIAL	*OFS*	*RELSIZE*	*YENSIZE*	*LMV*	*DEBT*	*LD(−1)*	*LD(+1)*	*TD*	*W/Sales (−2)*	*W/Sales −1)*	*W/Sales (+1)*
LINITIAL	1.00	0.06	0.19	−0.01	−0.09	0.09	−0.12	0.07	−0.07	−0.17	−0.16	−0.14
Prob.	0.00	0.22	0.00	0.83	0.06	0.07	0.05	0.25	0.29	0.00	0.00	0.01
N	396	396	396	396	396	366	249	249	249	335	337	333
OFS		1.00	0.09	0.00	0.00	0.01	−0.06	0.07	0.00	0.03	0.03	−0.01
Prob.		0.00	0.07	0.95	0.98	0.78	0.37	0.28	0.95	0.60	0.53	0.98
N		396	396	396	396	366	249	249	249	335	337	333
RELSIZE			1.00	0.04	−0.32	0.02	0.09	−0.02	0.07	−0.04	−0.04	0.03
Prob.			0.00	0.10	0.00	0.75	0.15	0.79	0.24	0.34	0.44	0.60
N			396	396	396	366	249	249	249	335	337	333
YENSIZE				1.00	0.90	−0.30	0.09	0.16	0.20	−0.14	−0.15	−0.06
Prob.				0.00	0.00	0.00	0.16	0.01	0.00	0.01	0.01	0.31
N				396	396	366	249	249	249	335	337	333
LMV					1.00	−0.28	0.06	0.16	0.17	−0.13	−0.14	−0.07
Prob.					0.00	0.00	0.36	0.01	0.01	0.01	0.01	0.20
N					396	366	249	249	249	335	337	333
DEBT						1.00	−0.22	0.05	−0.17	−0.19	−0.02	−0.22
Prob.						0.00	0.00	0.40	0.01	0.00	0.00	0.00
N						366	248	248	249	332	334	330
LD(−1)							1.00	−0.30	0.74	0.17	0.15	0.11
Prob.							0.00	0.00	0.00	0.01	0.03	0.10
N							249	249	249	233	234	235

LD(+1)	1.00	0.42	–0.08	–0.10	–0.07
Prob.	0.00	0.00	0.23	0.14	0.30
N	249	249	233	234	235
TD		1.00	0.11	0.07	0.06
Prob.		0.00	0.09	0.27	0.38
N		249	234	235	236
W/SALES(–2)			1.00	0.98	0.94
Prob.			0.00	0.00	0.00
N			335	332	326
W/SALES(–1)				1.00	0.96
Prob.				0.00	0.00
N				337	328
W/SALES(+1)					1.00
Prob.					0.00
N					333

Note: See Table 4(a) for definitions of the variables.

example (and not surprisingly), the three size-related variables (RELSIZE, YENSIZE and LMV) are highly correlated with one another, as are the three officers' shareholdings variables (LD(–1), LD(+1) and TD), and the three officers' explicit compensation variables (W/SALES(t) for t=–2, –1, +1). A notable exception is the OFS (offers for sale) variable, which is not highly correlated with most of the other explanatory variables.[12] The correlation coefficients displayed in Table 4–3(b) are important because highly correlated explanatory variables should not be jointly used in regression analysis. Further, certain explanatory variables which appear to be significant in single variable regressions, may lose their significance when more fundamentally important variables are included in multiple variable regressions.

5. EMPIRICAL TEST RESULTS

A. Single Variable Tests of the Six Empirical Predictions

Section 2's model predicts that an IPO's initial returns are an increasing function of its *ex ante* uncertainty. Beatty-Ritter (1986) assert that the inverse of an issue's proceeds may be a good proxy for its *ex ante* uncertainty. Hence Prediction 1: Initial returns and IPO size are negatively correlated.

In Table 4–4, Panels A1 (total sample) and A2 (excluding financial service companies and "indirect" exchange-listings, which previously traded OTC) present single variable regression results employing three different size variables: RELSIZE, YENSIZE and LMV (defined in Table 4–3(a)). The RELSIZE coefficient is positive and significant in both panels, YENSIZE is negative but not significantly so in either panel, and LMV is negative but only significantly so in Panel A1. The lack of support provided for Prediction 1 by the single variable regressions is surprising. Particularly since many U.S. studies have found supporting evidence using similarly defined size variables; for example, Beatty-Ritter (1986) use a variable similar to YENSIZE.

Table 4–1 and Table 4–2 also provide indirect evidence related to Prediction 1. Typically IPOs listed on major exchanges are larger than those listed on regional exchanges, and issues listed on organized exchanges are larger than those registered for the OTC market. However, the evidence does not support the obvious implications of Prediction 1. On the contrary,

TABLE 4–4
Basic Relationships Between IPO Initial Returns and Size, Officers' Shareholdings and Compensation, and Risk—January 1981–July 1991

$$(\text{LINITIAL}_i) = \alpha_0 + \alpha_1(\text{Variable}_i) + \varepsilon_i$$

Independent Variable[a]	*N*	α_0	α_1	R^2	*RMSE*
A1 Size (all 396 sample companies)					
1) OFS	396	0.2373[b] (17.30)	0.0784 (1.24)	0.01	0.2390
2) RELSIZE	396	0.1095[b] (2.95)	0.6611[b] (3.87)	0.04	0.2350
3) YENSIZE	396	0.2866 (1.49)	–0.0027 (–0.21)	0.00	0.2454
4) LMV	396	0.6301[b] (3.98)	–0.0225[d] (–1.89)	0.00	0.2454
A2 Size (excluding financial companies and "indirect' listings, companies with OTC trading experience)					
1) OFS	321	0.2626[b] (14.94)	0.0171 (0.57)	0.01	0.2559
2) RELSIZE	321	0.1799[b] (3.48)	0.4024[d] (1.78)	0.01	0.2547
3) YENSIZE	321	0.2776 (1.17)	–0.0006 (–0.04)	0.00	0.2561
4) LMV	321	0.4192 (1.63)	–0.0089 (–0.59)	0.00	0.2559
B. Shareholdings (data unavailable for 147 companies, including all 29 financial companies)					
1) LD(–1)	249	0.2983[b] (17.29)	–0.1318[c] (–1.95)	0.01	0.2268
2) LD(+1)	249	0.2626[b] (18.07)	0.1047 (1.15)	0.01	0.2280
3) TD	249	0.2663[b] (17.39)	–0.0678 (–1.06)	0.01	0.2277

Continued, next page

[a] All variables are defined in Table 4–3(a). R^2 is the regression's coefficient of determination, which is adjusted for degrees of freedom, and RMSE is the regression's root mean squared error. *t*-statistic is in parentheses below the estimate of each coefficient.
[b] Significantly different from zero at the 1% level.
[c] Significantly different from zero at the 5% level.
[d] Significantly different from zero at the 10% level.

TABLE 4–4, concluded

$$(\text{LINITIAL}_i) = \alpha_0 + \alpha_1(\text{Variable}_i) + \varepsilon_i$$

Independent Variable[a]	*N*	α_0	α_1	R^2	*RMSE*
C. Compensation (data unavailable for approximately 60 companies, including all 29 financial companies)					
1) W/Sales (–2)	335	0.2880[b] (18.06)	–0.0529[b] (–3.11)	0.03	0.2571
2) W/Sales (–1)	337	0.2867[b] (18.07)	–0.0527[b] (–3.02)	0.03	0.2332
3) W/Sales (+1)	333	0.2756[b] (18.73)	–0.0304[b] (–2.52)	0.02	0.2362
D. Risk (excluding financial companies)					
DEBT	365	0.1985[b] (5.53)	–0.1180[c] (–1.80)	0.01	0.2425

[a] All variables are defined in Table 4–3(a). R^2 is the regression's coefficient of determination, which is adjusted for degrees of freedom, and RMSE is the regression's root mean squared error. *t*–statistic is in parentheses below the estimate of each coefficient.
[b] Significantly different from zero at the 1% level.
[c] Significantly different from zero at the 5% level.
[d] Significantly different from zero at the 10% level.

although neither of the differences is statistically significant, the mean initial return is larger for major exchanges than for regional exchanges (Table 4–1, Panels K and L) and also, the mean return is larger for organized exchanges than for the OTC market (Table 4–2, Panel II). A corresponding result is obtained in Table 4–5; the coefficient for the dummy variable ED (ED=1 if the IPO is listed on a regional exchange, and is zero otherwise) is negative, and significant at the 1% level.

Next we test Prediction 2: Initial returns are increasing in OFS. Recall that OFS denotes the proportion of the IPO that consists of offers for sale. Single variable regression results are provided in Panels A1 and A2 of Table 4–4. In both regressions the OFS coefficient is positive, but not significantly so. A corresponding result is obtained in Table 4–5; the coefficient for the dummy variable UD (UD=1 if the IPO includes offers for sale, and is zero otherwise) is positive, but again not significantly so. Note that, while the evidence from single variable regressions employing Japanese data does not provide statistically significant support for Prediction 2, the U.S. data rejects it outright. For example, Carter and Manaster's (1990;1061) OFS variable (labelled "insiders") is negative, and significant at the 10% level.

As discussed in Section 2, two recent regulatory changes made it more difficult for informed investors to exploit their information advantage, thus reducing the adverse selection problem facing uninformed investors. In particular, in March 1989 IPO regulations were changed dramatically. Hence Prediction 3: Pre-March 1989 mean initial returns are greater than post-March 1989 returns.

From Panels F and G of Table 4–1, the pre-March 1989 subperiod's mean initial return (43.14%) is more than three times as large as the post-March 1989 subperiod's mean return (12.62%). In Table 4–5, a corresponding result is obtained from a single variable regression. The coefficient for the dummy variable SD (SD=1 if the IPO occurred post-March 1989, and is zero otherwise) is negative, and significant at the 1% level. Additional evidence supporting Prediction 3 is presented below when the multiple variable regression results are discussed.

Next we test Prediction 4: Mean initial returns are lower for IPOs of security companies and banks, than for IPOs of non-financial companies. While Muscarella and Vetsuypens' (1989) test (using U.S. data) of Baron's (1982) model only examines security companies, we have included banks to recognize their prominent role in Japanese corporate finance (see, for example, Aoki (1989)). Also, unlike Muscarella and Vetsuypens we do not possess data on which security company IPOs were self-marketed.

To test Prediction 4 the data set is classified into four subsamples. The logarithmic mean initial return and standard deviation (in parentheses immediately following the mean) for the four sample groups are as follows: Group One (13 securities companies), a mean of 17.45% (14.67%); Group Two (14 banks, one finance company, and one casualty insurance company), a mean of 5.27% (3.17%); Group Three (all 29 financial service companies), a mean of 10.73% (11.77%); and Group Four (all 321 nonfinancial companies), a mean of 26.84% (25.53%).

We now test four versions of the following null hypothesis, H_0: Group i's and group j's mean initial returns are equal.[13] First, the null hypothesis that the first group's (security companies) and second group's (banks) mean initial returns are equal is rejected at the 1% level of significance (the *t*-statistic is $|t| = 3.12$). This result suggests that banks may be, on average, better informed than securities companies. This is consistent with the prominent role of banks in Japanese corporate finance. Alternatively, Rock's (1986) model suggests that this may occur because, on average, banks' IPOs

TABLE 4–5
Relationships between IPO Initial Returns and Various (Dummy) Variables: Single Variable Regressions for January 1981–July 1991 (including all 396 Companies)

Definitions of Dummy Variables:

UD = < 0, else 0;
ID = 1 if the IPO is "indirect" (i.e., company's shares previously traded in the OTC market), else 0;
HD = 1 if the IPO occurred during a "hot" market period, else 0;
SD = 1 if the IPO occurred after the regulatory change of April 1, 1989, else 0;
ED = 1 if the company's shares are listed on one of the regional stock exchanges, else 0; and
FD = if the company belongs to the financial services industry, else 0.

$$(\text{LINITIAL}_i) = \alpha_0 + \alpha_1(\text{Variable}_i) + \varepsilon_i$$

Independent Variable[a]	*N*	α_0	α_1	$R^{2\,b}$	*RMSE*[b]
(1) UD	396	0.2369[c] (16.28)	0.0266 (1.03)	0.00	0.2392
(2) ID	396	0.2551[c] (20.45)	–0.0883[d] (–2.23)	0.01	0.2380
(3) HD	396	0.1835[c] (17.41)	0.3896[c] (14.72)	0.35	0.1924
(4) SD	396	0.3021[c] (22.89)	–0.1986[c] (–8.04)	0.14	0.2220
(5) ED	396	0.2609[c] (19.73)	–0.0829[c] (–2.71)	0.02	0.2373
(6) FD	396	0.2563 (20.78)	–0.1490 (–3.27)	0.02	0.2363

[a] *t*-statistic is in parentheses below the estimate of each coefficient.
[b] R^2 is the regression's coefficient of determination, which is adjusted for degrees of freedom, and RMSE is the regression's root mean squared error.
[c] Significantly different from zero at the 1% level.
[d] Significantly different from zero at the 5% level.

possess less *ex ante* uncertainty than security companies' IPOs. Note, for example, that the bank subsample's standard deviation (3.17%) is much smaller then the security companies' standard deviation (14.67%).[14]

Second, the null hypothesis that the first group's (securities companies) and the fourth group's (non-financial companies) mean returns are equal cannot be rejected at any conventional significance level (the *t*-statistic is only $|t| = 1.31$, even though the security companies' mean return is 9.39%

lower). This is similar to Muscarella and Vetsuypens' (1989) result using U.S. data; they also find that the subsample means are not significantly different from one another.

Third, the null hypothesis that the second group's (banks) and the fourth group's (nonfinancial companies) mean returns are equal can be rejected at the 1% level of significance (|t|=3.37). Fourth, the null hypothesis that the third group's (all financial companies) and the fourth group's (nonfinancial companies) mean returns are equal can be rejected at the 1% level of significance (|t| =3.36).

The second result above is similar to a result obtained in Muscarella and Vetsuypens' (1989) test of Baron (1982). However, one should exercise caution when comparing results obtained using U.S. data and designed with U.S. financial institutions in mind, with results for the Japanese market. In the Japanese context it is conceivable that banks are, on average, better informed than security companies regarding conditions prevailing in capital markets. This view is consistent with the evidence presented above. However, this evidence is only preliminary as more reliable tests require a larger sample and, like Muscarella and Vetsuypens, data on which security company's IPOs were self-marketed.

From the recapture theory developed in Section 3 we obtained two predictions, which are now tested using data on officers' total shareholdings and their total wage. Officers' total wage at time t is represented by W/SALES(t), where W denotes the total wage (salary and bonus) paid to the issuer's officers. W is divided by the firm's sales because data on the number of officers employed at each company is not available in our data set. The IPO takes place at $t = 0$; $t = +1$ denotes the end of the fiscal year during which the IPO occurs; $t = -1$ denotes the previous fiscal year-end; and $t = -2$ denotes the fiscal year-end one year prior to $t = -1$. Figure 4–2(a) displays the mean value W/SALES(t) for $t = -2, -1, +1$; observe its V-shaped pattern.

To obtain a very rough estimate of the informed trading profits obtained by a company's officers, let S_t denote the total number of shares held by the issuing company's officers at time t. Figure 4–2(b) plots changes in S_t, as represented by $\log(S_t/S_2)+1$, for $t = -2, -1, +1$ (without loss of generality, the $t = -2$ value is set equal to one). On average officers' total shareholdings increase dramatically between $t = -2$ and $t = -1$,[15] and then decline slightly between $t = -1$ and $t = +1$ (recall the IPO occurs at $t = 0$). Consequently, as displayed in Figure 4–2(b), officers' total shareholdings exhibit an inverted V-shaped pattern and, on average, they increase over the

FIGURE 4–2a
Changes in Relative Officers' Compensation Around the IPO Event—January 1981–July 1991, N = 335 (data unavailable for 61 companies, including all 29 financial companies)

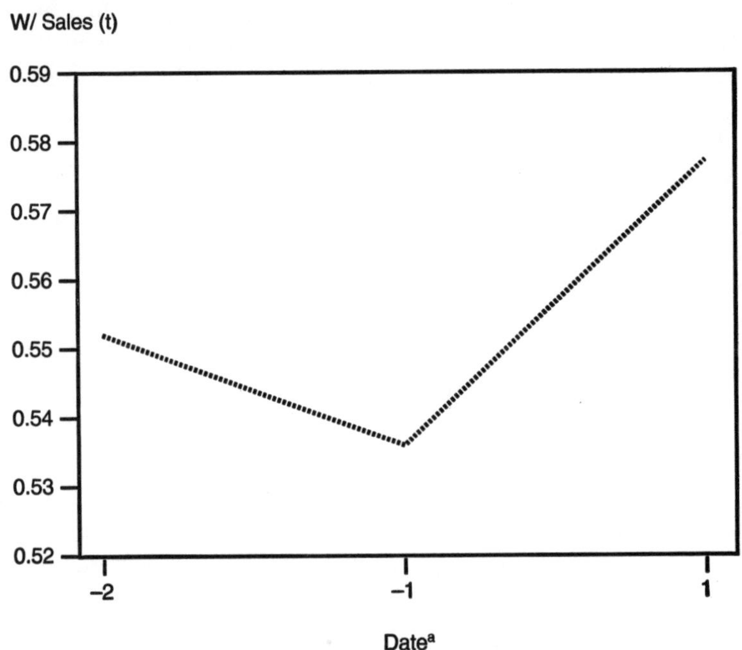

Note: The horizontal axis measures time relative to the IPO date ($t = 0$).

full period from $t = -2$ to $t = +1$. This inverted V-shaped pattern contrasts with the V-shaped pattern exhibited by the officers' total wage variable [W/SALES(t)] in Figure 4–2(a).

Recall Prediction 5: Initial returns and the total wage received are negatively correlated. Officers' total wage is represented by W/SALES(t), with the sample size reduced from 396 observations to 333-337 observations (because officers' compensation data is not available for approximately 60 companies, including all 29 financial service companies). Panel C of Table 4–4 presents single variable regression results for W/SALES(t) for $t = -2, -1, +1$. Consistent with Prediction 5, all three coefficients are negative, and significant at the 1% level. Further evidence regarding Prediction 5 is presented below when the multiple vari-

FIGURE 4–2b
Changes in Company Officers' Shareholdings Around the IPO Event—January 1981–July 1991, N = 249 (data unavailable for 147 companies, including all 29 financial companies)

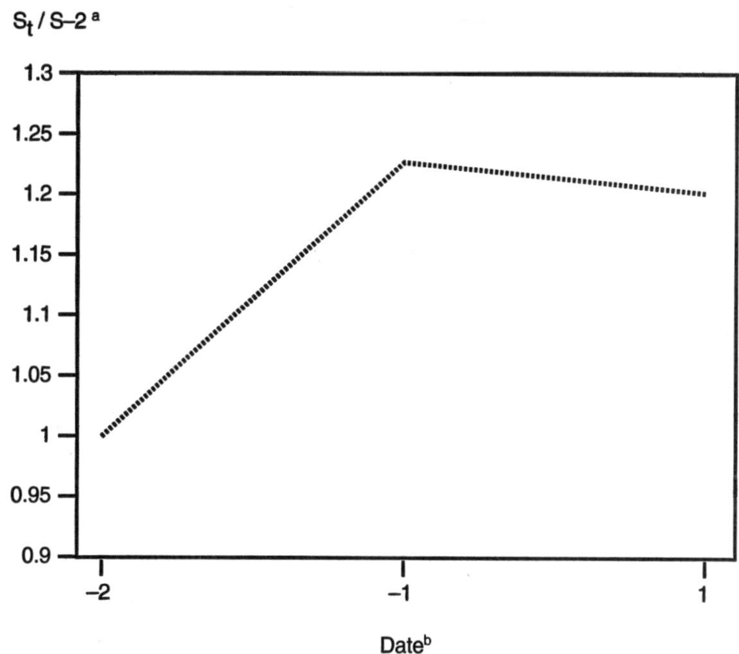

Note: The horizontal axis measures time relative to the IPO date ($t = 0$). The vertical axis measures S_t / S_{-2} for $t = -2, -1$, and $+1$, where S_t denotes the number of shares held by company officers at time t.

able regression results are discussed.

Next we test Prediction 6: Initial returns and total expected informed trading profits are positively correlated. For a very rough estimate of the officers' trading profits we define LD(–1) = log(S_{-1}/S_{-2}), LD(+1) = log(S+1/ S_{-1}), and TD = LD(–1)+LD(+1), where S_t denotes the total number of shares held by company officers at time t. The sample size is reduced from 396 observations to 249 because data on officers' shareholdings is not available for 147 companies (including all 29 financial service companies).

Panel B of Table 4–4 presents single variable regression results for LD(–1), LD(+1) and TD. The coefficient for LD(–1) is negative and significant at the 5% level, LD(+1)'s coefficient is positive but not significantly so, and TD's coefficient is negative but not significantly so. Since none of the three coefficients is significantly positive, Prediction 6 is not supported by the single variable regressions. It is possible that supporting evidence has not been identified because LD(–1), LD(+1) and TD provide only a very rough estimate of officers' total trading profits.

B. Multiple Regression Results

Table 4–6 presents the results of six multiple variable regressions with LINITIAL, logarithmic initial returns, as the dependent variable. The two regressions in Panel A include all 396 exchange-listed IPOs, and are designed to determine whether the two size variables, RELSIZE and LMV, retain their statistical significance when additional explanatory variables are incorporated.

The first regression in Panel A of Table 4–6 includes the relative size variable RELSIZE (IPO shares/total shares), with five control dummy variables: UD (offers for sale), ID ("indirect" listings, previously traded OTC), HD ("hot" markets), SD (regulatory shift, March 1989) and FD (financial service companies). The dummy variable ED (regional stock exchanges) is excluded from Panel A because it is highly correlated with the size-related variables. The second regression in Panel A is similar to the first; it includes the same five dummy variables, but replaces RELSIZE with the absolute size variable LMV (log of the total value of the issuer's shares).

In the first regression in Panel A of Table 4–6 the coefficient estimated for RELSIZE is positive, but is not statistically significant. In the second regression the coefficient estimated for LMV is positive, and significant at the 1% level. These results are very different from Table 4–4's uncontrolled (single variable) regression results. The RELSIZE coefficient was significantly positive in both Panels A1 and A2 of Table 4–4, while LMV's coefficient was negative in both panels, but only significantly so in Panel A2. Hence, the Japanese evidence from our multiple variable regressions rejects Prediction 1 (initial returns and IPO size are negatively correlated). We are unable to explain why the Japanese evidence is so different from the U.S. evidence, which is generally supportive of Prediction 1.

Five dummy variables were employed in the two regressions in Panel A of Table 4–6. The results for these variables are very similar to the results obtained in the single variable regressions of Table 4–5. The

TABLE 4–6
Multiple Variable Regression Analysis for IPO Initial Returns: January 1981–July 1991

A: $(LINITIAL_i) = \alpha_0 + \alpha_1 UD_i + \alpha_2 ID_i + \alpha_3 UD_i + \alpha_4 SD_i + \alpha_5 FD_i + \alpha_6 RELSIZE_i + \alpha_7 LMV_i + \varepsilon_i$
(including financial companies and "indirect" listings through OTC markets)

Reg.	*N*	α_0	α_1	α_2	α_3	α_4	α_5	α_6	α_7	R^2	*RMSE*
1)	396	0.205[a]	0.026	−0.062[b]	0.334[a]	−0.123[a]	−0.075[c]	0.132		0.42	0.183
		(5.64)	(1.27)	(−2.08)	(12.66)	(−5.71)	(−1.90)	(0.86)			
2)	396	−0.360[a]	0.020	−0.085[a]	0.338[a]	−0.152[a]	−0.131[a]		0.035[a]	0.44	0.180
		(−2.07)	(1.42)	(−2.93)	(12.99)	(−6.75)	(−3.50)		(3.43)		

B: $(LINITIAL_i) = \beta_0 + \beta_1 UD_i + \beta_2 HD_i + \beta_3 SD_i + \beta_4 ED_i + \beta_5 DEBT_i + \beta_6 RELSIZE_i + \beta_7 LMV_i + \beta_8 LD(-1)_i + \beta_9 W/SALES(-2)_i + \varepsilon_i$
(excluding financial companies, "indirect" listings through OTC markets, and 86 (87) other companies for which the necessary data is unavailable)

Reg.	*N*	β_0	β_1	β_2	β_3	β_4	β_5	β_6	β_7	β_8	β_9	R^2	*RMSE*
1)	235	0.326[a]								−0.099	−0.094[a]	0.04	0.223
		(14.80)								(−1.45)	(−2.95)		
2)	235	0.333[a]				−0.071[b]				−0.086	−0.080[b]	0.06	0.222
		(15.01)				(−1.95)				(−1.27)	(−2.78)		
3)	234	0.254[a]	−0.013	0.337[a]	−0.115[a]	−0.054[c]	−0.059	0.170		−0.046	−0.025	0.47	0.168
		(4.25)	(−0.25)	(11.50)	(−3.80)	(−1.87)	(−0.97)	(0.81)		(−0.86)	(−0.95)		
4)	235	−0.362		0.338[a]	−0.153[a]	−0.035			0.036[a]	−0.040	−0.006	0.48	0.165
		(−1.52)		(11.80)	(−4.75)	(−1.19)			(2.59)	(−0.78)	(−0.26)		

Note:
R^2 is the regression's coefficient of determination, which is adjusted for degrees of freedom, and RMSE is the regression's root mean squared error. *t*-statistic is in parentheses below the estimate of each coefficient.
[a] Significantly different from zero at the 1% level.
[b] Significantly different from zero at the 5% level.
[c] Significantly different from zero at the 10% level.

coefficients for ID, HD, SD, and FD are all significant, and possess the same sign as they did in Table 4–5. Further, the results for SD (regulatory shift, March 1989) and FD (financial service companies) remain supportive of Predictions 3 and 4, respectively. The coefficient for UD (offers for sale) exhibits the same properties obtained in Table 4–5; it is positive, but not significantly so and hence, again, is not supportive of Prediction 2.

Panel B of Table 4–6 contains the results from four multiple-variable regressions, designed to determine whether Table 4–4's results regarding officers' total wage and their total expected trading profits remain when additional explanatory variables are incorporated. The sample size is reduced from the 396 observations used in Panel A, to 234 or 235 observations for two reasons. First, the 46 "indirect" (via the OTC market) exchange listings are excluded from the sample and second, the data required to compute the officers' shareholdings and wage variables [LD(–1) and W/SALES(–2)] are not available for about 115 companies (including all 29 financial service companies). Consequently, the dummy variables ID ("indirect" listings) and FD (financial service companies) are excluded from the four regressions. Finally, the dummy variable ED (regional exchanges) which was not included in Panel A, is added to three of the four regressions in Panel B.

Only two independent variables are included in all four regressions in Panel B of Table 4–6. The first variable, LD(–1), represents the change in officers' shareholdings between $t = -2$ and t = –1. It is included because of its significance in Panel B of Table 4, and is designed to provide a rough estimate of officers' total expected trading profits. The second variable, W/SALES(–2), represents the officers' total wage, and is included because of its significance in Panel C of Table 4–4. W/SALES(–1) and W/SALES(+1) were also significant in Panel C of Table 4 however, since the three variables are highly correlated (see Table 3(b)) only W/SALES(–2) is included here.

The first regression in Panel B of Table 4–6 includes only the two variables LD(–1) and W/SALES(–2). Both coefficients are negative, but only the coefficient for W/SALES(–2) is significantly negative. Recall that in Panels B and C of Table 4–4, both of these variables' coefficients were negative and significantly so. Panel B's second regression is similar to the first regression, but it adds the dummy variable ED (regional exchanges). ED's coefficient is negative, and significantly so (as it was in Table 4–5's single variable regression). The second regression's results for LD(–1) and W/SALES(–2) are similar to those obtained in the first regression.

The third regression in Panel B of Table 4–6 includes eight independent variables. Coefficients for the officers' shareholdings [LD(–1)] and wage [W/SALES(–2)] variables both remain negative, but now neither are significantly so. The fourth regression includes three dummy variables and the size variable LMV (log value of total shares outstanding). Again the coefficients for LD(–1) and W/SALES(–2) are negative, but not significantly so. LMV's coefficient is positive, and significant at the 1% level (as it was in Panel A of Table 4–6). In this regression the LMV variable is more important than both LD(–1) and W/SALES(–2), and further, when LMV is included in Panel B's regressions, the dummy variable ED (regional exchange) ceases to be significant. Finally, among the four dummy variables included in Panel B's regressions, only HD ("hot" markets) and SD (regulatory shift, March 1989) are consistently significant.

Consequently, from our multiple variable regression analysis, three explanatory variables appear to be particularly important for explaining variations in Japanese IPO initial returns: the size variable LMV, and the dummy variables HD ("hot" markets) and SD (regulatory shift, March 1989).

6. CONCLUSION

This chapter examines the Japanese IPO market. Our principal findings are that: First, contrary to the U.S. evidence [e.g., Beatty-Ritter (1986)], initial returns are not inversely related to IPO size. In fact, in multiple variable regressions, returns are positively and significantly related to the size variable employed. Second, mean initial returns statistically significantly decreased following the March 1989 regulatory changes affecting the Japanese IPO market. The regulatory changes made it more difficult for informed investors to exploit their information advantage and hence, this result is consistent with Rock's (1986) adverse selection model of IPO pricing.

Third, initial returns are not positively and significantly related to the proportion of the IPO which consists of offers for sale. This finding is inconsistent with our third empirical prediction, which also appears to be rejected by the U.S. evidence [e.g., Carter and Manaster (1990)]. Fourth, the mean initial return for both the bank subsample and for the financial company subsample are significantly lower than the return for the non-financial company subsample. The mean initial return for the security company subsample is also lower than the return for the non-financial company subsample, but not significantly so. These results are largely consistent with Baron (1982), particularly if the prominent role of banks in Japanese corporate finance is taken into account.

In Rock (1986) underpricing occurs because uninformed investors require a price discount as compensation for their expected losses to informed investors. We assert that some informed investors (e.g., officers and directors, and executives) may receive valuable information as a costless by-product of providing certain contractual services to the firm. If the firm knows the statistical properties of the value of the information received by these individuals, then the firm can recapture the information's value by reducing, by the expected value of the information, the wage paid for their services. Consequently, we predict that initial returns are: inversely related to the total wage (explicit compensation) received by such investors; and positively related to their total expected informed trading profits (implicit compensation). Supportive results are obtained for the first empirical prediction, but not for the second. Our modification of Rock also implies that the cost of going public may be exaggerated if one does not take into account how the firm can "recapture," from informed investors with whom it has a contractual relationship, a portion of the money "left on the table."

NOTES

1. See, for example, Beatty and Ritter (1986), Ritter (1984, 1987, 1991), Rock (1986), Tinic (1988), and Welch (1989, 1991).
2. For example, variations in: issue size; industry; time-period ("hot" market periods); contract features (best effort with or without a minimum sales constraint, or firm commitment with or without an over-allotment option); underwriter quality; venture capital holdings; subsequent equity offerings; and so on.
3. See, for example, Hiraki (1985) and Jenkinson (1990).
4. Uninformed investors are necessary participants in the IPO market because the informed investors, it is assumed, do not possess sufficient wealth to finance the IPOs by themselves.
5. The Securities and Exchange Council's Special Committee on Unfair Trading recommended the following four measures:

   1. To lengthen the period restricting the transfer of pre-floatation shares and third-party allocations of new shares;

2. To obligate recipients of third-party allocations of pre-floatation shares to hold them;
3. To disclose the transfer of their shares and the names of third parties to which new shares were allocated prior to the issuing company's going public; and
4. To revise the method for determining the offering price, including the introduction of a system for auctioning shares to the public. (Japan Securities Research Institute (1991; 63–65))

6. For example: other types of employees; consultants to the firm; or the firm's suppliers or customers.
7. For example, security analysts or the firm's competitors. Rock (1986) implicitly assumes that all informed traders belong to this subset.
8. The first subset, top shareowners, requires a slightly different interpretation. While still private, the firm allots shares to them at some price *p*. Conventionally *p* is the present value of the share's expected future dividend stream. Here, *p* also includes the present value of expected informed trading profits.
9. Manne (1966) presents a theory which is similar, in spirit, to the argument developed here. More recently Demsetz (1986) asserts that insider trading constitutes a "secondary" form of compensation to controlling shareholders, key employees, bankers and others who do business with the firm. He questions how profitable trading by corporate insiders actually is since "economist should be suspicious of free lunches. The appearance of one often reflects our inability to observe the price easily."
10. Informed investors from the sixth subset are similar to the railway, depicted by Coase (1960), which is "not liable for damages by fires caused by sparks from its engines." The train imposes a social cost if its net value added, the value of the services it provides less the expected value of crops it destroys, is negative. Similarly, informed investors from the sixth subset impose a social cost because they are non-excludable, the firm cannot contract with them, and their net value added is negative.
11. Also, the percentage of IPOs with negative initial returns is much smaller in Japan (in our sample, 3 out of 350 IPOs, or less than 1%) than in the U.S. (for example, in Carter and Manaster's (1990) sample, 156 out of 501 IPOs, or over 30%).
12. This may occur because the OFS variable is set equal to zero for the 237 IPOs without offers for sale. It only has a non-zero value for the 113 IPOs that were accompanied by offers for sale.
13. Although we adjust for differences in sample size between groups, the problems associated with small sample size are unavoidable here.
14. Also, since Japanese banks are highly regulated their IPOs may possess, on average, less *ex ante* uncertainty than, for example, security companies' IPOs.
15. From $t = -2$ to $t = -1$ company officers can increase their shareholdings through "under-the-counter" transactions, or through offers for sale from existing major shareholders. However, during this period the discretionary allocation of new shares (*dai-sansha wari-ate*) is prohibited. Officers can receive discretionary allocations of new shares, but only well before (at least two fiscal periods) the IPO event. The discretionary allocation of new shares is typically used to create or maintain cross-shareholding arrangements with related companies (customers, suppliers and financial institutions) and, to a lesser extent, to compensate officers and provide them with appropriate incentives [see Capital Market Research Association (1989;28)].

REFERENCES

Allen, F. and G. Faulhaber. "Signalling by Underpricing in the IPO Market." *Journal of Financial Economics* (1989), pp. 303–23.

Aoki, M. *Information, Incentives, and Bargaining in the Japanese Economy.* Cambridge University Press, 1988.

Baron, D. "A Model of the Demand for Investment Banking Advising and Distribution Services for New Issues." *Journal of Finance* (1982), pp. 955–76.

Beatty, R., and J. Ritter. "Investment Banking, Reputation, and the Underpricing of Initial Public Offerings." *Journal of Economics* (1986), pp. 213–32.

Capital Market Research Association (ed.). "Kabushiki Koukai Sedo no Ariakata ni tsuite (Report to Minister of Finance)." Shihon Shijou Kenkyu-kai (Capital Market Research Association), Tokyo, 1989.

Carter, R., and S. Manaster. "Initial Public Offerings and Underwriter Reputation." *Journal of Finance* (1990), pp. 1045–67.

Coase, R. "The Problem of Social Cost." *Journal of Law and Economics* (1960), pp. 1–44.

Demsetz, H. "Corporate Control, Insider Trading, and Rates of Return." *American Economic Review* (1986), pp. 313–16.

Fama, E. "Efficient Capital Markets: II." *Journal of Finance* (1991), pp. 1575–1618.

Hiraki, T. "Pricing Problems for Primary and Secondary Market Efficiency." *Japane Financial Review* (1985), pp. 1–28.

Japan Securities Research Institute. "Securities Market in Japan." 1992.

Jegadeesh, N., M. Weinstein, and I. Welch. "An Empirical Investigation of IPO Returns and Subsequent Equity Offerings." UCLA Working Paper 22-90 (1991).

Jenkinson, T. "Initial Public Offerings in the United Kingdom, the United States, and Japan." *Journal of the Japanese and International Economies* (1990), pp. 428–49.

Manne, H. *Insider Trading and the Stock Market.* New York, 1966.

Megginson, W., and K. Weiss. "Venture Capitalist Certification in Initial Public Offerings." *Journal of Finance* (1991). pp. 879–903.

Muscarella, C., and M. Vetsuypens. "A Simple Test of Baron's Model of IPO Underpricing." *Journal of Economics* (1989), pp. 125–35.

Ritter, J. "The 'Hot Issue' Market of 1980." *Journal of Business* (1984), pp. 215–41.

Ritter, J. "The Costs of Going Public." *Journal of Economics* (1987), pp. 269–81.

Ritter, J. "The Long-Run Performance of Initial Public Offerings." *Journal of Finance* (1991), pp. 3–27.

Rock, K. "Why New Issues are Underpriced." *Journal of Economics* (1986), pp. 187–212.

Semkow, B. "New MoF Agenda to Deregulate Japanese Financial Institutions and Markets." *Journal of International Banking Law* (1992).

Snedecor, G. and W. Cochran. *Statistical Methods.* Iowa State University Press, 1980.

Swan, W. "The 1988 Japanese Insider Trading Amendments: Will Japan See Results From These Tougher Laws?" Jou*rnal of International Business Law* (1991), pp. 275–302.

Tinic, S. "Anatomy of Initial Public Offerings of Common Stock." *Journal of Finance* (1988), pp. 789–822.

Welch, I. "Seasoned Offerings, Imitation Costs, and the Underpricing of Initial Public Offerings." *Journal of Finance* (1989), pp. 421–49.

Welch, I. "An Empirical Examination of Models of Contract Choice in Initial Public Offerings." *Journal of Financial and Quantitative Analysis* (1991), pp. 497–518.

CHAPTER 5

WHY JAPANESE COMPANIES FINANCE ABROAD

Roy C. Smith

During the seven year period 1984-1990, Japanese corporations raised a total of ¥116,600 billion ($720 billion) in capital markets in Japan and other countries. More than half of this amount (53.7%) was raised in capital markets abroad, chiefly in the Eurosecurities markets, at a time when the rest of the world was in awe of Japan's large capital surpluses, which were being invested in portfolio and direct investments all over the world, and of its low cost of capital, which many economists and government officials believed was the secret to Japan's great success as a manufacturing nation. If money was so abundant in Japan, and the cost of capital so low, many observers wondered, why did Japanese companies go abroad to raise it?

Equity and equity related securities (common stock, convertible debentures, and bonds issued with equity purchase warrants) accounted for ¥100,000 billion ($688 billion), or 83.3% of the external issues and 87.0% of the domestic issues (see Table 5–1). The Japanese total new equity financing during the period was more than three times the comparable volume of equity issues in the United States, an economy nearly twice as large as Japan's with its own bull market going on. These data make us wonder: why so much equity?

Straight debt issues, on the other hand (even those including equity

The author gratefully acknowledges the kind assistance of John Ehara of Goldman, Sachs & Co., Tokyo, in preparing this chapter.

TABLE 5–1
Sources of Finance for Japanese Companies (¥ billion)

	Domestic			*External*		
Fiscal	*Shares*	*Convertibles (cum-warrants)*	*Straight bonds*	*Shares*	*Convertibles (cum-warrants)*	*Straight bonds*
1984	815 (3)	1,615	720	49	1,661 (434)	1,135
1985	651 (55)	1,641	944	11	1,814 (866)	1,439
1986	632 (104)	3,572	980	1	2,478 (1,993)	1,639
1987	2,084 (0)	5,055	915	39	4,516 (3,439)	824
1988	4,564 (0)	6,995	749	17	6,049 (4,982)	843
1989	7,560 (915)	8,537	729	336	10,009 (8,270)	1,120
1990	447 (395)	1,306	2,006	0	3,172 (2,652)	2,805
Total	16,783 (1,472)	28,721	7,043	453	29,699 (22,636)	9,805
Total Equity Securities:		46,976[a]			52,788[b]	
Total Domestic:		54,019		Total External:	62,593	

[a] 87.0% of total
[b] 83.3% of total

Source: Normura Securities Co., Ltd.

purchase warrants), only amounted to 13% of the Japanese domestic new issue volume during the period. Both the amount and the percentage were tiny by comparison to new issues in the United States, where in 1990 new corporate debt issues raised more than ten times as much capital as did equity issues. Another question, then, is: if the Japanese equity market is so good, why is the straight bond market so poor?

This chapter attempts to address these three issues. It will do so by addressing the effects on issuers of comparative differences in pricing, regulation, and innovation between capital markets in Japan, the United States and Europe. Japanese firms have been active in all three markets over the years.

PRICING DIFFERENCES

In the mid 1960s, many foreign corporations sold securities in the U.S. capital markets. This was done because their national capital markets were small and undeveloped, and what limited amounts of financing that were possible, were costly. Issues sold in the U.S. market (at a return to investors of 100 to 150 basis points above rates paid by comparable U.S. corporations) still provided a lower cost of funds to the issuer than was available at home. To control the adverse balance of payments effects of foreign capital market financing, the U.S. Treasury in 1963 imposed the "interest equalization tax" (IET) which assessed issuers for the amount of interest savings realized, thus of course closing the U.S. market to foreigners.

Ten years later, the IET was repealed and foreign corporations resumed financing in the United States. However, the U.S. market was no longer always the cheapest market for foreigners to use—they could often do better in the Eurosecurities market, which had grown to maturity during the time when the IET was in effect and borrowers from Europe and Japan (and numerous U.S. borrowers as well) turned to it. The Eurosecurities market was an unregulated (though it soon became effectively self-regulated), over-the-counter market in bearer securities that had to be free of national withholding taxes. U.S. securities laws prevented Americans from purchasing the securities. Investors were mainly nondollar based European and other clients of the major European banks. These investors were interested in the securities of well known companies, and the preferred maturity of bonds was 5–7 years, as compared to much longer maturities preferred by investors in the United States.

In the 1970s, significant pricing differences existed between, for example, a 7-year U.S. issue by General Motors Acceptance Corporation registered with the SEC (and not available in bearer form), and a 7-year Eurobond issue by the same company. The latter issue might be 25 to 30 basis points more expensive to GMAC. On the other hand, issuers such as the European Coal and Steel Community might find it cheaper to issue 7-year Eurobonds than to approach the U.S. market where it was less well known and would have to pay a premium rate. On the other hand, the European Coal and Steel Community could not issue 15-year bonds in the Euromarket at a cost as low as that available in the United States.

Japanese issuers during the 1970s, for regulatory reasons to be discussed, frequently issued bonds with bank guarantees in the European market, or convertible debentures, and these issuers became better known in Europe than they were to American investors. As a result, the Euromarket often offered better pricing to the Japanese issuer than the U.S. market. Japanese corporate issuers were also disinclined to undergo the considerable expense and disclosure required for an SEC registration if they didn't have to, so their appearance in the U.S. market was very limited.

As the yen gained in strength relative to the dollar, the gap between U.S. and Japanese interest rates widened. Japanese financial managers were unwilling to pay a fixed-rate of 10% for dollar bonds, if they could borrow at 6% in yen, or at a small spread over the 3 month London Interbank Rate. A dollar denominated convertible debenture, however, might be available for a coupon of 4.5%. Japanese executives in the late 1970s and early 1980s looked for the coupon first, regardless of currency, conversion obligations or other factors. The proposal with the lowest coupon would almost always win.

This attitude was confusing to Western investment bankers who did not at first understand that Japanese investors did not mark down the price of a stock when the company announced that a significant number of new shares would be issued. There was no immediate correction in the price of the shares for the dilution. This being the case, the conversion feature was virtually free, and therefore the only real cost was the coupon, which in the case of foreign issues was usually denominated in dollars, deutsche marks or swiss francs. The Japanese executives invariably believed that their stock price would rise well above the conversion price (usually a modest 5-10% above the market) and therefore the obligation to repay the principal amount in foreign currency was of little importance. Coupons on foreign issues, as long as the yen continued to rise against the dollar and most other currencies during the period, were actually depreciating in yen terms.

Thus, Japanese companies in the 1970s and early 1980s had a natural reason to prefer equity related financing, and to prefer foreign financing when convertibles were to be issued. Regular corporate practice limited each company to a single domestic equity issue in a year, and to a single overseas issue, usually a convertible debenture or warrant bond.

In the 1980s, however, after the explosion of the stock market, and of corporations participating as investors as well as issuers, a new development occurred. Euromarket issues by Japanese corporations were sold directly back to Japanese investors. Ultimately as much as 80% to 90% of such issues were placed in Japan. For this to work best, however, the equity conversion feature had to be separated from the straight bond feature. Japanese retail investors were not especially interested in the fixed income or the foreign currency feature of convertible bonds. So to attract these investors, and to eliminate some higher pricing levels for Japanese issues in Europe as compared to Japan, straight bonds with detachable stock purchase warrants replaced the convertibles. Japanese investors could then buy only the warrants, with the straight debt portion sold to other investors, e.g., banks which would purchase the bonds at a discount to yield a market rate for a fixed income security, which would be swapped into a floating rate security which could be financed profitably in the Eurodeposit market.

This innovation substantially improved the pricing on the bonds with warrants as compared to the convertible debentures. For example, five year warrants to buy a Japanese stock in a bull market at only 2.5% above the market would be worth quite a lot, perhaps 25–30% of face value. This being the case, the straight bonds could be unbundled for a price of 70-75%. Such a large discount would mean that the issuer could substitute a very low coupon for the 4.5% to 5% level that had become common for Japanese convertibles. For a five year dollar straight bond to yield 8.5%, at a discount of 30%, the coupon on the bond would only have to be 1%. This coupon would be more than fully covered by investing the proceeds of the issue in government securities. A few Japanese blue chip companies did succeed in financing warrant bond issues with 1% coupons, but most had to pay a bit more. Warrant bonds, nonetheless, were extremely popular with Japanese issuers and investors and before long the rate differences between Europe and Japan were substantially narrowed.

Interest rate and currency swaps have also contributed to the narrowing of rate differentials between domestic Japanese and overseas straight bond markets. Table 5–2 illustrates these differentials as they would have applied to Nippon Telegraph & Telephone Co (NTT) as of March 31, 1992. Gross spreads and all-in cost of funds are shown on the basis of fixed-rate reoffer pricing, a concept first introduced to Japan in November 1991. The table shows four ways on that date to obtain 5 or 7 year straight bond financing in yen.

The cheapest route to follow, by 35 basis points, was to issue Euroyen 7-year bonds, at a coupon 27 basis points lower, and a gross spread 20 basis points lower than domestic yen bonds. Dollar issues

TABLE 5–2
Comparison of Capital Market Alternatives—Nippon Telegraph & Telephone Co. Ltd., March 31, 1992

	Japan		*USA*		*Eurobond Market*			
			(Dollars Swapped to Yen)		*(Dollars Swapped to Yen)*		*(EuroYen)*	
	5 years	*7 years*	*5 years*	*7 years*	*5 years*	*7 years*	*5 years*	*7 years*
Coupon	5.70%	5.90%	7.30%	7.60%	7.25%	7.65%	5.50%	5.63%
Spread over Gov't Bond	0.33%	0.40%	0.40%	0.43%	0.32%	0.35%	0.24%	0.20%
Gross Spread	0.50%	0.50%	0.63%	0.63%	0.25%	0.30%	0.25%	0.30%
All in cost ($ bond)			7.47%	7.75%	7.30%	7.61%		
Swap spread, net			0.55%	0.54%	0.38%	0.40%		
All-in Cost to NTT (Yen bond equivalent)	5.82%	5.99%	5.80%	5.88%	5.62%	5.74%	5.56%	5.65%

Source: Goldman, Sachs & Co.

swapped into yen were competitive with the domestic market at the time, but were more expensive to NTT than Euroyen bonds.

The domestic market is saddled by a rigid new issue pricing structure, which is difficult to change because it is strongly supported by all the underwriting firms and banks which benefit from it, and an insufficiently liquid secondary market. The Euromarket, on the other hand, has had little opportunity to acquire fixed-rate, bearer securities of well-known, AAA-rated Japanese corporations and accordingly is prepared to acquire them at 23 basis points over the benchmark Japan Government Bond (JGB) rate, as compared to Japanese investors who require 40 basis points over the JGB rate. Inevitably, this rate differential will close as more Japanese issuers discover the opportunity, and more Euro investors satisfy their requirements for fixed-rate Japanese corporate bonds.

It should be noted, however, that despite the fact that domestic bond rates for high grade borrowers are higher in Japan than comparable financing opportunities overseas, the medium-term, fixed-rate bank lending rate (called "long-term prime rate") is even higher. On March 31, 1992 the posted long term prime rate was 6.0% (18 basis points higher than NTT's five year cost of funds from the bond market), but the actual bank lending rate may have been higher if the funds were offered at a price less than par. Long-term prime rate is usually set to reflect a spread of about 70 basis points over the banks' long term funding rate (as determined by the sale of bank debentures, usually at about 50 basis points over the JGB rate). Thus the effective cost of funds might be as high as 120 basis points over the JGB rate. Such rate differentials should certainly encourage the further development of the corporate bond market in Japan, but only when the Eurorates are not cheaper still.

REGULATORY DIFFERENCES

In many countries with large, powerful banks (e.g., Germany, France, Britain), the development of national fixed-rate capital markets lags well behind those of other countries in which the banks are less dominant, such as the United States. Japan's domestic bond market has always suffered from the fact that the principal financial institutions in the country were its big banks, especially the long term credit banks which had special authority to issue "bank debentures" with which to fund their industrial loans. The Japanese government, too, was a frequent issuer of bonds and did not wish to encounter competition for fixed-rate funds in the market that might raise its cost of financing.

Regulators in Japan at the Ministry of Finance, ever seeking balance between the interests of the long term credit banks, the city banks, the trust banks, and the securities firms, have acted as a traffic director, in many ways holding up market forces to protect one interest or another. Thus there is the situation in which new issue rates have to be within a strictly governed hierarchy, and corporate bonds have to be more expensive than the others, regardless of differences between issuers. Lobbying and trade-offs over the years have introduced operating practices and inefficiencies that are not required by the market itself.

Japanese bond market regulation operates in three parts (see Table 5–3).

First, there is the requirement for registering the securities (as in the United States) and applying for permission to enter the market. Neither requirements exist in the Eurosecurities market; both exist in the U.S. market. Japanese registration requirements have been simplified considerably in recent years. In the past, the waiting period could be up to several months, now it is much shorter, only one week for routine registrations. However, since the Ministry of Finance introduced "shelf registrations," which in effect enables companies to pre-register their securities, the waiting period has been eliminated altogether. A kind of shelf registration (called an "offer for sale") also applies to those portions of Euroissues sold into Japan.

Second, Japanese issuers have to meet certain eligibility tests which are quite restrictive. These are not required in the Euromarkets or in the United States, though market conditions may limit what companies can do at any given time. Issues in Japan must not exceed one-times the company's net asset value; Euroissues, however, can be twice as large (another compromise). All straight bond issues in Japan must be fully collateralized, unless the company obtains a single A or higher bond rating. Rating agencies began in Japan about ten years ago. Issuers must also agree to certain restrictive covenants which require the maintenance of a minimum level of net assets and profits, and limits the payments of dividends.

Third, in Japan issuers must retain the services of "commission banks" (banks which act as trustees, for a significant fee), and incur higher expenses for mechanical services such as paying agents, etc. Commission banks and trustees are generally not required in the Euromarket or in the United States.

Regulation, designed to keep different financial players each in his own place in the domestic market, have greatly heightened the appeal of markets

TABLE 5–3
Comparison of Nonfinancial Terms and Conditions for New Issuers in Different Capital Markets

	Japan	*USA*	*Eurobonds*
Registration	Yes	Yes	none
Waiting Period	can be reduced by shelf registration	can be reduced by shelf registration	none
Variety of Securities	limited	unrestricted	unrestricted
Size Limits	1 × net assets	none	none (Japanese issuers 2 × net assets)
Eligibility	ratings or collateral	none	none
Required Covenants	maintain minimum net assets; maintain minimum profits; dividend restrictions	none	none
Commission banks	expensive and inflexible	none	none
Pricing	hierarchy; little difference between companies	depends on issuer	depends on issuer

abroad. Indeed, the same condition existed in the United States in the early 1980s, when a majority of AA or better rated bonds issued by U.S. companies were Eurobonds. The absence of any waiting period, the low costs of accessing the market and the lessened threat of litigation made the markets in Europe much more attractive to U.S. companies, which were also finding a strong demand for their paper and very competitive interest rates. To counter these developments the SEC decided not to restrict U.S. companies in Europe, but to deregulate domestic market access requirements instead through introduction of the shelf registration process (Rule 415, 1982).

Japan, too, will have to deregulate further, especially in terms of eligibility requirements and issuing costs, if it is to see its capital markets develop further and its companies make greater use of the home market. As of December 31, 1991, of 309 Japanese companies eligible for shelf registration, only 27 (8.7%) have taken advantage of it.

DIFFERENCE IN INNOVATION

The present structure of the Japanese corporate bond market is such that almost all innovations must be introduced from abroad. This has been true for more than thirty years (when the first convertible bond was issued by a Japanese company in the Eurosecurities market). To regulators, and other players in Japan, experimentation can occur outside the domestic market, or involve nonJapanese issuers inside the market, as in the case of the first unsecured corporate bond issue which was done by Sears Roebuck. It is quite rare for a Japanese company to issue a new type of security in the domestic market, and when it does happen there is usually a foreign connection somewhere (as in the recent cases of NTT's fixed reoffer rate bond issued in November 1991, led by Morgan Stanley and Sakura Bank's exchangable preferred stock issue, led by Goldman Sachs).

Most of the bond market innovations that spread to Japan originated in the Eurosecurities market. These include bank guaranteed bonds, convertible bonds, bonds with warrants, and zero-coupon bonds. As in the preceding example of substituting bonds with warrants for convertible bonds, significantly better pricing can be the result. Even when there is no regulatory advantage, or ostensible pricing advantage to be gained by issuing abroad, the opportunity to try something new often results in economic advantage to the issuer. Japanese banks and securities firms do not have much reputation for innovation in corporate bond markets.

CONCLUSIONS

For the past several years Japan's capital markets have been subordinate to the "bubble economy," and much of the development that it might have enjoyed in the areas of free market pricing, deregulation, and innovation have been deferred. These have to be addressed over the next few years if Japan hopes to keep up with advanced capital market developments in the United States and Europe.

The equity markets offered special financing opportunities to Japanese corporations during the 1980s, but these advantages have now disappeared with the bursting of the bubble. Following the recent decline of the stock market, and with Japanese banks facing restrictions of the availability of funds to lend, Japan could be facing a significant increase in its cost of capital, which no longer is advantageous relative to other countries. The best remedy for this problem is to accelerate further changes and reforms to promote the development of the domestic capital market, especially the coprorate bond market.

One obstacle that appears to continue to block progress is a final resolution of the matter of large scale Japanese financial market reform, including the full repeal of Article 65 and the abolition of various barriers that now separate the permitted activities of different types of banks. By protecting banks, securities firms and other players from the need to compete with each other, the Ministry of Finance only prolongs the time when Japan's capital markets will be able to function on an equal basis with the principal markets in Europe and the United States.

The access to and use of foreign capital markets has been good for Japan, and has resulted in significant imported financial innovation and deregulation. It is important that this access be maintained for the future. To assure that it is, Japan's financial regulators must continue to be mindful of the need for its markets to become fully integrated into the emerging global marketplace. This will require further convergence with the regulatory systems of the United States and Europe.

PART TWO

GLOBAL COMPETITIVENESS BENCHMARKS

CHAPTER 6

EFFICIENCY, STABILITY, AND COMPETITIVENESS OF UNIVERSAL BANKING: LESSONS FROM THE GERMAN EXPERIENCE

Ingo Walter

Universal banking can be defined as the conduct of a range of financial services that today may comprise provision credit to an array of borrowers, trading of financial instruments and foreign exchange (and their derivatives), underwriting of debt and equity new issues, brokerage, investment management, insurance, and possibly extending to real estate, leasing, management consultancy, and other services. The functions a universal bank chooses to perform in an open, competitive environment depend on patterns of demand, the structure of the market, and the microeconomics of the financial intermediation process.

The linkage between corporate structure and competitive performance in financial services has long been actively debated. For example, Herring and Santomero [1990] review three basic types of structures that cover multi-product financial services firms:

- The *fully-integrated financial conglomerate*, legally capable of supplying all types of financial services from the same corporate entity, but with the possibility of creating separate subsidiaries or affiliates when warranted by market conditions—the *German-Swiss model*, or "true universal." Management has complete freedom to structure the organization to achieve maximum competitive advantage, which may or may not involve the creation of separate legal or functional entities, firewalls or other forms of fragmentation. Under this arrangement, the optimum delivery system from the standpoint of competitiveness dictates the form of the organization.

- The *bank-subsidiary structure*, where the core of the organization is a bank, and a broad range of non-banking financial activities is carried out through subsidiaries of that bank. This is the *British model*, or "financial universal." The affiliates are legally separate entities.
- The *bank holding company model*, under which a holding company owns both banking and non-banking subsidiaries that are legally separate, insofar as non-banking activities are permitted by law—the so-called *American model*.

Functional universality along the lines of one of these three prototypes can be—but is not necessarily—coupled to geographic spread across the domain covered by the relevant regulatory authorities. Another consideration is whether industrial companies are allowed to own banks, and whether banks or their holding companies may own or control significant equity stakes in industrial companies. Among the three prototypes the German system is least restricted, with a tradition of universality dating back at least to the early 19th Century, and contrasts starkly with the two countries that remain subject to important constraints on universal banking activities, the United States and Japan. It is often forgotten that both Japan and the United States have had, and continue to have, elements of universal banking in their financial systems.

The United States had long experience with universal banking, as American commercial banks provided investment banking services directly from 1812 to nearly the turn of the century, and thereafter though securities affiliates until 1933. The passage of the Glass-Steagall provisions of the Banking Act of 1933 (and later the 1956 Bank Holding Company Act) separated "banking"—defined as taking deposits and making commercial loans—from everything else, defined as "commerce." Over the years, the dynamics of the financial intermediation process juxtaposed against the static regulatory framework have left commercial banks with a vastly diminished share of U.S. national financial flows.

It is equally useful to recall that, prior to World War II, Japan had no substantive separation between banking and securities activities. Banks monopolized the underwriting of corporate as well as government securities under a cartel arrangement initially established in 1911. Securities distribution, brokerage and related functions were carried out by securities firms, as were equity underwriting and bond trading, mainly because banks were wary of the perceived risks involved. Acceptance of proposals by the General Headquarters of the Occupation to introduce Article 65 of the Securities and Exchange Law of 1947 was based on the view that underwriting (even of bonds) was excessively risky for banks. However, Article 65 did not place limits on bank holdings of either debt or equity securities for investment purposes—an important source of competitive strength of Japanese banks in the 1980s and weakness in the 1990s.

Another apparent purpose of Article 65 was to prevent bank monopolization of the securities industry by favoring non-bank securities houses. This was later reinforced by "administrative guidance" from the Ministry of Finance to prevent banks from underwriting local and government-guaranteed bonds, evidently in order to provide the securities firms with a monopoly that would help assure their competitive survival.

Today, banks in Japan may hold up to 5% of their assets (10% prior to 1987) in the form of equity shares in industrial companies—about equal to the 4.9% limitation for U.S. bank holding companies. They may in addition have equity holdings in affiliated insurance companies. About 30% of the equity of Japanese industrial companies has been held by banks in this manner, frequently within *keiretsu* cross-holding structures. [Pozdena, 1989]

In this chapter, our purpose is to examine a number of salient characteristics of the German-style universal banking system, and to attempt to draw some conclusions regarding the implications of universality for (a) static and dynamic efficiency of financial institutions, (b) global competitiveness, and (c) financial stability. The lessons are important for ongoing efforts to achieve financial reform in Japan and the United States, in search of improved performance against all three of these benchmarks on the basis of which financial systems are usually judged.

INSTITUTIONAL BACKGROUND

The term "universal bank" in Germany is applied to the principal classification of financial institutions in that country (which in 1991 accounted for about 78% of Germany's banking assets). Its members are engaged in commercial banking (deposit gathering and extending credit) as well as investment banking (securities underwriting and dealing), and investment management. The "universal" designation is used to distinguish them from "specialist" banks, which usually perform only one type of financial activity.

Far from comprising a homogeneous category of financial institutions, there are three broad classifications of German universal banks—commercial banks (*Grossbanken*), savings banks and cooperative banks. German *Grossbanken* took shape in the early 1800s, during the country's initial period of industrialization, and they have remained a dominant force ever since—despite efforts by the Allies in the immediate postwar period to break them up, as part of a policy to reduce the power of German industry and what were then regarded as its banking-sector tools. The *Grossbanken* today include Deutsche Bank, Dresdner Bank, and Commerzbank, and comprise the institutions most often cited when the subject of German "universal banking" is raised. Their activities span virtually the entire range of commercial and investment banking activities throughout the modern, unified Federal Republic of Germany.

The principal activities of the *Grossbanken* include retail deposit gathering, lending, investments, current accounts, discounting, brokerage, custody and transactions services, as well as underwriting and distributing equity shares and fixed-income securities. They dominate these activities domestically, and have had a strong presence in the Euromarkets. Still, the three large German banks have a market share, in terms of transactions value, of only about 9%. Over half of Germany's financial institutions remain in the state-owned sector.

Beyond the highly visible *Grossbanken*, there are five other classes of universal banks in Germany:

- **Regional banks** include two large Munich-based banks, Bayerische Vereinsbank, and Bayerische Hypotheken und Wechsel Bank, which are licensed to operate as mortgage banks in addition to the normal range of universal banking activities. With the exception of the Bank für Gemeinwirtschaft in Frankfurt (which has branches throughout the country) the regional banks are geographically limited.
- **Foreign-based banks** can likewise carry out the full range of commercial and investment banking activities, competing with local institutions. One exception is domestic securities underwriting, where they have been prohibited by law.

- **Private banks** provide individual and middle-market financial services. They are usually restricted as to customer, region, and types of activities.
- **Savings banks** are universal only in the sense that they issue mortgage-backed securities and underwrite local government bonds, in addition to deposit-taking and commercial and individual lending. Each savings bank is restricted to a specific region, and is prevented from making certain types of investments. Savings deposits are guaranteed, either by the local government or by the 12 regional *Gironzentralen*, with which each savings bank is affiliated. The **Giro** institutes hold the savings banks' reserves and function as the clearing banks. The largest *Giro* institute is also the fourth largest commercial bank in Germany, Westdeutsche Landesbank und Girozentrale. Like the *Grossbanken*, WestLB has undertaken considerable Euromarket and foreign activities, including its 1989 acquisition of the capital market activities of Standard Chartered Bank of the United Kingdom.
- **German cooperative banks** were established as mutual societies, to give support to their members rather than to earn profits for shareholders. Like the savings banks, they are organized into a tree-tier structure with each urban cooperative bank (*Volksbank*) and rural cooperative bank (*Raiffeisenbank*) affiliated with a regional cooperative bank (*genossenschaftliche Zentralbank*), which in turn is associated with a national clearing cooperative. Since the late 1970s, considerable consolidation of this structure has occurred. The central clearing institution, the Deutsche Genossenschaftsbank (DG Bank), is the eighth largest bank in Germany, with substantial dealings in domestic securities, the Euromarkets, and national financial markets abroad.

Under German universal banking statutes, all financial activities can be carried out within the structure of the parent bank except employee savings (where the employees themselves provide the bulk of the funds), building society activities (where the providers of funds acquire the right to take loans), mortgage and communal bond issuance (reserved for saving and cooperative banks), investment trust business, and insurance. Separate, wholly or partially owned subsidiaries of universal banks can, however, undertake all of these activities.

German universals may conduct insurance business through subsidiaries that are subject to the federal regulatory framework for the insurance industry. Among the *Grossbanken*, only Deutsche Bank has opted to set up a wholly owned life insurance subsidiary, Deutsche Lebensversicherungs AG and has control of two other insurers—life insurance presumably having the highest cross-selling potential against other retail financial services and requiring a tolerable level of capitalization. The other major German universals have chosen to form strategic alliances with insurance companies, whereby the banks sell a range of insurance products while the insurance companies take on pension plans, mutual funds and related financial services created by the banks. Among these are the acquisition of Bank für Gemeinwirtschaft (formerly owned by labor unions) by the Aachener & Münchener insurance group and (later) Crédit Lyonnais, and joint marketing ventures by Dresdner Bank with the Allianz Versicherungs AG—Germany's largest insurer and owner of a large block of Dresdner Bank shares—in five federal states and with three other insurers in the remainder of the Federal Republic.

The Regulatory Apparatus

Supervision of banking activities in Germany is conducted by the Bundesaufsichtsamt für das Kreditwesen—the Federal Bank Supervisory Office (FBSO) in Berlin—in cooperation with the Deutsche Bundesbank in Frankfurt. The legal framework for supervision stems from the Banking Act of 1961 as amended in 1984.

The German regulatory regime was traditionally comparatively lax and reliant on self-regulation and dates from 1974, when the Euromarkets were subjected to their first major crisis—the failure of the Herstatt Bank in Germany, caused by losses in the foreign exchange markets. Besides comprehensive supervision applied to banks, mortgage lending, insurance, building and loan associations and investment companies are subject to other supervisory agencies. The savings bank system falls under additional state laws, while leasing and factoring falls entirely outside FBSO jurisdiction. Bank mergers must be approved by the FBSO and, if they are likely to lead to a reduction in competition, by the *Bundeskartellamt* (Federal Cartel Office).

German banks can access liquidity via the Bundesbank through rediscount of eligible paper, within limits and quotas. This is in the absence of a broad and deep Fed Funds market, such as exists in the United States, as a source of liquidity. For banks suffering temporary liquidity difficulties, the

Liquiditäts-Konsorialbank, a joint venture between the Bundesbank and banks from all sectors, can also provide relief assuming it has satisfied itself as to the distressed bank's underlying solvency. The FSBO has the power to intervene in any bank's activities in order to prevent insolvency, and a financial institution's bankruptcy can be filed only through the FSBO. Should a bank failure endanger the economy or the payments system, the federal government may intervene directly.

Deposit insurance is not a federal government function. Since 1966, the commercial banks have had a voluntary deposit insurance scheme funded by an annual fee of 0.03% of each participant bank's non-bank customer deposits. Coverage is for 100% of all non-bank deposits up to 30% of bank capital for any single depositor. The savings bank system, as noted above, has deposit guarantees extended by regional giro institutes, and a similar system prevails for the cooperative banking system.

THE GERMAN INDUSTRIAL-FINANCIAL ALLIANCE

There are three attributes of the German financial system that make the German form of universal banking unique: (a) the *Hausbank* system, (b) bank ownership of non-bank stock, and (c) proxy voting of depository shares.

The Hausbank Relationship

Perhaps similar to Japan, there exists a long-standing alliance between the large universal banks and German industrial corporations. Unlike Japan, however a corporation can access both capital market services (stock and bond new issues, mergers and acquisitions transactions) and bank credit facilities by using the services of the same financial institution. This so-called *Hausbank* relationship has as its basis a nonfinancial firm's reliance on only one principal bank (its *Hausbank*), which is its primary supplier of all forms of financing.

Lending by the German universal banks to non-financial firms tends to be dominated by short term credit facilities. Current accounts (with overdrafts) represent the principal instrument for supplying permanent working capital to enterprises, and thus is a ready substitute for term lending. It has often been called "quasi-equity." Term credits (six months to four years) are often used for bridge financing. Long term credits are usually in the form of promissory notes placed by commercial banks with insurance companies, regional giro institutions, savings banks and regional banks. Bank credit facilities thus come with an implicit "insurance" feature, and the client is expected to pay an appropriate premium for them. If the client firm faces collapse, the *Hausbank* may well convert its debt into equity and take control, with a view to restructuring it or selling it to other investors.

The *Hausbank*, in turn, is deeply involved in its corporate client's business affairs and, in times of adversity, tends to remain more committed to the continued well-being and survival of the company as a going concern than would an institution with a looser, arms-length, profit-maximizing and risk-minimizing banking relationship.

German banks often gain *Hausbank* standing by providing all of the financing needs to start-up companies—subscribing seed capital, initial public offerings of stock, bond underwritings, and supplying working capital (with a rolling line of credit often constituting permanent financing). A *Hausbank*, in short, is expected to be loyal to its client, and the client is expected to be loyal to its bank.

Bank Share Ownership

German universal banks may own a significant block of client companies' voting stock in their investment portfolios. Table 6–1 shows the participations of the largest German universal banks in German non-banking firms. It is estimated that about 5% of the equity of the top 100 companies is owned by banks. This is in part a result of the "German solution" to corporate financial distress under the *Hausbank* arrangement, as banks' holdings of non-bank equity shares increased during debt workouts and financial restructurings in the past.

Overall, however, the German universal banks' ownership of equity in industrial companies is not particularly large. In 1976 it was about 1.3% of the outstanding shares, and by 1986 this had been reduced to 0.7% and by 1989 to 0.6%. In 1989, the total nominal value of the ten largest universal banks' shareholdings amounted to DM 1.68 billion, as compared with the nominal share capital of BASF alone of DM 2.85 billion. Consequently, the EC's 10% cap on bank shareholdings in industrial companies [see Walter and Smith, 1989] may not be as important as sometimes supposed.

The archetype of the German bank-industry share ownership arrangement is perhaps Deutsche Bank's relationship with Daimler-Benz AG, in which Deutsche holds a 28% equity stake.

TABLE 6–1
Current Valuation of Principal Industrial Equity Shareholdings

Investment	*Percent Owned*	*Number of Share*	*Price*	*Value*	
Commerzbank					
Boge	15.00	534,000	420	33,642,000	
Didier	10.30	1,848,000	263	50,060,472	
Hochtiel	12.50	4,000,000	1,025	512,500,000	
Holzman	5.00	1,800,000	1,250	112,500,000	
Horten	6.25	5,000,000	318	99,375,000	
Hutschenreuther	12.50	426,000	440	23,430,000	
Karstadt	25.00	7,200,000	669	1,204,200,000	
Linde	10.00	4,760,000	882	419,832,000	
Linotype	10.00	1,600,000	737	117,920,000	
MAN	7.50	13,490,000	458	463,381,500	
Salamander	10.00	1,452,000	549	79,714,800	
Thyssen	5.00	31,300,000	272	425,680,000	
Total				3,542,235,772	51.7%
Commerzbank		22,612,000	303	6,851,436,000	100%
Per share value				156.65	
Deutsche Bank					
Daimler Benz	28.1	42,360,000	820	9,960,591,200	
Hapag-Lloyd	12.5	9,200,000	370	425,500,000	
Heidelberger Zement	20.0	2,600,000	1,350	702,000,000	
Holzman	30.0	1,800,000	1,250	675,000,000	
Horten	18.8	5,000,000	318	298,125,000	
Hutschenreuther	24.9	416,000	440	45,576,960	
Karstadt	25.0	7,200,000	669	1,204,200,000	
Leonische Drahtwerk	12.5	360,000	565	25,425,000	
Linde	10.0	4,760,000	878	417,928,000	
Metallgesellschaft	10.6	5,600,000	618	366,844,800	
Suedzucker	20.0	1,716,000	780	267,696,000	
Munich Re	8.0	27,398,000	2,415	5,293,293,600	
Allianz	10.0	15,000,000	2,475	3,712,500,000	
Total				23,194,680,560	72%
Deutsche Bank		38,292,800	844	32,319,123,200	100%
Per share value				606	
Dresdner Bank					
Bilfinger & Berger	25.00	1,400,000	714	249,900,000	
Brau & Brunnen	27.20	3,020,000	486	399,219,840	
Degussa	10.00	7,300,000	497	362,810,000	
Dyckerhoff	3.00	1,852,000	825	45,837,000	
Fuchs Petrolub	10.00	800,000	250	20,000,000	
Hapag-Lloyd	12.50	2,400,000	370	111,000,000	
Heidelberger Zement	25.10	3,000,000	1,350	1,016,550,000	
Metallgesellschaft	23.10	5,600,000	618	799,444,800	
Total				3,004,761,640	20.4%
Dresdner Bank		33,820,000	436	14,745,520,000	100%
Per share value				88.85	

Source: Barclays de Zoete Wedd, 1990

Voting Rights

As in other parts of the world, share custody is a standard banking function in Germany, and large portfolios of stock are held by the universal banks in trust for individuals and institutions. An unusual feature of the German system is that—although the ultimate shareholders theoretically have the right to vote stock—in fact the voting rights of depository shares are typically exercised by the banks through proxy voting (*Auftragsstimmrecht*). This gives the banks a degree of control over industrial enterprises that is typically several times larger than their own proportionate share ownership.

The German universal banks have been prepared to discuss changes in their right to vote fiduciary shareholdings for some time, but point out that they actually do attend shareholders meetings (unlike most shareholders) and vote in an informed manner, as against uninformed proxy voting that is frequently the case in the United States. They are prohibited from voting fiduciary shares in their own shareholders meetings.

Supervisory Board Membership

The Hausbank relationship, share ownership and voting of fiduciary shares in client companies is cemented by bank membership on the supervisory boards (*Aufsichtsratsmandate*). Bank representatives on client company boards are frequently called upon to provide advice on questions of financial management and capital markets. Advisory board members are required by law to act in the interests of the firm and its shareholders.

Measured in terms of the share of board memberships, the role of the universal banks is not as large as is commonly supposed. Of 1,496 supervisory board seats among the 100 largest German industrial companies in 1988, 104 were occupied by representatives of the universal banks (114 in 1986) as compared with 729 seats occupied by employee representatives—including 187 by representatives of the labor unions. [Roeller, 1990]

Nevertheless, bank supervisory board memberships appear to be concentrated among the largest German firms, so that these figures may not be inconsistent with a high degree of control in certain sectors or individual corporations. Banks also have large numbers of board memberships in companies below the German top-100.

Kumulation

The combination of the Hausbank relationships, share ownership, voting of fiduciary shares and supervisory board memberships allegedly creates *Kumulation*, the potentially significant tiering of bank influence through multiple bank-corporate relationships. [Krümmel, 1980]

According to Wolfgang Roth, economic spokesman of the opposition Social Democratic Party, "Every supplier of Daimler Benz/MBB/AEG/Dornier/MTU...has of course a good chance [of doing business] if he gives Deutsche Bank as his main banking relationship, takes on Roland Berger (a Deutsche Bank subsidiary) as his management consultant, signs up for employee life insurance policies with Deutsche Lebensversicherungs AG, takes someone from Deutsche Bank into his advisory council, and when he lets his factory and office buildings be built by Philip Holzmann AG, which belongs one-third to Deutsche Bank." Along the same lines, as stated by Count Otto Lamsdorff, former Economics Minister and chairman of the Free Democratic Party, "...the combination of providing equity, providing credit, the seats on the supervisory boards, the exercise of proxy votes at shareholders meetings, that in all this an accumulation of economic power has been constituted that carries in it the possibilities of abuse."

A 1979 Banking Commission report (*Studienkommission für Grundsatzfragen der Kreditwirtschaft*, or Gessler Commission), on the other hand, confirmed the results of an earlier 1976 investigation that found no evidence of excessive cumulative influence on the part of the universal banks which could be interpreted as inimical to the interests of shareholders, employees, suppliers or the nation as a whole. The checks and balances implicit in market competition among some 4,000 German financial institutions, as well as insurance companies and other nonbanks, together with German banking and commercial law, were deemed to constitute sufficient safeguards. The Gessler Commission did, however, point to information advantages obtained by banks in the course of their credit business, and advocated strengthening of insider trading rules. It also recommended that information about all board memberships be published annually.

German universal banks justify their share ownership, voting and supervisory board roles with three arguments:

- It permits orderly restructuring of enterprises and saves jobs. Firms that get into trouble are taken over by banks, restructured, and then resold to new shareholders.

- It supports poorly capitalized mid-size companies (*Mittelstand*) directly though bank shareholdings and lending that would not otherwise be bankable.
- It can efficiently prepare state-owned enterprises (SOEs) for privatization.
- It provides an efficient vehicle for the sale of privately held companies to the public, with shares taken over by the bank and subsequently sold in a public offering.

The influence of the German universal banks nevertheless remains controversial on the ground of concentration of economic and political power.

Regarding economic power, there is the argument that they may be able to influence the structure of the economy in ways that run counter to the national interest—similar to the criticisms levelled in the 1920s at U.S. universals such as J.P. Morgan. Counter-arguments generally refer to the vigor and sophistication of German antitrust enforcement, and the presence of concentrations in Japanese *keiretsu* despite prohibition of universal banking in that country.

Regarding concentration of political power, the argument is that universal banks, through their dominance of client relationships, have the ability to suborn the political process and ram-through political actions that shift the balance of risks and returns in their favor. This may include favorable tax legislation and access to government guarantees. Counter-arguments focus on the fact that special-interest pressures from other types of financial institutions (e.g., savings and loans in the United States) are no less capable of co-opting the political process, and that the root of any problem may thus lie in the political process itself.

GERMAN UNIVERSAL BANKING: STRENGTHS AND WEAKNESSES

Having described the basic characteristics of the German form of universal banking and some of the controversies surrounding it, we can attempt to make an assessment of its apparent strengths and weaknesses against other forms of financial organization, particular financial systems that require a more or less strict separation between core commercial banking functions and other types of financial services.

Performance Benchmarks

This can be done by calibration against a set of benchmarks that would appear to describe optimum, performance-oriented financial systems which are at once efficient, creative (in terms of generating innovative financial products and processes), globally competitive, and stable. The first three can be discussed in terms of Figure 6–1. *Static* efficiency is modelled in the diagram as the all-in, weighted average spread (differential) between rates of return provided to ultimate savers and the cost of funds to users. This "gap," or spread, depicts the overall cost of financial intermediation. In particular, it reflects the direct costs of producing financial services (operating and administrative costs, cost of capital, etc.). It also reflects losses incurred in the financial process, as well as any monopoly profits earned and liquidity premia. Financial processes that are considered "statically inefficient" are usually characterized by high "spreads" due to high overhead costs, high losses, barriers to entry, and the like.

Dynamic efficiency is characterized by high rates of financial product and process innovation through time. *Product* innovations usually involve creation of new financial instruments (e.g., caps, futures, options, swaps) along with the ability to replicate certain instruments by bundling existing ones (synthetic securities) or to highlight a new financial attribute by rebundling existing instruments. *Process* innovations include contract design (e.g., cash settlement futures contracts), methods of settlement and trading, techniques for efficient margin calculation, new approaches to contract pricing, passive or index-based portfolio investment techniques, and a range of others. Successful product and process innovation broadens the menu of financial services available to ultimate borrowers and/or ultimate savers. Unsuccessful financial innovations include financial instruments that take substantial resources to develop but ultimately fail to meet a need in the marketplace. Probably the most powerful catalyst affecting the competitive dynamics of the financial services industry has been technological change.

Statically and dynamically efficient financial systems are those which minimize the "intermediation spread" depicted in Figure 6–1 and at the same time produce a constant stream of innovations that successfully address ever-changing needs in the financial marketplace. Indeed, one can argue that the most advanced financial systems approach a theoretical, "complete" optimum where there are sufficient financial instruments and markets which, individually and in combination, span the entire state-space of risk and return outcomes. Financial systems that are deemed inefficient or

FIGURE 6–1
Efficiency in Financial Intermediation

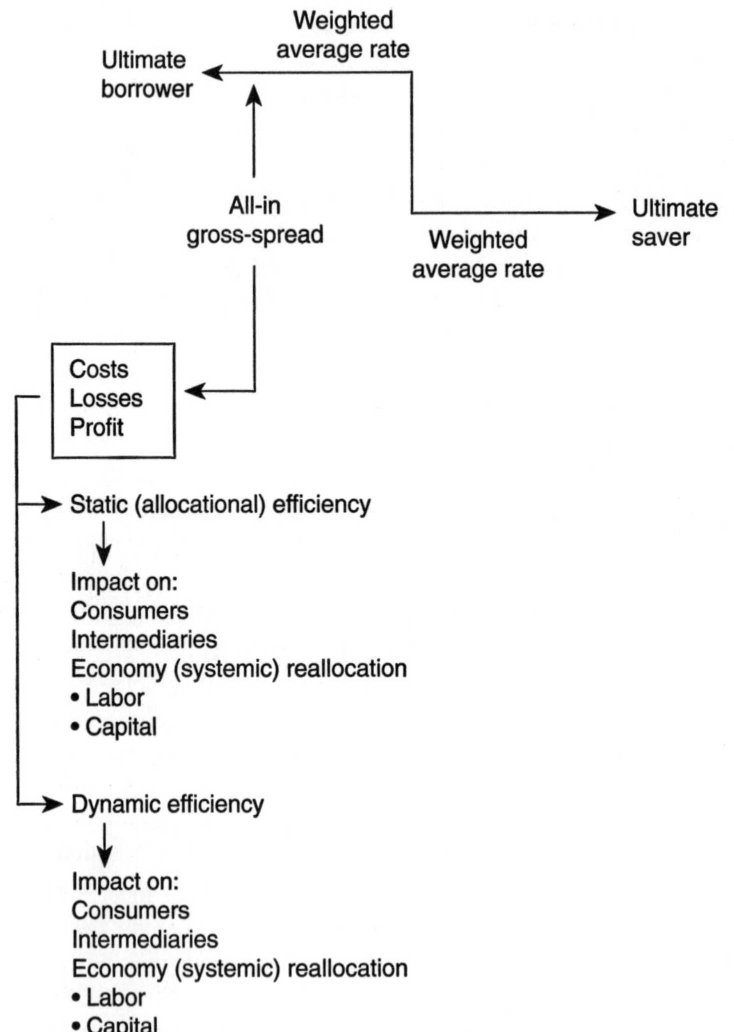

incomplete are characterized by a limited range of financial services and obsolescent financial processes.

Both static and dynamic efficiency are of obvious importance from the standpoint of national and global resource allocation, not only within the financial services industry itself but also as it effects users of financial services. That is, since financial services can be viewed as "inputs" to the overall production process of a nation, the level of national output and income—as well as its rate of economic growth—are directly affected by the efficiency characteristics of the financial services sector.

A "retarded" financial services industry, in this sense, can represent a major impediment to a nation's overall real economic performance. Such retardation represents a burden on the final consumers of financial services and potentially reduces the level of private and social welfare. It also represents a burden on producers, by raising their cost structures and eroding their competitive performance in domestic and global markets. As such, they distort the patterns of resource allocation in the national economy.

Financial system inefficiencies can be traced to a number of factors. These include:

- Regulations that prevent financial firms from complete access to alternative sources of funding or the full range of borrowers and issuers.
- Taxation imposed at various stages of the financial intermediation process, including securities transfer taxes, transactions taxes, etc.
- Lack of competition that reduces incentives to cut intermediation costs and promote innovation.
- Lack of market discipline imposed on owners and managers of financial intermediaries, leading to poor risk management and significant losses.

National financial systems that are statically and/or dynamically inefficient tend themselves to be disintermediated. Borrowers or issuers in a position to do so seek foreign markets or offshore markets that offer lower costs or a more suitable range of products. Investors likewise seek markets abroad that offer higher rates of return or improved opportunities to construct more efficient portfolios. Such systems can be termed "uncompetitive" as venues for financial intermediation in the context of global markets—although individual institutions based in them may be able for a time to cross-subsidize foreign activities from abnormal profits earned at home.

A final benchmark related to financial system stability, by which we mean the absence of *negative externalities*—costs imposed on society at large (the general public) that are attributable to either systemic failure or bailouts of individual institutions dictated by the political process. There are clearly tradeoffs between stability (which is often addressed via regulation) and efficiency, so that the task is to find a socially optimum balance in a globally competitive environment.

Capital Market Development

The importance of the *Hausbank* relationship and universal banking have clearly had an impact on the static and dynamic efficiency attributes of German capital markets. This has reinforced the Bundesbank's long-standing opposition to the development of a commercial paper market for monetary policy reasons. As a result, the German money market long remained almost entirely a market in deposits with the Bundesbank, until the introduction of DM commercial paper in 1990. Moreover, little activity has existed in the interbank treasury bill and government agency market.

The stock market in Germany is likewise poorly developed by industrial-country standards, and all stock transactions up to a certain size must be carried out through one of the German exchanges. Of the 2,000 joint stock companies, shares of only 400 were listed on the exchanges, and a large number of them have been inactively traded. German stock market capitalization amounted to only 5% of the global total in 1991. The fragmented German equity market has thus been comparatively thin and inefficient, although its securities clearance and settlement system is the fastest in Europe (2 days). It was not until the end of 1989 that the German universal banks established a screen-based information system, *Ibis*, which posts the prices of 14 blue-chip German companies. The German options and futures exchange, the *Deutsche Terminbörse* (DTB), was established only in 1990.

The German bond markets are more active, including issues of the federal government (*Bunds*), state and local governments, commercial banks and savings banks, including mortgage-backed bonds. Among these, the least developed sector is the corporate bond market.

Domestic capital markets in Germany have thus been perceived to be relatively inefficient, as indicated by the large volume of German issuer and investor transactions being done abroad. Debt and equity securities denominated in DM are traded heavily in London, where derivatives markets developed early and transactions costs are comparatively low. The German share of cross-border lending, at 4% of the world total in 1990, was smaller than that of France and about one-third that of Japan.

A country that has traditionally been the world's largest exporter of merchandise, Germany remains the world's largest importer of financial services. In part, this is due to German financial technology being perceived as uncreative and lacking in sophisticated financial engineering at the corporate level, especially in relation to the United States and the United Kingdom. This has frequently been attributed two factors:

- On the borrower side, a lack of the kind of tooth-and-nail competition for corporate business common in financial systems not subject to the Germanic *Hausbank* relationships.
- On the investor side, the lack of institutionalized, performance-driven asset pools—with a large share of retail portfolios managed by the universal banks themselves, and poorly developed corporate pension funds due to an adequate social security system and the prevalence of employer- and union-managed funds.

The ruling Christian Democratic party has strongly supported German-style universal banking, but has nevertheless focused criticism on the big banks' rear-guard actions in inhibiting the introduction of new financial instruments and markets, and the consequent role of Germany as "an industrial giant but a financial dwarf." [Delamaide, 1990] The point is made that the Bundesbank has been responsible to a significant degree for this state of affairs. By inhibiting the creation of money market mutual funds ostensibly for monetary policy reasons relating to the stability of the monetary demand function, its position was traditionally supported by the German banks, whose earnings such innovations could endanger—and which therefore had an incentive to maintain internalization of market functions and to combat threats attributable to financial innovation and competition from external financial markets.

Modernizations already undertaken include the aforementioned introduction of a computerized futures and options exchange, an auction process for government debt issues, and the abolition of the securities transfer tax [Levich and Walter, 1990] but the full development of a creative, diverse financial market remains some distance away. In 1991 and 1992, the German Finance Ministry announced a series of further measures intended to address this issue with a series of reforms intended to make the German capital markets significantly more efficient and competitive.

There may of course be positive aspects of German universal banks' impact on financial market efficiency. For example, investment banks in the process of securities underwriting serve to close the information gap that exists between the true value of securities and their perceived value in the market. Accurate pricing of securities based on superior information is what underlies an underwriter's franchise, and hence its value as a going concern with respect to this function. One can argue that universal banks have access to more and better information about a prospective issuer by virtue of their commercial banking relationships than do unaffiliated investment banks, and hence can price new securities issues more accurately—especially in initial public offerings. The benefits would be reflected in lower costs to issuers and/or higher returns to investors, thereby enhancing the efficiency of the underwriting process.

Economic Performance

To an extent far greater than in the United States (but not Japan), the interests of German finance, industry and government are perceived to be largely coincident. The need to separate capital markets from credit markets has never been perceived as a prerequisite to the maintenance of financial stability. In fact, the years when domestic banks have been powerful have also been years of exceptional growth and stability for Germany. And banks have been left largely to their own devices in preserving the integrity of deposits, with little apparent loss of social welfare.

The economic restructuring process in Germany has always reflected corporate finance that has been heavily bank-oriented, with financial institutions having universal banking powers engaged in corporate lending as well as equity investments for their own and fiduciary accounts. This pattern has provided the universal banks with both non-public information and (indirectly and through their external board memberships) potential influence over management decisions involving corporate restructuring. Under such a system, firms that do not meet bank performance expectations find themselves under pressure to restructure—activity that may be initiated, orchestrated and implemented by the banks. [Rybczynski, 1989] Indeed, the German universal banks have repeatedly been relied upon to carry out industrial restructurings in the absence of well-functioning capital markets in the past, following periods of war or economic collapse, and so are accustomed to this role.

The idea that the Hausbank, bank shareholding, and proxy voting systems impart stability to industrial concerns is predicated on the view that markets are short-sighted and dynamically inefficient, and that by placing a significant degree of corporate control in the domain of bankers greater social welfare will be achieved over the long term. This view is supported to some degree by financial theoreticians who have argued that a strong benefit may arise in resolving information asymmetries when the bank is both an equity insider and a creditor—i.e., the notion of an "internal capital market" that is more efficient than the external capital market. [Cable, 1983]

This view is at variance with the experience in the United States and the United Kingdom, where banks have not had a comparable tradition in corporate finance, and capital markets have played a constructive role in industrial development for well over a century. Corporate debt financing has relied much more heavily on the securities markets, with debt-holders exerting limited influence on managerial decisions, and public equity holders exposed to the agency costs associated with management pursuing interests other than those which would maximize the value of their shareholdings. At the same time, accounting and disclosure standards are such that the financial affairs of public companies are relatively transparent, while banks under Glass-Steagall in the United States and pre-Big Bang restrictions in the United Kingdom have been limited in their ability to exert influence on management even remotely comparable to that of some of their German counterparts—notwithstanding their traditionally powerful exercise of control in the context of restructuring via loan workouts. Consequently, changes in corporate control have been accomplished by the capital market, often through hostile takeovers by unaffiliated parties. Even if unsuccessful, existing management may engage in corporate restructuring activity not dissimilar to what an unaffiliated acquirer would do.

Among recent studies of this issue, Steinherr and Huveneers [1992] were unable to reject the hypothesis that universal banks better support the long-term financial strategies of the non-financial sector than financial systems based on capital markets. They also found that universal banks achieve a superior risk-return tradeoff than more specialized financial institutions, probably due to better collection of information and monitoring of exposures, and that they benefit significantly from size and a strong capital base.

The transaction that has epitomized the contrast between the two systems was Deutsche Bank's involvement in the acquisition of Messerschmitt-Bölkow-Blohm (MBB), Germany's largest aerospace firm, by Daimler-Benz AG in 1989. Apparently convinced of MBB's strategic "fit" with the Daimler-Benz group, the acquisition was allegedly engineered (including replacement of the firm's chief executive) and executed by Deutsche Bank and the late Alfred Herrhausen. It was then politically approved by the Federal government over the strenuous objections of the Federal Cartel Office, evidently as a result of heavy political lobbying by the bank. Skeptics argued that the transaction (a) pulled Daimler-Benz into the middle of the politically-charged European Airbus consortium; (b) created "synergies" of dubious value in the light of experience in aerospace by General Motors and Ford, and (c) established Daimler-Benz as Europe's premier weapons supplier at a time of declining international tensions and rising concerns about the prospective European military role of a reunified German state. All of this coincided with substantially greater competition in other parts of the Daimler-Benz portfolio, particularly motor vehicles, given its extraordinarily high-cost production base in Germany.

What has been viewed in this context by critics as an industrial "blunder" of first magnitude could never have occurred, it is argued, under the transparent conditions of dominant "external" capital markets. Proponents are just as insistent that the same strategic move represents a stroke of industrial genius, one which would never have occurred under the transparency and short-term-results orientation of an Anglo-Saxon style of corporate control.

Economies of Scale and Scope

Do economies of scale and scope exist in financial services? This question lies at the heart of strategic and regulatory discussions about optimum firm size and structure in the banking sector. If economies of scale and scope are indeed important determinants of competitive performance, then geographic and functional limits may create significant disadvantages for scope-restricted financial systems such as Japan and the United States against the Germanic and other forms of universal banking. In an information- and distribution-intensive industry such as financial services with substantial fixed costs, there is ample potential for *scale* economies—as well as for diseconomies attributable to administrative overhead, agency problems and other cost factors. Similarly there is ample potential for economies and diseconomies of *scope*, which may arise either through supply- or demand-side linkages.

Individually or in combination, economies (diseconomies) of scale and scope may be passed along to the buyer in the form of lower (higher) prices resulting in a gain (loss) of market share, or absorbed by the supplier to increase (decrease) profitability. If all other factors are held constant, firms enjoying either supply- or demand-side economies of scale or scope should enjoy faster rates of growth than those that do not. Moreover, supply-side scale and scope economies should be directly observable in cost functions of financial services suppliers.

- With respect to scale economies, the consensus of empirical research has been that significant economies of scale tend to be exhausted at a relatively small size—i.e. less then $100 million in total deposits—and that no overall scope economies were available, although strong evidence existed for pair-wise scope economies between certain products of certain financial institutions [Clark, 1988]. By avoiding a bias toward smaller institutions, more recent studies find scale economies in evidence for banks with assets up to $6 billion [Noulas et al., 1990] and from $15 billion to $37 billion [Schaffer and David, 1991].
- The identification of scope economies continues to be highly dependent on the definition of products. Mester [1992], examined U.S. banks and Nathan and Neave [1990] surveyed Canadian banks, and both studies identify strong diseconomies of scope between traditional and non-traditional banking activities.

In an assessment of comparative growth rates and scale/scope economies among the world's 200 largest banks in the 1980s, Thomas and Walter [1992] found that (a) very large banks have grown more slowly than the smaller among the large banks, while (b) *positive* supply-side economies of scale and *negative* supply-side economies of scope have been the rule for large banks. Banks have tended to diversify, thereby possibly incurring the diseconomies of scope that were found in the study. This finding is confirmed by Steinherr and Huveneers [1992], who likewise confirmed the existence of diseconomies of scope with respect to the share of commission income and the size of the distribution network.

The evidence regarding economies of scale and scope is clearly critical in assessing the efficacy of German-style universal banking. As a form of organization that is viable in globally and regionally competitive markets that are likely to dominate at the end of the 1990s, the presence of significant scale and scope economies will do much to determine the competitive performance of the universals against their smaller, quicker, more specialized (by geography, by product and by client) rivals.

Conflicts of Interest

It has been argued that conflicts of interest which arise from serving various clients increase with the breadth of activities of a financial services firm. Examples include conflicts between the fiduciary responsibilities of a bank and its role as investment banker, conflicts between its interest in completing a hostile M&A transaction where the target company is or has been a client, and conflicts that result in stuffing and churning portfolios are only a few of a range of issues extensively explored in the literature. [Walter, 1985]

Some see an example of the German universal banks' ability to profit unfairly from their "insider" positions in the case of Deutsche Bank's rescue in late 1988 of Kloeckner & Co. The bank took over all of the equity of the foundering firm and restructured it. Although perceived at the time as a Hausbank fulfilling its side of the loyalty bargain in times of corporate difficulty, Deutsche Bank stood to make large profits from a transaction that was well removed from the transparency of the capital market, while preventing others from participating. According to one (anonymous) German observer, "The only difference between Deutsche Bank and corporate raiders ... is that it has a triple-A rating."

Economists generally rely on adverse reputation-effects and on legal sanctions to check the incentives to exploit such conflicts. Whether these checks operate satisfactorily in the German system is one focus of the debate.

Safety and Stability

Limitations on activities can affect the risk profile of financial firms, and hence financial stability. By limiting product diversification and geographic diversification, there is evidence that the cost-of-capital aspect of competitiveness may be impacted as well—and that large universal banks may in this way obtain a competitive advantage.

That the German financial system has shown a high level of stability, with few taxpayer bailout costs is not subject to debate—certainly in comparison to the United States. With only two significant bank failures in about two decades (Bankhaus I.G. Herstatt & Co. in the 1970s and Schoeder, Münchmeyer, Hengst & Co. in the 1980s), stability is as much a part of the German financial heritage as the country's fear of inflation. Stability may nevertheless come at the cost of static and dynamic efficiency through high levels of market power and excess returns.

At the same time, German-style universal banking relationships may improve the monitoring of lending risks by virtue of the shareholding and underwriting function—as opposed to relying largely on loan covenants and the option of withdrawing lending facilities in adverse circumstances. This may reduce the moral hazard problem associated with management taking on excessive risks in the absence of viable controls on the part of lenders.

There is also the issue of access to the safety net. That is, large universal banks will not be permitted to fail due to the social costs of such failure ("too big to fail"), and that they therefore have an artificial advantage in competing with institutions that have no such access. Even in cases of failure of separately incorporated affiliates it may be necessary to bring the safety net into play, leading to unfair advantages in credit rating levels and in funding costs. If the market perceives this to be the case, the safety net effectively stretches under such affiliates as well and possibly under industrial companies. Counter-arguments focus on the view that a broader range of activities increases the stability of the financial institution and therefore decreases the likelihood that the safety net will come into play.

Finally, the supervision and regulation that goes along with the safety net may be more difficult in the case of large, complex and heterogeneous financial institution than those which are more narrowly defined.

SUMMARY: COMPETITIVE PERFORMANCE AND FORMS OF ORGANIZATION

The German experience with universal banking is clearly an amalgam of strengths and weaknesses. Against each of the static and dynamic efficiency, scale and scope, and stability benchmarks we have applied, the German style of universal banking demonstrates important contradictions.

In the 1990s there is likely to be some degree of convergence between the universal and separated approaches to organization of financial services firms. EC financial liberalization and wider use of the securities markets by continental European corporations—including German companies—together with increasingly performance-oriented portfolio management on the part of mutual funds, insurance companies and other institutional investors is leading to a gradual shift away from bank finance, and the appearance of unwanted takeover attempts through acquisition of shareholdings by unaffiliated (often foreign) investors.

At the same time, easing of bank activity-limits in the United Kingdom and the United States is beginning to allow them to play a larger role in industrial restructuring transactions, and to exploit some of the information and relationship advantages they have as lenders.

Certainly in terms of international competitive performance, financial institutions that are subject to legal or regulatory barriers on the lines of business they may pursue as well as how (and where) they may pursue them could well suffer at the hands of rival institutions that are freely able to choose the optimum organization form. The fact that regulatory environments which are totally unrestricted as to the organizational form of financial services firms are home to true universal banks suggests—assuming competitive markets—that structure-related sources of institutional competitive advantage and disadvantage do in fact exist. Assuming the inevitable organizational problems can be resolved as the universal banks pursue their objective of becoming world-class profitable players in the global financial markets at the end of the century, it would certainly be foolish to bet against them.

REFERENCES

Arthur Andersen & Co. *European Capital Markets: A Strategic Forecast* (London: Economist Publications Ltd., 1990).

Bank for International Settlements. *Recent Innovations in International Banking.* Basel: Bank for International Settlements, 1986.

William J. Baumol, J.C. Panzar and R. Willig. *Contestable Markets and the Theory of Industry Structure.* (New York: Harcourt Brace Jovanovich, 1982).

George Benston, G. Hanweck and D. Humphrey "Scale Economies in Banking" *Journal of Money, Credit and Banking,* No. 14, 1982.

George Benston, A. Berger, G. Hanweck and D. Humphrey "Economies of Scope and Scale" Federal Reserve Bank of Chicago, *Conference Proceedings,* 1983.

Allen N. Berger, George Hanweck, and David B. Humphrey "Competitive Viability in Banking," *Journal of Monetary Economics,* No. 20 (1987).

Allen N. Berger and David B. Humphrey, "The Dominance of Inefficiencies Over Scale and Product Mix Economies in Banking," Board of Governors of the Federal Reserve System, Working Paper, November 1990.

Ernest Bloch. *Inside Investment Banking* (Second Edition). (Homewood, IL: Dow Jones-Irwin, 1989).

Jeffrey Clark. "Economies of Scale and Scope at Depository Financial Institutions: A Review of the Literature," *Federal Reserve Bank of Kansas City Review,* September-October 1988.

Kerry Cooper and Donald R. Fraser. *Bank Deregulation and the New Competition in Financial Services.* (Cambridge, MA: Ballinger, 1986).

Christine M. Cumming and Lawrence M. Sweet. "Financial Structure of the G-10 Countries: How Does the United States Compare?" *Federal Reserve Bank if New York Quarterly Review,* Winter 1987–88, pp.14–24.

Jean Dermine (ed.). *European Banking After 1992* (Oxford: Basil Blackwell, 1990).

General Accounting Office. *Banks Selling Insurance,* (Washington, DC: General

Accounting Office, 1990).

Thomas Gilligan and Michael Smirlock "An Empirical Study of Joint Production and Scale Economies in Commercial Banking" *Journal of Banking and Finance*, Vol. 8, 1984.

Thomas Gilligan, Michael Smirlock and William Marshall "Scale and Scope Economies in the Multi-Product Banking Firm" *Journal of Monetary Economics,* Vol. 13, 1984.

Daniel M. Gropper, "An Empirical Investigation of Changes in Scale Economies for the Commercial Banking Firm, 1979-1986, *Journal of Money, Credit and Banking*, Vol. 23, No. 4, November 1991.

Richard J. Herring and Anthony M. Santomero. "The Corporate Structure of Financial Conglomerates," paper presented at a Conference on International Competitiveness in Financial Services, American Enterprise Institute, May 31–June 1, 1990.

Beverly Hirtle, "Factors Affecting the Competitiveness of Internationally Active Financial Institutions," *Federal Reserve Bank of New York Quarterly Review,* Spring 1991.

Michael Jensen and Richard Ruback. "The Market for Corporate Control: The Scientific Evidence" *Journal of Financial Economics 11* (April 1983), 5–50.

H. Youn Kim "Economies of Scale and Scope in Multiproduct Financial Institutions," *Journal of Money Credit and Banking,* Vol. 18, 1986.

Hans-Jakob Krümmel. "German Universal Banking Scrutinized," *Journal of Banking and Finance,* March 1980.

Richard M. Levich. "Financial Innovation in International Financial Markets," in M. Feldstein (ed.), *The United States in the World Economy,* (Chicago: University of Chicago, Press, 1988).

Christopher Markwell. "Banking and Insurance: Marrying Corporate Cultures," paper presented at the International Insurance Society, Paris, 11 July 1990.

Loretta Mester "Traditional and Nontraditional Banking: an Information Theoretic Approach," *Journal of Banking and Finance,* (forthcoming).

John D. Murray and Robert S. White "Economies of Scale and Economies of Scope in Multiproduct Financial Institutions," *Journal of Finance*, Vol 38, 1983.

New York State Banking Department. "Briefing Papers on Financial Conglomerates, Large Credit Exposure, and Market Risk," International Conference of Banking Supervisors, Frankfurt, 10–12 October 1990.

Athanasios G. Noulas, Subhash C. Ray and Stephen M. Miller "Returns to Scale and Input Substitution for Large U.S. Banks," *Journal of Money Credit and Banking*, Vol 22, 1990.

Office of Technology Assessment, U.S. Congress. *International Competition in Banking and Financial Services.* (Washington, D.C.: OTA, July 1986 mimeo).

John C. Panzar and Robert D. Willig. "Economies of Scope," *American Economic Review,* May 1981.

Olivier Pastré. *Multinationals: Banking and Firm Relationships*, (Greenwich, Ct: JAI Press, 1981).

Olivier Pastré. "International Bank-Industry Relations: An Empirical Assessment." *Journal of Banking and Finance,* March 1981.

Randall J. Pozdena. "Do Banks Need Securities Powers?" *Federal Reserve Bank of San Francisco Weekly Letter,* 29 December 1989.

Raghuram G. Rajan, "Conflict of Interest and the Separation of Commercial and Investment Banking," University of Chicago, Working Paper, November 1991.

Wolfgang Roeller. "Die Macht der Banken," *Zeitschrift für das Gesamte Kreditwesen,* 1 January 1990.

Anthony Saunders. "The Separation of Banking and Commerce," New York University Salomon Center working paper (mimeo), September 1990.

Sherrill Shaffer and Edmond David, "Economies of Superscale in Commercial Banking," *Applied Economics,* Vol. 23, 1991.

Sherrill Shaffer, "Potential Merger Synergies Among Large Commercial Banks," Federal Reserve Bank of Philadelphia, Working Paper No. 91-17, October 1991.

Sherrill Shaffer. "A Revenue-Restricted Cost Study of 100 Large Banks," Federal Reserve Bank of New York (mimeo), February 1990.

Roy C. Smith and Ingo Walter. *Global Financial Services* (New York: Harper & Row, 1990).

J. Andrew Spindler, Jonathan T.B. Howe and David F. Dedyo, "The Performance of Internationally Active Banks and Securities Firms Based on Conventional Competitiveness Measures," Federal Reserve Bank of New York (mimeo), May 1990.

Alfred Steinherr and Christian Huveneers, "On the Performance of Differently Regulated Financial Institutions: Some Empirical Evidence," Université Catholique de Louvain, Working Paper (mimeo), February 1992.

Adrian E. Tschoegl "Size, Growth and Transnationality Among the World's Largest Banks," *Journal of Business*, Vol 56, 1983.

David J. Teece. "Economies of Scope and the Enterprise," *Journal of Economic Behavior and Organization,* March 1985.

Hugh Thomas and Ingo Walter. "The Introduction of Universal Banking in Canada: An Event Study," *Journal of International Financial Management and Accounting*, 1992.

Hugh Thomas and Ingo Walter, "Economies of Scale and Scope Among the World's Largest Banks," New York University Salomon Center working paper, January 1992 (mimeo).

Adrian E. Tschoegl. "Size, Growth and Transnationality Among the World's Largest Banks," *Journal of Business*, 1983, Vol. 56, No. 2.

U.S. Comptroller of the Currency. *U.S. Banks' Loss of Global Standing*, (Washington, DC: US Government Printing Office, for the Office of the Comptroller of the Currency, 1984).

Ingo Walter. *Barriers to Trade in Banking and Financial Services*. (London: Trade Policy Research Centre, 1985).

Ingo Walter (ed). *Deregulating Wall Street.* (New York: John Wiley & Sons, 1985).

Ingo Walter. *Global Competition in Financial Services,* (Cambridge, MA: Ballinger - Harper & Row, 1988).

Ingo Walter and Roy C. Smith. *Investment Banking in Europe: Restructuring for the 1990s* (Oxford: Basil Blackwell, 1989).

Kanji Yoshioka and Takanobu Nakajima "Economies of Scale in Japan's Banking Industry," *Bank of Japan Monetary and Economic Studies,* September 1987.

CHAPTER 7

INTERNATIONAL BANKING: A EUROPEAN VIEW

Jean Dermine

At the Council of Ministers held in Milan in 1985, the European Commission proposed a detailed timetable for the complete integration of European markets by January 1993. The aim was to dismantle the technological, regulatory and fiscal barriers which prevented the free flow of goods, capital and persons in the European Community, a group of 12 countries with 340 millions inhabitants. As concerns banking and financial services, a major issue arises as to whether regulation and supervision must be handled by a unique European authority, or whether it can be delegated to independent national Central Banks and supervisory bodies. After a frustrating experience in trying to harmonize banking regulations during twenty years, the European Commission (EC) adopted the principle of opening the borders with very minimal harmonization of regulations. Each country will recognize the competence of foreign authorities to regulate and supervise their own banks ("home country control" principle). In December 1991 at the Maastricht meeting, the heads of States or Governments signed a draft Treaty on Economic Union which includes the creation of a European System of Central Banks, a European Central Bank and a common currency by 1999 at the latest. However, the principle of decentralization of regulation and supervision is recognized in the Treaty. Under very special circumstances only would the European Central Bank be in charge of regulation and supervision. At a time when the North American Free Trade Agreement

(NAFTA) proposes to integrate further the economies of Canada, the United States and Mexico, and when financial services are the object of discussion at the GATT negotiation, it appears useful to have a critical review of the approach adopted for the integration of financial markets in Europe.

The chapter is structured as follows. The European banking industry is described in section one. An analysis of the early effects of European Financial Integration follows in section two. A description of the integration approach taken by the European Commission is developed in section three. The regulatory problems linked to the integration of national markets follows in section four.

The conclusions of the chapter are as follows. Early evidence on the effects of European financial integration demonstrates that the banking industry is undergoing a major restructuring caused by competitive deregulation. It is argued that a proper regulatory structure for open financial market needs to be developed further. Work remains to be done to ensure that the actions of independent Central Banks lead to the stability of financial markets. In the case of international banks with significant risks located in foreign offices, we recommend joint supervision by the host and home country authorities. Moreover, as domestic regulators will be responsible for controlling the ownership of banks (public or private) or their degree of market power in the domestic market, a European authority is needed to ensure that banks do not subsidize their international activities and that the terms of international financial services meet competitive criteria.

I. EUROPEAN BANKING STRUCTURE

The European banking industry includes 2,183 commercial banks and 3,323 savings or mutual banks. As is indicated in Tables 7–1a and 7–1b, it is still a fragmented market with leading financial institutions having a substantial market share in their domestic market (81 percent in the Netherlands or 79 percent in Denmark). At European Community level however, the five largest institutions control only 14 percent of the market. In Europe, banks play a major role in the financial system with a ratio of total assets to GDP of 1.7, compared to 0.81 in the USA and 2.8 in Japan.

The type of ownership of banks in Europe is rather diverse. Out of the 100 largest credit institutions, 49.6 percent are controlled by private interest, while the public sector controls 37.9 percent. (See Table 7–2.) This raises substantial issues of fair competition between private and public institutions.

TABLE 7–1a
Summary Statistics on Selected Banking Systems—End 1989

	Belgium	*Denmark*	*France*	*FRG*	*Greece*	*Ireland*	*Italy*
Number of commercial banks	85	76	404	299	34	33	267
Number of savings and mutual banks	29	165	421	594[a]		2	813
Assets of commercial banks (billion ECU)	238.7	93.2	771	518	39	20	588
Assets of other depository institutions (billion ECU)	40.6		411.5	1,085	19	13.7	246
GDP (billion ECU)	141.1	92.4	868.8	1,072	48.7	26.9	783
Total assets/GDP	1.98	1	1.89	2.4	1.2	1.25	1.07
Population (millions)	9.9	5.13	56.2	62	10	3.5	57.5
Market share of five largest institutions	58%	77%	43%	26%	63%	45%	53%
ECU rate (domestic currency per ECU)	43.4	8.05	7.02	2.07	179	0.77	1,510

[a] Does not include 3,225 cooperative credit institutions

Sources: OECD and national sources

Table 7–1b
Summary Statistics on Selected Banking Systems—End 1989

	Luxembourg	*Netherlands*	*Portugal*	*Spain*	*UK*	*EEC*	*USA*	*Japan*	*Switzerland*
Number of commercial banks	166	89	29	145	556	2,183	12,689	145[a]	236
Number of savings and mutual banks	49	53	1	188	163	2,478	3,323	1,080	214
Assets of commercial banks (billion ECU)	239	345	45	400	1,745	5,002.9	2,754	4,183	399
Assets of other depository institutions (billion ECU)		222.7		175.3	283.4	2,497	1,033	3,100	382
GDP (billion ECU)	5.43	203	39.4	343	764	4,387	5,720	2,623	170
Total assets/GDP	44	2.8	1.14	1.7	2.65	1.7	0.84	2.8	4.6
Population (millions)	0.37	14.8	10.5	38.9	57.2	326	247	123.5	5.5
Market share of five largest institutions	26%	84%	56%	39%	29%	14%	14%	25%	60%
ECU rate (domestic currency per ECU)	43.4	2.33	173	130.2	0.67		1.1	152	1.8

[a] Includes city and regional banks

Sources: OECD and national sources

TABLE 7–2
Sector Distribution of the 100 Largest EC Banks, 1987

		Total Assets	
Sectors	*Number of Banks*	*in Billions of ECU*	*in Percentages*
Public	42	1,691	37.9
Cooperative	9	489.7	11.0
Mutual	5	69	1.5
Private	44	2,432.4	49.6
Total	100	4,682.1	100.0

Source: J. Revell, "Bank Preparations for 1992; Some Clues and Some Queries," *Revue de la Banque*, March 1989.

In the recent past, banks in Belgium, Denmark, France and Spain have benefited very much from regulation or 'gentleman's agreement on interest rates paid on retail deposits. As Tables 7–3a and 7–3b document, interest margins on demand deposits have reached 11 percent on average in Belgium and France in the period 1980–1985.

TABLE 7–3a
Interest Margins and Operating Expenses

	Belgium	*Denmark*	*France*	*FRG*	*Greece*	*Ireland*	*Italy*
Average margin on demand deposits[a] (1980-85) (%)	11.2	16.2	11.7	6.5	-	-	4.3
(1987-91) (%)	8.7	9	9.7	7.2	-	-	-
Average margin on savings deposits[a] (1980-85) (%)	5.6	8.9	4.3	2.8	-	-	3.4
(1987-91) (%)	3.9	7	5.2	2.2	-	-	-
Population per branch	1,816	1,677	2,189	1,564	-	-	3,800
Operating expenses per asset in banks[b] (%)	2.6	2.8	3.2	2.5	-	-	3
Operating expenses as percentage of gross margin	0.66	0.65	0.65	0.65	0.76	-	0.63

[a] Current short-term rate minus interest rate paid on deposits

[b] Excludes interbank assets, expenses on non-interbank is calculated as follows: total expenses – (interbank assets × 1/8%)

TABLE 7–3b
Interest Margins and Operating Expenses

	Luxem-bourg	*Nether-lands*	*Portu-gal*	*Spain*	*UK*	*USA*	*Japan*	*Switzer-land*
Average margin on demand deposits[a]								
(1980-85) (%)	-	5.6	-	14.5	10.8	9	5.6	4.8
(1987-91) (%)	-	6.8	-	6	7	7.5	5.4	6.8
Average margin on savings deposits[a]								
(1980-85) (%)	-	2.5	-	10.7	2.5	1	3.5	1.3
(1987-91) (%)	-	4.7	-	9	2	1	2	2.6
Population per branch	-	2,000	6,031	1,127	-	-	8,700[b]	1,622
Operating expenses per asset in banks[c] (%)	1	2.5	2.5	3.5	4.2	3.5	1	1.95
Operating expenses as percentage of gross margin	0.41	0.65	0.47	0.6	0.65	0.61	0.61	0.55

[a] Current short-term rate minus interest rate paid on deposits
[b] Does not include 22,000 branches of postal savings banks
[c] Excludes interbank assets, expenses on non-interbank is calculated as follows: total expenses – (interbank assets × 1/8%)

In contrast spreads were much smaller in Germany and the Netherlands. The major reason is that the market (interbank) interest rate was much higher in some countries, allowing banks to realize major benefits from deposit rate control or pricing arrangements. Interestingly enough, in the more recent period 1987-1991, one observes a clear pattern of *convergence* due to deregulation and convergence of interest rate level. Interest rate margins are going down in Belgium, France, Denmark and Spain, but interest margins are going up in the Netherlands and Germany due to a higher interest rate level caused by German reunification. The profitability of banks did not reflect the high interest margins earned on retail deposits. Stock index data collected by the BIS (Table 7–4) shows that the banking industry has underperformed the market in the last ten years.

However, this general image should not hide that some institutions are doing remarkably well. As is documented in Table 7–5, banks in Spain, Lloyds in Great Britain or Credit Commercial de France did manage to raise substantially their capitalized market value. The poor performance of the

TABLE 7–4
Ratio of Banking Stock Index to National Stock Index (1980 = 100)

	1970	*1980*	*1990*
America	142	100	69
Japan	71	100	160
Germany	95	100	75
United Kingdom	85	100	87
Belgium	110	100	84
Netherlands	-	100	56

Source: BIS, 1990

Table 7–5
Ratio of Market Capitalization to Equity Book Value

	Market Capitalization/ Equity Book Value
United Kingdom	
Barclays	1.23
Lloyds	1.97
Midland	0.65
Natwest	0.88
USA	
Bankers Trust	1.92
Citibank	0.57
Morgan	2.08
Bank of America	1.4
France	
CCF	1.6
Société Générale	1.1
Crédit Lyonnais	0.6
Belgium	
Générale de Banque	0.9
Kredietbank	1.1
Spain	
BBV	1.47
Banco Popular	2.30
Santander	1.81
Netherlands	
ABN-AMRO	0.7
ING	0.9

Source: Salomon Brothers (1991)

banking system as a whole can be explained by three factors. The first is that an excessive branch network was built; the second, documented in Table 7–6, is that trade unions succeeded in increasing wages, especially in Belgium and France. A third reason is that margins on deposits were used to cross-subsidize corporate and international banking activities.

TABLE 7–6
Salaries in the Banking Sector, 1986

	Average Costs per employee (ECU)
B	37,672
D	26,000
F	31,716
I	37,631
NL	26,792
L	36,440
E	NA
K	NA
UK	27,854

Source: Association Belges des Banques, 1989

Although the effects of European financial integration will only be fully realized over the coming years, there is already a clear pattern emerging. This is discussed in the following section.

II. EUROPEAN FINANCIAL INTEGRATION—EARLY RESULTS

The major effect of integration is coming from competitive deregulation among national regulators who attempt to enhance the attractiveness of their home market. Two excellent examples concern the reduction of taxes on interest income and the deregulation of the Money Markets which used to be open only to financial institutions and the Treasury. The case of Belgium is symptomatic. Banks used to benefit from cheap tax-free savings deposits ("carnet de dépôts"), highly competitive vis-à-vis other instruments which were taxed at 25 percent. (See Table 7–7.) In April 1991, the Minister of Finance reduced the tax rate to 10 percent to reduce capital outflows to neighboring country of Luxembourg.

TABLE 7–7
Structure of Banks' Liabilities in Belgium[a] (in billions of Belgian francs)

	Deposits						Savings and Demand Deposits as % of Total
	Savings Accounts	*Demand Deposits*	*Term Deposits*	*Total*	*Bonds*	*Total*	
1986	607.3	450.9	677.6	1,735.8	447.6	2,183.4	48
1987	690.6	476.1	769.8	1,936.5	455.4	2,391.9	49
1988	766.6	517.7	805.0	2,089.3	465.0	2,554.3	50
1989	862.3	572.9	982.2	2,417.4	526.0	2,943.4	49
1990	757.5	581.2	1,229.3	2,568.0	673.3	3,241.3	41
1991 (August)	712	-	-	-	-	-	-
Variations over 12 months	–104.8	+8.3	+247.1	+150.6	+147.3	+297.9	

[a] Interbank excluded

Source: Commission Bancaire, Statistiques (1990)

As a result of the lost advantage, the banks have seen their cheap funding base reduced from 49 percent to 41 percent in just nine months!

The second example concerns the deregulation of the Money Markets. Table 7–8 gives the timing of deregulation of the Commercial Paper and Treasury Bills markets in Europe.

In France, Money Market Funds ("Sicav de Trésorerie") which were created in the early eighties, have increased from 10 percent of money supply (M2) in 1985 to 30 percent in 1990. The commercial paper market created in 1986 represents already 18 percent of short term bank lending to business firms. (See Table 7–9.)

This process has induced major mergers between national banks in several countries, with the clear intention to reduce their branch network and cost structure. In Denmark, the Netherlands or Spain, these domestic mergers concern the largest domestic banks. The impact on the competitive structure remains to be observed. It would appear that market power is less of an issue in the Netherlands, while the debate about the takeover of

TABLE 7–8
Introduction of Negotiable Money-Market Instruments

	Commercial Paper	*Treasury Bills*
France	1985	1986
Greece		1985
Italy		1975
Netherlands	1986	
Portugal		1985
Spain	1982	1981
United Kingdom	1986	1981

Source: Broker (1989)

TABLE 7–9
Money Market Funds and Commercial Paper in France

	Money Market Funds (FF billions)	*M2 (FF billions)*
1985	204	2500
1990	975	2948

	Commercial Paper (Billions)	*Short-Term Bank Lending to Business Firms (Billions)*
1986	24	488
1990	159	895

Source: Banque de France, *Bulletin Trimestrial*

Midland shows that competition issues do matter in the United Kingdom. This raises the need for a European authority to ensure that the terms of trade in international services meet competitive criteria. Indeed, one could argue that public ownership of banks or market power in the domestic market can help banks to subsidize their international activities. (See Table 7–10.)

These are early results of countries preparing for 1993. But as has been seen, the effects are quite substantial. European integration is leading to fundamental and permanent changes in the banking industry. A

TABLE 7–10
Domestic Mergers in Europe

Country	*Year*	*Merger*
Netherlands	1990	ABN-AMRO
	1991	NMB-Post Bank-ING
Denmark	1990	UniBank (Privatbanken, Sparekassen, Andelsbanken)
Spain	1988	Banco de Vizcaya
		Banco de Bilbao
	1989	Caja de Barcelona
		La Caixa
	1991	Banco Central - Banco Hispano
Italy	1992	Banca di Roma (Banco di Roma, Cassa di Risparmio di Roma, Banco di Santo Spirito)
	1992	IMI - Cariplo

detailed analysis of the approach pursued by the European Commission follows.

III. THE EUROPEAN APPROACH TO INTERNATIONAL INTEGRATION

The actions taken by the European Commission and the Council of Ministers can be divided in three time periods: Deregulation of entry on domestic markets from 1957 to 1973, various attempts toward harmonization of regulations from 1973 to 1983, and the recent proposals of freedom of cross-border services, single license, home country control and mutual recognition.

Deregulating Entry 1957–1973

The objective of the 1957 Treaty of Rome was the transformation of highly segmented national markets into a common, single market. This objective was achieved by two types of measures: The recognition of the right of establishment and the coordination of legislation whenever necessary.[1] In June 1973, the Council adopted a directive on the Abolition of Restrictions on Freedom of Establishment and Freedom to Provide Services in Respect of Self-Employed Activities of Banks and other Financial Institutions. This directive applies the national treatment principle which ensures the equal treatment of national firms of member states on entry in domestic markets and on conditions to which banks are submitted during their activity. It is explicitly recognized that subsidiaries of banks whose parents are established in non-member countries are to be recognized as EC undertakings in every way. Although in 1973 little discrimination remains as to entry in member states, the objectives of the initial treaty were still far from being met[2]. International competition through the supply of cross-border services was severely restricted by restrictions on capital flows. Furthermore, there was no coordination of banking supervision, so that banks operating in different countries could be subject to different rules. This led to the second phase of attempts to harmonize regulations.

1973–1983 Harmonization of Banking Regulations

Progress in harmonization came in 1977 with the adoption of the First Directive on the Coordination of Laws, Regulations and Administrative Provisions Relating to the Taking Up and Pursuit of Credit Institutions[3]. This directive establishes the principle of home country control. The supervision of credit institutions operating in several Member countries will gradually be shifted from the host to the home country of the parent bank. The 1977 directive is a first step towards the harmonization of regulations. It is a general program which, without providing any specific regulation, calls for further directives. Directives on Supervision of Credit institutions on a Consolidated Basis, on a Uniform Format for Bank Accounts and on Consumer Protection were adopted by 1986. The first banking directive initiated work on Winding up and Liquidation and on the Mortgage Market.

After the 1977 directive, the European banking markets were still fragmented for the following reasons:

- A bank wishing to operate in another country still had to be authorized by the supervisors of the other country.
- It remained subject to supervision by the host country and its range of activities could be constrained by host country laws.
- In most countries, branches had to be provided with earmarked capital as if it were a new bank.
- Finally, as already mentioned, the supply of international services was severely impaired by the restrictions on capital flows. For

instance, the 1984 exports of financial services represented 2 percent of output in France and Germany, while the market share of foreign institutions in the same two countries represented 16 percent and 4 percent respectively.

The task of complete harmonization of national regulations seemed to be a tentacular task which prompted a new approach towards European integration.

The Completion of the Internal Market by 1992: 1983–1992

While most international agreements have used the national treatment principle which ensures the equal treatment of all firms operating in one country, the European Commission has used a powerful method of integration: the opening of markets with very minimal harmonization of regulations.

In the context of *banking*, the 1985 White Paper calls for a single banking license, home country control and mutual recognition. These principles are incorporated in the Second Banking Directive[4]. All credit institutions authorized in one European country will be able to establish or supply financial services without further authorization[5]. The banking model adopted by the EC is the universal banking model. It permits banks to undertake investment banking activities and allows national supervisors to regulate the eventual links between insurance, commercial and industrial groups, and banks. For instance, it is known that the Bank of England would not favor the ownership of banks by industrial groups, while this would be allowed in France or Belgium. The second directive calls for home country control on solvency, but recognizes explicitly that host country regulations will apply for monetary policy reasons and for market position risks. Recognizing that fair competition requires a fair level playing field and minimal harmonization of regulations, the second banking directive calls for minimal equity, harmonized capital adequacy rules, supervisory control of major shareholders and of banks' permanent participation in the non-financial sector[6]. A proposal for a new directive on large risks is under discussion.

Along with this process is the complete liberalization of capital flows since June 1990. Exceptions include Ireland, Spain and Portugal (1992), and Greece (1995). It should be mentioned that this capital directive contains a safeguard clause authorizing Member States to take necessary measures in the event of balance of payments problems.

The integration of investment services (investment banking) and insurance proceeds in a very similar manner. As far as *investment services* is concerned, draft directives for Investment Services in the Securities Field and for Capital Adequacy provide for a single license, home country control on shareholders, capital adequacy, risk management and compliance with prudential rules. A major difference with the second banking directive is that substantial powers would be given to host authorities in terms of the design of the rules of conduct of business. These include share registration and new issues procedure, securities prospectuses, investment management, investor protection, insider trading and related market practices.

In the field of *insurance*, integration is somewhat lagging, although major progress is underway. Two fields have to be distinguished: Life insurance (including life insurance, pension and general annuities) and non-life insurance (including motor vehicle, fire and property, liability and accident). As regards the latter, the principle of single license, home country control and mutual recognition applies to large risks only (business firms with more than 250 employees). Host country authorization and supervision still applies for mass risks (second non-life directive). As regards life insurance, the second directive authorizes free cross-border sales when the initiative is taken by the applicant. Otherwise, host country authorization and supervision is the rule. A proposal for a third life insurance directive has been issued recently; it would allow the home country principle for life insurance by 1994, although marketing practices could be regulated for public interest. As concerns the choice of contract law, the general rule is that the law applying to the country where the risk is located will be chosen, unless it has been waived explicitly.

One would not be complete without making reference to the December 1991 Treaty on Economic and Monetary Union. Although "the primary objective of the European System of Central Banks shall be to maintain price stability," there are explicit references to regulation and supervision. "The European System of Central Banks shall contribute to the smooth conduct of policies pursued by the competent authorities relating to the prudential supervision of credit institutions and the stability of the financial system." "The national Central Banks are an integral part of the ESCB and shall act in accordance with the guidelines and instructions of the European Central Bank." "The ECB may offer advice to and be consulted by the Council, the Commission and the competent authorities of the Member States in the scope and implementation of Community legislation relating to the prudential supervision of credit institutions and to the stability of the financial system ... The ECB may fulfill specific tasks concerning policies relating to the prudential supervision of credit institutions and other financial institutions with the exception of insurance undertakings."[8]

From this review of the directives and recommendations, it appears that the objective pursued by the European Commission is threefold: Free entry and freedom of cross-border services throughout the Community, the establishment of a fair level playing field with single license, home country control, mutual recognition and minimal harmonization of regulations and, finally, consumer protection. In this respect, reference is often made (for instance in the 1985 White Paper) to the 1978 European Court of Justice "Cassis de Dijon" case[9] according to which control of the quality of a product is warranted, but can be met adequately by the supervisor of the home country. This path-breaking case strengthens considerably the economic integration process in recognizing a principle of limited sovereignty. However, references are also made to a 1986 non-life insurance Court case,[10] according to which control by the host authorities are acceptable as long as they are justified on the grounds of the "public interest": "Insurance is a sensitive area, and until more progress is made in achieving a common regulatory framework, the only way of safeguarding the interest of individual customers is to insist that policies sold in any Member State must accord with the rule prevailing in that country." A further illustration of the perceived need for consumer protection is the recommendation on deposit insurance:[11] "Member states shall ensure that the deposit-guarantee schemes that exist in their territory cover the deposits of branches of institutions having their head office in another Member state. As a transitional measure, pending entry into force of a deposit-guarantee scheme in all Member States, the latter shall ensure that the deposit guarantee scheme, in which the institutions that have their head office in their territory take part, extend cover to deposits received by branches set up in host countries within the Community which have no deposit-guarantee scheme, under the same conditions as those laid down to guarantee deposits received in the home country."

Both the European Commission and the European Court of Justice appear to accept the premise that consumers of financial services need to be protected. In case of public interest, it has been argued by the Court and recognized again in a draft proposal for a third life-insurance directive that host country regulations could be applied. In order to assess the economic coherence of the European framework, it is useful to review the literature on the sources of market failures calling for public interventions.

IV. THE ECONOMICS OF FINANCIAL SERVICES REGULATION

An analysis of the characteristics of financial services and of the market failures calling for regulations follows. It attempts to clarify the maxim: "Competition whenever possible, regulation wherever necessary." Although the services provided by banks are interrelated, it is convenient to distinguish four categories: Portfolio management, payment (transmission) mechanism, risk sharing and monitoring or information-related services (Eisenbeis, 1987).

Portfolio management At low cost, investors can acquire a diversified portfolio of liabilities issued by deficit spending units. The pure case is the mutual fund or unit trust (called SICAV in France and Luxembourg) which supplies a diversified portfolio to the holders of its shares.

Payment mechanism A second role for banks in the economy is the management of the payment system, that is to facilitate and keep track of transfers of wealth among individuals. This is the bookkeeping activity of banks realized by debiting and crediting accounts.

Risk sharing services An essential function of banks is to transform the risks faced by the parties, that is to supply risk sharing contracts. First, banks not only supply diversified assets, they also organize efficiently the distribution of the risky income earned on the asset pool. The deposit holders receive a fixed payment while the shareholders receive the residual income. Other insurance services would include liquidity insurance (option for the deposit holder to withdraw quickly at face value) and interest rate insurance (floating rate lending with various ceilings on interest rates).

Monitoring and information-related services Banks perform a useful function in reducing the costs of screening and monitoring borrowers. Private information held by borrowers results in contracting problems because it is costly to assess the solvency of a borrower and to monitor its actions after lending has taken place. The delegation of screening and monitoring to banks is an efficient allocation mechanism. In addition to the classical lending function of banks, one can include in the information-related services most of the 'investment services' activities, such as underwriting and distribution of securities, market making, trust or fiduciary services, and advisory services on corporate governance, merger and acquisition and risk management.

Two independent explanations have been advanced for the existence of market failure in the financial services industry: imperfect information and the need to protect consumers, and the potential for bank runs and systemic crisis.

Information and Consumer Protection

The economic literature recognizes that the inability of consumers to evaluate properly the quality of a product can create a market failure. The literature distinguishes three types goods: search goods, whose quality is apparent before purchase; experience goods, whose quality is apparent after consumption; and "trust" goods, whose quality is not always apparent even after consumption.[12] An inefficiency may arise because the quality of a service is not valued properly by the market and reflected into higher prices so that there are insufficient incentives for firms to produce quality. For instance, it may be difficult for depositors to assess the quality of the assets of a bank and its degree of solvency. Or it could be difficult to evaluate the quality of incompetent or dishonest financial advisors.

Such situations create the need for two types of regulations to protect consumers. Regulations can control entry in a market (the 'fit and proper' criterion) or conduct behavior (capital adequacy, risk taking, insider trading...). In this context, there is an important issue as to whether this regulatory task should be performed by private or public organizations, and in an international and global marketplace, whether there is a need to harmonize regulations.

The analysis of the "consumer protection" argument will proceed in three steps. First, a private market solution to the information problem is sought. Next, we analyze the set of circumstances under which the regulation of entry and conduct is justified. Finally, the conditions requiring an international harmonization of regulations are analyzed.

A natural solution to the imperfect information problem is the provision of information and regulation of disclosure. However, the evaluation of bank risks is a costly activity which has the nature of a public good. Since it is available to consumers at a very low transfer cost, the evaluation of banks should not be undertaken by each depositor but could be delegated to a public agency or a private rating firm. Furthermore, since small account holders may find the cost of interpreting the rating high and/or since they care about risk free deposits only, two alternatives could be developed. The first is to have deposit insurance. The second is to create risk free banks, that is intermediaries investing all deposits in risk free securities. Depositors would have the choice between banks offering a higher but risky return and those providing quasi-risk free deposits. It would appear that the evaluation of risks is not inherently more difficult in banking than in other industries. A main difference is that it is quite likely that a large fraction of depositors care for risk free deposits, but these could be provided by the markets.

In addition to the disclosure and evaluation of information, there are two alternative private ways to reduce the imperfect information problem: reputation and industry insurance-warranty. Reputation implies that firms who care for the value of their franchise and long run profits have an incentive to build internal control systems to reduce risks and fraud. However, a trade-off will exist between (high) short term fraudulent profit and the benefits of long term reputation. An alternative is for a firm or an industry to provide a warranty to guarantee the quality of the services offered. For instance, the fund of a stockbrokers association guarantees clients against potential dishonest behavior of its employees. Peer monitoring or industry self-regulation prevent deviant behavior.

This analysis has shown that the information problem can be solved privately on the market in several different ways. However, whenever there is evidence that the market cannot discriminate among firms, then there is a case for the government to regulate entry and ensure a minimal quality, as is done for instance in the medical and legal professions (Goodhart, 1985). The argument is that regulation is necessary to maintain a minimum desired level of quality. A question arises as to whether this should be done privately or quasi-privately as in Great Britain with the Self-Regulatory Organizations (SRO) or whether it should be public. The benefits of flexibility and industry expertise provided by private self-regulations have to be balanced against the risk of capture by the SROs whose members have an obvious incentive to limit entry and competition. As there is currently no empirical evidence in favor of one system or another, we suggest that the national regulatory structures compete.

Competitive (de)regulation raises immediately the issue of the need to harmonize regulations at the international level. The answer to this question is again related to imperfect information. Competition among national regulators or private clubs is desirable whenever the parties can evaluate the quality of regulatory systems. For instance, competition among regulators in Paris, Frankfurt, London and New York will shape the development of local stock exchanges and the outcome will be optimal if participants can discriminate among different regulatory systems. Harmonization of rules to ensure minimal quality would be necessary only if the market cannot discriminate. This suggests that the degree of international harmonization could vary for different activities and classes of investors, the 'informed' and the "non-informed."

It is fair to recognize that different countries may wish different degrees of protection and regulations, so that an international harmonization is unlikely to satisfy fully all members. But the alternative to free international trade with (imperfect) international harmonization is a "closed economy" with domestic regulation. The author has little doubt that the benefits of international trade and competition will weigh favorably against the benefits provided by a possibly more satisfactory domestic regulation in a "closed" economy.

As regards the market failure related to imperfect information, one has to be extremely careful to avoid permanent regulatory interference which can create the *raison d'être* of public intervention. For instance, the creation of a safe and publicly insured deposits market reduces the market for information gathering and the creation of risk free funds. A clear example of a potentially perverse effect of intervention is the money market funds market in France which, so far, is virtually risk free. In a case where a distribution company CODEC was close to defaulting on its commercial paper (held by money market funds), the banks intervened to absorb the losses. The argument was that this was necessary to stabilize the money market funds market. The argument of market stability is understandable, but the intervention creates a false sense of safety and reduces the private incentives to create rating agencies evaluating the riskiness of money market funds.[13]

Facing a remarkably similar situation in May 1970, the Federal Reserve Bank of New York refused to lend to Penn Central which was defaulting on its commercial paper. It only created a liquidity cushion available to banks to absorb temporary disturbances on the commercial paper market.[14] This laissez-faire policy should not imply that there is no ground for public intervention to compensate the unlucky or imprudent investors. The argument is that transitory transfer policies should be used in these cases rather than direct and permanent interference with the functioning of private markets.

It is striking to observe that the motivation for regulation advanced by the European Commission is the need to protect consumers against losses. Although the principle of home country control is recognized as an efficient way to foster integration, there are several references to "public interest" and the possibility to rely on host country rules to restrict competition and protect consumers. In contrast, the banking literature is less concerned with risk per se. As long as information flows properly, the risk will be priced into higher deposit rates and investors will have a menu ranging from risk-free to "junk" banks. The case for imperfect information and regulation should apply only to the small "uninformed" investor. The provision of the third life insurance directive which applies the law of the applicant (except when it has been waived explicitly) and leaves a time to cancel the policy seems in this respect quite effective. In banking, risk-free funds or banks whose assets are invested exclusively in risk-free government securities could be created to meet the needs of investors who care for riskless asset or who are uninformed.

The second major argument for the regulation of financial institutions is the fear of systemic risk in the banking industry.

The Stability of Financial Markets

Banks are special because the financial contract that emerges—illiquid loans funded by short-term deposits—creates potential market failure and the need for public intervention. The financial contract creates the risk that depositors run to withdraw their funds. A run can be triggered by bad news about the value of bank assets or by any unexplained fear. In both cases, there may be a loss since illiquid assets will be sold at a discount. Moreover, a bank failure could eventually trigger a signal on the solvency of other banks, leading to a systemic crisis. A market failure exists because a cooperative solution among depositors cannot be enforced. Collectively, there is no incentive to run, but individually, there is the incentive to be the first on the line to collect the deposits at full value.

This market failure explains banking regulations and the establishment of safety nets to guarantee the stability of banking markets. They have taken the form of deposit insurance and lender of last resort interventions. In Europe, deposit insurance systems have been created recently in most countries. (See Table 7–11.)

Three features of the European insurance systems make them unique. The first is that, contrary to the FDIC in the United States or the CDIC in Canada, they are totally ignored by the public. Publicity is even forbidden in Germany. The argument seems to be that the announcement of their creation could reduce confidence in the banking system. Since the coverage per deposit is small and even incomplete in the United Kingdom and Italy, they are unlikely to contribute much to the stability and one would have to rely on lender of last resort intervention of central banks to ensure stability. Secondly, since the coverage is different across countries, it could be desta-

TABLE 7–11
Deposit Insurance Systems in Selected Countries

Country	*Coverage (Domestic Currency)*	*Coverage (ECU)*
Belgium	BEF 500,000	11,520
Denmark	DKR 250,000	31,056
France	FF 400,000	56,980
Germany	30% of equity per deposit	
Ireland	£IRL 10,000	12,987
Italy	Lit 1 billion (100% for first 200 mil. and 75% for next 800)	662,000
Luxembourg	FLUX 500,000	11,520
Netherlands	DG 40,000	17,167
Spain	Pta 1,500,000	11,536
United Kingdom	75% of deposits up to £20,000	22,388
Greece	No system	
Portugal	No system	
Japan	¥ 10,000,000	65,789
United States	$100,000	90,909

bilizing if depositors start to chase the best coverage. A third feature of the deposit insurance systems is that they cover the deposits of domestic and foreign banks operating locally. This could create an "accountability" problem. Indeed, any insurance activities require the monitoring of risks taken by the insurer, but the principle of home country supervision would not allow the control of the foreign entities by the domestic lender of last resort or the deposit insurance agency. The failure of BCCI involves a bank chartered in Luxembourg, with significant activities in Great Britain. Its liquidation creates a liability for the British deposit insurance fund. Current discussion seems to suggest the organization of European deposit insurance on a consolidated basis. For instance, the deposits of an international bank chartered in Luxembourg would be insured by the deposit insurance system from Luxembourg wherever their location. If this was the case, there would be an appropriate matching between supervision and insurance, but one has to realize that deposit insurance on a consolidated basis requires an identity of coverage, otherwise Italian banks benefiting from a large coverage (ECU 526,400) would compete away Belgian banks (insurance coverage of ECU 11,870).

One is left wondering about the creation of deposit insurance systems in Europe. As has been argued, they are unlikely to contribute to the stability of the banking systems. Deposit insurance systems can be interpreted as a tool to create small risk free deposits while putting the cost of bailing out on the insurance fund funded by the banking industry.

It seems to us that the creation of safe deposits should be done *without* recourse to insurance. European deposit insurance mechanisms should be dismantled. Risk free funds can be created and the market will decide how much will flow into these funds. As to risky banks, they will be evaluated by rating agencies who can provide adequate information.

As there remains a need to foster stability, discretionary lenders of last resort will be necessary. The major advantage of a discretionary safety net as opposed to a more systematic insurance is that it increases the private incentives for monitoring and evaluating bank riskiness. The stability system through deposit insurance or lender of last resort creates two additional problems. They concern the *potential liability* of the lender of last resort and the *implicit subsidy* that can be given to domestic banks.

As lenders of last resort will be concerned primarily with their domestic markets and banks operating domestically[1], it would seem legitimate that they keep some supervisory power on <u>all</u> institutions operating domestically. That is, host country regulation could apply[15] to limit the exposure of the domestic central bank. A first alternative to host country control is to harmonize completely the solvency standards, but experience has shown that it would be very difficult to reach an agreement on common harmonization of regulations and supervisory practices. A second alternative is to pursue further the process of harmonization and delegate supervision and regulation to a European Central Bank. The problem of accountability would be solved at the European level but not at the world level. Moreover, we do not believe that a centralized regulation at the level of a European Central Bank is necessary, nor desirable. Competition between national regulators will produce efficient standards and prevent the regulatory capture by the regulatees as has happened so often in banking in the last sixty years. It thus seems reasonable to let domestic lender of last resorts keep some host supervisory powers on international banks having substantial risks located in foreign offices. Equivalently, the European Central Bank could organize the prudential supervision of these international banks, in accord with the principle of subsidiarity.

A second and related issue is the recognition that public safety net or deposit insurance systems can provide an implicit subsidy that can alter competition. For instance, the leverage of a bank (increased degree of indebtedness) reduces the cost of funding loans, transferring the cost of eventual bank failure to the lender of last resort. To create a level playing field, the Bank for International Settlements and the European Commission have enforced minimal capital requirements and are working on lending limits to a single borrower. The harmonization of prudential regulations is warranted when the objective is to create a level playing field. But harmonization should only be limited to that objective. For instance, the current effort to harmonize the regulation on interest rate risk and foreign exchange exposures does not appear desirable because it does not provide clear competitive advantage to banks (Dermine, 1991). Quite often the identification of a regulatory subsidy will be questionable. For instance do links between banks and industrial groups provide a competitive advantage which is subsidized by the central bank who takes a greater risk? It would seem to us that there is no case for harmonization as long as the joint existence of a competitive advantage and a subsidy is not demonstrated. Such a case was pretty clear in the context of loan funding and capital adequacy. It is much debatable in the context of the links between banks and industrial groups.

CONCLUSION

The purpose of this chapter has been to analyze the integration of European financial markets. While most international agreements have used the national treatment principle and kept domestic authorization and supervision, the European Commission has used a powerful innovative method of integration. The opening of markets with single license, home country control, mutual recognition and very minimal harmonization. Our analysis of the financial services industry has shown two main sources of economic failure calling for national regulations and the eventual harmonization of regulations. The first source of market failure is the traditional need to protect consumers. *It has been argued that domestic regulation of quality is only warranted in those cases where consumers cannot evaluate the quality of a product. Similarly, international harmonization of regulation is necessary if the market participants cannot discriminate among different regulatory structures.* It is the author's view that information disclosure, competition between public or private regulators and the creation of risk free funds will be satisfactory in most situations. In any case, different products and classes of consumers will require different regulatory treatment. A call has been made to limit the "public interest" argument which not only may limit competition but also harm the spontaneous development of private markets. A second market failure calling for regulation and harmonization comes from the need to provide a safety net and the legitimate need to limit moral hazard and risk taking. *From this angle, host regulation may be justified to limit the exposure of domestic lender of last resort and the international harmonization of regulations may be necessary to limit implicit public subsidies.* It has been argued that harmonization of prudential regulations should only be done when there is a clear case of implicit subsidy and competitive advantage. The international integration of financial markets is going to lead, as the early results of the European experience shows, to significant gains for consumers; however, it remains necessary to develop further the proper international regulatory structure.

NOTES

1. See Dassesse and Isaacs (1985).
2. See Clarotti (1984).
3. Directive 77/780, O.J.L. 32/30 of 17 December 1977.
4. COM (87) 715, 16 February 1988.
5. As concerns non-EC banks, the "single" passport applies only to subsidiaries authorized in one country of the EC. Branches do require national authorization.
6. See Dermine (1990a,b).
7. It is symptomatic to observe that the draft Treaty (EC, 1992) refers explicitly to the exclusion of insurance. Although the Governors of Central Banks wanted to leave open the possibility of consolidated supervision of financial conglomerate, the European Commission was in favor of keeping separate insurance regulation.
8. Rewe-Zentral AG v Bundesmonopolverwaltung Fur Branntwein (Case 120/78) [1979] ECR 649.
9. EC Commission v Germany (Case 205/84) [1986] ECR 3755.
10. Recommendation on deposit-guarantee schemes in the Community, 87/63, J.O.L. 33/16 February 4,1987.
11. See Kay-Vickers (1986) and Mayer-Neven (1991).

12. The first ratings on French money market funds were made public in April 1991, ten years after the creation of the market.
13. See Brimmer (1989).
14. It is well known that the Bank of Italy did not intervene to prevent the collapse of the Luxembourg-based Banco Ambrosiano Holdings.
15. A provision in the second banking directive allows host country control for "public policy" or "monetary policy" reasons. The control of the liability of the lender of last resort could fall in these cases.

REFERENCES

Association Belge des Banques, *Rapport Annuel,* Brussels, 1989.

Bank For International Settlements, *Annual Report,* Basle, 1990.

Banque de France, *Bulletin Trimestriel,* June 1991.

Brimmer, Andrew F., "Central Banking and Systemic Risks in Capital Markets," *The Journal of Economic Perspectives,* Spring 1989.

Broker, G., *Competition in Banking,* OECD, Paris, 1989.

Dassesse, Marc, and Stuart Isaacs, *EEC Banking Law,* London: Lloyds of London Press, 1985.

Clarotti, Paolo, "Progress and Future Developments of Establishment and Services in the EC in Relation to Banking," *Journal of Common Market Studies,* 1984.

Dermine, Jean, "The Specialization of Financial Intermediaries, the EC Model," *Journal of Common Market Studies,* March 1990a.

Dermine, Jean (editor), *European Banking in the 1990's,* Oxford: Basil Blackwell, 1990b.

Dermine, Jean, "The BIS Proposals for the Measurement of Interest Rate Risk, Some Pitfalls," *Journal of International Securities Markets,* Spring 1991.

Eisenbeis, Robert A., "Eroding Market Imperfections: Implications for Financial Intermediation, the Payments System, and Regulatory Reform," in *Restructuring the Financial System,* Federal Reserve Bank of Kansas City, 1987.

European Commission, *Traité sur L'Union Européenne,* Brussels, 1992.

Goodhart, C. A., *The Evolution of Central Banks,* The London School of Economics and Political Science, London, 1985.

Kay, John, and John Vickers, "Regulatory Reform in Britain," *Economic Policy,* 7, 1988.

Mayer, Colin, and Damien Neven, "European Financial Regulation: A Framework for Policy Analysis" in A. Giovanini and C. Mayer (eds.), *European Financial Integration,* Cambridge: Cambridge University Press, 1991.

CHAPTER 8

UNITED STATES BANK REFORM: GETTING BEYOND THE OXYMORON

Bevis Longstreth
Ivan P. Mattei
David P. Mason

The 1980s represented a decade in which excesses became commonplace across the entire spectrum of commercial endeavor: hostile takeovers; management entrenching defenses such as the poison pill; golden parachutes and other enriching compensation packages for top executives; management and other highly leveraged buyouts financed with junk bonds; program trading strategies promising the capture of gains no matter how over-priced the equity market became, without risk of loss when the market turned. The Government did its part with ever-increasing deficits, both in absolute terms and as a percentage of GNP.[1] And, of immediate relevance here, first the S&Ls and then the commercial banks failed on a grand scale unparalleled since the Great Depression.

At the outset of the 1990s, then, with the country turning from its excesses, and more open to reforming itself, one would have thought major bank reform possible, if reform was needed. And consensus there was on the question of need.

- The cost to taxpayers of protecting depositors in S&Ls is expected to reach $200 billion plus interest on the federal borrowing necessary.[2] $200 billion! (Remember the intense debate over whether, in 1980, to provide Chrysler with up to $2.3 billion in government guarantees.) It was obvious that something had to be done to fix a financial system that had allowed the S&L catastrophe to occur.

- The cost to taxpayers of protecting depositors in commercial banks has yet to be determined, but the FDIC's insurance funds are depleted, Congress has enacted legislation to increase the FDIC's borrowing authority to $70 billion,[3] and bank failures continue to rise. From 1942 through 1980 bank failures totalled 198. During the 1980s the cost and number of bank failures grew dramatically, with 206 banks failing in 1989, 169 in 1990 and 127 in 1991.[4] More recently, between September 30, 1991 and January 31, 1992, the total assets of institutions on the FDIC's problem list jumped 26% to $613 billion.[5] Something was obviously wrong with the banks too.
- A particularly perplexing aspect of these events was the fact that the comprehensive regulatory scheme to which banks and S&Ls were subject, making them among the most highly regulated commercial enterprises in the country, had been designed to assure their safety and soundness. Plain to all was the fact that this regulatory scheme wasn't working as intended.

However fertile the ground, the seed of real reform has failed to germinate. Despite a strong consensus as to the need for reform, there has developed no consensus as to what "banking reform" means. The Bush Administration's proposal to authorize banks to undertake new financial activities is a "reform" proposal,[6] but so too is the "core bank" proposal, which would impose much greater restrictions on banks than now pertain as the price for allowing them to affiliate with non-bank financial institutions permitted a broader range of activities.[7] Treasury Secretary Brady endorses consolidation in the banking industry,[8] but Representative Henry Gonzalez is opposed.[9] Hugh McColl wants to be able to take NationsBank nationwide,[10] but he faces the formidable Independent Bankers Association of America.[11]

Looking back to 1992 and to the failure of the Bush Administration's reform package to find favor in the 102nd Congress, and to all the previous failed attempts to improve the banking system, one can fairly characterize banking reform in the United States as an oxymoron. Why this is so is a large and separate topic not central to this chapter. But brief comment is in order to set the stage for what follows.

A British philosopher—F.M. Cornford—captured a general problem for legislative bodies with a quip: "nothing is ever done until everyone is convinced that it ought to be done, and has been convinced for so long that it is now time to do something else." Compounding this legislative inertia in the case of bank reform is the success of post-Depression reforms. Perhaps the hardest thing to do in government is to repeal or overhaul legislation that has proved successful but is no longer necessary or appropriate. In the first days of law school, we were taught a Latin maxim: *Cessante Ratione Legis, Cessat et Ipsa Lex.* "The reason of the law ceasing, the law itself also ceases." However true as a matter of common law, this maxim doesn't work with statutes, because they can only be repealed by the legislative body that wrote them. We seem to be held in thrall by laws that once succeeded, however outmoded, unnecessary or positively hurtful they become. The Public Utility Holding Company Act of 1935 is one example. But ExhibitA in support of this claim is the set of banking laws put in place after the Great Depression and elaborated in numerous pieces of legislation ever since.

Despite enormous changes in the nature of banking since the early 1930s and its diminishing role in the dynamic financial services sector, the regulatory approach to banking has remained essentially the same.[12] The shift away from traditional banking is well known and can be captured by a couple of statistics. Between 1974 and 1989 financial assets held by U.S. depository institutions as a percentage of the total financial sector fell from 57% to 41%,[13] a remarkable loss of business to non-banks. Perhaps even more telling is the shift in business over this period that occurred at J.P. Morgan, the only U.S. money-center bank that still has a AAA credit rating.[14] Between 1975 and 1990, Morgan's interest revenue as a percentage of total revenues dropped from 77% to 36% and loans as a percentage of earning assets dropped from 65% to 33%.[15] Today, J.P. Morgan's three "engines of growth"—M&A, public underwriting and global trading of financial instruments—can all be done by non-banks outside the bank regulatory scheme.[16] Indeed, the time is long past when our costly and restrictive regulatory scheme was offset by the special value of a banking franchise. Almost any banking activity today can be undertaken by non-banks without these regulatory burdens, with the exception of deposit taking, which itself has been undermined by the attractions of money-market and short-term bond mutual funds offering superior rates of return and check-writing privileges.

While these facts lead some to conclude that bank regulation has become an impediment to the health of those it regulates, there are many powerful policy makers who believe the lesson of the S&L and bank failures in the 1980s is a need not just for better supervision but for tighter bank regulation rather than the reverse.

Confusion, of course, can serve a purpose.[17] In the case of bank reform, confusion has led to stalemate in Congress. If the banking system were not under such severe stress, perhaps we could be grateful for this outcome. Unfortunately, the increasing inability of our banks to compete in either domestic or global markets means that the status quo is becoming perilous.[18] Nor can we forget that our trading partners have learned from our mistakes and have taken advantage of the weakened condition of our banks to gain valuable experience and capture market share at the expense of U.S. banks (near-term) and the U.S. economy as a whole (long-term).[19]

In part, the problem is that traditionally the United States has been virtually alone among its trading partners in debating regulatory, tax and other conditions affecting banks with little reference to the potential consequences they hold for the industry's ability to compete internationally.[20] (It's the financial analog to our national disdain for learning foreign languages.) The easy assumption of our nation's pre-eminence, built up in the early post-war period, makes it hard for national policy makers to see that regulatory structures serving the parochial interests of one part of the financial services industry increasingly threaten the overall national interest of having a first rate, globally competitive system. Unless the banking industry is to go the way of Detroit, real reform must take place.

To a very limited degree the banking industry has been able to work within the current statutory and regulatory framework to achieve incremental reform. For example, banks have gained limited powers to underwrite commercial paper and securities,[21] and there will probably be some continued advancement in this area. Some banks have been able to make an end run around the Douglas Amendment by "relocating" rather than branching across state lines.[22]

For all the small advances, however, there have been retreats as well, as in the case of bank insurance powers.[23] And more generally, one finds in the FDIC Improvement Act fresh evidence of a Congressional instinct to embrace regulation as the solution of choice to problems rather than one of last resort. Tucked away in this law is the new requirement that federal banking agencies prescribe by August 1, 1993 standards for compensation, fees and benefits paid by banks and S&Ls to their officers and directors and define what constitutes excessive compensation levels, the payment of which will be deemed an "unsafe and unsound practice."[24] It's ironic to find within our market-oriented system serious pressure building for government control of compensation, while elsewhere we applaud the global dash away from command economies, government-run businesses and government-imposed levels of price and compensation.

This process of one step forward, two steps back will not suffice. If U.S. banks are to be and remain profitable, competitive and safe, Congress must enact a meaningful and comprehensive reform package.[25] Our thesis is that effective reform requires *first*, an understanding of the proper role of regulation in serving the public interest and *second*, an application of that understanding to the banking industry in order to determine what reforms will best achieve that goal. The balance of this chapter will address these two topics.

THE PROPER ROLE OF REGULATION

Regulatory intervention in the financial services sector of a free market economy is justified if, *but only if*, the individual pursuit of economic gain by market participants will lead to socially inefficient outcomes[26]. In general, this will be the case only in the presence of one or more specified "market failures." Absent such a diagnosis, the strong presumption should be against regulatory intervention. Hence, our first task is to return to basics and ask:

Why Should Banks Be Regulated?

The catalog of justifications commonly offered for bank regulation is well known, although the economic soundness of those justifications is not always clearly articulated. Without attempting a full critique of the arguments, there follows a list of the most prominent justifications proffered in the literature.

Instability Inherent in Fractional Reserve Banking

Almost by definition, banks are institutions whose assets and liabilities are mismatched in terms of maturity, interest rate, currency of denomination or other attributes (i.e., they provide "portfolio transformation services"), while simultaneously providing payments services through the creation of liquid deposits or "transactions balances."[27] This joint production of portfolio intermediation and payments services yields significant transaction cost savings for the economy that could not be achieved through the more limited intermediation provided by checkable money market mutual funds. Stated otherwise, we need a class of institutions to intermediate between the money supply and the longer-term capital needs of the economy. This role is assigned to banks. However, when coupled with the illiquidity of traditional bank assets, it creates a risk of insolvency in the event of a depositor run. If such a run occurs and depletes a bank's reserves against deposits, insolvency is inevitable unless assets can quickly be disposed of at book value.

Banks are unique in the degree of their susceptibility to depositor runs.[28] Moreover, even healthy banks are susceptible to such runs in the event of a sudden loss of depositor confidence. This is often explained by reference to the well-known "prisoner's dilemma"—a situation in which the best strategy for an individual depositor (in light of his lack of information about what others will do) is to take an action that is individually optimal (withdraw one's deposited funds immediately), but collectively disastrous (a bank run leading to insolvency).[29] This "market failure" has two principal consequences. Banks themselves suffer because, in the event of a depositor run, they may be forced to liquidate assets or obtain alternate funding on uneconomical terms.[30] The depositors' perspective is somewhat different. A depositor is concerned about the return of its principal (and interest) as well as maintaining the liquidity of its deposit. If a deposit is by definition a liquid asset of the depositor, then the failure of a depository institution will transform that liquid asset into an illiquid claim against the bank in receivership.

A depositor run leads to different conclusions regarding the appropriate regulatory response, depending upon whether or not the run is economically justified. The risk posed to a healthy bank is alleviated by providing an interim source of liquid funds—i.e., the Federal Reserve[31] as lender of last resort. In the event of an irrational depositor run on a healthy bank, the Federal Reserve in effect breaks the prisoner's dilemma by substituting its own resources for those of myopic depositors. However, in the case of a failing bank, the risk of illiquidity to the depositor suggests a different regulatory response. In the event of insolvency, deposit insurance provides immediate liquidity to depositors who would otherwise be unsecured creditors in a possibly protracted receivership proceeding.

Systemic Risks

It is often asserted that the failure of a bank can have potential spillover effects (what economists refer to as "negative externalities") affecting unaffiliated banks and financial institutions. These external costs are not factored into the economic calculations of bank management, shareholders or creditors (including depositors). Hence, actions taken by each of these constituencies on the basis of a private assessment of likely costs and benefits, though individually rational, can lead to collectively inefficient outcomes. These outcomes can take at least two forms. First, it can be argued that a bank-specific prisoner's dilemma might degenerate into a multi-bank or system-wide prisoner's dilemma. Second, even in the absence of a system-wide depositor run, the failure of one bank might initiate a chain reaction of failures by other institutions with significant financial exposures (through the payments system, for example) to the failing bank. These possibilities are also said to justify regulatory intervention.

Although these concerns are easily seen to be valid in theoretical terms, it is much more difficult to assess how seriously they should be taken as a practical matter. Citations of prior experience in the nineteenth century and during the Great Depression are inapposite in today's world, where the Federal Reserve stands ready to provide liquidity to any bank in the event of a depositor run or a significant disruption in the payments system[32] and where credit risk in the payments system is either assumed by the government (through Fedwire) or reduced to a negligible level (through CHIPS, for example). Prior to 1913, we had no such lender of last resort, and during the Great Depression the Federal Reserve failed to act forcefully to forestall depositor panics.[33] In any event, modern bank runs tend not to drain reserves from the banking system as a whole (as they did in the nineteenth century), but rather result in a redeployment of deposits from one institution to another.[34]

Deposit insurance is no doubt a factor in helping to explain the absence of systemic runs in recent times. However, because our system of deposit insurance has also created serious incentive distortions (e.g., "moral hazard"[35]) which have produced *enormous and clearly quantifiable social costs,* it bears asking whether deposit insurance, at least in its current form, is a necessary part of the remedy for the theoretical systemic risks identified above.

The threat of a system-wide prisoner's dilemma is asserted to arise because the failure of a bank or a group of banks might undermine depositor confidence in the banking system as a whole. The basis for this assertion is twofold. First, it is argued, a depositor could well assume that a problem in one bank is due to a regional economic downturn that is likely to affect all neighboring banks.[36] Second, it is presumed that depositors tend to act irrationally. Paradoxically, the vitality of the first argument derives in no small part from the geographic restrictions we have chosen to impose on our banks, making them vulnerable to economic downturns in specific regions or industries. And the premise of depositor irrationality should be regarded with suspicion.[37] If a group of depositors did in fact act "irrationally" and withdraw funds from a healthy bank, there are other rational investors (including, as a last resort, the Federal Reserve) that can supply alternative funds to the bank. There would be some cost to the bank because it would have to pay a marginally higher interest rate, but this is a part of the cost of being a bank. In the past it may have been true that runs happened too quickly to permit such a market correction. The current highly developed national market for bank certificates of deposit, however, suggests that the market itself, if not constrained, could now respond with sufficient speed.[38]

Systemic risks are also thought to arise because the interdependence of banks through the payments system creates a possible "negative externality" in the event of a bank failure.[39] However, this line of reasoning is subject to attack on both theoretical and empirical grounds. First, it can be argued that increased interdependence through the payments system creates *positive* "network externalities"[40] and that, if anything, we should encourage greater interdependence.[41] Second, as an empirical matter, the banking industry itself has moved to minimize the risks inherent in the payments network.[42] Because banks themselves have both the incentive and the ability to manage payments system risks through private ordering, a generalized fear of such risks should not be invoked as justification for otherwise unnecessary regulatory intervention.[43]

Market Concentration

A substantial portion of the state and federal bank regulatory apparatus can be seen as a direct outgrowth of an historical fear of concentration in the financial sector. This fear has been a unifying theme in the Glass-Steagall Act's separation of commercial banking and investment banking,[44] the branching restrictions of the McFadden Act[45] and the interstate banking limitations of the Douglas Amendment.[46] What is left unclear, however, is why banks are special in this respect. By almost any measure, the banking industry in the United States is far from concentrated: today there are approximately 12,000 commercial banks in operation in the United States, compared with approximately 150 in Japan, 550 in the United Kingdom, 65 in Canada and 900 in Germany.[47] As discussed in more detail below, the burden of proof has not been sustained by those who would impose regulatory constraints on the banking system in order to prevent concentration.

Credit Allocation Biases

The Bank Holding Company Act enshrines the policy of separating banking from commercial and industrial activities. This policy is premised in substantial measure on the view that banks' decisions regarding the extension of credit should be made on the basis of market criteria and not influenced by the interests of controlling or affiliated industrial concerns. This solution is unnecessarily severe if one looks at the success in other fields of less intrusive ways of containing undue influences, which is simply another name for conflicts of interest.[48]

Conflicts of Interest

As one of the authors observed in testimony before the Federal Reserve Board:

> Potential conflicts of interest inescapably arise whenever a financial firm—be it primarily an insurance company, broker-dealer or bank—is permitted to offer multiple services. Some potential for conflicts of interest often accompanies the potential for market efficiencies and synergies. The goal of regulation, however, is not to deny the potential for efficiencies in order to escape the possibility of conflicts, but rather to filter the multiple activities through the least intrusive regulatory scheme that can protect against actual harm from the conflicts. In devising that screen, regulators should be practical in their assessment of risk, looking first to the protections afforded by the firm's self-interest—that is, the economic disincentives to exploit potential conflicts of interest. For the financial firm, those disincentives are powerful....[49]

These observations remain true. Potential conflicts will arise whenever firms offer multiple services. Yet, in most cases, the firm's self-interest provides a countervailing incentive sufficient to preclude exploitation of those conflicts.

In situations where it is determined that self interest will not alone deter undesirable behavior, the appropriate regulatory response should be to craft a scheme based on disclosure, customer consent and, where necessary, criminal sanction, but not (except as a last resort) a prohibition of the activities that give rise to conflicts.

Six Guidelines for Coherent Regulation

In our view, regulatory intervention in the market for banking services should be consistent with the six guidelines described below. In the next section of this chapter we will apply these guidelines to the "market failures" identified above, with a view to developing proposals for sound bank reform.

Harness Competitive Market Forces

Strong, competitive and efficient financial institutions are the product of vigorous competition in open (and increasingly international) markets. They cannot be legislated into existence. Wherever possible, our system of bank regulation should seek to harness competition as a force to produce stronger, more efficient institutions. We can no longer afford a bank regulatory policy founded on outdated antitrust notions that we must prevent "destructive competition," that "big banks are bad banks" or that "independent" community banks must be preserved.

Regulatory policy should not be based on the assumption that economic actors, particularly retail depositors, do not understand their self-interest. As developed below, the ability of undercapitalized banks to impose costs on the federal safety net through inefficient risk-taking can be mitigated by returning to depositors some incentive to monitor bank soundness.

Limit the Medicine to Just What's Needed to Cure the Ill

Once a market failure is identified, the regulatory response should be limited to that which is necessary to remedy it. As we discuss in more detail below, the appropriate response to the risk of *irrational* bank runs is to assure that the central bank stands ready to act as a lender of last resort and instill investor confidence through full and timely disclosure of banks' financial condition. However, providing 100% deposit insurance is not necessary. Nor is it necessary to prevent every bank failure—in some cases depositor runs *are* rational.

Price Controls Are Bad

Price controls are perhaps the least reputable and most dangerous tool in the regulator's arsenal. The S&L debacle can be attributed in no small measure to the pernicious effects of Regulation Q[50], which for many years capped the interest rates payable on certain deposits and granted thrifts a 25 basis point advantage over banks with respect to the interest rates that could be offered to depositors.[51] As a result, the incentive to manage interest rate risk—through the use of variable rate mortgages, for example—was attenuated. The S&L's were in effect set up for a fall when, during the course of the 1970s, nominal interest rates skyrocketed along with inflation, money market funds not bound by Regulation Q were able to cut into the thrifts' deposit base and, ultimately, Regulation Q was repealed.[52] The net effect was to render a substantial part of the thrift industry insolvent on a mark-to-market basis virtually overnight.[53]

Other examples of the pernicious effects of price controls may be cited. In the 1960s, for example, Congress imposed the interest equalization tax, which produced the unanticipated side-effect of driving capital formation offshore into the waiting arms of a fledgling Eurobond market. The business didn't return when the IET was removed. Indeed, since 1986 the volume of Eurobond offerings has exceeded that of the U.S. domestic corporate bond market.[54] In 1992, we saw the value of major bank stocks tumble when the Senate voted to approve Senator Alfonse D'Amato's legislative cap on credit card interest rates.[55]

The lessons of these experiences are straightforward. Firms forced to operate subject to price regulation are likely to vent competitive pressures through non-price or service-based competition in ways that may be socially undesirable. And perhaps most importantly, price controls are particularly dangerous when applied to financial instruments.

Prohibitions Are Suspect

Regulation should proceed with surgical exactitude—not by amputation. Prohibiting an activity (other than in the context of criminal matters) should be a last resort, taken only after a determination has been made that a market failure exists that cannot be rectified by means of any lesser intervention. Prohibitions (of which the so-called "section 20 firewalls" are the most notorious example) should be regarded as the bank regulatory equivalent of the "suspect classifications" receiving strict scrutiny under the U.S. Constitution.

Diversification Is Good

The risk in a bank's portfolio of assets will be smaller, the lower the covariance among those assets.[56] This principle applies equally to a portfolio of business lines. To the extent a bank is able to broaden the mix of its product offerings to encompass lines of business with low (or even negative) covariance with the bank's other business lines, the risk to the enterprise as a whole is correspondingly reduced.

In the wake of hundred billion dollar bailouts of financial institutions, regulatory constraints on the attainment of greater diversification should be vigorously resisted.

Permit Dynamic Efficiency

Regulation should not merely seek to foster what economists refer to as "static" or "allocative" efficiency—assuring that resources are channeled to their most productive current use. Rather, a sensible regulatory system should be conducive to the attainment of "dynamic efficiency"—a situation in which firms are allocating resources in an efficient manner to the development of new products or services ("product innovation") or to the production of existing products or services more efficiently ("process innovation").[57]

A regulatory system that inhibits banks from pursuing business into related or new markets creates not only static inefficiency (in the form of lost economies of scope), but also dynamic inefficiency through the elimination of a force tending to foster innovation. Such a policy is particularly dangerous in a world of international competition against institutions from countries not having similar inhibitions.

In designing a sensible system of bank regulation, we cannot afford to ignore evolutionary forces. Consider the World Bank statistics[58] in Table 8–1, setting forth the percentage of gross assets in the financial systems of several countries that are held by various institutions within those countries. According to this data, banks in developing countries tend to hold a much larger share of all financial assets than they do in industrial economies, particularly if central bank assets are included[59]. On the other hand, long-term debt and equity securities account for a substantially larger fraction of financial system assets in industrial economies than in developing economies. Moreover, collective investment vehicles, such as mutual funds, play virtually no role in most developing countries, but are a significant part of the financial system in most industrialized countries.

We can draw a simple lesson from these statistics. As financial systems mature, securities markets and collective investment vehicles will tend to account for a larger share of capital formation. A corollary is

TABLE 8–1
Assets as a Percentage of Total Gross Assets of the Financial System, 1988

	Central Banks	*Deposit Banks*	*Specialized Lending Institutions*	*Contractual Savings Institutions*	*Collective Investment Institutions*	*Long-Term Debt Securities and Equities*
Developed markets						
Australia	5	31	14	17	1	33
Canada	1	33	2	26	8	30
France	6	56	10	7	5	16
Germany, Fed. Rep. of	4	41	14	9	2	30
Japan	2	45	9	6	7	30
Sweden	4	27	18	16	1	35
United Kingdom	1	35	1	26	3	34
United States	2	28	7	19	4	40
Average	3	37	9	16	4	31
Emerging Markets						
Argentina	32	43	11	5	0	10
Brazil	27	32	12	2	4	23
Chile	14	44	1	11	1	28
India	10	47	6	12	1	24
Korea, Rep. of	9	53	14	4	10	10
Malaysia	7	34	12	13	3	32
Nigeria	23	46	2	3	7	19
Pakistan	21	65	1	2	1	11
Philippines	30	38	14	3	3	14
Portugal	20	72	1	2	1	4
Thailand	16	55	12	1	0	17
Turkey	33	54	4	6	0	3
Venezuela	20	46	25	1	0	8
Average	20	48	9	5	2	16

that banks will come under increasing competitive pressure from securities firms and other intermediaries. Prudential Securities, in a recent company report on J. P. Morgan, put the matter very simply: "Commercial banking and investment banking have 'fused.'"[60] "[J.P. Morgan] has distanced itself from money center banks in general—via its AAA debt rating and its transformation into a global securities firm and investment bank, with commercial banking contributing less than half of net income."[61]

Given this natural evolutionary path for financial systems, a regulatory policy that restrains a parallel evolution in the banking franchise is misguided.

PROPOSALS FOR SOUND REGULATION

We now apply the six guidelines for regulatory intervention identified in Section I to develop specific reform proposals regarding deposit insurance, interstate banking, industry consolidation, product restrictions, universal banking and the bank regulatory structure. We then close with a brief critique of the so-called "core bank" proposal.

Deposit Insurance Reform

The centerpiece of any banking reform proposal must be the reform of our deposit insurance system. The current system of Federal deposit insurance does not withstand scrutiny under the guidelines for regulatory intervention we have presented. Although some form of insurance is appropriate medicine to protect depositors from insolvency, our system, with fixed premiums, explicit coverage up to $100,000 and implicit coverage of all amounts in excess of $100,000, is not the right cure. [62] As the Treasury Department's recent study so succinctly stated, the current fixed-rate system of deposit insurance is "perverse."[63] The system needs to be restructured to mitigate moral hazard and encourage private sector monitoring and discipline among banks as much as possible. As we try to demonstrate in the remainder of this chapter, it has been the absence of market discipline in the deposit insurance system that has provided the most frequently heard current justification for diverse regulation of depositary institutions in order to guard against the many unwanted side effects of providing deposit insurance without regard to risk. This effort has proved difficult, much like trying to push a string instead of pulling it, because market forces were not engaged to do all that they could do in serving the goals for which regulation was substituted. Thus, with the restructuring of deposit insurance recommended below, market forces should importantly assist by diminishing the level of regulatory supervision required, by establishing capital adequacy and by eliminating the need for product restrictions based upon either a fear of unfair competition or a fear that highly risky activities will endanger the insurance fund.

Prescribing sound reform of the deposit insurance system requires that we identify with specificity the market failures to be remedied, a subject to which we now turn.

The Need for Deposit Insurance

Systemic Risks Although fear of a system-wide "spillover," where one bank pulls down many others, may have been justified sixty years ago, market evolution and technological developments have largely eliminated this risk. As noted above, inter-bank risk in the payments system has been substantially eliminated through joint industry efforts.[64] To the extent systemic risks are thought to arise outside the payments system as a result of excessive uncollateralized extensions of credit (including off balance sheet exposures) among individual banks, the "problem" is not substantially different from that sought to be addressed by lending limits.[65] Deposit insurance is not the proper regulatory response to these concerns. Moreover, recent studies suggest that depositors are not so irrational as to cause runs on healthy banks in response to a run on a failed or failing bank.[66] Therefore, in crafting a sound system of deposit insurance, our focus should be on the causes and effects of individual bank runs, rather than systemic concerns.

Depositor Runs on Healthy Banks Caught in a prisoner's dilemma, depositors may be prompted to act by a misperception that their (healthy) bank is in risk of failing. The first line of defense for a bank facing such misperceptions is to assure its depositors that it is sound, just as any firm must be able to reassure its creditors. While typically this will prove hard to achieve, it can on occasion prove to be easy. As this chapter was being written, rumors circulated that a large money center bank faced substantial exposure to the real estate developer Olympia & York, which was itself rumored to be experiencing financial difficulties. The response of the bank was simply to *disclose* its actual exposure, which was not substantial, thus allaying creditor and shareholder concern.[67]

Even if disclosure of its financial condition does not reassure skittish depositors, a healthy bank should be able to avoid a liquidity crisis by obtaining funds from more rational firms, including other banks, or from the Federal Reserve as lender of last resort. The Federal Reserve's ability to lend is an adequate and narrowly tailored regulatory response that is consistent with the principles of regulation that we are advocating.[68] Deposit insurance is not a necessary part of the regulatory response to the problem of irrational depositor runs on healthy banks, particularly in light of the observation that "many countries have managed to avoid runs without the existence of deposit insurance."[69]

Orderly Liquidation of Failing Banks In the case of an unsound bank, no amount of reassurance from bank management will be able to stop a depositor run, because the run is economically justified. Moreover, collateralized borrowing from the Federal Reserve will not stave off insolvency because, by definition, the failing bank lacks the necessary collateral to support such borrowing. In such cases, the goal of regulatory intervention should not be to prevent a bank failure, but rather to promote a prompt and orderly liquidation of the failing bank.[70] This leads to the further conclusion that the Federal Reserve should be assigned a supervisory role, in addition to its central banking functions, in order to be able to distinguish accurately (and with dispatch) between situations warranting liquidity support and those in which such support should be withheld.[71] Absent an informational advantage over the market, Federal Reserve lending might simply prolong the life of insolvent institutions while losses continue to mount. Moreover, the effectiveness of discount window lending as a tool to resolve true liquidity problems is enhanced if its use is perceived by the market as a signal that the institution in question has been judged viable. If discount window lending sends an ambiguous signal, it might have the perverse effect of further weakening the troubled institution because borrowings from the Federal Reserve must be collateralized and, therefore, tend to deplete the unencumbered asset base available to unsecured claimants.[72]

No exception from this policy should be made for banks deemed "too big to fail." To the extent failure of such a bank is thought to create secondary *liquidity* problems for other banks, the appropriate regulatory response is to provide discount window privileges to those deemed viable by the Federal Reserve. However, barring systemic disaster, the number of institutions whose continued *viability* is threatened by the extent of their uncollateralized *and* uncollectable exposure to a failing bank should ordinarily be quite small. If a situation to the contrary has developed, "the mistake was made prior to the crisis. Letting intermediaries maintain levels of capital and diversification that create an environment in which a single shock can cause a large number of failures is fundamentally a different problem than the temporary lack of liquidity healthy firms may be experiencing."[73]

In the case of nonbanking firms, the regulatory response to similar problems is quite different. The automatic stay provision of the Bankruptcy Code, 11 U.S.C. §362, and the rules regarding preferential transfers prevent creditors from taking unilateral action to protect their interests at the expense of others. In our view, this model is not sufficient in the case of a bank failure because, in most cases, a substantial portion of the claims on the bankrupt's estate consist of depositors' unsecured claims. Unlike trade creditors in a typical commercial bankruptcy, retail depositors may face unmanageable burdens if a significant part of their liquid assets are tied up in protracted bankruptcy proceedings.[74] Thus, appropriately structured deposit insurance has a legitimate role to play in the design of an orderly system to manage bank failures.

However, deposit insurance should not be allowed to dull depositor incentives to the point where regulatory intervention outpaces market discipline. The delay in waiting for regulators to close a bank imposes significant costs on society as bank losses continue to mount, management error compounds upon management error, and economic resources are tied up when they could be more efficiently deployed in alternative uses.[75] Moreover, because banks are able to alter the riskiness of their asset portfolio quite rapidly in comparison to typical commercial enterprises, the effectiveness of market discipline is clearly enhanced if ongoing monitoring is undertaken by a class of claimants holding assets of relatively short duration, i.e., demand deposits. Indeed, it can be argued that the institution of funding illiquid bank assets with demand debt subject to the so-called "sequential service constraint" (i.e., payment to depositors on a first-come, first-served basis) is an efficient form of private ordering designed to yield an equilibrium in which agents with superior information and opportunities for self-dealing (i.e., bank management) are induced to refrain from acting to the detriment of their principals (i.e., depositors), and depositors are simultaneously induced to refrain from initiating sudden withdrawals of deposited funds.[76] To the extent this equilibrium is disrupted by a system of de facto blanket insurance coverage, one would expect to find a persistent pattern of insider abuse—an expectation not at variance with the empirical record.[77]

The FDIC Improvement Act encourages early intervention by giving regulators expanded authority to close a bank before it has completely exhausted its capital.[78] Although we endorse prompt regulatory intervention, reliance on this step alone will not suffice. Intervention by regulators will invariably be inadequate. And regulators do, albeit infrequently, make mistakes. There is a risk that regulators will do "too much too soon" or "too little too late."

Unlike regulatory intervention, prompt market action will close a failing bank quickly and without the costs of a vast regulatory superstructure. Even the cost of annual bank examinations are increasingly burdensome on banks. In the FDIC Improvement Act, Congress mandated annual bank examinations for nearly all depository institutions.[79] The Office of the Comptroller of the Currency will be forced to raise assessments for examinations 30% in order to carry out this mandate.[80] In our view, mandating ever more frequent and comprehensive bank examinations is not a cost-effective regulatory response to the perceived problems of bank safety and soundness.[81] Instead, we should rely on the financial markets to assess the true financial condition of banks. To the extent this requires more thorough disclosure by banks, the appropriate response is to mandate the necessary level of disclosure. We can then rely on the discipline of depositors (under a suitably structured deposit insurance program) and other creditors to force prompt closure of failing banks.

Finally, it bears noting the obvious, but often overlooked, proposition that regulatory reform proposals should be evaluated on a "pro forma" basis—i.e., by reference to anticipated market outcomes after giving full effect to the market's adaptations to the new policies. Thus, under a system of deposit insurance that restores depositors' incentives to monitor bank risk on an *ongoing* basis, we would expect that fewer banks will in fact find themselves subject to market discipline in the form of a sudden loss of depositor confidence. Moreover, under a deposit insurance system of the type advocated below, we would expect many depositors to switch some or all of their transaction balances to checkable money market funds which, in turn, would invest some or all of their assets in bank certificates of deposit. In this way, small depositors could enlist the services of professional money managers to exercise depositor discipline and diversify risk. The net effect of these market adaptations would be to reduce the number of bank failures, as well as the extent of losses to bank creditors in the event of a failure.

We conclude, therefore, that deposit insurance should not be viewed as a tool to remedy perceived systemic risks or to prevent irrational depositor runs on healthy banks. Other forms of intervention are appropriate and sufficient to deal with those issues. Rather, deposit insurance is justified only as a mechanism to provide an essential level of liquidity to depositors in failed banks and to promote their orderly liquidation.

The Proper Scope of Deposit Insurance

In light of this analysis, several conclusions follow regarding the proper scope of deposit insurance.

Coverage Ceiling First, the current limit on deposit insurance of

$100,000 is much higher than needed to provide depositors with essential liquidity. Deposit insurance coverage could be reduced to $50,000 and still insure the overwhelming majority of individual and small business deposits. In the case of households, empirical evidence (although somewhat dated) suggests that more than 75% of all individual accounts would be covered if deposit insurance coverage were $50,000.[82] Similarly, nearly half of all small business deposits would be fully insured with a $50,000 coverage.[83] Insuring the full amount of a deposit (or a very high amount, as in the case of the current $100,000 limit available to several different accounts in the same institution) creates a systemic cost by relieving depositors of the role they could play, at an acceptable burden to society, in monitoring and disciplining their depository banks. Accordingly, we recommend capping deposit insurance at a level on the order of $50,000 per depositor.[84]

Coinsurance Second, in order for depositors to have an incentive to monitor the riskiness of bank activities, their deposits must likewise, at least to a limited extent, be at risk on an ongoing basis. The current $100,000 level of deposit protection is so high and so readily available to different potential accounts of the same individual,[85] that depositors effectively have no incentive to conduct even the most cursory analysis of the safety of a bank.

The appropriate remedy is to build an element of "coinsurance" into our system of deposit insurance.[86] If individual depositors took a "haircut" in the event of a bank failure, they would have an adequate incentive to monitor banks and help winnow out failing institutions.[87] We believe that the risk of losing 10% of deposited funds would give depositors sufficient incentive to act as if they were uninsured while still assuring them of a substantial level of liquidity in the event they make the wrong choice.[88]

Of course, Federal insurance of less than the full deposit does not mean that individual depositors will actually lose ten cents on the dollar in the event of a bank failure.[89] Banks may well compete for deposits by offering fully insured accounts through a combination of Federal *and* private insurance. Brokerage firms now provide private insurance coverage against losses due to insolvency, beyond the limits of SIPC.[90] The incremental cost that a depositor or bank would pay for this supplemental insurance is justified because the depositor is choosing to insure himself fully. The monitoring and disciplining that the private supplemental insurer would bring to bear would in effect be a substitute for what the fully-insured depositor has chosen to escape.[91] Moreover, as noted above, we would expect that under a system of deposit insurance of the type advocated here, many depositors would chose to hold some or all of their transaction balances through money market funds that would, in turn, hold a diversified portfolio of bank certificates of deposit and other money market instruments. In the event of a bank failure, such depositors would likely suffer losses substantially smaller than ten cents on the dollar.

Protecting the small depositor through 100% Federal deposit insurance may seem sacrosanct, but it is neither necessary, desirable, nor, in our judgment, politically unavoidable, especially as part of a comprehensive reform package advocated by strong leadership in Congress and at the highest level of the Executive Branch (something the Bush Administration's proposal lacked).

Pricing of Deposit Insurance

The risk of loss to the insurance fund is a function of the behavior of at least three groups: bank management, stockholders and depositors. Under the current system of deposit insurance, the cost of FDIC deposit insurance to the bank (and, indirectly, to its shareholders) is not affected by the level of risk imposed on the insurance fund through the actions of these three constituencies. Depositors have little incentive to monitor or exert meaningful discipline over bank management. Management has only its self interest in avoiding a failure, which depends mainly on the size of its capital stake.[92] And the effectiveness of bank stockholders as monitors of risk is impaired by the many statutory and regulatory limitations on the acquisition of significant equity stakes in banks or bank holding companies.[93] Moreover, in the case of a failing bank with zero or negative net worth, the current system of deposit insurance gives bank stockholders (and management) an incentive to gamble with depositors' (i.e., the FDIC's) resources in an effort to reattain solvency.

Our proposals to modify the scope of deposit insurance are designed to restore to depositors a role in monitoring and constraining the incurrence of risk by bank management. Realigning shareholder and management incentives with market norms requires the further step of pricing deposit insurance according to the risk imposed on the insurance fund.

There is general agreement in most quarters that banks should be assessed a risk-based deposit insurance premium. That is how private insurance works, and federal deposit insurance should be no different. The Bush Administration[94], the FDIC[95] and the General Accounting Office[96] have acknowledged the need for risk-based deposit insurance. Congress has mandated studies[97] and, in 1991, called for risk-based deposit insurance assessments starting in 1994.[98]

The actual mechanism for setting an institution's risk-adjusted premium is a more difficult question, but not an insurmountable one. The Bush Administration proposed that the ratio of risk-based capital to risk-weighted assets be the basis for setting a risk-adjusted insurance premium.[99] Although convenient, and a familiar concept, risk-based capital will not accurately establish the proper premium that a given institution should be assessed.

Under the so-called international Basle Accord[100], all banks are expected to maintain total risk-based capital equal to at least 8% of their risk-weighted assets. Risk-based capital is the total of a bank's Tier1 or "core capital" (essentially its common stockholders equity, non-cumulative perpetual preferred stock and certain qualifying intangibles) plus its Tier2 or "supplementary capital" (cumulative preferred stock, allowance for loan and lease losses and certain other capital instruments). A bank's risk-weighted assets are determined by assigning each asset to one of four risk categories (based on the type of obligor, guarantors and collateral) and then discounting the total assets assigned to each category by a corresponding weight indicative of the relative riskiness of the assets in that category.[101]

But merely categorizing assets in this manner does not accurately identify their inherent riskiness—it implicitly assumes, for example, that all commercial loans are equally risky. Premiums based solely on capital levels would fail to take into account other factors that would normally influence the cost of insurance, such as interest rate risk, quality of bank management and asset diversification. Moreover, as the Government Accounting Office has observed, a bank's capital is usually a lagging indicator of the quality of the underlying assets. Therefore, the Bush Administration's proposal to use risk-weighted capital and risk-weighted assets is likely to prove an inaccurate measure of overall risk, and thus an inappropriate tool for determining the cost of deposit insurance.

However, the market itself, if stimulated to address the matter, can accurately determine the proper price that an institution should pay to insure deposits. One way to invoke the market would be to require banks to issue relatively short-term subordinated debentures in amounts that bear a relation to their assets. The market would determine the interest rate that these debentures must pay based on the relative risk profile of the issuer. The deposit insurance premium of the bank could then be determined by reference to this rate.[102] Unlike a system in which insurance premiums are tied to a regulatory definition of capital—developed through a slow process of inter-agency and international consultation—insurance assessments based on market indicators could respond rapidly to any changes in a bank's asset portfolio that affect its overall riskiness, even if those changes are not reflected in the calculation of risk-weighted assets for capital purposes.

Implementation of such a system would require careful attention to the disclosure requirements applicable to banks, particularly those which are not publicly owned. However, compliance with an appropriate disclosure system would not impose an unreasonable net regulatory burden on banks, particularly to the extent the deposit insurance reforms advocated in this article permit a substitution of market oversight for (expensive) regulatory oversight.

Capital Adequacy and Moral Hazard

As noted above, in the case of a failing bank with zero or negative net worth, the bank's uninsured residual claimants (i.e., management and shareholders) have an incentive to engage in high risk activities at the expense of the insurance fund in an effort to reattain solvency. In the past, the market has tolerated such cases only because (1) the other principal claimants on the bank (i.e., depositors and, to a lesser extent, other debtholders) have enjoyed a de facto government guaranty *and* (2) regulators have not intervened on a timely basis. It follows logically that one possible remedy for this problem is to insist on early regulatory intervention whenever clearly articulated capital adequacy standards are not satisfied. Here the problem is that those standards, however clearly articulated they may be, remain an inaccurate measure of riskiness. But it also follows that an alternative, *sufficient* remedy is to restore market discipline. If the de facto government guaranty implied by the current system of deposit insurance is eliminated (including the "too big to fail" policy), it would be farfetched to assume that the market will continue to allow undercapitalized banks to remain in operation. As between these two possible remedies, our guidelines for sound regulation argue in favor of a policy mix that stresses the market solution over the regulatory solution (i.e., early intervention tied to rigid capital standards).

Although it is essential that banks have sufficient capital both to insure that shareholders have a serious stake in the enterprise and to act as a cushion between the insurance fund and bank creditors, an over-emphasis on capital per se can be misplaced. In particular, bank leverage ratio requirements, which can range from 3% to 5% and higher depending on regulators' assessment of an institution, may well be doing more harm than good.[103] As Martin Feldstein has observed, excessive capital requirements create problems for the economy.[104] Artificially high capital requirements limit the ability of banks to expand lending and, in some cases, require banks to shed assets.[105] Indeed, Feldstein reports that if banks in New England were required to meet only the international risk-weighted capital standards and a three percent leverage ratio they could more than *double* their business lending.[106]

There is a respectable body of opinion to the effect that banks today are generally undercapitalized because the federal safety net has weakened market discipline. However, setting the optimal level of bank capital is beyond the scope of this chapter. It will suffice simply to observe here that if market forces can be brought to bear, banks will be driven toward the level of capital demanded of unsubsidized enterprises with similar risk characteristics. If depositors bear some risk of loss, they will focus on bank capital in assessing the safety and soundness of the bank. Similarly, with risk-based insurance premiums, banks will pay the price for operating with insufficient capital. Thus, the proposals to reform deposit insurance discussed above will also operate to drive banks towards adequate levels of capital, replacing artificial regulatory guesswork.

Geographic Restrictions on Banking

Restrictions on interstate banking remain a testament to the triumph of special interests over the common good. Forced geographic atomization of the banking industry and the much ballyhooed dual banking system have provided sinecures for State legislators and regulators.[107] Geographic restriction of banking is not a response to market failure; it is an unjustified regulatory intervention that thwarts competition and undercuts the important regulatory goal of fostering dynamic efficiency. Although geographic restrictions may purport to foster strong local cartels, many of the banks so protected continue to weaken and fail. In any event, protectionism for small community banks is antithetical to any sensible competition policy.

Despite the restrictions of the Douglas Amendment and the McFadden Act, interstate banking is becoming a reality, but only where states have expressly authorized it and then only through the unwieldy and inefficient bank holding company structure. In the case of national banks, the

McFadden Act prohibits direct interstate branching.[108] Almost all states now permit interstate banking through holding companies, although often only available to those with banks within given regions. Some have chosen to exclude non-U.S. banks.[109] This patchwork of restrictions is an unnecessary drag on the banking system.

The Bush Administration proposed true interstate banking: interstate branching by national banks and, if permitted by the laws of the chartering State, by State banks; interstate banking by holding companies; and the abolition of state "foreigners not welcome" rules.[110]

The benefits of interstate banking (including interstate branching) are obvious. Interstate banking promotes geographic diversification and, in some cases, may permit the attainment of economies of scale.[111] If their retail core deposit base and assets (loan portfolio) are not restricted to given geographic regions, banks will be better able to withstand regional economic downturns.[112] A crisis in the oil patch need not have led to the failure of so many Texas and Oklahoma banks. And by being able to draw on regions where the economy is prospering, banks will be able to continue to provide credit to a region under economic stress, thus moderating the severity of regional downturns.[113] The credit crunch in New England would not be as severe as it has been if New England banks had a broader deposit and earnings base.

Unjustified by any sound basis for regulatory intervention, and empirically shown to have contributed to the weakness of our banking system, geographic restrictions on banking should be removed.

Consolidation

Consolidation of the banking industry has been predicted for some time. Although the pace of activity does appear to be picking up, the long-awaited consolidation has yet to occur. Geographic restrictions on banking are in part responsible.[114] In addition, the market for control of banks does not operate as efficiently as that for corporate control in general, thus permitting bank management to entrench itself deeper and longer than might otherwise be the case.[115]

Banking reform should permit market forces to shape consolidation, subject to the antitrust laws.[116] We do not propose the abolition of all regulatory approvals concerning bank mergers, acquisitions or changes in control. Instead, through the exercise of that approval authority, the regulators should permit market forces the greatest freedom possible. It is encouraging to note that Vice Chairman David Mullins of the Federal Reserve Board has acknowledged this, and has recognized that the Board for its part must adopt more flexible measures of market concentration, taking nonbank competitors into consideration in approving applications.[117]

Because banks compete with other banks and non-banking firms for the provision of financial services, substantial consolidation poses no real threat of oligopolistic behavior.[118] Automatic teller machines, the nationwide market for bank certificates of deposit, loan production offices, mutual funds that offer "800" numbers, all are part of a dynamic and competitive market. Thus, regulatory intervention to hinder the natural consolidation of the banking industry based on a fear of monopolistic behavior is unjustified.

Recognizing the cost savings and greater safety that can be achieved by consolidation, we believe that market forces, if allowed to operate freely within the constraints of the antitrust laws, will lead to substantial consolidation in the banking industry. McKinsey and Company's Lowell Bryan reports that large regional banks can operate at "significantly lower costs" than smaller regional banks.[119] The empirical evidence on scale economies is mixed, however.[120] Nevertheless, even in the absence of clearly demonstrable short-term cost savings from consolidation, bank mergers may make sense for a number of reasons, including geographic diversification, product diversification and the attainment of economies of scope, long-term competitive benefits from the development of regional or national (or, indeed, international) brand name loyalty and the ability to compete for larger corporate customers by increasing the applicable lending limit. In any event, the mere absence of scale economies, without a demonstration that *diseconomies* of scale or other undesirable consequences will result, is not an appropriate basis on which to prohibit bank mergers. In short, our guidelines for sound bank regulatory policy dictate that market forces be permitted to determine whether there are potential benefits to be obtained through consolidation, accepting the risk that at times the parties to a consolidation will "get it wrong."

Glass-Steagall and Other Product Restrictions

The Glass-Steagall Act prohibits banks and, together with the Bank Holding Company Act, bank holding companies and their non-bank affiliates from conducting significant investment banking activities. The proponents of this product line restriction long ago cast off whatever regulatory justification might originally have supported this interference with the market. These proponents, largely from markets benefitting from the protection against bank competition that the Glass-Steagall Act affords, argue that what *they* do without great risk of failure must not be undertaken by banks, because bank safety and soundness would be impaired by participation in such markets. The truth, in fact, is just the reverse. The efficiency-driven migration of corporate customers from being bank borrowers to issuers of debt securities, and the inability of banks to follow their customers across the Glass-Steagall barrier, have weakened the banks and will continue to do so until this law is repealed.[121]

It is useful to note that most of our global competitors permit banks to conduct a broad array of financial activities. For example, the European Economic Community's Second Banking Directive permits banks to trade, for their own account or for customers, in money market instruments, foreign currencies, financial futures and options and exchange and interest rate instruments, and to participate in securities issues and services related to securities issuance. Japan alone among our significant trading partners separates commercial from investment banking. Japan does so, however, because the U.S. imposed the restrictions in 1948,[122] perhaps, as others have observed, due to the "interesting American belief that a democratic regime not only required free elections, free speech and due process, but also antitrust laws and the Glass-Steagall Act."[123] The Japanese Ministry of Finance has recommended a liberalization of the Japanese version of the Glass-Steagall Act.[124] Already formidable competitors, Japanese financial institutions are certain to become even more so when they are no longer shackled by the Glass-Steagall Act.

Arguments in favor of product restrictions for banks are generally of three types. The first is that banks would have an unfair competitive advantage over other firms because they are effectively subsidized through Federal deposit insurance. The second is that the prohibited activities are somehow "riskier" than commercial banking and, thus, incompatible with the need for safety and soundness. The third is that permitting banks to perform such activities would open the door to what Supreme Court Justice William Brennan called the "subtle hazards."[125] We will consider these arguments in reference to the Glass-Steagall Act's prohibition against securities powers.

Unfair Competition To the limited extent, if any, that this argument has merit, its strength rests entirely on the current fixed premium deposit insurance system. Reforming the deposit insurance system as we have proposed would eliminate any possible claim of unfair advantage. Thus, as part of an overall reform package, permitting banks to conduct investment banking activities should not give rise to unfair competition.[126]

Safety The argument that separating investment banking from commercial banking makes the commercial bank safer is undermined by both economic theory and empirical data. If commercial banking is "special" because of its intermediation function between illiquid assets and liquid deposits, it only exacerbates the potential liquidity problem of a bank to deny it other fee-based sources of income. Forcing banks into a narrow range of assets and activities does not preserve or enhance their safety; it makes them riskier.[127]

Modern portfolio theory teaches that risk analysis must take account of the *combination* of all activities engaged in, rather than looking at the riskiness of each activity in isolation. Even if investment banking were somehow riskier than commercial banking, it would not lead to the conclusion that a combination of the functions would increase overall risk.[128]

Moreover, the idea that, as presently conducted, investment banking is riskier than commercial banking is highly dubious. Recent history suggests that commercial banking, in its current narrow form, is the riskier activity. In addition to credit risk, banks also face substantial interest rate risk because of the mismatch in interest rates between longer-term assets and short-term liabilities. Indeed it was just this interest rate mismatch that rendered so many institutions (thrifts in particular) insolvent during the late 1970s and early 1980s when interest rates sky-rocketed.[129]

One approach to the management of credit risk by commercial banks has been the syndication of loans. In this way the lead bank limits its exposure to just the portion of the loan it retains. By selling participations in its loans, a bank can also benefit by freeing up capital that can then be used to extend credit to other borrowers. Of course, to be successful at participating out a loan to other banks, the originating bank must "underwrite" the loan, both in the sense of carrying the credit risk of the full loan pending the sale of participations and in the sense of putting its reputation on the line in seeking buyers. This risk-reducing practice requires, in effect, that commercial banks function in much the same way as an investment bank does when it underwrites an offering of securities. In other words, both types of institutions manage credit risk by applying similar strategies of diversification and syndication. However, only commercial banks are handicapped in doing so for securities by the limitations of the Glass-Steagall Act.

Securitization is not the only illustration of the natural tendency of commercial banking firms to conduct investment banking activities in order to enhance safety and shareholder return. J.P. Morgan and Bankers Trust are prime examples of banking firms that have continuously "pushed the envelope" of permitted banking powers. Each has benefitted from doing so, and each is among the safest and most well-regarded banking firms in the world. In addition, data compiled by the Federal Reserve Board shows that, overall, non-banking subsidiaries of bank holding companies are slightly more profitable than banking subsidiaries.[130] The investor acceptance of these banks—relative to more traditionally and narrowly focused banks—suggests that the market does not credit the idea that investment banking is more risky than commercial banking.

Retention of the Glass-Steagall Act while traditional commercial banking becomes less profitable (and less safe) invites the prospect of the more innovative and successful banks relinquishing their banking charters in order to pursue the most profitable and innovative lines of business without regulatory interference. Indeed, Robert Clarke, former Comptroller of the Currency, predicted just such a development as he left office.[131] Effective bank reform should be possible without forcing the strongest banks to this point of choice.

Subtle hazards The remaining class of arguments in support of the Glass-Steagall Act rest on what are known as the "subtle hazards."[132] The fear is that banks will use the power to extend or deny credit in a way that is either predatory or otherwise a misallocation of resources, or that, confronted with a conflict of interest between the bank and its customers, the bank will favor itself.[133]

The "subtle hazard" of predatory behavior may be seen in the case of a bank extending credit to an affiliate at below-market terms to permit the affiliate to drive out competitors.[134] In the case of non-banking firms the anti-trust laws stand as a protection against such predatory behavior and should do so in the case of banking firms as well. Moreover, in today's globally competitive markets, it is unlikely that such predatory behavior could succeed.

The "subtle hazard" of credit misallocation is said to arise, for example, where the bank has an incentive to extend credit to an affiliate at below-market terms in order to prop up the affiliate. However, if a bank acts on this incentive, it will pay the price of doing so by foregoing profits from more profitable lending opportunities to unaffiliated borrowers.[135] Thus, rational bank managers would not extend credit to affiliates in such situations absent a determination that overall the firm will benefit.[136] We have no problem with an automobile manufacturer offering 0% financing on the sale of its products because the cost of the below-market loan is more than offset by the gain on the sale of the automobile. Why should banking be any different?

To view as an unacceptable "hazard" the possibility that banks will use their commercial banking operations to subsidize other activities also reflects a disturbing tendency to treat banks as public utilities. Rather than permit banks to determine for themselves where to allocate credit and other bank resources, product restrictions essentially force banks to allocate resources in limited areas. By prohibiting banks from offering certain products, banks have no choice but to lend to riskier or less desirable borrowers within the narrow market open to them.[137]

Banks, like any market participant, should be able to determine how best to allocate resources. Institutions that make errors in judgment fail, with the result that their remaining assets become deployed by others, in most cases with greater efficiency.[138] Restricting bank activities becomes de facto an indirect way of channeling bank credit; as such, it is a dangerous form of industrial policy. A misallocation of assets by a financial intermediary is particularly problematic for the economy because in addition to credit being extended to the *wrong* borrower (another strip mall on Route 1) it is unavailable to the *right* borrower (the next Apple Computer?). Tussing makes this observation in the case of allowing inefficiently managed institutions to fail.[139] It is no less true when it is Congress and the bank regulators, rather than bank management, that misdirect resources.

The attractions of this form of industrial policy in the banking sector underpin a recent study of banking consolidation by the staff of the House Committee on Banking, Finance and Urban Affairs. With unsuppressed satisfaction, Committee Chairman Henry Gonzalez reported his staff's conclusion (drawn on the basis of questionable empirical analysis) that bank holding companies with several banks drain lendable funds from local communities, with social costs resulting from the bank's sapping the community of its economic blood.[140] There is no place in a free economy for regulations forcing a bank to direct credit to certain sectors or regions of the economy. Neither insurance companies nor other financial institutions operate subject to such directions. Few would doubt the folly of directing General Motors to build a plant in Alaska solely because Alaskans buy GM cars or trucks. The basis for allocating credit services by regulatory fiat is no more respectable. If funds can be invested more efficiently or profitably outside a local community, then that is where they belong. Anchoring a bank to a small community will tend to make the bank more dependent on that community, with a concomitant increase in the risk of failure in the event of a regional economic downturn.

The broadest category of "subtle hazards" sought to be mitigated by product limitations in general, and the Glass-Steagall Act in particular, is the potential for conflicts of interest between the bank and its customers if the bank is permitted to offer multiple services. Faced with such conflicts, it is argued, the bank will succumb to the temptation to favor itself.[141] The concern is valid, but it is not unique to banks. The appropriate regulatory response is not to prevent the potential for conflict from ever arising by prohibiting banks from conducting additional activities or performing additional services. Doing so deprives the consumer of a potential vendor of those services and reduces competition. It also denies the bank the potential synergies and efficiencies that can be gained.

If banks are permitted to conduct additional activities and potential conflicts do arise, the bank's own self-interest—through the economic disincentives to exploit that conflict—will in most cases protect consumers.[142] However, some regulatory safeguard makes sense. A time-tested, conservative solution to the problem of conflicts of interest may be found in the securities laws. There the problem of conflicts is addressed by requiring full disclosure of the potential conflict and the consent of the client involved.[143]

Competitive forces and the economic disincentives for exploiting conflicts, together with the regulatory requirement of full disclosure and consent, should provide adequate protections against potential conflicts of interest that may arise if banks are permitted to conduct additional activities. As was true in the case of the other "subtle hazards," the potential for conflicts of interest does not justify the Glass-Steagall Act's wholesale prohibition of the increasingly important products offered by investment banking firms.

Insurance Activities

Just as banks could expand into investment banking without significant additional cost, banks are well-suited to many insurance activities, particularly insurance brokerage through retail branch networks. Some banks are currently permitted to conduct limited insurance activities.[144] And in recent years numerous States expanded the insurance powers of State chartered banks, exercised either directly or through subsidiaries. However, that trend has effectively been halted by the FDIC Improvement Act, which generally prohibits state banks from engaging in insurance underwriting activities except to the extent permissible for national banks. Both the banking system and consumers will benefit if banks are permitted to expand their insurance activities beyond the confines of present law.

For analytical purposes, insurance activities can be divided into two broad categories: brokerage or "agency" activities and underwriting or "principal" activities. Banks could be permitted to perform all insurance agency activities with virtually no incremental risk to the bank. If anything, doing so would enhance bank safety by providing an additional source of fee-based income and further diversifying the lines of business engaged in by banks. A bank with a large retail branch structure in place could easily and efficiently provide insurance agency activities. Indeed, recognizing this competitive threat, the insurance industry remains implacably opposed to bank entry into this business. In addition to these efficiencies, as the Treasury Study noted, banks could offer complementary packages such as automobile loans and automobile insurance, or mortgages and mortgage insurance.[145] Consumers would benefit through reduced costs and greater convenience.[146]

Insurance underwriting of actuarially quantifiable risks is also a natural complement to banking. The Federal Reserve has recognized this fact in its RegulationK, which authorizes bank holding companies to underwrite life insurance through their overseas affiliates. The asset portfolios of banks and insurance companies are in many respects quite similar. Both insurance companies and banks make largely illiquid investments, although insurance companies are not subject to the same restrictions as banks. The principal differences between these two classes of financial intermediaries are found on the liability side of the balance sheet. Insurance companies receive premiums over time, and policy holders have only a limited immediate claim on the value of their insurance contracts. Although the actuarial expertise needed to price insurance differs from credit analysis, banks could develop such expertise without significant capital expenditure. Indeed, savings banks have underwritten life insurance for many years, and, as noted above, many banks have taken advantage of the limited opportunities to underwrite insurance that are currently available to them, and thus have already developed such expertise.[147]

Bank Organization

Most proposals for expanded bank powers contemplate their exercise through separate affiliates in a bank holding company structure with elaborate "firewalls" to separate the bank from its affiliates.[148] This separation is thought necessary for a number of reasons, including a perceived need to insulate the bank (and the federal safety net) from the risks of the non-banking businesses and in order to prevent the federal safety net from being used to subsidize non-banking activities. Without attempting a comprehensive treatment of this subject, we turn now to a brief consideration of these arguments.

As a preliminary matter, we question the basic premise that a separate affiliate can really be entirely separate—the "watertight" theory of corporate compartments. Among the problems in achieving a full separation are the following:

- Each member of a holding company group would be liable for the pension liabilities of other members of the group upon termination of any member's pension plan, up to 30% of the group's net worth.
- If the holding company group is consolidated for tax purposes, each member of the group, including the bank, would be jointly and severally liable for the federal taxes owed by the entire group.
- "Controlling person" liability under the securities laws could affect the holding company and, through it, the bank.
- In the case of multi-bank holding companies, the cross-guaranty provision of FIRREA effectively pierces the watertight compartment between affiliated depositary institutions.

The Federal Reserve's "source of strength" doctrine further erodes traditional concepts of corporate "separateness." Thus, even in the best of circumstances, mandatory compartmentalization of financial activities can be expected to produce only an incomplete insulation of the bank.

But more importantly, requiring non-banking activities to be conducted in a separate affiliate ignores the lessons of diversification. Structural separation prevents banks from realizing the benefits of diversification that would be available whenever the returns to non-banking activities exhibit low (or negative) covariance with the bank's core business. Moreover, such separation can reduce, if not eliminate, the efficiency gains and synergies that would otherwise be expected from the exercise of expanded powers.[149] This is particularly true in the case of product combinations, such as retail banking services coupled with insurance or real estate activities, which offer the prospect for significant economies of scope by cross-marketing such products through established retail branch networks. In addition to foregone efficiency gains, forced structural separation can impose additional costs in the form of duplicative facilities, particularly where legislative or regulatory "firewalls" mandate a physical separation of offices (in order not to "confuse" customers) or prohibit management interlocks. "Mandating that non-traditional banking activities be performed through a separate subsidiary may result in an uneconomical duplication of costs or an uneconomical decision not to offer the product or service at all."[150]

Of course, some institutions might choose to conduct some or all of their non-banking activities in separate affiliates or subsidiaries, even if permitted to do so directly in the bank. Indeed, we would expect that rational bank managers would make such decisions (as do rational managers of any other multi-product enterprise) by comparing the expected net benefit to the firm from conducting new activities through a separate department within the bank, a new or existing operating subsidiary of the bank or, as is typically required under current law, an affiliated corporation under a common holding company. An important consideration in that calculation would be the ability of the firm's top management and board to control effectively the various activities undertaken by the firm, either within the bank or through its affiliates.

The problem of designing optimal organizational structures for multi-service institutions is one which will have different answers in different cases, depending on diverse and constantly changing factors.[151] It is not a problem appropriate for decision by regulatory fiat and should be left in the realm of private ordering, subject to the discipline of market forces and, where appropriate, narrowly tailored regulation to preclude exploitation of conflicts of interest to the detriment of the firm's customers.[152] If the benefits of conducting expanded activities directly through the bank did not outweigh the perceived risks of doing so, or if greater net benefits could be obtained by moving such activities into a separate entity, banks would be driven by market forces to adopt a more efficient organizational structure. This would be particularly true if, as we propose, the bank's deposit insurance premiums are adjusted to reflect the market's perception of risk.[153]

The Dual Banking System

The chief justification for the dual banking system has been that competition among regulators will lead to the optimal level of regulation. However, as

Henry Butler and Jonathan Macey have ably demonstrated, competition between Federal and State regulators is more myth than reality.[154] Indeed, the trend seems to be toward a further erosion of the ability of States to "compete" in any way with their Federal regulatory overlords.[155] Without any of the promised benefits from the dual banking system, there seems no real justification for maintaining 51 bank regulatory structures.

Moreover, retaining a dual banking system can be affirmatively debilitating. For example, the failure of the Federal Reserve to act forcefully as a lender of last resort during the Great Depression was due, in part, to the fact that many failing banks were state chartered institutions that did not belong to the Federal Reserve System. Similarly, we question the desirability of permitting state-sponsored deposit insurance schemes to coexist with the revised federal scheme advocated in this chapter. Our experience with these systems has not been a happy one. Witness the failure in 1985 of the Ohio Deposit Guarantee Fund, the failure in 1985 of the Maryland Savings Share Insurance Corp. and, most recently, the failure in 1991 of the Rhode Island Share and Deposit Indemnity Corp. The fact that ultimate financial responsibility for failed State experiments tends to be assumed by the federal government argues strongly against permitting the establishment of parallel deposit insurance schemes that have not been structured to address satisfactorily the incentive distortions discussed above. Moreover, even if state-sponsored schemes were to be "cloned" from the federal model proposed in this chapter, the lessons of risk diversification (particularly geographic diversification, pending repeal of the McFadden Act and the Douglas Amendment) suggest that insured risks should nonetheless be pooled at the national level.

Despite the seeming political infeasibility of abolishing the dual banking system, we would expect that the dual banking system would gradually wither away if interstate banking is authorized, because of the additional regulatory costs that State banks would bear if they were to branch across State lines. If a state-chartered bank branched into another State, it would be subject to regulation by its chartering state and any out-of-state branches would be subject to regulation by the other states as well.[156] A national bank, on the other hand, would not face this additional level of regulatory oversight. Thus, as a result of reduced regulatory burden, we would expect a national bank charter to be significantly more attractive than a state charter.

The "Core Bank" Proposal

We turn now to a brief critique of the so-called "core bank" proposal advanced in various quarters, but perhaps most forcefully by Lowell L. Bryan.[157] The core bank concept is worthy of attention because it found favor among many in Congress during the bank reform debate in 1991, and may do so again in future legislative sessions.

The core bank proposal would address the incentive distortions created by federal safety net by restricting deposit insurance to a new class of "core banks." In order to contain the risk to the federal safety net, core banks would be limited to certain traditional banking activities, including home mortgages, credit cards and small business lending. Real estate lending to local developers would be allowed, but subject to strict regulation of the terms and conditions of such loans[158]. These activity restrictions would be complemented by regulation of interest rates on core bank deposits—which henceforth would be pegged to floating rates on Treasury securities. The purpose of regulating interest rates would be to prevent destructive competition among banks seeking to attract deposits by bidding up interest rates. Absent such competition, core banks would be under less pressure to engage in high risk lending in order to cover their cost of funds.

Under the core bank proposal, "bundled banks" that today offer services beyond those permitted to core banks would be required to split their operations into two or more entities in order to segregate their core banking operations in a separate corporate compartment. Non-core services would be conducted through uninsured and largely unregulated "money market investment banks" and "finance companies." However, such institutions would be subject to disclosure-based regulation by the Securities and Exchange Commission.

Although appealing on the surface, these proposals are seriously flawed because they do not forthrightly address the incentive distortions which lie at the core of our current predicament—in short, they do not satisfy our guidelines for sound bank regulation. The core bank proposal correctly diagnoses the moral hazard problem created by our system of deposit insurance. But rather than reform that system by addressing the incentive problem, its prescription is to create a new class of heavily regulated financial intermediaries operating under a similarly flawed deposit insurance program. Under the core bank proposal, the task of policing the safety and soundness of core banks would fall almost exclusively to bank regulators. Fully insured depositors would have little incentive to monitor bank risk.

Nor would market forces be harnessed to constrain bank management through risk-based insurance premiums or a market assessment of capital adequacy. And the re-regulation of interest rates ignores the lessons of the recent past. How will regulators determine the proper cap? If the cap is set low enough to matter, will core bank depositors migrate to money market funds and other "unregulated" competitors? Will this create pressure to extend regulation of interest rates beyond deposits at core banks? Will core banks' incentives to manage interest rate risk (through adjustable rate mortgages, for example) be diminished or eliminated?

The activity limitations proposed for core banks ignore the basic lessons of diversification. It does not follow that narrowly focused core banks are safer than properly managed bundled banks. Forcing bundled banks to spin off their non-core businesses would, in many cases, come at the expense of substantial losses of economies of scope and other synergies. The proposed demarcation between core and non-core functions is arbitrary and suspect. One wonders, for example, why a core bank should not be permitted to market insurance products on an agency basis. Such a combination of services would almost certainly reduce the riskiness of the core bank's combined activities and would offer obvious economies of scope. Moreover, even if the demarcation of core banking functions could be appropriately fine-tuned in today's marketplace, the resulting legislative snapshot would unnecessarily constrict the ability of core banks to evolve in response to market demands and, *a fortiori,* would further retard the dynamic efficiency of our banking industry.

In our view, the core banking proposal falls short of the mark because (1) it fails to harness competitive forces, (2) it prescribes the wrong medicine for the diagnosed ill, (3) it calls for a return to interest rate regulation beyond the scope of regulatory competence, (4) it is founded on the precept that risk should be controlled through prohibitions rather than elastic incentive mechanisms, (5) it ignores the lessons of diversification, and (6) it is inconsistent with the goal of fostering dynamic efficiency. We acknowledge that the core bank proposal may be more feasible as a matter of politics than the direct approach to deposit insurance reform we prescribe. However, by extending the reach of regulation to a special class of banks, it carries with it the potential for further significant and lasting injury to our financial system. Accordingly, it is not the sort of political comprise that should be entertained.

This chapter has touched only on some of the most significant issues of banking reform. There remain a number of related issues that are important and deserve thorough analysis and discussion. Our hope is that any such analysis will proceed by applying the regulatory framework adopted here, using the six guidelines for regulatory intervention identified in the first part of this chapter.

NOTES

1. The Congressional Budget Office has projected that the U.S. budget deficit in the 1992 fiscal year will be 6.1% of gross national product, the second-highest percentage in post-war history. *See Congress' Budget Head Warns on Emergency Requests*, Reuters, Oct. 2, 1991, *available in* LEXIS, Nexis Library, Reuters File.
2. Martin Feldstein, *Introduction* to *The Risk of Economic Crisis* (Martin Feldstein, ed. 1991).
3. Federal Deposit Insurance Corporation Improvement Act of 1991, Pub. L. No. 102-242, §101, 105 Stat. 2236 (1991) [hereinafter the FDIC Improvement Act]. The FDIC's authority to borrow from the Treasury alone was increased by an astronomical 600% to $30billion.
4. The number of failed institutions is only a part of the story. Although the number of failures declined from 1990 to 1991, the size of the failed institutions leapt from a combined total assets of $16.8billion in 1990 to an astonishing $64 billion in 1991. *See Failures Fell in '91, But Institutions Were Larger*, American Banker, Jan. 3, 1992, at 1.
5. *Budget Office Foresees Giant Bank Failures*, American Banker, March 9, 1992, at 1.
6. The Bush Administration's legislative proposal, the Financial Institutions Safety and Consumer Choice Act of 1991, S. 713, 102d Cong., 1st Sess., was based on the Department of the Treasury's study, *Modernizing the Financial System: U.S. Treasury Department Recommendations for Safer, More Competitive Banks* (1991) [hereinafter *Modernizing the Financial System*].
7. In Congress, Representative Charles Schumer has been the leading advocate of core banking. *See, e.g., Efforts to Limit Interest Rates Picks Up Steam in Congress*, American Banker, June 18, 1991, 1. Outside of Congress Lowell L. Bryan has been the champion of core banking. *See* Lowell L. Bryan, *Bankrupt: Restoring the Health and Profitability of Our Banking System* (1991) [hereinafter *Bankrupt*].
8. *See, e.g., Who Says We Have Too Many Banks*, American Banker, June 13, 1991, at 4 (reporting speech before Securities Industry Association).
9. *See, e.g.*, Statement accompanying Staff of the House Committee on Banking, Finance and Urban Affairs Analysis of Banking Industry Consolidation Issues (March 2, 1992) ("trend towards consolidation raises the specter of a large-scale diversion of lendable funds from local communities").
10. *See, e.g., NationsBank's McColl Steps Up Criticism of ABA Over Branching*, American Banker, Feb. 20, 1990, at 1.
11. *See, e.g., Victory Festival for Small Banks*, American Banker, Feb. 14, 1991, at 2.

12. The distinctions among banks and thrifts (savings and loan associations, savings banks and credit unions) may have been justified once, but are now an historical anachronism reflecting balkanized regulatory turf more than anything else. Throughout this paper we use the term "bank" to include all depository institutions and depository institution holding companies.
13. *Modernizing the Financial System, supra* note 6, at 15, Figure 1.
14. Wachovia Corp. is the only other U.S. commercial banking firm with a AAA credit rating.
15. *See* Prudential Securities, *J.P. Morgan & Co. Company Report* 20, Table 8 (Aug.7, 1991).
16. *Id.* at 1. Indeed, according to the FDIC, gains on the sale of securities accounted for 16% of the total profits of the commercial banking industry in 1991. *See Bond Sales Pumped Up Bank Profits Last Year*, American Banker, Mar. 12, 1992, at 1. This is not a new phenomenon. One Federal Reserve staff study concluded that average rates of profit for non-bank activities exceeded those for affiliated bank subsidiaries of bank holding companies in 1986 and 1987. Nellie Liang and Donald Savage, *New Data on the Performance of Nonbank Subsidiaries of Bank Holding Companies* 6 (Staff Study No. 159) (Feb. 1990) [hereinafter Liang & Savage].
17. In the debate over bank reform legislation in particular, distortion, misinformation and confusion have been used effectively to protect special interests. The use of confusion in battle is a time-honored tradition. *See* Sun Tzu, *The Art of War* 51 (Thomas Cleary trans. 1988) ("use deception to throw them into confusion").
18. *See Modernizing the Financial System, supra* note 6, at ch. XVIII 9-12 (domestic market) and 18-19 (foreign markets). *See also* Committee on Banking, Finance and Urban Affairs, *Report of the Task Force on the International Competitiveness of U.S. Financial Institutions* 182-84 (1990).
19. The Department of the Treasury has recently reported that as of June 30, 1990, 284 foreign banks from 58 different countries conducted banking activities in the U.S., through branch and agency offices, loan production and representative offices, U.S. banking subsidiaries, Edge Corporations and New York State investment corporations. Department of the Treasury, *National Treatment Study: Report to Congress on Foreign Government Treatment of U.S. Commercial Banking and Securities Organizations* 76 (1990) [hereinafter *National Treatment Study*]. Total assets of U.S. banking operations of foreign banks and subsidiaries totaled a staggering $734 billion. *Id.* This represented 20.4% of all bank assets in the U.S., including 17.3% of all loans, 29.4% of all business loans, and an overall market share of 13.8% of bank deposits. *Id.* at 83.
20. Ingo Walter and Anthony Saunders, *National Global Competitiveness of New York as a Financial Center:Report to the Mayor's Committee on Financial Services Competitiveness* (1991) [hereinafter *Walter Report*].
21. For an intriguing discussion of one example of this, see David G. Litt, Jonathan R. Macey, Geoffrey P. Miller and Edward L. Rubin, *Politics, Bureaucracies, and Financial Markets: Bank Entry Into Commercial Paper Underwriting in the United States and Japan*, 139 U. Pa. L. Rev. 369 (1990) [hereinafter *Commercial Paper Underwriting*].
22. For example, U.S. Bancorp moved the headquarters of a Washington national

banking subsidiary into neighboring Idaho, taking advantage of 12 U.S.C. § 30(b) (national bank may relocate main office within 30 miles), with the tacit (albeit reluctant) approval of the Board of Governors of the Federal Reserve System. *See Fed Gives Interstate Issue a Push By Easing Bank Relocation Rule*, American Banker, Feb.27, 1992, at 1. *See also Synovus Financial Corp. v. Board of Governors*, 952 F.2d 426 (D.C. Cir. 1991) (Douglas Amendment does not give Board authority to disapprove relocation authorized by the Comptroller under 12 U.S.C. § 30(b)).

23. *Independent Insurance Agents of America v. Clarke*, No. 90-5209, 1992 U.S. App. LEXIS 1432 (D.C. Cir. Feb. 7, 1992) (calling into question *all* national bank insurance powers).
24. FDIC Improvement Act, *supra* note 3, §132, 105 Stat. 2266 (codified at 12 U.S.C. § 1831s(c)).
25. Moreover, looking chiefly to regulators such as the Comptroller of the Currency and the Board of Governors of the Federal Reserve System to provide relief from unnecessary regulation through creatively aggressive legal constructions of the statutes they are charged to administer raises troubling questions of legitimacy and respect for Congress.
26. In more technical terms, this view is based on the two so-called fundamental theorems of neoclassical welfare economics: first, that every competitive equilibrium in an economy with complete markets will produce a Pareto-efficient allocation of resources and, second, that absent nonconvexities in consumption or production, such an economy can be made to achieve any one of many efficient competitive equilibria through appropriate wealth redistributions. *See* K. Arrow, *The Coordination of Economic Activity: Issues Pertinent to the Choice of Market Versus Nonmarket Allocation*, in R. Haveman and J. Margolis (eds.), *Public Expenditure and Policy Analysis*, 67-81 (1977); G. Debreu, *Theory of Value: An Axiomatic Analysis of Economic Equilibrium*, 94-96 (1959). Under this framework, the design of regulatory policy calls for a focus on market failures (*i.e.*, situations in which the requirement of complete markets for all goods is not satisfied) in order to deduce minimum sufficient conditions for the attainment of efficient equilibria, with a view to providing guidance regarding when to intervene in the markets. *See* S. Breyer, *Regulation and its Reform* (1982) for an excellent example of this analytic framework.
27. *See generally* M.K. Lewis and K.T. Davis, *Domestic and International Banking*, 20-51 (1987) [hereinafter Lewis & Davis]. Lewis & Davis define "portfolio transformation services" broadly to include all situations where "financial intermediaries, acting as principals, . . . bridge the gap between the types of financial assets that lenders [*i.e.*, depositors] prefer to acquire and the forms of debt that borrowers want to issue, where the two do not match up in size, duration or in other respects." *Id.* at 27.
28. Insurance companies, broker-dealers, money market mutual funds and other financial institutions are, in general, not subject to this threat, either because they do not have demand liabilities (*e.g.*, insurance companies), because their assets are liquid (*e.g.*, money market mutual funds) or because they do not issue fixed claims and the volatility of their assets is intentionally passed through to investors (*e.g.*, open end stock funds).

29. *See, e.g.*, Jonathan R. Macey and Geoffrey P. Miller, *Bank Failures, Risk Monitoring, and the Market for Bank Control*, 88 Col. L. Rev. 1153, 1157 (1988) [hereinafter Macey & Miller]; Daniel R. Fischel, Andrew M. Rosenfield and Robert J. Stillman, *The Regulation of Banks and Bank Holding Companies*, 73 Va. L. Rev. 301, 307-10 (1987) [hereinafter Fischel, Rosenfield & Stillman]. William Poundstone presents a fascinating overview of the prisoner's dilemma and its application to a variety of situations. William Poundstone, *Prisoner's Dilemma: John von Neumann, Game Theory and the Puzzle of the Bomb* (1992).
30. Macey & Miller, *supra* at 1156.
31. For convenience, we use the term "Federal Reserve" to refer to the Board of Governors of the Federal Reserve System and the Federal Reserve Banks interchangeably.
32. *See* 12 C.F.R. § 201.3(a). Lewis & Davis, *supra* note 27, at 168 recount one episode in 1985 when a computer malfunction caused the Bank of New York to incur a daylight overdraft of $23 billion at the Federal Reserve Bank of New York (an amount 23 times the size of its capital). Systemic damage was prevented, however, as a result of an overnight loan from the Federal Reserve's "discount window" at a cost to the Bank of New York of $5 million in overnight interest.
33. *See* M. Friedman and A. Schwartz, *A Monetary History of the United States, 1867-1960* at 355-59 (1963).
34. Macey & Miller, *supra* note 29, at 1159 (citing George Kaufman, *Implications of Large Bank Problems and Insolvencies for the Banking System and Economic Policy* 12 (Federal Reserve Bank of Chicago, Staff Memorandum No. 85-3, 1985)). Even if withdrawn deposits are held in the form of currency, leading to a reduction in monetary reserves, the central bank can quickly offset the resulting contraction in the money supply through open market operations.
35. In this paper we use the term "moral hazard" loosely to refer to numerous principal-agent incentive problems arising in the context of deposit insurance, without seeking to categorize those problems more precisely in terms of "hidden action", "hidden information", "adverse selection" and other situations distinguished in the literature on information economics. *See generally*, J. Pratt and R. Zeckhauser (eds.), *Principals and Agents: The Structure of Business* (1985).
36. *See, e.g., Modernizing the Financial System*, *supra* note 6, at 16.
37. Macey & Miller, *supra* note 29, at 1198-99 (citing various empirical studies showing that investors are able to recognize the existence of financial problems in banks — signalled by stock price declines — well in advance of regulators).
38. We note that the FDIC Improvement Act would constrain this market by restricting "brokered deposits". FDIC Improvement Act, *supra* note3, §301. This is an unfortunate reaction to the problems of our present scheme of deposit insurance, made necessary by our inability to address those problems directly.
39. *See, e.g., Modernizing the Financial System*, *supra* note 6, at 42.
40. "Network externalities" arise when a collective good is produced through the establishment of a "network" whose value is an increasing function of the number of participants. The classic example is the telephone network. The value of having a telephone is greater, the larger the number of other persons having a telephone, and each new subscriber creates a "positive externality" for other subscribers merely by

joining the network. *See e.g.*, Jean Tirole, *The Theory of Industrial Organization* at 404-409 (1990) [hereinafter *Theory of Industrial Organization*].

41. This is particularly true in the case of industry-sponsored wire transfer systems in which settlement risk is shared by participating banks. Thus, an increase in the size of the network not only enhances its value as a payments system, but also as a mechanism to self-insure against counterparty risk.
42. *See, e.g., Modernizing the Financial System, supra* note 6 at 42; J.P. Morgan, *World Financial Markets*, January 25, 1991 [hereinafter *World Financial Markets*], observing that "[b]anks have established limits on the daylight overdrafts they incur over Fedwire and on the net debit positions they incur on CHIPS. They have also agreed to limits on the net debit position they maintain over both systems. [Moreover, in 1991] participants in CHIPS signed a loss-sharing agreement, written into CHIPS rules, to provide additional funds necessary to complete settlement if any bank (or limited number of banks) is unable to settle its position at the end of the day. CHIPS participants have also posted collateral in the form of Treasury securities with the Federal Reserve to assure that each bank is able to meet its additional settlement obligations under the loss-sharing program." In an effort to further reduce risks in the payments system, the Federal Reserve and CHIPS are exploring the possibility of settling CHIPS transactions several times each business day (rather than merely at closing) and opening the Fedwire system earlier each business day in order to increase the hours of overlap with Europe.
43. Of course, the Federal Reserve can play a valuable role by encouraging the further development of industry-based mechanisms to control payments system risk. And in extreme cases, recourse to the Federal Reserve's discount window may also be warranted. *See, e.g., supra* note 32.
44. Banking Act of 1933, 48 Stat. 162 (1933) (codified principally at 12 U.S.C. §§ 24(Seventh), 12, 78, 377 and 378) [hereinafter the Glass-Steagall Act].
45. Act of Feb. 25, 1927, c. 191, 44 Stat. 1244 (codified at 12 U.S.C. § 36(c)) [hereinafter the McFadden Act]. *See generally, Investment Co. Inst. v. Camp*, 401 U.S. 617, 629-34 (1971) (interpreting legislative history of the Glass-Steagall Act).
46. Bank Holding Company Act of 1956, ch. 240, § 3(d), 70 Stat. 133, 135 (1956) (codified as amended at 12 U.S.C. § 1842(d)) [hereinafter the Bank Holding Company Act].
47. *Economic Report of the President* 158 (1991). These figures, if anything, exaggerate the number of banks in other countries. Of the 65 banks in Canada at the beginning of 1990, for example, eight were Canadian-owned and 57 were subsidiaries of foreign banks. *National Treatment Study, supra* note 19, at 123. The eight domestic Canadian banks held 90% of total bank assets in Canada. *Id.*
48. We also note a disturbing tendency to use bank regulation to direct credit allocations in certain legislatively prescribed directions. *See infra*, notes 134-36 and accompanying text.
49. Bevis Longstreth, *Testimony Before the Board of Governors of the Federal Reserve System* (Feb. 3, 1987). This testimony took place in the context of an application to the Federal Reserve for a bank holding company subsidiary to conduct certain securities activities under Section 20 of the Glass-Steagall Act.
50. In 1966 Congress enacted legislation authorizing the Federal Reserve, FDIC and

Federal Home Loan Bank Board to issue joint regulations establishing ceilings on interest paid on deposits. Pub. L. No. 89-597, 80 Stat. 823 (1966) (codified at various sections of 12 U.S.C.). This authority was implemented in Federal Reserve Regulation Q, 12 C.F.R. §526.5.

51. On the lighter side, interest rate controls led to such practices as the proverbial toaster for a new deposit — in effect, the payment of interest in kind. This is an example of the more general principle that price controls will often lead to non-price or service-based competition. *See, e.g.*, L.J. White, *Quality Variation When Prices Are Regulated*, Bell J. Econ. 425 (Autumn 1972).
52. Depository Institutions Deregulation and Monetary Control of 1980, Pub. L. No. 96-221, 94 Stat. 132 (1988).
53. *See, generally*, Carl Felsenfeld, *The Savings and Loan Crisis*, 54 Fordham L. Rev. 7 (1991) [hereinafter Felsenfeld].
54. *Walter Report, supra* note 20, at 17.
55. *See, e.g., Bankers Take Offensive Against Card Rate Cap*, American Banker, Nov. 15, 1991, at 1; *Tough Week for Bank Stocks*, American Banker, Nov. 22, 1991, at 1.
56. J.C. Francis and S. H. Archer, *Portfolio Analysis* 43 (2d ed. 1979). *See also* D.R. Harrington, *Modern Portfolio Theory, The Capital Asset Pricing Model & Arbitrage Pricing Theory, A User's Guide* (2d ed. 1987).
57. *See Theory of Industrial Organization, supra* note 38, at 389. The concept of dynamic efficiency provides a benchmark for the design of optimal patent systems and other regulatory interventions designed to create and protect intellectual property rights.
58. International Bank for Reconstruction and Development, *World Development Report 1989: Financial Systems and World Development Indicators*, Table 2.4 (1989).
59. In many developing countries, the central bank performs substantial commercial banking functions in addition to its public role as a lender of last resort and regulator of the payments system.
60. Prudential Securities, *J.P. Morgan & Co. Company Report, supra* note 15, at 7.
61. *Id.* at 3.
62. The original coverage of $2,500 per insured account was raised to $5,000 in 1934, when coverage for thrift institutions was adopted, and six times thereafter, most recently in 1980 when the current ceiling of $100,000 was established by the Depositary Institutions Deregulation and Monetary Control Act of 1980. *World Financial Markets, supra* note41, provides an excellent discussion of U.S. deposit insurance reform. In 1935 only 45% of domestic deposits were explicitly insured compared to 75% today. In addition, because of the FDIC's preference for handling bank failures through mergers or assisted transactions, there is *de facto* insurance for deposits in excess of $100,000. Thus, between 1985 and 1989 the FDIC protected 99.5% of the uninsured deposits in failed U.S. banks from losses. *Id.* at 2-3.
63. *Modernizing the Financial System, supra* note 6, at 43.
64. *See* sources cited *supra* note 42.
65. In this context, we endorse the recent addition of section 23 to the Federal Reserve Act, directing the Federal Reserve to "prescribe standards that have the effect of limiting the risks posed by an insured depository institution's exposure to any other

depository institution." FDIC Improvement Act, *supra* note 3, §308. For these purposes, "exposure" is defined to include "(A) all extensions of credit to the other depository institution,...; (B) all purchases of or investments in securities issued by the other depository institution; (C) all securities issued by the other depository institution accepted as collateral for an extension of credit to any person; and (D) all similar transactions that the Board by regulation determines to be exposures for purposes of this section." *Id.*

66. *See* Macey & Miller, *supra* note29, at 1159 and n.20. *See World Financial Markets, supra* note41, at 45, for various evidence that the market does discipline banks through the price paid for uninsured deposits and bank holding company debt.
67. *See J.P. Morgan Shares Soar on Votes of Confidence*, American Banker, Mar.11, 1992, at 12.
68. We are not sanguine about the prospects for the development of industry-sponsored liquidity support mechanisms that could fully supplant the lender of last resort function of the Federal Reserve. Lewis & Davis, *supra* note 27, at 139-140, briefly review the historical experience with such mechanisms prior to the establishment of the Federal Reserve System and describe how "[t]he New York Clearing House was originally instituted in 1853 to facilitate [check] clearing, but soon evolved into acting in addition as an organizer of liquidity support. During crises, loans were made to member banks by issuing clearing house certificates which other members agreed to accept in place of currency." However, the efficacy of such industry-sponsored mechanisms is clearly impaired by the natural incentive of potential members to "opt out" of rescue efforts, the difficulty of organizing quick support through collective action, the limited resources of market participants and the likelihood that rescue decisions will fail to incorporate all relevant social costs and benefits. In addition, as we discuss below, to discharge its lender of last resort function effectively, the Federal Reserve must be assigned a supervisory role over banks in order to be able to distinguish between illiquid (but healthy) banks worthy of support and unsound banks that should be allowed to fail. Committing such discretion to politically unaccountable industry-sponsored organizations may be unwise. Hence, "after the panic of 1907 in the United States, bankers perceived the need for a bankers' bank to assume the liquidity support operations performed by the loan committee of the New York Clearing House. From these plans resulted the Federal Reserve System, created in 1913." *Id.*
69. S. Smith and L. Wall, *Financial Panics, Bank Failures and the Role of Regulatory Policy*, Federal Reserve Bank of Atlanta, 77 Economic Review 1, 4 (1992) [hereinafter Smith & Wall].
70. In this connection, we endorse the recent amendments to the Federal Reserve Act designed to discourage the Federal Reserve from making discount window advances to undercapitalized banks. FDIC Improvement Act, *supra* note 3, § 142.
71. A comprehensive analysis of the proper allocation of functions among the various bank regulatory agencies (or the desirability of consolidating some or all of those agencies) is beyond the scope of this paper.
72. Smith & Wall, *supra* note 69, provide a fuller treatment of these issues.
73. Smith & Wall, *supra* note 69, at 8. As noted above in note 65, the concern about inadequately diversified inter-bank exposures has now been addressed directly in

the FDIC Improvement Act.

74. Deposit insurance is not the only solution to this problem. For example, if a trade creditor of a failed or failing commercial enterprise cannot afford to bear the time delay in recovering its claims from a bankrupt firm, it may sell the claim (at a discount reflecting the delay and risk of recovery) to a third party. Individual depositors of a bank, however, would not be well-suited for this kind of solution.
75. Felsenfeld, *supra* note 53, at 36-38, 48, provides an illuminating discussion of the significant costs of regulatory forbearance.
76. C. Calomiris and C. Kahn, *The Role of Demandable Debt in Structuring Optimal Banking Arrangements*, 81 American Econ. Rev. 497 (1991).
77. In a 1989 study, the Government Accounting Office found that "institutional conflict situations" (*e.g.*, economic tie-ins, customer favoritism, acting on customer confidential information or making uneconomic loans to issuers or purchasers of securities underwritten by the bank) appear to be neither significant nor widespread, in large part due to the disciplining effect of competition. On the other hand, the available evidence suggests that insider abuses (including fraud) were present in a majority of national bank failures from 1979 to 1987. United States Government Accounting Office, *Conflict of Interest Abuses in Commercial Banking Institutions* (1989) [hereinafter *GAO Conflicts Study*].
78. FDIC Improvement Act, *supra* note 3, §131, 105 Stat. at 2253-67.
79. FDIC Improvement Act, *supra* note 3, 105 Stat. at 2240, § 111 (codified at 12 U.S.C. § 1820(c)).
80. *See Comptroller Unveils Rise in Regulation Fees*, American Banker, Mar. 10, 1992, at 2.
81. Among other adverse effects, excessive regulatory monitoring can inhibit otherwise desirable bank lending. Federal Reserve Chairman Alan Greenspan has acknowledged that bank examiners played a significant role in bringing about the recent credit crunch. *See Calling Bank Supervision Archaic, Greenspan Seeks Major Change*, New York Times, Feb. 10, 1991, at 32.
82. *Modernizing the Financial System, supra* note 6, at ch. III 26 and Table 1 (summarizing data presented in Alan Greenspan, *Testimony by the Chairman, Board of Governors of the Federal Reserve System, before the Subcommittee on Commerce, Consumer, and Monetary Affairs* Appendix I (Oct. 3, 1990)).
83. *Id.* at ch III 26-27 and Table 2.
84. To make such a limitation effective, it must be applied on a basis that aggregates all of a depositor's accounts with a given bank. Although clearly important, the details of such aggregation rules are not central to our analysis in this paper.
85. *Modernizing the Financial System, supra* note6, at 24 and 36, Figure10. As Representative Gonzalez has observed, a family of four could obtain as much as $1.4 million of insurance coverage at a single institution. *Gonzalez Introduces Bill to Toughen Personal Limit on Deposit Insurance*, American Banker, Mar. 12, 1992, at 2. Representative Gonzalez has proposed to limit the maximum deposit insurance to $100,000 per individual at any one institution. *Id.* Although laudable, any proposal that would maintain full $100,000 coverage without any provision for coinsurance will still fall short because small depositors will not monitor the depository bank, and large depositors will simply break up their deposits into

$100,000 blocks at several institutions (as they do now through brokered deposits).

86. The use of coinsurance or risk sharing payments to structure optimal contracts between risk neutral principals (*e.g.*, an insurance company) and risk averse "agents" (*e.g.*, insured parties) whose behavior affects the return to the principal is a well-established proposition in the field of information economics. *See, e.g.*, Shavell, *Risk Sharing and Incentives in the Principal and Agent Relationship*, 10 Bell J. Econ. 55 (1979). The analogy to the types of insurance policies that have been developed in other markets (*e.g.*, medical insurance) in order to address the problem of moral hazard is obvious.
87. The use of coinsurance in the context of depositor protection is by no means unprecedented. Risk sharing schemes in one form or another are in place in Argentina, Chile, Colombia, Ireland, Italy and the United Kingdom. *Modernizing the Financial System, supra* note 6, at ch. XXI, Table 2; United States General Accounting Office, *Deposit Insurance: Overview of Six Foreign Systems* (1991).
88. On the surface appealing, one thought might be to insure deposits up to a lesser amount, *e.g.*, $25,000 fully, but have the depositor bear a portion of loss of every dollar thereafter. Doing this, however, would undercut the goal of depositor discipline. Just as large depositors now can break up their deposits into fully insured blocks of $100,000, depositors will simply break up their deposits into smaller $25,000 pieces. This is particularly true given the low-cost and ease of electronic transfers and other technological developments. Therefore, as politically unpalatable as it may seem, it is essential that depositor coinsurance apply to the entire deposit and not just a portion.
89. Although we propose Federal deposit insurance, private insurance could do the job just as well. *See, e.g.*, *A Plan to Bankroll Deposit Insurance*, New York Times, Mar. 11, 1992, at D2 (discussing Bert Ely's industry-wide self-insurance); Peter Wallison, *Private Deposit Insurance*, Wall Street Journal, Aug.16, 1990, at A14.
90. In the Securities Investor Protection Act of 1970, Pub. L. No. 91-598, 84 Stat. 1636 (1970) (codified as amended at 15 U.S.C. § 78aaa *et seq.*), Congress established the Securities Investor Protection Corporation (SIPC) to provide comprehensive insurance coverage to customers of brokerage firms.
91. Section 322 of the FDIC Improvement Act directs the FDIC, in consultation with the Treasury Department and private sector experts, to conduct a study of the feasibility of establishing a private reinsurance system. The FDIC is also directed to conduct a demonstration project which may include engaging in actual reinsurance transactions.
92. Including, of course, its commitment of "human capital" to the enterprise.
93. Under the Federal Reserve Board's Regulation Y, a presumption of control is triggered when (1) a shareholder acquires more than 5% of the outstanding shares of any class of voting stock of a bank holding company, (2) no other shareholder holds 5% or more of any class of voting stock of the bank holding company, and (3) the shareholder in question establishes a director or management interlock with the bank holding company. 12 C.F.R. §225.31(d)(2)(iii). Under these and related rules governing the acquisition of "control" over banks, large institutional investors find it difficult to exert a voice in bank management. In one recent example, as a condition to obtaining Federal Reserve Board permission to acquire a significant

equity interest in Wells Fargo Bank, Berkshire Hathaway was forced to enter into a series of "passivity commitments" that effectively stripped it of the ability to influence Wells Fargo's management.

94. *See Modernizing the Financial System, supra* note6, at ch.VIII.
95. *See* Federal Deposit Insurance Corporation, *Perspectives on Financial Restructuring*, 176-79 (1987).
96. United States General Accounting Office, *Deposit Insurance: A Strategy for Reform* (1991).
97. Financial Institutions Reform, Recovery and Enforcement Act of 1989, Pub.L. No.101-73, §1001, 103 Stat. 183 [hereinafter FIRREA]. *Modernizing the Financial System, supra* note 6, was the result of this mandate.
98. FDIC Improvement Act, *supra* note3, §302, 155 Stat. 2345.
99. *Modernizing the Financial System, supra* note6, at 44.
100. Basle Committee on Banking Regulations and Supervisory Practices, *International Convergence of Capital Measurement and Capital Standards* (July 1988).
101. For example, claims guaranteed by the United States are assigned to a 0% risk category against which a bank need hold no capital. An asset secured by a first mortgage on a one-to-four family home, on the other hand, is given a 50% risk-weighting. Thus a bank must have capital equal to at least 8% of 50% of the value of the mortgage loan.
102. This proposal is not too far from the FDIC's conclusion in 1983 that unsecured debt holders could provide needed market discipline over banks. Federal Deposit Insurance Corporation, *Deposit Insurance in a Changing Environment*, ch.III (1983). However, in addition to market discipline, we believe subordinated debentures could be used to set the price for the insurance itself.
103. A bank's leverage ratio is the ratio of its total Tier 1 and Tier 2 capital to its total assets.
104. Martin Feldstein, *Revise Bank Capital Standards Now*, Wall Street Journal, Mar.6, 1992.
105. Federal Reserve Chairman Alan Greenspan has made the same observation: "The major element underscoring the credit crunch is the desire on the part of commercial banks to enhance their capital position. Individual banks are very concerned about the status of their capital and have pulled back in lending in a number of instances. Ultimately, this process must lead to a loss of creditworthy customers." *See* Wall Street Journal, Jan. 18, 1991.
106. *Id.*
107. *See generally*, Henry N. Butler and Jonathan R. Macey, *The Myth of Competition in the Dual Banking System*, 73 CornellL.Rev. 677 (1988) [hereinafter Butler & Macey].
108. *See generally*, *Modernizing the Financial System*, *supra* note 6, at ch. XVII.
109. *See, e.g.*, *National Treatment Study*, *supra* note 19, at 34-35.
110. Financial Institutions Safety and Consumer Choice Act, *supra* note 6, §§ 261-265.
111. The number of branches per bank differs markedly between the U.S. and its competitors, suggesting that U.S. banks are "under-branched." For example, the Organization for Economic Cooperation and Development has reported that the average U.S. bank maintains approximately 6 branches, while the average bank in

Japan has 6, in Germany 8.5, in France 17 and in the U.K. 31. *See Who Says We Have Too Many Banks*, American Banker, June 13, 1991, at 4 (reporting OECD study). The results of empirical studies seeking to document the existence and extent of scale economies are mixed, however. *See generally* sources cited *infra*, note 120.

112. *See, e.g., Modernizing the Financial System, supra* note 6, at ch. XVII 9.
113. *Id.* FIRREA's cross-guarantee provision (12U.S.C. §1315(e)), which make insured bank subsidiaries of a bank holding company liable for any loss incurred by the deposit insurance funds due to a failure of an insured sister bank imposes all of the down-side of interstate branching without any of the benefits. For a discussion of the cross-guarantee and related issues, see William R. Keeton, *Bank Holding Companies, Cross-Bank Guarantees, and Source of Strength*, Federal Reserve Bank of Kansas City Economic Review 54 (May/June 1990).
114. *See supra* notes 107 – 113 and accompanying text.
115. *See generally*, Macey & Miller, *supra* note 29 at 1202-25.
116. *See, e.g.*, William M. Isaac, *Outmoded Policies Thwart Needed Bank Consolidation*, American Banker, Dec. 6, 1990, at 4.
117. *Mullins Says Merger Route Has Few Antitrust Obstacles*, American Banker, Aug.13, 1991, at 2.
118. In only the most recent example of this competition from nonbanking firms, AT&T, through its finance subsidiary AT&T Capital Corp, which has more than $6.8 in assets, plans to introduce a small business lending program. *AT&T Unit to Woo Franchise Owners*, American Banker, Mar. 4, 1992, at 6.
119. *Bankrupt, supra* note 7, at 85.
120. A recent study by two economists on the staff of the Federal Reserve Bank of Atlanta failed to find any evidence that bank mergers significantly lower expenses. *See* A. Srinivasan and L. Wall, *Cost Savings Associated with Bank Mergers* (Federal Reserve Bank of Atlanta, Working Paper 92-2, 1992). *See also* Lewis & Davis, *supra* note27, at 199-209 (reviewing 19 empirical studies with inconsistent results).
121. Although the Glass-Steagall Act and the Bank Holding Company Act most significantly restrict competition in the market for investment banking services, they can unexpectedly restrict competition even within the banking industry. For example, the Netherlands NMB Postbank may be forced to give up its U.S. banking charter because it recently merged with a Netherlands insurance company — an impermissible affiliation under the Bank Holding Company Act. *See Dutch Bank May Drop U.S. Banking License*, American Banker, Mar.13, 1992, at 6.
122. Securities Exchange Law of 1948 (Law No.25).
123. *Commercial Paper Underwriting, supra* note 21, at 380 (citations omitted).
124. The liberalization proposed by the Ministry of Finance is by no means complete. For example, while banks would be allowed to underwrite securities through majority-owned subsidiaries, they would not be allowed to engage in brokerage transactions, despite this being a virtually inseparable part of the securities business.
125. *Investment Co. Inst. v. Camp, supra* note 45, at 630 (1971) ("subtle hazards that arise when a commercial bank goes beyond the business of acting as fiduciary or managing agent and enters the investment banking business"). *See generally*, Fischel, Rosenfield & Stillman, *supra* note 29, at 323-30.
126. Indeed banks might well be competitively disadvantaged because of their high costs

for regulatory supervision and the requirement that they maintain non-interest bearing reserves with the Federal Reserve. We agree with Chairman Greenspan that the Federal Reserve Board should pay interest on reserves. *See* Wall Street Journal, 3/11/92.

127. This is one of the principal reasons why we join those who disagree with the "core banking" proposal of Lowell Bryan. See, *e.g.*, William Isaac, *Core Banking: The Wrong Rx*, American Banker, July 3, 1991, at 4.
128. *See generally*, sources cited *supra* note 56.
129. Felsenfeld, *supra* note53.
130. Liang & Savage, *supra* note 16.
131. *Clarke's Final Days: A time for Forecasts*, American Banker, Mar. 2, 1992, at 7.
132. *Investment Co. Inst. v. Camp*, *supra* note 45, at 630.
133. Fischel, Rosenfield & Stillman classify the "subtle hazards" as follows:

    (1) biased advice to clients—providing misleading information to clients of the bank to induce them to purchase nonbanking services from the bank or its affiliate; (2) uneconomical transfers—the making of loans by a bank to a commonly controlled, financially troubled nonbanking affiliate at less than the market rate of interest; a bank trust department paying more than the market price for securities of an underwriting sponsored by a commonly controlled separate underwriting subsidiary; the making of loans to purchasers of these securities to ensure that the underwriting will be successful; (3) predation—extending credit to an affiliate at less than the market rate of interest in order to injure rivals of the affiliate; and (4)tie-in sales—requiring customers of the bank to purchase goods and services from commonly controlled nonbanking business affiliates as a condition of obtaining credit from the bank.

    Fischel, Rosenfield & Stillman, *supra* note 29, at 324 (footnote omitted).
134. Fischel, Rosenfield & Stillman, *supra* note29. If the bank were conducting the activity directly, it could use the profits from one activity to offset losses at the other.
135. *Id.*
136. If a bank were able to make such a loan using insured deposits without paying an attendant additional cost for its deposit insurance, then the bank may have an incentive to "gamble." Reform of deposit insurance as we have proposed, however, would remove this potential incentive to "bet the bank." It may be noted that under a bank holding company structure, a bank's below market loan to a non-bank affiliate will help only the affiliate (and indirectly its parent) to achieve profits, while the bank will be exposed to excessive risk of loss and may call upon the Federal Reserve's safety net for protection. Absent effective reform of deposit insurance, this problem would suggest the usefulness of requiring that banking and related activities be conducted through a single entity such as a "universal bank."
137. As Robert P. Forrestal, president of the Federal Reserve Bank of Atlanta, has observed, overcapacity in the banking industry also plays a part in forcing banks to search out riskier assets. *See Atlanta Fed Sees a Tough Future for Banking Industry*, American Banker, Mar. 12, 1992.
138. Macey & Miller, *supra* note29, at 1155.
139. Tussing, *The Case for Bank Failure*, 10 J.L. & Econ. 129, 146 (1967).

140. Staff of the House Committee on Banking, Finance and Urban Affairs *Analysis of Banking Industry Consolidation Issues* (1991).
141. *See, e.g., Investment Co. Inst. v. Camp, supra* note45, at 633-34.
142. *GAO Conflicts Study, supra* note 77.
143. *See, e.g.*, section 17(a) of the Securities Act of 1933; sections 10(b) and 15(c)(1) of the Securities Exchange Act of 1934.
144. The OCC currently permits national banks to underwrite and sell title insurance, property insurance related to loan collateral and financial guaranty insurance. Until a recent judicial set-back national banks were also able to sell insurance products nationwide from a small-town branch. *See Independent Insurance Agents of American v. Clarke, supra* note 23.
145. *Modernizing the Financial System, supra* note 6, at ch. XVIII 16-17.
146. *Id.* at ch. XVIII 17 (*citing* United States General Accounting Office, *Banking Powers: Issues Relating to Banks Selling Insurance* 17-19 (1990)).
147. A recent and intriguing example of current bank entry into insurance is found in the recent acquisition by Bankers Trust of a variable life insurance company from Mutual Benefit Life. Because Bankers Trust acquired the company in satisfaction of a debt previously contracted with Mutual Benefit Life (swap contracts), Bankers Trust will be able to retain the insurance company for up to five years as "DPC" stock. *See Bankers Trust Gains Variable Life Insurance Unit in a Trade for Debt,* American Banker, Mar.9, 1992, at 16.
148. *See, e.g.*, Financial Modernization Act of 1988, S. 1886 (commonly known as the Proxmire-Garn Bill); Financial Institutions Safety and Consumer Choice Act, *supra* note 6.
149. Fischel, Rosenfield & Stillman, *supra* note29, at 322.
150. *Id.* at 323.
151. *See generally*, O. Williamson, *Markets and Hierarchies* (1975).
152. In keeping with our guidelines for sound regulation, we would expect such intervention to draw heavily on our experience with similar problems in the field of securities regulation by emphasizing policies of disclosure and customer consent. Of course, many adjustments—largely technical in nature—to existing regulations would be necessary in order to implement our proposals. For example, the scope of current rules regarding *lending* limits should be expanded to cover financial exposure to individual customers on a more comprehensive basis commensurate with the wider array of services that could be offered by banks. A discussion of those adjustments is beyond the scope of this paper.
153. As discussed above, our proposals for deposit insurance reform should also dispose of any remaining concern that the federal safety net might be used to subsidize non-banking activities.
154. *See generally*, Butler & Macey, *supra* note 107.
155. For example, the FDIC Improvement Act gives the FDIC the authority to restrict state innovations if it determines the new activity to be unsafe.
156. Financial Institutions Safety and Consumer Choice Act of 1991, *supra* note 6, §264.
157. *See* Lowell L. Bryan, *A Blueprint for Financial Reconstruction*, Harv. Bus. Rev. (May-June 1991); *Bankrupt, supra* note 7.
158. Bryan suggests that regulators might develop numerical guidelines requiring, for

example, that real estate developers provide 30% of the equity for real estate projects, that disbursement of construction loans be withheld until a project is 90% preleased and that committed leases provide 100% coverage of principal and interest payments.

PART THREE

FINANCIAL MARKET DIMENSIONS OF THE COST OF CAPITAL

CHAPTER 9

THE EVOLVING JAPANESE FINANCIAL SYSTEM AND THE COST OF CAPITAL

Jeffrey A. Frankel

Americans became concerned in the 1980s with the question whether Japanese corporations had an advantage in the ease with which they could raise funds to finance investment. The majority of studies found that Japanese firms did indeed have a financial advantage, and disagreed only over what was the key element that constituted the difference in the two countries' financial systems.[1]

Many approached the question by quantifying the cost of capital, defined for example as a weighted average of the market cost of debt and the

Parts of the chapter draw on parts of three earlier papers: "Japanese Finance: A Survey," in *The U.S. and Japan: Has the Door Opened Wider?*, edited by Paul Krugman, University of Chicago Press, Chicago, 1991; "The Japanese Cost of Finance: A Survey," *Financial Management*, Spring 1991; and "The Japanese Financial System and the Cost of Capital," forthcoming in *Handbook of Japanese Capital Markets*, edited by Shinji Takagi, Basil Blackwell Inc., Cambridge, MA. (Those papers include also sections on land and private saving.) I would like to acknowledge financial support from the Center for Pacific Basin Monetary and Economic Studies at the Federal Reserve Bank of San Francisco, and the Japan-United States Friendship Commission, an agency of the U.S. Government.

I gratefully acknowledge advice and suggestions from David Meerschwam, and comments on earlier drafts from: James Ang, Alan Auerbach, Sudipto Bhattacharya, Robert Dekle, Ken Froot, Michael Kinsley, Ryutaro Komiya, Paul Krugman, Hiro Lee, Eiji Ogawa, Yuzuru Ozeki, Ulrike Schaede, Hiroshi Shibuya, and Shinji Takagi. I would also like to thank Shang-Jin Wei for research assistance. A disclaimer that the survey is not completely exhaustive applies, in particular, with respect to writings that appear only in Japanese.

market cost of equity. A few such studies failed to find evidence of a significantly lower cost of capital in Japan. It is easy enough to come up with a negative finding like this, if one measures the required rate of return on equity by the observed *ex post* return on equity, because stock prices are so volatile that statistical significance is limited. But most studies did find lower real interest rates and other measures of required rates of return in Japan. Indeed, this conclusion in the finance field corresponded well to a conclusion of mainstream macroeconomists: that a shortfall in the U.S. national saving rate in the 1980s drove the rate of return in the United States above that prevailing in Japan and elsewhere, thereby attracting the large capital inflow that was the counterpart of the infamous trade imbalance.

Others argued that the standard concept of the cost of capital was not relevant to Japan, where long-term relationships such as that between a firm and its main bank predominated over Anglo-American style securities markets.[2] But these writers generally subscribed to the view that such relationships helped Japanese firms to achieve a level of investment that was even higher than what one would expect from the observed cost of capital. Thus the main-bank relationship theory was not in competition to the cost-of-capital theory, in the sense that they were two parallel ways of explaining a greater apparent ease of funding investment in Japan.

Much has changed since December 1989. In that month, a new governor arrived at the Bank of Japan, determined to tighten monetary policy and burst the 1980s stock market bubble. Interest rates rose sharply, and the Japanese stock market fell in three precipitous drops (dated roughly at January 1990, August 1990, and April 1992). The result is that standard measures of the cost of debt and the cost of equity show that they have now rise to the same level prevailing in the United States. It seems likely that the specifics of Japanese monetary policy mainly affected the timing, and that the convergence of Japanese and world rates of return was the inevitable eventual outcome of the preceding ten-year trend of financial liberalization. The point is that the equalization of Japanese and U.S. rates of return has rendered obsolete much of the cost-of-capital literature that is only a few years old.

For those who have always believed that the measured cost of capital is less relevant in Japan than main-bank and other relationships, the events of 1990-92 seem more supportive. Many Japanese corporations have come home from the Euromarkets, where they were busy issuing equity-linked bonds in 1989, and resumed borrowing from their banks.

This chapter reviews the literature on cost of capital, beginning with the issue of access to cheap borrowing, shifting to a consideration of the equity markets (including such issues as dividend-payout rates, P/E ratios, and corporate taxation), and then considering domestic and international determinants of the real interest rate. It concludes with a discussion of banking relationships. Measurement and accounting problems occur from the beginning, and will be discussed as we proceed. But throughout, the chapter attempts to concentrate on those trends in financial prices that are so strong that one cannot easily attribute them entirely to measurement problems.

The chapter raises a number of puzzles. First, if low interest rates explain the high level of the Japanese stock market in the late 1980s, what explains the *increase* in stock market prices during the decade? Second, if banking relationships represent a more efficient way to raise capital, why did Japanese corporations move away from them in the 1980s, and rely more heavily on securities markets for their funds? Third, do the developments since 1989 constitute a reversal of the trends of the late 1980s? Which situation more accurately indicates the longer-run reality, 1987-89 or 1990-92?

I. THE STANDARD WEIGHTED-AVERAGE MEASURE OF THE COST OF CAPITAL

The claim that the cost of capital was lower in Japan, perhaps giving Japanese firms an "unfair" advantage, arose with some American businessmen in the early 1980s.[3] Some of the original statements focused only on differences in interest rates. Later versions were more complete.[4]

A traditional measure of the cost of capital is a weighted average of the cost of borrowing and the cost of equity:

$$r_c = w\, r_d + (1-w)\, r_e\,, \tag{9.1}$$

where r_d is the cost of debt, r_e is the cost of equity, and w is the relative weight of debt in total financing. Under this definition, the claim can be broken down into some combination of the following three possibilities: (a) the cost of borrowing was lower in Japan, (b) the cost of equity was lower in Japan, or (c) the weight on debt-financing (versus equity-financing) was higher in Japan. All three statements contain some truth.[5]

Real Interest Rates

Nominal interest rates in Japan have been below those in the United States during most of the postwar period, and continuously from 1977 to 1989. Japanese inflation has also been relatively low since 1977, and it is of course the real interest rate, not the nominal rate, that matters for investment. But calculations suggest that Japanese real interest rates were below U.S. real rates virtually continuously from 1967 to 1989.[6]

It should be noted that some of these calculations may understate the Japanese real interest rate in the 1960s and 1970s. The actual inflation rates that are used overstate expected inflation rates, and the government bond rates that are used were too low to be willingly absorbed by private investors. Also, for the case of borrowing from banks, firms were required to maintain "compensating balances," which did not pay interest.[7] But for the 1980s one can use interest rates that do not have such problems.

In the period 1982-84, the U.S. long-term real interest rate rose substantially above that in Japan and other G-7 countries. The differential in real interest rates is widely considered to have been the result of a U.S. fiscal expansion, at a time of fiscal contraction in Japan and some major European countries.[8]

The U.S.-Japan real interest differential was smaller after the midpoint of the 1980s than it was in the first half of the decade.[9] This differential, even if small, was still present however in 1989. In early 1989, the long-term real interest differential was over one point, as is illustrated in Figure 9–1, and the short-term differential was larger. We postpone until the fourth section the question of how such a differential could have persisted despite the apparent international integration of financial markets. As discussed below, further narrowing of the real interest differential took place in the second half of 1989. (The long-term nominal interest rates in the graphs are 10-year government bond yields. Expected inflation is measured by a survey of forecasters conducted by *Currency Forecasters' Digest*.[10])

The standard capitalization formula for the equity price/dividend ratio and the price/rental ratio is

$$\frac{1}{r-g}, \tag{9.2}$$

where r is the real interest rate used to discount expected future divi-

FIGURE 9–1
Real Interest Rates in the United States and Japan, February 1988–April 1992

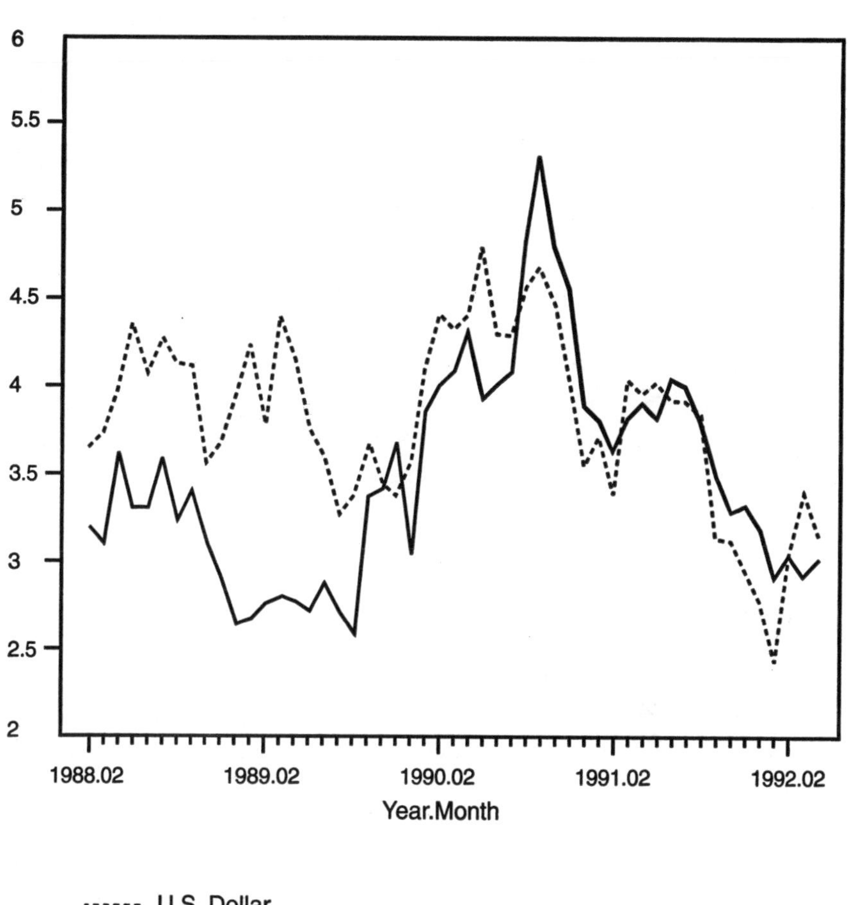

Source: Currency Forecasters Digest

dends to the present, and g is the expected growth rate of dividends. The formula is also sometimes used to think about the price/earnings ratio for equities. ("Earnings" would better be defined asnet profits after new investment. See note 15.)

Sometimes the best we can do to get an idea of the expected growth rate of dividends is assume that it is equal to the expected growth rate of the economy. If $r - g$ were a number like .02 in the world economy at large, then the Japanese interest rate would only have to be lower by .01—or the growth rate higher by .01 (quite plausibly)—to explain a doubling of the price/earnings ratio. French and Poterba (1991) point out that a lower real rate of interest in Japan might be able to explain the high level of Japanese stock prices *on average* during their sample period (the 1970s and 1980s). But it cannot explain the *increase* during the last three years, 1986–88.

Because the real interest differential is thought to be small, with the exception of the early 1980s, those who argue that the cost of capital is low in Japan and that this has presented a problem for the "competitiveness" of U.S. industry ever since 1973, e.g., Krugman, Hatsopoulos, and Summers (1988) and Poterba (1991), tend not to emphasize the real interest rate. They choose, rather, to emphasize the cost of equity financing and the relative weight of debt versus equity in corporate financing. We return to the role of the real interest rate later, however.

Leverage (Debt/Equity Ratios)

In the past, Japanese corporations have had a much higher ratio of debt to equity than U.S. corporations, that is, they have been much more highly leveraged. (In terms of equation 9.1 earlier, the debt/equity ratio is $w/(1-w)$.) In the period 1970–72, for example, debt/equity ratios in Japan were four times as high as in the United States. This commonly-observed characteristic of the Japanese system is one major reason why calculations often show a lower overall cost of capital in Japan than in the United States; equity-financing is known to be more expensive than debt-financing in any market, presumably because portfolio investors demand a higher expected return on equity to compensate them for higher risk. It must be noted from the outset that the apparent conclusion that a given firm can lower its cost of capital by increasing the weight on debt is illusory. It would only hold if both the cost of equity and the cost of debt could be assumed to be independent of leverage. To the contrary, both would in fact be expected to rise: the former as the firm's levered beta rises, and the latter as its credit rating falls (McCauley and Zimmer, 1989, p. 24). Kester and Luehrman (1992, pp. 9–14) think that most of the cost-of-capital literature is crippled by a failure to realize that the costs of debt and equity themselves depend on the degree of leverage, which they refer to as the "mismatch" problem.

How have Japanese firms been able to rely so heavily on debt? As a number of authors have pointed out, a particular debt/equity ratio that would be very risky for a U.S. firm would have been less risky for a Japanese firm. There are several reasons for this.

(1) Much of the borrowing was from the firm's main bank. A main bank would not cut off lending in time of financial difficulty; to the contrary it would do all it could to see the company through. Hoshi, Kashyap and Scharfstein (1990) examined a sample of 125 Japanese firms that ran into financial trouble over the period 1978–85. They found that those who had a main bank—and especially those who were members of a keiretsu—were buffered from their financial distress and enjoyed subsequent recovery of earnings as compared to other firms.[11]

(2) Until recently, all loans had to be collaterized. This certainly reduced the risk from the viewpoint of the bank, which in turn helps explain the reduced danger from the viewpoint of the corporation that bank lending (as well as the ability to sell bonds) would dry up in time of difficulty.

(3) Such government policies as allowing the formation of cartels in event of recession reduced the risk of financial difficulty or bankruptcy.[12]

(4) The practice of paying workers a substantial fraction of their compensation in the form of twice-yearly bonuses that vary with the success of the company acts as a sort of profit-sharing mechanism, and again reduces the risk of bankruptcy.

Abegglen (1985, p. 165) offered an accounting reason why a given corporate balance sheet that might spell excessive risk in the United States would not be as worrisome in Japan: a typical Japanese firm does not consolidate the financial assets held by its subsidiaries into its own balance sheet—where a corresponding U.S. firm might do so—and carries land and securities on its books at original cost. He thinks that such a firm is in a stronger financial position than its balance sheet would suggest. Some of these accounting questions are discussed under the heading of price/earnings ratios below.

In any case, it is important to note that the seemingly robust regularity that "Japanese firms are much more highly leveraged" appears to have died out in the course of the 1970s and 1980s. The debt/equity ratio fell throughout most of these two decades, and by one measure had by 1986 fallen *below* the level in the United States, as shown in the last two columns of Table 9–1 (from French and Poterba).[13] This reversal was due only in part to the increase in corporate leverage in the 1980s that generated so much alarm in the United States. The reversal was due

TABLE 9–1
Price-Earnings Ratios, Japan and the United States, 1971–1990

	United States		*Japan*[a]	
	Reported	*Adjusted*	*Reported*	*Adjusted*
1971	15	15	na	na
1972	14	14	na	na
1973	10	12	na	na
1974	6	11	na	na
1975	6	8	na	na
1976	6	8	23	8
1977	6	7	21	8
1978	5	7	20	10
1979	5	7	19	24
1980	6	10	15	9
1981	7	10	20	12
1982	10	12	21	16
1983	10	10	24	18
1984	10	8	25	15
1985	12	9	30	18
1986	16	11	48	23
1987	13	11	52	36
1988	11	10	52	32
1989	14	14	58	37
1990	14	15	33	21
1970–74	11	13	na	na
1975–79	5	7	22	10
1980–84	9	10	21	14
1985–89	13	11	49	30

a Daiwa firms.

Source: K. French and J. Poterba, *Journal of Financial Economics*, 1991, Table 6.

primarily to the decline in Japan, which was in turn due, at least in an arithmetic sense, to the soaring value of Japanese equities in the late 1980s and to decreased reliance on the main bank system, as well as to the reduced need for external financing of any sort after 1973. Each of these factors will be discussed below.

II. EQUITY CAPITAL

The Rate of Return on Equity: Stock Prices and Dividends

The third of the standard components of the overall cost of capital, after leverage and the cost of debt, is the cost of equity financing, r_e in the standard equation 9.1. It is the most ambiguous of the components to measure. One approach has been to use the realized market rate of return on equity, i.e., the dividend/price ratio plus the rate of increase of equity prices. Baldwin (1986) and Kester and Luehrman (1991) were unable to reject the hypothesis that the level of expected return on equities for any given level of risk was similar in the two countries. Ando and Auerbach (1988a) found, for the period 1966-1981, that returns were actually considerably *higher* in Japan. (In addition to their calculation of the average rates of return, they also looked at earnings/price ratios, discussed below.)

Subsequently, on a much larger sample of firms than that used in their earlier study, but with a similar methodology and time period, Ando and Auerbach (1988b) found that the overall rate of return on capital was substantially lower in Japan than in the United States after all. (The time period was 1967–83.)

Stockholders' realized rate of return on equity is a very noisy indicator of their ex ante expectations. As McCauley and Zimmer (1989, p. 9) and Poterba (1991, p. 24) pointed out, an increase in the discount rate, by causing an immediate fall in stock prices, would even show up perversely in the short run as a lower rate of return rather than a higher one. Friend and Tokutsu (1987, p. 317) remarked that while realized market rates of return on equity were higher in Japan (over the period 1962–1984) than in the United States, a reverse answer results if the dividend/price ratio is added to the rate of growth of dividends per share, rather than to the rate of growth of prices. Looking at the problem from the viewpoint of the market investor rather than the firm might give the wrong answer if the stockholders' return to capital measured over a finite sample differs from what managers perceive as their required rate of return. Hatsopoulos and Brooks (1987) and Hodder (1988b, 1990) dissented from the Baldwin and Ando-Auerbach approaches on these grounds.[14]

In the absence of a speculative bubble, stock prices can be thought of either as the present discounted value of expected future dividends, or the present discounted value of expected future free cash flow, where the latter is often proxied by earnings. (Free Cash Flow is defined as profit after tax, minus changes in working capital, minus other capital spending, plus depreciation.[15]) We consider the subject of dividends first, and turn to earnings in the next subsection.

There has been little upward trend in Japanese dividends per share over the last 20 years.[16] This made it especially difficult to explain the high level of Japanese stock prices, if one followed the common approach of choosing the present-discounted-value-of-future-dividends formula and estimating expected dividends from actual realized dividends. On the other hand, the observed high level of prices relative to dividends would be perfectly understandable if the increase in dividends were thought still to lie in the future.

If dividends are treated as expected to grow at a constant rate g_d from now on, then the current dividend/price ratio should equal $r_e - g_d$, where r_e is the required rate of return on equity capital (which may be higher than the real interest rate because of a risk premium). As of 1988, the dividend price ratio was only .006 in Japan, as compared to .030 in the United States (from French and Poterba). If r_e is assumed to be the same in the two countries, then the 1988 levels of stock prices make sense if and only if the dividends were expected to grow at a rate 2.4 per cent faster in Japan than in the United States.

Why should Japanese dividends grow rapidly in the future, given that they have not done so in the past? We have no good theory of how shareholders wish to receive the return on their equity investment, i.e., in the form of dividends or capital gains, or of how managers choose to pay dividends. In a sufficiently abstract (Modigliani-Miller) world the payout rate is indeterminate. On the one hand, tax considerations point to postponing the payment of dividends. On the other hand, the hypothesis that managers sometimes use funds for purposes other than maximizing shareholder welfare points to shareholders insisting on early payment of dividends.

Corporations do determine dividends, one way or another. One hypothesis is that some shareholders like to receive quarterly checks for liquidity reasons. They could instead sell some stock to generate cash, but there are transactions costs to doing so.

The payout rate, i.e., the ratio of dividends to earnings, has been declining gradually in Japan since the early 1960s, and is lower than in the United States. Over the period 1980-88, it averaged .357 for Japan and .469 for the United States. This difference would be larger if Japanese earnings were adjusted upward for the factors described in the next section.[17]

The ratio of retirees to working-age people is close to a minimum in Japan now, and will soon begin to rise until, by 2020, it will be the highest of the major industrialized countries. It is plausible that wealthy Japanese retirees in the future will wish to receive high dividend payments on their holdings. Thus it is not entirely implausible that the expected future growth rate of dividends in Japan should be almost as high as the rate of return on capital, or that it should be 2.4 per cent higher than the growth rate in the United States, notwithstanding the dividend record of the past 20 years.

Another, consistent, explanation as to why Japanese dividends might rise in the future even though they have been low in the past is that Japanese corporations have over the postwar period had many profitable investment opportunities, but until the late 1980s have not had sufficiently free access to securities markets to drive their cost of capital into equality with the rate of return on these investments. For this reason, they have chosen to finance investment out of retained earnings. Even in the United States, a rapidly-growing company may pay no dividends at all, for example, and rather re-invest all earnings into highly-profitable projects. Japan has been going through a collective life-cycle similar to such a company. At some point in the future, the extra growth opportunities of Japanese corporations will disappear, and they will be free to begin paying out a higher level of dividends. Akio Morita (1992, p. 8), Chairman of Sony, has recently suggested, "Wouldn't it be advisable for Japanese companies to increase the payout ratio to a level comparable with that of European and American companies?"

Such considerations suggest that looking at the past history of dividends may not be very useful. An alternative approach is to look at the amount of *earnings* the firm is required to generate per unit of equity, that is, the inverse of the price/earnings ratio.

Price-Earnings Ratios

The price/earnings ratio (like the price/dividend ratio) has been observed to be higher in Japan than in the United States ever since the early 1970s, and most dramatically in the late 1980s. Because this difference could be explained by a lower discount rate in Japan, it is often the basis of arguments that the cost of equity capital is lower in Japan. But the difference could also have other explanations, such as a higher expected growth rate in Japan. If a high growth rate were the complete explanation, one would not want to attribute the high P/E ratios to a low discount rate. More broadly, one would not want to attribute the superior performance of Japanese industry necessarily to a low cost of capital. The chapter now turns to the subject of the high and (in the 1980s) increasing P/E ratios in Japan, an important question in its own right.

Some, such as Ando and Auerbach, have looked at the price-earnings ratio because they are interested in the cost-of-capital question, and they consider P/E to be inversely related to the required rate of return r_e. Others, such as French and Poterba (1991) and Lawler, Loopesko and Dudey (1988) are interested in the price-earnings ratio for its own sake. As shown in the first two columns of Table 9–1, the reported price/earnings ratio for Japanese firms has been higher than the P/E ratio in the United States ever since the 1970s. It reached 58.6, three times as high as the U.S. level, in 1986. In the stock market crash of October 1987, the decline in Japan was smaller and shorter-lived, with the result that in 1988 and 1989 Japan's reported P/E was more than four times that in the United States or the rest of the world. (The developments of 1990-92 are discussed below. See Figure 9–2, which is borrowed from Hale.)

Such an apparent discrepancy would be difficult to explain. If earnings were expected to grow at rate g_e, then the earnings/price ratio should equal $r_e - g_e$. The end-1988 differential between reported earnings/price ratios in the United States and Japan was .06 [=.078 – .018]. The real growth rate of the Japanese economy had averaged 1.6 per cent faster than the U.S. economy over 1980-88; there was no particular reason to expect the real growth rate of the economy to increase in the future, or to expect the growth rate of earnings or cash flow to be higher than the growth rate of GNP. Thus the required rate of return on capital r_e would have to have been more than 4 percentage points lower than in the United States to explain the difference in reported P/E ratios. Such a finding would support the cost-of-capital-advantage school, but seems too large to be plausible.

Hatsopoulos and Poterba (1991, p. 11–12) point out that stockholders' required rate of return on equity will differ from the earnings/price ratio to the extent that some part of earnings is reinvested by managers rather than paid out, and is reinvested at a rate of return that differs from the stockholders' required return. They acknowledge that the earnings/price ratio will accurately reflect the required return in the special case when the return on reinvested earnings is the same as the stockholder return. But they focus on an example where the stockholders cannot prevent managers from undertaking projects that are not profitable at current required returns. This case, which implies that the earnings/price ratio understates the true required rate of return, would appear to be more applicable to the United States than Japan, if the literature on information and incentive problems described in

FIGURE 9–2
Price/Earnings Multiples in Japan and the United States, Ratio of Price to Cash Earnings (3-Month Average), 1970–1991

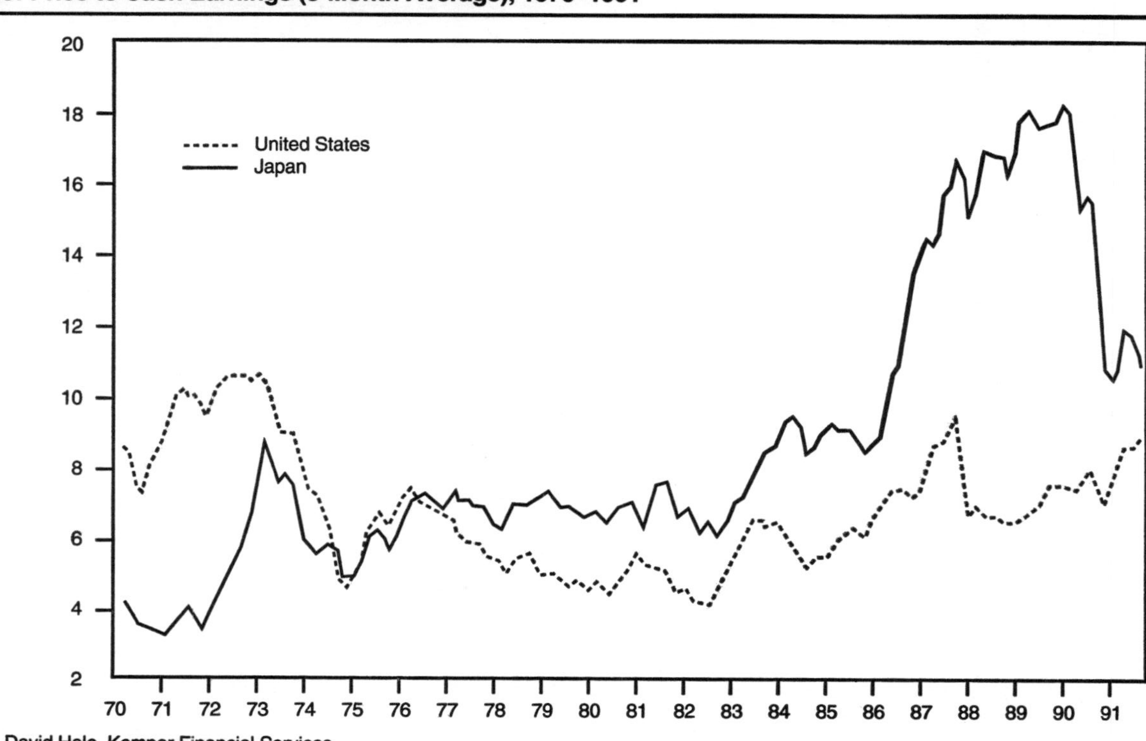

Source: David Hale, Kemper Financial Services

the fourth section of this chapter is to be believed. It would appear to follow that the U.S.-Japanese difference in required rates of return on equity is even larger than E/P ratios imply.[18]

French and Poterba (1991), Ando and Auerbach (1988a, 1988b, 1990), Lawler, Loopesko and Dudey (1988), and Hatsopoulos and Poterba (1991) all emphasized the importance of correcting earnings for a number of measurement problems. Ando and Auerbach (1988ab) focussed on three distortions related to inflation: depreciation accounting, inventory accounting, and accounting for nominal liabilities. They found that correcting for these distortions increased estimated earnings, and therefore increased the E/P ratio, for virtually all the Japanese firms in their sample, while it had no systematic effect for the U.S. firms.[19] The principle apparent source of the effect was that the Japanese firms relied more on debt than equity (see above), so the fact that inflation reduced the real value of their outstanding liabilities was more important for them. Apparently the fact that the inflation rate was lower in Japan had less of an effect than the higher debt/equity ratio. If reliance on debt is indeed the source of the effect, then the fact that the debt/equity ratio in Japan appeared to have fallen below that in the United States by 1986 (and that inflation fell in both countries in the 1980s), suggests that the inflation accounting may no longer be as important for the P/E comparison.

French and Poterba had some other corrections to make to reported earnings and therefore P/E ratios. First was the point that earnings reported by U.S. corporations include the profits of subsidiaries, while those reported by Japanese firms do not (only actual dividends received from subsidiaries), so their earnings look smaller. A calculation to convert P/E ratios to what they would have been if there were no cross-holding of corporate equity (which required adjusting both earnings—by removing intercorporate dividends—and share prices) reduced the Japanese P/E ratio.

Second, reported Japanese earnings also look smaller because they deduct (both on the firms' tax returns and on their financial statements) generous allowances for special reserves for such possible future contingencies as product returns, repairs, and retirement benefits. But this effect was relatively small.

Third, Japanese firms often take greater depreciation allowances. This factor, like the previous two, works to reduce reported earnings. (Unlike U.S. firms, when a Japanese firm claims a high depreciation allowance for tax purposes, it must do the same on its income statement.) The effect of all three corrections together was to reduce the 1989 P/E ratio in Japan from 58 to 37. Lawler, Loopesko and Dudey (1988, p. 24) made their own adjustments for depreciation and consolidation of earnings, which produced a very similar result. The analogous downward adjustment in U.S. P/E ratios was much smaller. Overall, these accounting differences in earnings explained about half of the difference between Japanese and U.S. ratios.[20] This still left Japanese equities about 2.6 times as high as U.S. equities at the end of 1989. Or, if our interest is in the cost-of-capital question rather than in the was-Japan's-market-too-high question, the correction still left 1988 Japanese earnings/price ratios at about half U.S. levels.

Once we get the corrected Japanese earnings/price ratio up to the neighborhood of .027, it becomes slightly easier to explain the differential vis-à-vis the United States (which was at .071 when similarly adjusted by French and Poterba). If, for example, the expected rate of growth of earnings g_e in Japan were 2 per cent faster than in the U.S. and the rate of return required by shareholders were 2 per cent lower, that would explain the differential. But if it is true that the required rate of return was lower by, say 2 per cent, what might have been the source of this difference?

We consider six possible explanations, relating to: the equity risk premium, land prices, tax treatment, the low real interest rate, a possible speculative bubble, and nonmarket finance. The latter four topics merit their own sections below. We begin with the first two.

One possible explanation of a low required rate of return on equity is that the "equity premium" (defined as the expected rate of return on equity minus the risk-free interest rate) was smaller for Japan. In theory this would require either a lower level of risk in the Japanese market, or a lower price of risk. The latter hypothesis would in turn require that Japanese stocks—for whatever reason—are held primarily by Japanese investors (i.e., markets are segmented) and that Japanese investors are less risk-averse than American investors. This hypothesis has the virtue that, in commonly specified intertemporal utility functions, the parameter determining risk-aversion is the same as the parameter determining the rate of time preference; the claim that Japanese are less impatient than Americans sounds more familiar than the hypothesis that they are less risk-averse.

In any case, Baldwin (1986) and the appendix to Ando and Auerbach (1988b) found no sign that the expected rate of return on Japanese securities was lower for a given amount of risk. Similarly, Kester and Luehrman (1991) were statistically unable to reject the hypothesis that the price of risk was the same in Japan as the United States.

Thus the risk-premium hypothesis would seem to require the Japanese stock market to have been less risky than the American stock market. Ueda

(1990, pp. 362–64) argued that the risk premium in the Japanese stock market declined sharply between 1982 and 1988, but could find little evidence of a corresponding decline in riskiness. Lawler, Loopesko and Dudey (1988, pp. 26–27) concluded that uncertainty in the two stock markets was roughly similar in the late 1980s (despite some possible differences in the past), whether estimated from the standard deviations of monthly changes or expected volatilities implicit in stock index options. So there is little evidence of the smaller uncertainty in the Japanese market that would normally be required to justify a smaller risk premium.

Another explanation that could explain an apparently low required rate of return on equity in the 1980s is the rise in land prices. Firms hold a lot of land, which they usually carry on their books, not at current market price, but at the price of acquisition (which, in the case of land held since the 19th century, is essentially zero). French and Poterba thus tentatively concluded that the puzzle as to why equity prices rose so much in the 1980s may be the same as the puzzle why land prices rose so much in the 1980s. Ando and Auerbach (1990) reached a similar conclusion—that even a conservative calculation to adjust corporate earnings for land appreciation can fully account for the apparent differential in rate of return vis-à-vis the United States—while admitting that this answer only pushes the question of the source of the 1980s run-up from the stock market onto the land market.[21] Hamao and Hoshi (1991) report evidence of linkage between stock prices and land prices. But Ziemba (1991) finds evidence that stock prices lead land prices, rather than the reverse.

Theories regarding Japanese land prices are reviewed in section II.E of Frankel (1991a). The price of land, analogously to the price of equity, should equal the present discounted value of future rents (in the absence of a speculative bubble). If rents are expected to grow at rate g_r, then the price/rental ratio should be given by

$$P_{\text{land}}/\text{rent} = \frac{1}{r - g_r}$$

In terms of the above equation, either a high value for g_r or a low value for the discount rate r could explain the high price/rental ratio. Ito (1989), Sachs and Boone (1989) and Boone (1989b) attribute Japanese land prices to such macroeconomic factors. But, even though the expected-growth argument favored by both Boone and Ito tells us why land price/rental ratios in Japan were high as of 1989, it does not tell us why they should have *in-*

creased so much in the 1980s. According to the theory, the price and rent should each rise proportionately with economic growth. Instead, while land and housing prices sky-rocketed, the rental rate remained approximately constant in real terms. Furthermore, since low interest rates and high expected growth rates are the same factors used to explain the high level of the stock market, the consideration of the land market does not move us ahead in understanding the Japanese cost of capital.

We now consider in turn three remaining serious possibilities to explain the apparently lower required rate of return on equity capital in Japan in the 1980s: more favorable tax treatment, a lower real interest rate, and financing that is cheaper than the rate of return required on securities markets. We will see that the third explanation seems especially appropriate for the period before liberalization, and the second explanation for the period since liberalization. But there is also a fourth possibility to consider, that the increase in stock prices in the late 1980s was a speculative bubble.

Corporate Taxation

Corporate taxation is one of the respects in which the effective cost of capital facing the firm can differ from the observed rate of return on investment: it is of course the *after*-tax cost of capital that should matter for investment decisions. It would presumably be more convenient for any American businessman who wished to claim that Japanese industry had an "unfair advantage" in the form of a low cost of capital, if the source of the advantage were more favorable tax treatment by the Japanese government.

In the past, the corporate income tax rate in Japan has been much *higher* than in the United States, especially after the more favorable U.S. tax treatment of business adopted in 1981. In 1985, the Japanese government raised 5.9 per cent of its tax revenue from corporations, as compared to only 2.1 per cent in the United States.[22] This has made it difficult to claim a tax advantage for Japanese industry.

Indeed, when Ando and Auerbach (1988a) computed after-tax earnings/price ratios and after-tax return-to-capital rates, they found that "it is Japanese, not American, firms that are taxed more heavily on their real incomes." They registered two possible qualifications. First, one would prefer to look at the marginal effective tax rates that are relevant to the firm's decision whether to invest, rather than the average tax rate. They noted that such measures were unavailable for Japan. Second, their calculations apply to the unlevered firm; but a corporation derives tax advantages from borrowing since interest payments are tax-deductible and one might expect these advantages to be larger for Japanese firms (both because they have had higher debt/equity ratios until recently and because the corporate tax rate that they are deducting against was higher). But Ando and Auerbach computed an upper bound on this tax advantage, and claimed that it was very small. Thus they felt able to "rule out" the claim that the corporate tax system gave Japanese firms a cost-of-capital advantage. Noguchi (1985), taking into account the advantages of borrowing, also concluded that the tax burden was higher on Japanese, not U.S., corporations.

Other authors have ascribed more importance to the tax advantages of borrowing in Japan. Hatsopoulos and Brooks (1987), for example, emphasized that the definition of tax-deductible borrowing is more permissive in the Japanese tax code than in the American.

Bernheim and Shoven (1986) disputed the prevailing approach in public finance of presupposing that the (pre-tax) real interest rate must be constant across countries, in light of the observed failure of this condition. They first computed the after-tax cost of capital under the 1980 tax codes, using the actual interest rates and inflation rates that held on average for the 1970s (which entails assuming a U.S.-Japan real interest differential of 1.5 per cent). They found a smaller tax wedge on capital in Japan than the United States, with the result that the after-tax cost of capital in Japan was negative.[23] They attributed this result to the greater importance of interest payments in Japan.

Bernheim and Shoven then repeated the computations for 1985 tax codes, using the actual interest and inflation rates for the early 1980s. Despite the adoption of accelerated depreciation allowances in the U.S. tax code in 1981, the estimated U.S. cost of capital rose substantially in the 1980s, as a result particularly of the much higher real interest rate (5.0 per cent, as compared to 2.0 per cent in the 1970s). The real interest rate was higher in Japan as well, but there remained a substantial difference in the after-tax costs of capital in 1985 (5.5 for the U.S. versus 2.8 for Japan).

The central message of Bernheim and Shoven was that variation in real interest rates tends to dwarf variation in corporate tax laws as determinants of the cost of capital. They subsumed in this message the changes in the 1986 tax reform (including the removal of the investment tax credit that had been increased in 1981), which was under debate at the time that they were writing. Takenaka (1986) concluded that the impact of the investment tax credit on Japanese investment was negligible. Fukao (1988, 339-341) found a less favorable tax wedge (less negative) for Japan than the United States during the period 1981-84, but found that the combination of the 1986 U.S. tax reform and lower inflation rates brought the post-1986 tax wedge in the United States very close to that in Japan.

In December 1988, the Japanese Diet approved a tax reform which had been long sought by the ruling Liberal Democratic Party. The reform, among other things, cut the Japanese corporate tax rate from 42 per cent[24] to 37 1/2 per cent (with the full cut not effective until 1990). This left the tax rate only slightly higher than the current rates in the United States (34 per cent) or the United Kingdom (35 per cent). When state and local taxes on corporations are added in, the Japanese rate is about 50 per cent and the U.S. rate about 40 per cent. (These numbers are taken from Shoven, 1988.) One of several motives for the Japanese tax reform is that the Ministry of Finance fears that, in the absence of international harmonization of corporate tax rates, business would increasingly be able to find ways to arbitrage across tax jurisdictions.

Shoven (1989) updated his calculations of the effective tax rates on corporate investment. He found that the effective tax rate on investments in Japan was up sharply to 32 per cent in 1988 (as compared to 5 per cent in 1980). Part of the reason was the tax reform: in Shoven's calculations—unlike Ando and Auerbach's—the high *average* corporate tax rate in Japan worked to reduce the effective *marginal* tax rate on new investment, because it increased the value to the corporation of borrowing to finance the investment and deducting the interest payments from its taxable income. He thus estimated that the reduction in the average corporate tax rate in itself raised the effective tax rate 9 percentage points.

The major reason for the increase in the marginal effective tax rate on investment was not the tax reform, however, but rather the sharp decline in expected inflation relative to the 1970s. This decline was estimated to have raised the effective tax rate by 23 percentage points. The fall in the inflation rate in Japan (from 9% in the 1970s to 1%) means that the favorable distortion caused by the tax-deductibility of nominal interest payments was reduced. This left the effective Japanese tax rate still somewhat below the U.S. rate, which was at 41 per cent in 1988 (up from 29 per cent before the Tax Reform Act of 1986).

It is possible that the moderate tax advantage that remained in Shoven's numbers did not adequately take into account the downward trend in the Japanese reliance on debt,[25] and that by now little is left of the Japanese tax advantage. Ando and Auerbach (1988a, 1988b) dismissed the importance in this context of taxes altogether. Bernheim and Shoven (1986, p.3) concluded that "under prevailing tax systems, differences in the cost of capital between countries are largely attributable to differences in domestic credit market conditions, rather than to taxes."

Since the time that these papers were written, the difference in tax treatment between the two countries has, if anything, narrowed further. The Japanese tax reforms that took effect in April of 1988 and April of 1989 raised the tax rate on Japanese saving in a number of ways.[26] Iwata and Yoshida (1987) calculated that the abolition of the pro-saving bias in the (then-proposed) reforms would increase the total tax wedge in Japan, and thereby narrow the differential in the corporate cost of capital vis-à-vis the United States, despite the accompanying reductions in Japanese corporate taxes. (They, unlike Shoven, found that the latter work to reduce the after-tax cost of capital in Japan.)

If the public finance experts think that taxes are of at best second-order importance in comparing the cost of capital between the U.S. and Japan—or that the difference has, if anything, gone *against* Japanese corporations—why should an international economist disagree?

Speculative Bubbles

There is the serious possibility of a speculative bubble in the 1980s, to explain the price of land, the price of equity, or both. In surveys of institutional investors conducted by Shiller, Kon-ya and Tsutsui (1991b) in mid-1989, late 1989, and early 1990, many respondents chose the statement, "Stock prices in Japan, when compared with measures of true fundamental value or sensible investment value, are too high." (In August 1990, when the Japanese market fell precipitously, the percentage of respondents finding the market "too low" rose sharply, and the percentage finding it "too high" fell.)[27]

It is sometimes argued that special institutional features of the Japanese stock market, such as the dominance of trading by the big four security firms and administrative guidance by the Ministry of Finance,[28] keep prices artificially high. It has been argued, for example, that such features might explain why the Japanese market "was not allowed" to fall as far in the crash of October 1987 as other countries' markets.[29] From a 1989 survey of 139 Japanese institutional investors, Shiller, Kon-ya and Tsutsui (1991a, pp. 12-13) report that 68 per cent agreed with the statement "The Ministry of Finance will take steps to assure that stock prices in Japan will not lose too much of their value in another crash," while only 12 per cent disagreed.[30]

What means does the Japanese government have to control the stock market, aside from monetary policy? Hardouvelis and Peristiani (1989, p. 19) found that "Margin requirements in Japan have proved to be an effective tool of controlling wild gyrations in stock prices." Hardouvelis and Peristiani (1990, p. 27) also found that "margin policy in Japan has been useful even during the 1980s, a period when Japanese capital markets were increasingly deregulated." But it is not clear that adjustment of margin requirements has helped to stabilize the stock market in the 1990-92 decline.

Financial economists have not yet been able to construct good models of what gets speculative bubbles started, or what causes them to collapse. We do not even have much idea whether bubbles are more or less likely in perfectly competitive "efficient" markets than in markets where trading is characterized by turnover taxes, larger transactions costs, oligopolistic market-makers, and government intervention (all of which characteristics are attributed to Japanese stock markets).[31] Amihud and Mendelson (1992) find that such aspects of the Japanese stock market as the securities transfer tax and fixed commission rates, by raising transactions costs and reducing liquidity, artificially *depress* the level of the market.

In 1990–92, the Japanese stock market lost half its value. At first consideration, this plunge could be interpreted as clear evidence that the run-up of prices in the late 1980s was indeed a speculative bubble. Unfortunately for this view, the macroeconomic fundamentals changed dramatically at the same time. A new Bank of Japan governor, less enthusiastic about buying dollars to support the U.S. currency than some others in the Japanese government and more intent on fighting inflation, began to tighten Japanese monetary policy in the second half of 1989, raising real interest rates to a sharply higher level in 1990. Notice from Figure 9–1 that the long-term real interest differential vis-à-vis the United States vanished at the end of 1989. The Japanese stock market fell sharply at the beginning of 1990, presumably as a result of the increase in interest rates, and fell again in August, presumably as a result of the beginning of the Kuwait crisis. It then fell a third time in the Spring of 1992. Before we attribute the 1980s ascent in Japan's equity (and land) prices to a speculative bubble, we should consider the possibility that the cycle can be explained by interest rates.

We can try some simple calculations to see if the changes in macroeconomic fundamentals can explain the decline of the Japanese stockmarket between late 1989 and the end of 1990. The calculations use monthly survey data collected from a sample of banks, multinational corporations by *Currency Forecaster's Digest* of White Plains, New York.

The Japanese 10-year real interest rate is estimated to have been 2.6 per cent in September 1989, and the 10-year expected rate of economic growth to have been 3.7 per cent. One is tempted to take the difference $r - g$ as an estimate of $r_e - g_e$ and see if it equals the ratio of earnings to prices. But the difference, –1.1, is less than zero, and would thus apparently be capable of explaining any P/E ratio, no matter how high. Clearly the real interest rate must underestimate the required rate of return on capital—presumably due to a risk premium of the sort discussed above in the section on price/earnings ratios—or else the GNP growth rate must overestimate the rate of growth of earnings.[32]

The comparable calculations for the United States show that the differential between the real interest rate and the expected growth rate was 0.7 per cent in September 1989. The French and Poterba (1991) figures, after adjustment of earnings, show that the U.S. E/P ratio exceeded the Japanese E/P ratio by about .044 in 1989. Thus at the end of the 1980s there was an apparent "overvaluation" of the Japanese stock and land markets that could be attributed either to (1) a speculative bubble, or (2) a higher equity risk premium for the United States than for Japan, or some other source of bias in $r - g$ (as an estimate of the difference between the relevant discount and growth rates) that is greater for the United States.

Let us consider the second hypothesis, and assume that the difference in risk premiums (or other source of bias) between the two countries remained the same at the end of 1990 as in late 1989: about 2.6 per cent if adjusted figures are used (3.6 per cent with unadjusted earnings). Is the 1990 increase in Japanese real interest rates capable of explaining the collapse of the Japanese market? French and Poterba's figures show that the international difference in E/P ratios fell by .025 in 1990 if adjusted figures are used (.013 with unadjusted figures). Calculations in Frankel (1991, Table 3) suggest that the increase in real interest rates in Japan (1.3 %) can explain a large fraction, but not all, of the decline in the stock market in 1990 vis-à-vis the United States. It would seem to follow that there is not necessarily a need for recourse to the hypothesis of a burst speculative bubble. Suzuki (1991, p. 10–11) comes to this conclusion.

It should be noted that it is the intrinsic nature of such calculations that nearly-inconsequential changes in the computed macroeconomic fundamentals are apparently capable of "explaining" large changes in the stock market. Perhaps the appropriately-balanced judgment would conclude that there may have been a bubble component in the late 1980s, coming on top of a rise in the stock market that occurred for fundamental reasons, and point out that the decline was deliberately triggered by the authorities, by raising interest rates in order to head off a still-larger bubble.

What are the implications of the 1990 developments for the cost of capital question? The difference in real interest rates between the United States and Japan has disappeared completely. As of mid-1992 there is probably now little left also of the difference in P/E ratios once the accounting adjustments are made to Japanese earnings.[33] Some may continue to believe that the standard weighted average of debt and equity is not relevant for Japan because many corporations still get much of their financing from main banks. This point is developed in the last part of this chapter. Even in the case of bank borrowing, however, there is reason to think that the era of cheap finance may be over. Japanese banking was itself the industry hardest-hit in the 1990 stock market collapse, and is now under pressure to restrict lending in order to meet stringent new international standards for capital adequacy.[34]

In short, though by most measures the cost of finance in the 1980s was lower in Japan than in the United States, this appears no longer to be the case. Whether this is cause for rejoicing among American businessmen is another question. Given the high degree of international integration that has taken place over the last ten years, fluctuations in saving are reflected in capital flows between Japan and the rest of the world as easily as in domestic investment. In other words, corporate borrowers in Japan are not the only ones to feel the effect of a decreased availability of Japanese savings; borrowers in the United States and elsewhere in the 1990s will feel it as well.

III. DETERMINANTS OF THE REAL INTEREST RATE

If one thinks of the real interest rate as equilibrating the various sources and uses of funds, then a low real interest rate in the 1970s and 1980s would be explained by some combination of four factors: a high corporate saving rate net of investment, a high public saving rate, a high household saving rate, or a high availability of savings from abroad. Each factor probably has played a role at one time or another in Japan.

We know that the government was a source of cheap capital for many firms in the 1950s and 1960s, but that it went sharply into deficit and became a big *user* of funds after 1973. The Ministry of Finance took pains to cut the government budget deficit in the early 1980s, but the deficit has nevertheless been relatively high throughout the post-1973 period, and thus cannot explain a low real interest rate during this period.

The corporate sector was in deficit in the postwar period until the first oil shock. We know that the corporate deficit has been sharply lower since then,[35] as the result of a fall-off in the previously-high level of investment, which helps explain cheap capital after 1973. But the high Japanese household saving rate is the factor most often cited as applying throughout the period.

The Japanese household saving rate is among the highest of industrialized countries: saving (expressed net of depreciation) averaged 16.0 per cent of disposable income over the period 1980–89. By comparison, net saving in the United States averaged only 6.0 per cent of disposable income over the same period. The question of why the saving rate is so high in Japan is another major topic in itself. Horioka (1990) offers a comprehensive survey. Section III.A of Frankel (1991) offers a condensed survey, including some measurement issues and an enumeration of six arguments that have been suggested to explain the high saving rate, though it must be admitted that none of them is entirely convincing.

Even if the Japanese level of household saving were to be reduced toward that in Western countries, for example by a tax reform or a land-use reform, there is a serious further question as to whether such a change would lower the Japanese real interest rate or the cost of capital to firms. If capital is perfectly mobile internationally, it is argued, then a decline in national saving should not put any upward pressure on the rate of return within Japan, but rather should be entirely offset by increased borrowing from abroad (and decreased lending) at an unchanged rate of return. However it is fairly clear that such a decrease in saving *would* reduce the Japanese current account surplus—and all the more so if capital is highly mobile—which is what many Americans want.

Feldstein and Horioka (1980) initiated what has proven to be a long-lasting debate by observing that changes in countries' rates of national saving in fact had large effects on their rates of investment, and interpreting the finding as evidence of low capital mobility. The paper was subjected to many econometric attacks, but the basic results seemed to hold up. The "saving-retention" coefficient did finally begin to decline in the 1980s however, according to the latest studies: Feldstein and Bacchetta (1989) and Frankel (1991a). (The latter paper contains 65 references on the subject, many of them demonstrations that one can have a high correlation between saving and investment despite perfect capital mobility.)

It is possible to test the international equalization of rates of return more directly. Many studies have documented the failure of real interest rates to be equalized across countries,[36] seeming to confirm the Feldstein-Horioka results. We saw in the first section that the Japanese real interest rate was below the U.S. rate throughout the 1980s. But the Japanese government announced the removal of controls on international capital movements in 1979–80, and further liberalization measures in 1983–84, partly in response to pressure from the U.S.Treasury.[37] It is often argued that if capital markets are open, international arbitrage should eliminate real interest differentials. Is it possible that the announced Japanese liberalization has failed to be genuine or complete?

A number of studies have shown, using data on *covered* interest differentials, that the 1979–80 and 1983–84 liberalizations did indeed have the effects advertised.[38] By now covered interest parity holds as well for Japan (vis-à-vis the Eurodollar market) as it does for such major countries as Canada, Germany and the United Kingdom: the differential between the dollar interest rate and the interest rate on domestic currency is equal to the discount on the dollar in the forward exchange market. This finding suggests that Japan is highly integrated into world financial markets with respect to the movement of capital across national boundaries.

The finding still leaves open the possibility of differences associated with the *currency* in which an asset is denominated, as opposed to the *political* jurisdiction in which it is issued. For example, investors' expectations that the dollar may in the future depreciate against the yen in nominal terms almost certainly explain why the yen interest rate was less than the dollar interest rate in the 1980s.[39] Similarly, expectations that the dollar may depreciate against the yen in *real* terms may explain why the yen *real* interest rate was less than the dollar real interest rate. In that case, the original Feldstein-Horioka view is correct—real interest rates are not necessarily equalized internationally and changes in saving (even if truly exogenous) need not be offset by borrowing from abroad and thus may be heavily reflected as changes in investment—and yet the explanation may be the imperfect international integration of goods markets that allows failures of purchasing power parity, rather than imperfect international integration of financial markets. If there is no way of arbitraging directly among countries' goods or among their plant and equipment, and if plant and equipment are imperfect substitutes for bonds *within* each country, then perfect international arbitrage among countries' bonds is not sufficient to equalize real rates of return among countries' plant and equipment.

It is quite likely that, by the 1980s, investors had come to hold an expectation of future yen appreciation. The issue is discussed elsewhere.[40] One piece of evidence is survey data on investors' forecasts.[41]

We have argued that, even if Japanese corporations are now no more highly levered than American corporations, and even if international arbitrage now equates the Japanese and foreign nominal interest rates (when expressed in a common currency), the Japanese real interest rate could still lie below the foreign rate. A real interest differential in the 1980s—whatever its source—could in turn help explain high average price/earnings ratios in the Japanese stock market, high price/rental ratios in the Japanese land market, and a lower cost of capital to some Japanese firms.[42]

The argument about the low real interest rate might seem to apply to the past in Japan as much as, or more than, to the 1980s. Similarly, the argument that the expected rate of real economic growth in Japan is high applies to the past as much as, or more than, to the 1980s. How can one explain that price/earnings ratios and price/rental ratios were not also high in the past, i.e., that they rose sharply in the 1980s? We address this question in the course of the next part of the chapter.

IV. MAIN BANK RELATIONSHIPS, VS. SECURITIES MARKETS

The standard formula for the price/earnings ratio and the price/rental ratio, $1/(r - g)$, assumes that r, the real interest rate (or a required rate of return equal to the real interest rate marked up by a risk premium), is relevant for discounting expected future returns. This assumption is appropriate for economies where corporate finance is oriented around a unified central market, i.e., a common pool of funds into which most savers deposit and from which most investors draw off.[43] This description applies relatively well to the United States, and it applies increasingly to Japan today. But it did not apply very well to Japan in the 1970s, and still less so in the 1960s, as Meerschwam (1989) explains at greater length. In terms used by Zysman (1983), Japan has a "credit-based" financial system such as Germany and France have, rather than a "capital market-based" financial system such as the United States and the United Kingdom have.[44]

The existence of lending by government agencies to favored firms in favored industries at subsidized rates, and the artificial "repression" of other interest rates through regulation and administrative guidance, have always been major ways that Japanese corporations have been thought to have an "unfair" cost-of-capital advantage in the past. Twelve government financial institutions as recently as 1980 supplied 17 per cent of funds for investment in plant and equipment—of which the Japan Development Bank and the Small Business Finance Corporation were particularly notable in channeling subsidized investment funds to selected industries (Lee, 1988, p. 25–36). The general low-interest rate policy of the government before 1973 was explicit.[45]

Equally familiar is the claim that large corporations or keiretsu take profits from one activity and cross-subsidize investment in another.[46] But it has often been unclear why Japanese industry should want to do this. If the investment is expected to be profitable in the long run, then it should be undertaken in a market-oriented financial system such as the United States, with the investment funded by borrowing in the market if necessary, as readily as under the Japanese system.

How the Japanese System Has Avoided Information and Incentive Problems

Recent theoretical developments have helped us understand better how the cost of internal finance can be less than the cost of external finance.[47] One route is asymmetric information between the firm's managers and the typical stockholder or bondholder in the market regarding the rate of return on an investment. Another route is incentive or "agency" problems.

"Internal finance" is the corporation's financing of an investment out of retained earnings (or out of depreciation charges), as opposed to financing at market rates by borrowing from a bank or issuing securities.[48] Retained earnings explain why the Japanese cost of capital was low in the 1970s. When the Japanese economic growth rate fell off with the oil shock of 1973, the number of profitable investment projects fell relative to the supply of funds available. (In the national savings identity, the offset to the increase in the saving-investment balance of the corporate sector was primarily a large increase in the government budget deficit in the 1970s, followed by a large increase in the current account surplus in the 1980s.) In other words, since 1973 firms have been able to finance investments out of retained earnings to a much greater extent than previously.[49] Retained earnings can be a cheaper source of financing than issuing corporate debt or equity, because they are not penalized by problems of incomplete information or incentive incompatibility.

It can be argued that, in Japan, borrowing by a firm from its main bank under a long-term relationship avoids incentive and information problems as effectively as does internal finance. The reasoning is that the main bank, like a large shareholder—which, in fact, it often is—can keep close tabs on what goes on inside the firm, thus largely obviating the information and incentive problems.[50] Japanese financial institutions (including not just banks, but also life insurance companies and other institutional investors), unlike their U.S. counterparts, are allowed to take large debt *and* equity positions in the same firm. Prowse (1989) and Kim (1992) argue that this difference constitutes in itself a way that the Japanese system is better able to circumvent agency problems.[51]

Hodder (1988b) concludes that the advantages of "lender monitoring" are key, and that they may explain why studies like Ando and Auerbach (1988b) find that the cost of capital is lower in Japan than the United States. His argument is that the advantages of lender monitoring may show up in part as low reported earnings/price ratios because banks receive payments for their services in the form of "compensating balances" and transactions fees, which come out of reported corporate earnings, rather than in the form of interest payments.[52]

Aoki (1990, pp. 17-18) describes an equilibrium whereby a main bank preserves its reputation as a reliable monitor of firms by voluntarily foregoing the priority of its claims in the process of reorganization or liquidation of a troubled client firm. Aoki (1992) suggests that this equilibrium is delicate, and is only preserved by (implicit) Ministry of Finance regulation. The Ministry keeps the list of eligible banks (primarily 12 city banks) from changing, regulates them as a natural monopoly, and even stands ready to punish a main bank that defects from the cooperative equilibrium (by withholding licenses for branch office openings).

Empirical evidence in support of the proposition that internal and main-bank finance are cheaper than external or market finance is offered by some recent microeconomic studies of the determinants of firm investment. The new theories of information and incentive problems now provide the desired rigorous theoretical basis for including cash flow in econometric equations to explain business fixed investment, rather than just the real interest rate or Tobin's Q.[53]. Fazzari, Hubbard and Petersen (1988) have recently estimated regression equations for investment on a cross-section of U.S. firms. They distinguish firms that pay low dividends, which they assume are liquidity-constrained, from others. They show that cash flow is a more important determinant of investment in the former group, which they interpret as evidence in favor of the internal-finance hypothesis. (Tobin's Q, the ratio of the market price of equity to replacement cost, is also included as an explanatory variable, to capture expectations of the return to investment.) One can interpret such findings as analogous to the Feldstein-Horioka result: just as a high correlation of national saving and investment across countries suggests that there may exist some barriers that separate individual countries from the worldwide capital market, so does high correlation of corporate saving and investment across firms suggest that there may exist barriers that separate individual firms from the nationwide capital market.

Hoshi, Kashyap and Sharfstein (1989a) apply a similar methodology to Japan, where the segregation of firms can be more definitively accomplished. They break down a sample into two groups. One consists of 121 "affiliated" firms, those with ties to large banks (typically a main bank) that are part of its keiretsu. The other consists of 25 "independent" firms, without close links to any particular bank. They find that among the independent firms, cash flow positively affects investment (and Tobin's Q does not), while among the affiliated firms cash flow has no significant effect (while Q does have an effect).[54] The conclusion is that the first group faces a barrier between the cost of financing investment out of retained earnings and the cost of borrowing, like American firms do, while the latter can borrow from their affiliated banks as easily as financing out of retained earnings. The authors conclude that one possible implication is that "the institutional arrangements in Japan may offer Japanese firms an important competitive advantage (p. 24)."

The Loosening of the System and the Shift Toward Market Finance

The hypothesis that internal and indirect finance (especially from the main bank) is cheaper than direct or market finance can thus support the claim that the true cost of capital to Japanese corporations (at least those that are members of keiretsu) has been low in the past. But established banking relationships have begun to break down in Japan and the market has begun to take their place, as corporations begin to use banks less and bond markets more, a process that accelerated in the 1980s as the result of international liberalization as well as domestic deregulation.[55] In the 1970s, the non-financial corporate sector issued stock and marketable debt securities on a scale that averaged only 12.8 per cent of total outside financing including borrowings from banks; in 1987 that ratio increased to 30.1 per cent, as many firms found they could raise funds more easily or more cheaply on the open market (Bisignano, 1990, p. 41 and Table 10).

But if the relevant cost of issuing debt was higher in the more market-oriented 1980s than it was in the past era of cheap bank finance, this raises some difficult questions. The first question, which we now consider, is how one explains the fact that price/earnings and price/rental ratios were lower in previous decades than in the late 1980s.[56] The second, why firms would voluntarily abandon advantageous banking arrangements, is addressed subsequently.

We must ask who would have had the opportunity to arbitrage between the low "cost of capital" and the high expected future return to holding land or equities. For those who had the opportunity to buy land, plant and equipment, or equity, the *opportunity cost* of funds was high, a number more like the observed rate of return on equity than like the observed interest rate or the still lower cost of internal finance.[57] The individual small investor did not have such opportunities; he was given little alternative to depositing his savings in a low-interest-rate account.[58] The same was to a certain extent true of institutional investors such as pension funds and insurance companies, and in any case the pool of available savings in such institutions was far smaller than in the 1980s. A corporation that was favored with access to cheap loans from the government or from its main bank was not generally free to use those funds to "speculate" in land or in the shares of other corporations. Nor was the firm allowed to buy back its own shares, when it should have had plenty of profitable new projects in which to invest.[59] Thus the arbitrage between the interest rate and real assets that we take for granted in a market-oriented system was not entirely relevant in the earlier period.

As noted, firms have begun to rely less on banks for their financing, and more on marketplace borrowing, due in large part to deregulation and internationalization. The most important liberalizations include: (1) the removal of ceilings on interest rates after 1978 (in response to growing reluctance on the part of banks to absorb growing quantities of government debt at artificially low interest rates), (2) the switch to a presumption that firms were allowed to sell bonds to foreign residents (as part of the Foreign Exchange Law Reform) in 1980, (3) the legalization of warrant bonds in 1981, (4) the legalization of non-collateralized bonds for sufficiently safe corporations beginning in 1983, and (5) the liberalization of issues of Euro-yen bonds as part of the Yen/Dollar negotiations between the Ministry of Finance and the U.S. Treasury in 1984. More recent measures taken pursuant to the Yen/Dollar Agreement include: (6) establishment of new short-term financial markets (in yen-denominated banker's acceptances, June 1985,[60] short-term bonds, November 1986, and commercial paper, November 1987), (7) further liberalization regarding the Euromarket (such as allowing foreign companies to lead-manage Eurobond issues in December 1986, and introducing rating systems for Eurobonds in 1987), (8) establishment of an offshore market in Japan (December 1986), (9) the admission of major American securities companies to the Tokyo Stock Exchange (approximately 22 by the end of 1987), and (10) inclusion of foreign firms in the syndicate through which the Japanese government sells its bonds and in the trust business (9 banks authorized after October 1985). In addition, (11) the Ministry of Finance liberalized restrictions on what share of their portfolios Japanese insurance companies and trust banks could hold in the form of foreign securities (in 1986 and 1987).[61]

Even for those steps that represent domestic innovation or deregulation as opposed to international liberalization, foreigners have been an important driving force. There has been both direct political pressure on the Japanese government from foreign governments and competitive pressures on Japanese financial institutions from the activities of foreign rivals.[62]

By 1989 Japanese bond issues in the Euro-yen market, which had been growing rapidly for ten years, reached 40 per cent of total public corporate issues.[63] Often the Eurobonds issued by Japanese corporations, particularly convertible and warrant issues, were ultimately acquired by *Japanese* residents. Hale (1990, p.5) estimates that 60 to 70 per cent of Japanese corporate bonds issued in the Euromarket in 1989 were bought by Japanese investors. In this way internationalization facilitated an end-run around remaining domestic Japanese rigidities, and made Japanese finance more competitive, even when neither the borrower nor the lender was foreign. The transactions costs that remained in Japanese financial markets were large enough to be exploited by major corporations who took money raised at a low interest rate offshore and invested it in other financial instruments, an example of earning profits by "zaiteku" or financial engineering.[64] Aoki and Sheard (1992, p. 7) identify the transactions costs leading to Eurobond issues: still-restrictive collateral requirements on domestic bond issues.

In a follow-up to their first paper, Hoshi, Kashyap and Sharfstein (1990b) address the gradual weakening of the links between banks and affiliated firms that has been taking place in Japan. Choosing 1983 as the first year in which the effects of deregulation were fully felt, they begin with their sample of firms that had close banking ties during the period 1977-1982, and divide it into a sub-sample who shifted emphasis thereafter from bank-borrowing to direct market finance, and a sub-sample who continued to rely primarily on their banks. They find that the former group developed a strong sensitivity of investment to cash flow after 1983, while the latter group did not. This constitutes further evidence that bank-borrowing in Japan obviates some of the usual costs of external financing.

Is the Shift to Market Finance Good or Bad?

Some have surmised that if public policy and the main-bank system have kept the cost of capital artificially low in Japan in the past, the deregulation and internationalization of Japanese financial markets must now have eliminated that advantage. Even if we could be confident that the Japanese cost of capital has been raised in this manner, that would still leave open the question of whether or not the traditional system produced a greater level of economic efficiency for the economy overall. On the one hand, any way of obviating information or incentive problems must represent a gain. On the other hand, the exclusion of certain firms and certain industries from the privileges of cheaper financing is only beneficial if there exists some decision-making mechanism superior to the market to decide who is worthy of inclusion and who is not, a debatable proposition.

It is also possible that the previous system of denying Japanese savers, banks, and taxpayers an opportunity to earn an equilibrium rate of return on their savings, even if inefficient in the economists' sense that it failed to maximize intertemporal welfare, nevertheless produced a high level of investment. Zielinski and Holloway (1991, p. 152) speak of "chronic overinvestment in plant and equipment" resulting from cheap capital, at the expense of the Japanese public. Such a proposition would be consistent with the legendary Japanese corporate emphasis on maximizing market share at the short-run expense of current profits.[65] Blinder (1991) also argues that Japanese corporations maximize growth rather than profits, and includes among the implications the proposition that Japanese firms act *as if* they have a lower cost of capital than American firms. Horiuchi (1990, p.26) attributes a corporate emphasis on growth rather than shareholder profits to managers maximizing their own personal objectives, protected from the sort of merger-and-acquisition activity that disciplines managers under the U.S. system.

An alternative line of argument is that it is the U.S. system that is inefficient. Krugman, Hatsopoulos and Summers (1988) argue that the U.S. market system gives rise to an inefficiently low level of investment because of excessive concern with short-term profits and capital gains, at the expense of longer-term investment opportunities. McKinnon (1989) argues that excessively short investment horizons in the United States (in contrast to Japan) are attributable to high interest rates, which are in turn attributable to the risk of dollar depreciation against the yen under the floating exchange rate system.[66] If it is the U.S. system that is inefficient, it would appear to follow that American pressure on Japan to speed financial liberalization constitutes an effort to "drag the Japanese down to the U.S. level." Kaplan (1992), on the other hand, examines rewards to Japanese and American managers, as reflected in executive turnover rates and compensation, and finds no significant differences in their degrees of sensitivity to performance measures such as the prices of their stocks.

In any case, a puzzle remains. If the effective cost of capital under the traditional system is less than the market interest rate under the new system, why are Japanese firms voluntarily giving up their advantageous main-banking relationships for the difficulties of the marketplace? Hodder (1988b) concludes that if firms are leaving their main bank relationships, it must be because it is advantageous to do so, though he also concludes that it must have been advantageous for them to enter into these relationships in the first place.

Hoshi, Kashyap and Sharfstein (1990a) suggest a possible explanation to the paradox: there are hidden costs to the system of bank monitoring, and a cheaper way of overcoming the information and incentive obstacles to borrowing—which is available only to older, well-established, successful firms—is to take advantage of the firm's reputation by issuing highly-rated bonds. It is noteworthy that agencies that rate the creditworthiness of corporations (the analogues of Moody's or Standard and Poor's) did not develop in Japan until recently. In yet another paper, Hoshi, Kashyap and Sharfstein (1991) put forth the hypothesis that older, more successful, firms that have "reputational capital" at stake are the ones who issue bonds rather than borrowing from banks. They claim supporting evidence in a finding that Japanese firms with more "collateralizable assets" in place seem to have moved away from banks during the period of deregulation.[67]

Perhaps national financial systems pass through a life cycle. In Stage 1, business investment is financed out of family savings or—in a country where the government plays a more *dirigiste* role—by official loans. In Stage 2, financial intermediation by investment banks allows a more effective channeling of funds from savers to business. U.S. firms relied on investment banks for much of their finance a century ago.[68] In Stage 3, well-established corporations find that it is more efficient still to disintermediate. They switch from reliance on bank loans to issuing securities directly in developed financial markets, where a corporation with a good reputation and credit-rating can obtain capital cheaply.

There are alternatives to the hypothesis that the corporate migration in Japan away from reliance on banking relationships is the manifestation of newly-exploitable reputations. It is possible that the trend is not even desirable from the viewpoint of the well-established firms. One approach would be to model cooperation between a firm and its main bank as an equilibrium which is only sustainable in a repeated game if the relevant discount rate is sufficiently low. There is a temptation in each period for defection from the relationship: when the corporation is experiencing bad times, the bank will be tempted to defect, and when the corporation is experiencing good times it will be tempted to defect. Only if the discount rate is low will the prospective future benefits of continuing the relationship (the avoidance of information problems via monitoring) be sufficiently important to sustain the cooperation. It could then be argued that, because the interest rate has in the past been lower in Japan than in the United States, it has been easier to sustain such cooperative relationships. But now that the relevant interest rate in Japan has risen to the world level, it is harder to sustain such cooperation, and long-term banking relationships are coming apart.

It may not be possible for trust and long-term relationships to survive in an environment where new-comers deal only in explicit contracts. Rajan (1991) develops a model with precisely this property. In this model, the private information that a bank obtains with regard to a firm's sequence of investment projects gives the bank some monopoly power, which it is able to exploit by extracting rents from the firm in the terms of short-term loans. When an armslength bond market is then introduced, some firms will switch their financing to it (notwithstanding the problem that investors lack information about the firm) in order to get out from the bank's clutches. Even though such firms find it in their private interest to switch, the result may be a net loss in efficiency for the economy, due to the loss of banks' monitoring role. It is likely that some firms will gain from a switch to a market system and others lose. Wells and Frankel (1993) attempt to model the process whereby entrepreneurs, whose investment was successfully financed before financial deregulation, can fall victim to credit-rationing in the new, more competitive equilibrium.

Meerschwam (1990, pp. 6-7) acknowledges the possibility that "insiders," those corporations with access to preferentially priced funds may have in the past had an advantage over "outsiders," and that this advantage was lost when the latter gained access to the escape route of borrowing abroad. If the outsiders had previously been subsidizing the insiders, their escape from the closed system may have driven up the cost of capital for the former.[69]

Finally, an additional hypothesis is that the fundamental structure of the system of main bank relationships has not in fact changed radically after all. Aoki (1992) and Aoki and Sheard (1992) argue essentially that firms which prosper are able to move up a hierarchy from less-desirable financial states into better ones, where they are less dependent on their main banks, but that the same main bank monitoring system prevails throughout. When many firms were able to decrease their bank borrowing in the 1980s, or to reduce the frequency with which they were induced to accept managers from their main bank,[70] this was an indication that times were good, not that the fundamental structure had changed. Hsieh and Wells (1992) offer evidence that firms' reliance on bank loans is negatively related to performance (profitability and growth rates). The key point, in the view of Aoki and Sheard, is that the main bank remains the device to discipline the firm (by takeover of management or liquidation) in the event that it falls into a critical state in the hierarchy, and that the existence of this hierarchy provides incentives to the team of managers and workers.

This hypothesis deserves particularly serious consideration in light of the recent reaction to the 1990–92 collapse of the stock market and the onset of a Japanese recession. New equity issues fell 48 per cent in the fiscal year ended March 1992, and Eurobond issues have also fallen dramatically. Some firms have returned to bank borrowing in place of securities issues. Aoki and Sheard would presumably view this development as an example of firms moving back down the hierarchy when times are bad. Perhaps the apparent shift away from banks in the late 1980s was a transitory deviation, in part an artifact of the stock market bubble, rather than a longer-lasting trend.

V. CONCLUSIONS

The overall conclusions that emerge from the literature of the 1980s on the cost of capital may be summarized as follows. (1) required rates of return were lower in Japan than in the United States. (2) Two aspects of this difference were lower real interest rates and lower required returns on equity. (3) Low real interest rates and high expected growth rates can go far toward explaining the high *levels* of equity prices, but not the great *increases* of the 1980s. (4) The high Japanese saving rate was responsible for the low rates of return; Japanese tax policy plays no clear role. (5) The increased availability of funds that can be used for asset-market arbitrage allowed the great run-up in equity prices in the 1980s. (6) Financial liberalization narrowed cost-of-capital differences in the 1980s; now fluctuations in the availability of Japanese saving affects investment abroad almost as easily as at home. (7) Many believe that the measured cost of capital is less relevant in the post-war Japanese system to managers' decisions than are long-term banking relationships, which are thought to obviate problems of managers' incentives and imperfect information regarding projects, thus further easing the financing of investment. (8) In the 1980s, large successful corporations were able to move on to a stage where they could issue bonds more cheaply than borrowing from their banks, though this trend may have endangered the cooperative equilibrium between firms and their main banks.

Recent events suggest some additional conclusions. (9) Increases in interest rates and declines in the stock market in Japan during 1990-92 have left the cost of capital there approximately as high as in the United States. (10) Given the earlier international financial liberalization and integration, the 1990 increase in the cost of capital in Japan may hurt borrowers in the U.S. and elsewhere almost as much as Japanese corporate borrowers. (11) Japanese firms withdrew from the securities markets in 1990–92; the loosening of banking relationships that was widely reported in the late 1980s may turn out to have been in part transitory.

In the 1980s, the banking-relationships theory was not in competition with the cost-of-capital arguments: both pointed to ease of financing investment. Some argue that the banking relationships have gradually broken down over time, an argument that is appealing in that it parallels the trend observed in the cost of capital. Others argue that observed swings in the share of bank borrowing versus securities issues do not reflect fundamental long-term changes in the main-bank relationship, but only short-term fluctuations in firms' fortunes. This view has its own appeal, in that it can explain developments of the late 1980s and early 1990s as changes within a specified structure, rather than as postulated changes every few years in the structure itself. A verdict will have to wait until more evidence is available.

NOTES

1. Concise summaries are offered by Poterba (1991) and Frankel (1991c). Kester and Luehrman (1992) offer a skeptical survey, with a series of criticisms of the studies that purport to find a difference in the cost of capital.

2. E.g., Meerschwam (1989, 1990) and Hodder (1988b, 1990).
3. Early, highly influential, claims that Japanese firms had a cost-of-capital advantage over American competitors included Hatsopolous (1983) and Semiconductor Industry Association (1980).
4. For example, Hatsopoulos and Brooks (1986, 1987) and, especially, Hatsopoulos, Krugman, and Summers (1988). Lippens (1990) argues that a wide variety of estimates from different studies support the claim that U.S. industry labors under a higher cost of capital than Japanese industry.
5. The three-way breakdown was calculated by Friend and Tokutsu (1987), among others.
6. Bernheim and Shoven (1986) for the periods 1971-84, Lawler, Loopesko and Dudey (1988, 26) for the 1965-1988 period; Friend and Tokutsu over the period 1970-1984. Luehrman and Kester (1989) found no systematic difference in real interest rates.
7. McCauley and Zimmer (1989) correct observed interest rates for the cost of compensating balances, to obtain a comprehensive measure of borrowing costs.
8. References on the forces behind the flow of capital from Japan to the United States are given in Frankel (1988).
9. E.g., French and Poterba, 1989, p.40 .
10. Edited by Alan Teck, White Plains, N.Y.. I obtained this data by subscription by the Institute for International Economics. The reported data on inflation expectations come from surveys conducted every third month. Prior to June 1989, long-term forecasts of inflation are not available, so 12-month forecasts are used instead.
11. Other references include Abegglen (1985), Bisignano (1990, p. 38), Borio (1990, p. 26–31), Crum and Meerschwam (1987), Frost (1987, p. 41), Gerlach (1989, p. 153-54), Meerschwam (1989), McCauley and Zimmer (1989, p. 21) and Nakatani (1984).
12. Caves and Uekusa (1976, p.480) suggested that highly leveraged firms are more likely to collude, as a way to reduce risk. However Japanese firms are generally considered to be relatively competitive in their product markets (as opposed to factor markets). Gilson and Roe (1992), for example, see product-market competition as a more important discipline on Japanese firms than monitoring by main banks, and see it as an important difference between the Japanese and German systems, which others describe as similar.
13. The debt/equity ratio actually fell to half the U.S. level in an estimate for 1988 [according to French and Poterba, 1991 (p. 8 and Table 4), and Bisignano, 1990, Chart 3]. Others' figures show the Japanese ratio still above the U.S. level (e.g., Frost, 1987, p. 41, and McCauley and Zimmer, 1989, p. 13). Borio (1990, 8–11) also shows the Japanese debt/asset ratio still above the U.S. level as of 1987, even for the measure that uses market values (which shows greater convergence).
14. We save until later the argument that firms may have access to some funds that are cheaper than the expected rate of return on capital (that internal financing is cheaper than *either* the cost of debt or the cost of equity).
15. How does the use of Price/Earnings ratios bias the calculation, relative to a more correct calculation that would use Free Cash Flow, which subtracts off investment, in place of Earnings? More of earnings are thought to go to net investment in Japan than in the United States, in line with its higher growth rate. The implication is that the true equity cost of capital r_e was even lower in Japan than would appear from our attempt

in the next section to apply the capitalization formula to the P/E ratio.

16. Minimum dividend-payout rates were established in the early 1970s (Meerschwam, 1989).
17. E.g., Zielinski and Holloway (1991, p. 167).
18. This is the same direction of bias suggested in footnote 15.
19. When Ando and Auerbach applied a corresponding correction for their measure of total return to capital, on the other hand, they found that the median rate for Japan fell more than that for the U.S..
20. When Aron (1989) converted the Japanese P/E ratio to U.S. accounting practices, and adjusted for crossholding, he lowered it from a reported 49.6 in 1989 to 19.1 (compared to 13.5 in the United States).
21. Ueda (1990, p.357) found that the market value of corporate shares after 1983 surpassed the officially-reported value of corporate assets including land. But in the final version of his paper he did not rule out the possibility that land prices were a major factor in the rise in stock prices, in light of claims that the official land prices greatly understate true land values.
22. Shoven (1989). See also Noguchi (1985).
23. Consistent with the findings of Shoven and Tachibanaki (1988). Kikutani and Tachibanaki (1990, pp. 287–88) fine-tune the earlier calculations [particularly with regard to depreciation]; they conclude that the 1980 marginal tax rate on capital in Japan was again lower than in the United States, primarily due to the tax-advantage of debt. They also find the Japanese marginal tax rate to have been as low in 1961 as in 1980.
24. The tax rate on undistributed profits during the period 1984 to 1987 was 43.3 per cent. (Homma, Maeda and Hashimoto, 1986, p.14., and Homma, 1987, p. 21.) However, it had been lower in the 1950s and 1960s, ranging from 35 per cent to 40 per cent. (Homma et al., 1984, p.124, Table 2.39, and Shoven and Tachibanaki, 1988, Table 3.6.)
25. Recall the figures from French and Poterba that by 1988 the debt/equity ratio in Japan had fallen below that in the United States. Noguchi (1985, p. 9, 18) listed the fall in the debt/equity ratio as one of several reasons why the tax burden on Japanese investment increased in the late 1970s and early 1980s (though, like Ando and Auerbach, Noguchi thought that the Japanese burden had been higher than the U.S. burden all along). The most important of the reasons (as with Shoven) was the fall in the inflation rate.
26. The previously existing pro-saving bias in the Japanese tax system, compared to the American system, constituted part of the difference in "tax wedges" computed by Bernheim and Shoven (1986). Determinants of saving are surveyed in Part III of Frankel (1991a).
27. Interestingly, *American* respondents at all survey dates are far more pessimistic about the Japanese market than Japanese respondents. Shiller, Kon-ya and Tsutsui interpret this finding as support for the claim of French and Poterba (1990)—based on the observation that investors in each country each hold most of their portfolios in their own country's assets—that investors in each country expect the rate of return on their own stock market to be higher than on the other's.
28. The Ministry of Finance began to look after the stability of the Japanese stock market

after a crash in 1965. S. Takagi (1989) discussed the history and institutional features of the market.

29. Lawler, Loopesko and Dudey (1988, 31-33), Murphy (1989) and Zielinski and Holloway (1991, 71-74).
30. The Japanese respondents attribute their October 1987 crash to contemporaneous U.S. developments. But, like American respondents, they rate news of price movements themselves as a more important influence on their behavior than news regarding fundamentals.
31. Aggarwal, Rao and Hiraki (1990) found evidence in the Tokyo Stock Exchange that stocks with low P/E ratios had higher returns than stocks with high P/E ratios (as others have found in the United States).
32. As noted earlier, the capitalization formula does not strictly apply to P/E ratios, because the portion of earnings that are reinvested are not available as returns to the stockholder. (This just makes the gap between the discount rate—growth rate differential and the E/P ratio that much harder to explain.) One would be on firmer theoretical foundations to match up the calculations reported in this section to observations on the price/dividend ratio, for the case of stocks, or the price/rental ratio, for the case of land.
33. Hatsopoulos and Poterba (1991, Table 6) report adjusted P/E ratios up through 1990 (while adjusting accounting earnings in a way that they now regard as better than the adjustments made in French and Poterba, 1991). They conclude that the adjusted P/E ratio, even after the 1990 crash, is still higher in Japan than in the United States. But the difference is much smaller than it was during the period 1983-89, and it undoubtedly diminished further in 1992.
34. In 1988 Japan agreed with other major countries, through the Bank for International Settlements in Basel, to raise the minimum capital/asset ratios of its international banks to 8 per cent by 1993 (the same as other countries' international banks). Japanese banks were initially able to attain this ratio easily by issuing large amounts of equity on the booming stock market. But the 1990 stock market plunge put many of the banks back below the 8 per cent capital/asset ratio. Hale (1990) and Zielinski and Holloway (1991, pp. 179–88).
35. Indeed, Balassa and Noland (1988, p. 84) reported that the Japanese corporate sector was in surplus in the years 1974–77, although others showed only a declining deficit (where both financial and nonfinancial corporations were included; Lincoln, 1988, Table 3-2, pp. 76–77).
36. Glick (1987) and Glick and Hutchison (1990) examine real interest differentials among Pacific countries.
37. The story of the U.S. Treasury campaign for the liberalization of Japanese financial markets, which began in October 1983, is told in Frankel (1984).
38. Otani and Tiwari (1981), Frankel (1984, 1988) and Ito (1986).
39. The interest differential could in theory be explained by either of two terms (after the possibility of a covered interest differential, or political premium, has been eliminated), both of them associated with the currency: expected depreciation or an exchange risk premium. The possible exchange risk premium between the dollar and yen is examined by Fukao and Okuba (1984), Frankel and Froot (1987), Ito (1988), and Frankel (1988).

40. The section on long-term real appreciation of the yen in Frankel (1991b) attributes the 1950-1989 trend (which averaged in excess of 3.5 per cent per year) to a steady increase in the Japanese price of non-traded goods relative to traded goods.
41. By 1989, however, expectations of future yen appreciation according to surveys had disappeared. Survey data on the yen are used in Frankel and Froot (1987), Ito (1990), and Froot and Ito (1989).
42. One must note, however, that if "the" real interest rate was lower in Japan than the United States only because of an expected rate of real appreciation of the yen in terms of a basket of goods that includes non-traded goods, it can only explain high equity prices or a low cost of capital *within the nontraded goods sector*, or for the average across the entire economy. It cannot explain a low cost of capital for Japanese firms producing *traded* goods, which are the ones from whom American businessmen fear competition.
43. Note that this does not preclude some firms having projects with rates of return greater than the market rate or internal funding sources at costs less than the market rate; it requires only that the market rate be the marginal cost of funds for most firms.
44. Other cross-country studies of corporate finance structure include Mayer (1988) and Bisignano (1990).
45. For example, Tamura, 1987.
46. Abegglen and Stalk (1985) and Hodder and Tschoegl (1985).
47. For example, in the finance literature, Myers and Majluf (1984) and Jensen and Meckling (1976). The first focuses on information costs, the latter on incentive problems. For a concise statement of this literature, see Hubbard (1990).
48. More net financing of investment comes from retained earnings in the United States (and the United Kingdom) than in Japan and other countries with bank-oriented financial systems. Mayer (1988) argues that the absence of long-term banking relationships in the former countries is a handicap that forces corporations to rely on retained earnings.
49. Aoki (1984, p. 195, 219; 1988, pp. 99-138) examines the increased reliance on internal finance in the 1970s. He argues that firms could have advantageously cut dividend payout rates in the 1960s and obtained more of their financing internally, but were kept from doing so by powerful banks who encouraged their clients to overborrow.
50. For example, Crum and Meerschwam (1986), Hamada and Horiuchi (1987), Hodder (1988a,b), and Hoshi, Kashyap and Sharfstein (1990a,b).
51. Horiuchi, Packer and Fukuda (1990) test the alternative hypothesis proposed by some that the key element of the main bank relationship is risk-sharing (e.g., Nakatani, 1984, who finds that the profit rates and growth rates for group-affiliated firms are less variable than for independent firms), as opposed to minimizing information problems. They find no evidence to support the alternative.
52. On the general point that the apparent cost of borrowing is understated in Japan by the requirement of compensating balances, see, e.g., Bronte (1982, p. 17). The fraction of loan contracts with compensating balances declined steadily in the 1980s (A. Frankel and Morgan, 1991, p. 36).
53. Traditional investment equations are surveyed by Jorgenson (1971).
54. Hayashi and Inoue (1989) find that Q is significantly related to firm growth, and that much, though not all, of the power of cash flow to explain investment in a cross-section

of Japanese firms disappears when correcting for the endogeneity of cash flow. They do not segregate affiliated and non-affiliated firms.

55. Crum and Meerschwam (1986) and Meerschwam (1989), for example, discuss the decline of "relationship banking," and its replacement by the market. Also Kyuno (1989, p. 5).
56. Despite the diminished importance of subsidized government lending and the main bank system, the era of cheaper capital through internal finance was prolonged past 1973 in Japan by the greater availability of retained earnings when the number of profitable investment projects that needed to be financed diminished after the oil shock. The share of funds coming from internal finance narrowly-defined (retained earnings and depreciation charges), as opposed to external finance (securities-issues and borrowings), rose from 32.9 per cent in the period 1970-74 to 46.3 per cent in the period 1975-78, and stayed in that neighborhood subsequently. (1979-85. The source is Tamura, 1987, p. 3.) It is the changes of the 1980s that need explaining, not the changes after 1973.
57. When markets in government bonds and other instruments did begin to develop, especially in the 1970s, the observed interest rate was presumably somewhere between the low cost of internal and subsidized finance and the high rate of return to physical investment.
58. As noted in Meerschwam (1989), only pre-existing shareholders received advantageous new-share subscription rights.
59. The commercial code still prohibits companies from buying back their own shares. (Hatsopoulos and Brooks, 1987, p. 12, and Zielinski and Holloway, 1991, p. 106, 226.)
60. Volume in the yen-denominated BA market soon began to decline, however, in favor of other instruments, and it died out completely in November 1989. *Nihon Keizai Shimbun* (December 14, 1989.)
61. Lincoln (1988, 130-210), Shinkai (1988), Hoshi, Kashyap and Sharfstein (1990a), Crum and Meerschwam (1986), Feldman (1986), Frankel (1984), Sakakibara and Kondoh (1984), Suzuki (1987), Ido (1989) and Bisignano (1990, pp. 41–45), among many other sources.
62. Rosenbluth (1989) examines the various political and market forces that brought about Japanese financial liberalization.
63. Bisignano (1990, p.42 and Table 8).
64. Emmott (1989, 108-112) suggests that only government regulation kept Japanese corporations until the 1980s dependent on bank borrowing, and that all parties in Japan subsequently benefitted from the changes. Deregulation of domestic securities markets and, especially, the opportunity to issue securities abroad allowed corporations to obtain cheaper funds in the Euromarket in the late 1980s. (See also Rosenbluth, 1989, pp. 137-166.) The shift also benefitted Japan's securities firms. Even Japan's banks were compensated for the loss of domestic loan business by the opportunity to underwrite corporate securities abroad, a business that they are still excluded from at home under Article 65 (the equivalent of the American Glass-Steagall Act, which was written into Japan's financial system during the post-war occupation).
65. For example, Abegglen and Stalk (1985), Crum and Meerschwam (1986) and Meerschwam (1989).

66. Stein (1989) offers a theory with more rigorous foundations.
67. One might interpret the finding of Ando and Auerbach (1990) that the required rate of return in Japan declines with the size of the corporation as evidence that larger companies are indeed better able to develop reputations and thereby overcome obstacles to borrowing.
68. DeLong (1991).
69. To validate this hypothesis, one would like evidence that banks and other financial institutions are supplying less credit to their previously-privileged domestic clients (or offering less favorable terms), and instead taking advantage of the higher interest rates in the United States by lending abroad.
70. Aoki and Sheard (1992, p. 11) report that large firms decreased their employment of main-bank managers in the mid-1980s, by an average of 3.3 per cent, while small and medium firms increased theirs, by an average of 9.4 per cent. In a similar connection, Okazaki and Horiuchi (1992) examine the strength of main-bank relationships in the 1980s for a sample of 38 companies, using as a measure the frequency with which the main bank sent executives to the management of the firm (in addition to the usual measures of lending and shareholding).

REFERENCES

Abegglen, James, and George Stalk, Jr., 1985, *Kaisha, The Japanese Corporation,* New York: Basic Books.

Aggarwal, Raj, Ramesh Rao, and Takato Hiraki, 1990, "Regularities in Security Returns on the Tokyo Stock Exchange: P/E, Size, and Seasonal Influences," *Journal of Financial Research 13*, Fall (forthcoming).

Ando, Albert, and Alan Auerbach, 1988a, "The Corporate Cost of Capital in the U.S. and Japan: A Comparison," NBER Working Paper no. 1762. In J. Shoven, (ed.), *Government Policy Towards Industry in the United States and Japan,* New York: Cambridge University Press, 21–49.

Ando, Albert, and Alan Auerbach, 1988b, "The Cost of Capital in the U.S. and Japan: A Comparison," NBER Working Paper no. 2286. In *Journal of the Japanese and International Economies* 2, no.2 (June), pp. 134–58.

Ando, Albert and Alan Auerbach, 1990, "The Cost of Capital in Japan: Recent Evidence and Further Results," NBER Working Paper No. 3371. *Journal of the Japanese and International Economies 3,* no. 4 (December), pp. 323–50.

Aoki, Masahiko, 1984, "Shareholders' Non-Unanimity on Investment Financing: Banks vs. Individual Investors," in M.Aoki (ed.), *The Economic Analysis of the Japanese Firm,* Amsterdam: North-Holland, pp. 193–224.

Aoki, Masahiko, 1989, *Information, Incentives and Bargaining in the Japanese Economy*, Cambridge University Press.

Aoki, Masahiko, 1990, "Toward an Economic Model of the Japanese Firm," *Journal of Economic Literature 28* (March), pp. 1–27.

Aoki, Masahiko, 1992, "Ex Post Monitoring by the Main Bank," ["very preliminary"], paper presented at conference on Corporate Governance: New Problems and New Solutions, Center for Economic Policy Research, Stanford University, CA., May 1-2.

Aoki, Masahiko, and Paul Sheard, 1992, "The Role of the Main Bank in the Corporate Governance Structure in Japan," paper presented at conference on Corporate Governance: New Problems and New Solutions, Center for Economic Policy Research, Stanford University, CA., May 1-2.

Aron, Paul, 1989, "Japanese P/E Multiples: The Tradition Continues," *Japanese Research Report No. 35*, Daiwa Securities America, Inc., October 23.

Balassa, Bela, and Marcus Noland, 1988, *Japan in the World Economy*, Washington, DC: Institute for International Economics.

Baldwin, Carliss, 1986, "The Capital Factor: Competing or Capital in a Global Environment," in Michael Porter (ed.), *Competition in Global Industries*, Boston, MA: Harvard Business School Press, 185–223.

Bernheim, Douglas, and John Shoven, 1987, "Taxation and the Cost of Capital: An International Comparison," in C. E. Walker and M. A. Bloomfield (eds.), *The Consumption Tax: A Better Alternative?*, Cambridge, MA: Ballinger, pp. 61–85.

Bisignano, Joseph, 1990, "Structures of Financial Intermediation, Corporate Finance, and Central Banking," Basle: Bank for International Settlements (December).

Boone, Peter, 1989, "High Land Values in Japan: Is the Archipelago Worth Eleven Trillion Dollars?" Harvard University (November).

Borio, C.E.V., 1990, "Leverage and Financing of Non-Financial Companies: An International Perspective," *BIS Economic Papers No. 27* (May), Basle: Bank for International Settlements.

Bronte, Stephen, 1982, *Japanese Finance: Markets and Institutions*, London: Euromoney Publications.

Caves, Richard and Masu Uekusa, 1976, "Industrial Organization," in Hugh Patrick and Henry Rosovsky (eds.), *Asia's New Giant*, Washington, DC: The Brookings Institution, 459–523.

Crum, M. Colyer, and David Meerschwam, 1986, "From Relationship to Price Banking: The Loss of Regulatory Control," in T.McCraw (ed.), *America vs. Japan*, Boston: Harvard Business School Press.

DeLong, J.Bradford, 1991, "The Great American Universal Banking Experiment," from *Inside the Business Enterprise*, Chicago: University of Chicago Press.

Emmott, Bill, 1989, *The Sun Also Sets: The Limits of Japan's Economic Power*, Times Books.

Fazzari, Steven, R. Glen Hubbard, and Bruce Petersen, 1988, "Investment and

Finance Reconsidered," *Brookings Papers on Economic Activity, 1*, pp. 141–96.

Feldman, Robert, 1986, *Japanese Financial Markets: Deficits, Dilemmas, and Deregulation*, Cambridge, MA: M.I.T. Press.

Feldstein, M. and P.Bacchetta, 1989, "National Savings and International Investment," forthcoming, D. Bernheim and J. Shoven (eds.), *National Saving and Economic Performance,* Chicago: University of Chicago Press.

Feldstein, M. and C. Horioka, 1980, "Domestic Saving and International Capital Flows," *Economic Journal 90,* pp. 314–29.

Frankel, Allen, and Paul Morgan, 1991, "A Primer on the Japanese Banking System," *International Finance Discussion Papers,* no. 419 (December).

Frankel, Jeffrey, 1984, "The Yen/Dollar Agreement: Liberalizing Japanese Capital Markets," *Policy Analyses in International Economics*, no. 9, Washington, DC: Institute for International Economics.

Frankel, Jeffrey, 1988, "U.S. Borrowing From Japan," KSG Working Paper 174D, Harvard University. In G. Luciani (ed.), *Structural Change in the American Financial System*, Rome: Fondazione Adriano Olivetti (1989); excerpts (translated to Japanese) in *Kinyu Journal*, July 1988 and February 1989.

Frankel, Jeffrey, 1991a, "Japanese Finance: A Survey," in Paul Krugman (ed.), *The U.S. and Japan: Has The Door Opened Wider?*, Chicago: University of Chicago Press; related papers appear in *Financial Management*, Spring 1991; and forthcoming in Shinji Takagi (ed), *Handbook of Japanese Capital Markets*, Cambridge, MA: Basil Blackwell Inc.

Frankel, Jeffrey, 1991b, "Quantifying International Capital Mobility in the 1980s." In D. Bernheim and J. Shoven (eds.), *National Saving and Economic Performance*, Chicago: University of Chicago Press.

Frankel, Jeffrey and Kenneth Froot, 1987, "Short-term and Long-term Expectations of the Yen/Dollar Exchange Rates: Evidence from Survey Data," *Journal of the Japanese and International Economies 1*, pp. 249–74.

French, Kenneth and James Poterba, 1990, "Japanese and U.S. Cross-Border Common Stock Investments," *Journal of the Japanese and International Economies 4* (December), pp. 476–93.

French, Kenneth and James Poterba, 1991, "Were Japanese Stock Prices Too High?" *Journal of Financial Economics*. Earlier versions appeared as "Are Japanese Stock Prices Too High?" ["preliminary"], CRSP Seminar on the Analysis of Security Prices, Univ. of Chicago, April 1989; revised, M.I.T. Economics Working Paper No. 547 (February 1990); and NBER Working Paper No. 3290 (March 1990).

Friend, Irwin, and Ichiro Tokutsu, 1987, "The Cost of Capital to Corporations in Japan and the U.S.A.," *Journal of Banking and Finance 11*, no. 2, pp. 313–27

Froot, Kenneth and Takatoshi Ito, 1989, "On the Consistency of Short-Run and Long-Run Exchange Rate Expectations," NBER Working Paper no. 2577. In

Journal of International Money and Finance 8, no. 4 (December), pp. 487–510.

Frost, Ellen, 1987, *For Richer, For Poorer*, Council on Foreign Relations, New York.

Fukao, Mitsuhiro, 1988, "Balance of Payments Imbalances and Long-term Capital Movements: Review and Prospects," in Masaru Yoshitomi (ed.), *Correcting External Imbalances*, Tokyo: Economic Planning Agency.

Fukao, Mitsuhiro and T. Okubo, 1984, "International Linkage of Interest Rates: The Case of Japan and the United States," *International Economic Review 25* (February).

Gerlach, Michael, 1989, "Keiretsu Organization in the Japanese Economy: Analysis and Trade Implications," in Chalmers Johnson, Laura d'Andrea Tyson and John Zysman (eds.), *Politics and Productivity: The Real Story of Why Japan Works*, Ballinger Books.

Gilson, Ronald, and Mark Roe, 1992, "Comparartive Corporate Governance: Focusing the United States - Japan Inquiry," paper presented at conference on Corporate Governance: New Problems and New Solutions, Center for Economic Policy Research, Stanford, CA., May 1-2.

Glick, Reuven, 1987, "Interest Rate Linkages in the Pacific Basin," *Federal Reserve Bank of San Francisco Economic Review No. 3*, pp. 31–42.

Glick, Reuven, and Michael Hutchison, 1990, "Financial Liberalization in the Pacific Basin: Implications for Real Interest Rate Linkages," *Journal of the Japanese and International Economies 4*, pp. 36–48.

Hale, David, 1990, "Economic Consequences of the Tokyo Stock Market Crash," U.S.-Japan Consultative Group on International Monetary Affairs, Washington, DC, July 23.

Hamada, Koichi, and Akiyoshi Horiuchi, 1987, "The Political Economy of the Financial Market," in Kozo Yamamura and Yasukichi Yasuba (eds.), *The Political Economy of Japan: Volume 1. The Domestic Transformation*, Stanford, CA: Stanford University Press, pp. 223–60.

Hamao, Yasushi, and Takeo Hoshi, 1991, "Stock and Land Prices in Japan," Graduate School of Business, Columbia University (October).

Hardouvelis, Gikas, and Steve Peristiani, 1989, "Do Margin Requirements Matter? Evidence from the Japanese Stock Market," Federal Reserve Bank of New York (October).

Hardouvelis, Gikas, and Steve Peristiani, 1990, "Margin Requirements, Speculative Trading and Stock Price Fluctuations: The Case of Japan," Federal Reserve Bank of New York Research Paper No. 90-06, July (rev. January 1991).

Hatsopoulos, George, 1983, "High Cost of Capital: Handicap of American Industry," Study sponsored by the American Business Conference and Thermo Electron Corp. (April).

Hatsopoulos, George, and Stephen Brooks, 1986, "The Gap in the Cost of Capital: Causes, Effects, and Remedies," in Ralph Landau and Dale Jorgenson (eds.), *Technology and Economic Policy*, Cambridge, MA: Ballinger, pp. 221–80.

Hatsopoulos, George and Stephen Brooks, 1987, "The Cost of Capital in the United States and Japan," Kennedy School of Government, Harvard University. In Dale Jorgenson and Ralph Landau (eds.), *International Comparisons of the Cost of Capital*, Washington, DC: Brookings Institution (Spring 1992).

Hatsopoulos, George, Paul Krugman, and Larry Summers, 1988, "U.S. Competitiveness: Beyond the Trade Deficit," *Science* (July 15), pp. 299–307.

Hatsopoulos, George and James Poterba, 1991, "Rates of Return on Japanese and U.S. Nonfinancial Companies: New Evidence on International Cost of Capital Differences," Harvard/Stanford Workshop on Economic Policy, Kennedy School of Government, November.

Hayashi, Fumio, 1990, "Taxes and Corporate Investment in Japanese Manufacturing," NBER Working Paper No. 1753; in Charles Hulten (ed.), *Productivity Growth in Japan and the United States*, NBER Studies in Income and Wealth Vol. 53, Chicago: University of Chicago Press, pp. 295–316.

Hayashi, Fumio, and Tohru Inoue, 1990, "The Relationship of Firm Growth and Q With Multiple Capital Goods: Theory and Evidence From Panel Data on Japanese Firms," Institute for Empirical Macroeconomics Discussion Paper 13, Federal Reserve Bank of Minneapolis; and NBER Working Paper No. 3326 (April).

Hodder, James, 1988a, "Corporate Capital Structure in the United States and Japan: Financial Intermediation and Implication of Financial Deregulation," in J. Shoven (ed.), *Government Policy Towards Industry in the USA and Japan*, Cambridge University Press, Ch. 9, pp. 241–263

Hodder, James, 1988b, "Capital Structure and Cost of Capital in the U.S. and Japan," Stanford University (July).

Hodder, James, 1991, "Is the Cost of Capital Lower in Japan?" *Journal of the Japanese and International Economies 5*, no.1, March, 86–100.

Hodder, James and A. Tschoegl, 1985, "Some Aspects of Japanese Corporate Finance," *Journal of Financial and Quantitative Analysis 20*, no.2, pp. 173–190.

Homma, Masaki, 1987, "An Overview of Tax Reform in the U.S. and Japan," US-Japan Core Group, San Diego, Feb.

Homma, M., N. Atoda, F. Hayashi, and K. Hata, 1984, *Setsubi Toshi to Kigyo Zeisei* [Investment and Corporate Tax Structure], Economic Planning Agency: Tokyo.

Homma, M., T. Maeda, and K. Hashimoto, 1986, "The Japanese Tax System,"Brookings Discussion Papers in Economics, June.

Horioka, Charles, 1990, "Why Is Japan's Household Saving Rate So High? A Literature Survey," *Journal of the Japanese and International Economies 4*, no. 1 (March), pp. 49–92.

Horiuchi, Akiyoshi, 1990, "Some Aspects of the Capital Market Mechanism in Japan," Hawaii Conference on International Financial Markets, The Center for Japan-U.S. Business and Economics Studies, New York University.

Horiuchi, Akiyoshi, and Ryoko Okazaki, 1992, "Corporate Investment and the Main Bank Relationship in Japan," Bank of Japan (January).

Horiuchi, Akiyoshi, Frank Packer, and Shin'ichi Fukuda, 1990, "What Role Has the 'Main Bank' Played in Japan," *Journal of the Japanese and International Economies 2,* no.2 (June), pp. 159–80.

Hoshi, Takeo, Anil Kashyap, and David Sharfstein, 1988, "Corporate Structure, Liquidity, and Investment: Evidence from Japanese Panel Data," Sloan WP #2071-88, *Quarterly Journal of Economics* (September 1990).

Hoshi, Takeo, Anil Kashyap, and David Sharfstein, 1989, "Bank Monitoring and Investment: Evidence from the Changing Structure of Japanese Corporate Banking Relationship," NBER Working Paper No. 3079, August. In R. G. Hubbard (ed.), *Asymmetric Information, Corporate Finance, and Investment,* Chicago: University of Chicago Press, (1990).

Hoshi, Takeo, Anil Kashyap, and David Sharfstein, 1990, "The Role of Banks in Reducing the Costs of Financial Distress in Japan," NBER Working Paper No. 3435. *Journal of Financial Economics* (September).

Hoshi, Takeo, Anil Kashyap, and David Sharfstein, 1991, "On the Choice Between Public and Private Debt: An Examination of Post-Deregulation Corporate Financing in Japan, ("preliminary"), November.

Hsieh, Psieh-Shun, and Robin Wells, 1992, "Japanese Financial Market Deregulation: Evidence on Financing Choice and Investment," University of Michigan.

Hubbard, R. Glen, 1990, "Introduction," in R.G. Hubbard (ed.), *Asymmetric Information, Corporate Finance, and Investment,* Chicago: University of Chicago Press, (1990), pp. 1–14.

Ido, Kiyoto, 1989, "Internationalization and Implementation of the New Foreign Exchange Control Law," *FAIR Fact Series: Japan's Financial Markets*, vol. 19.

Ito, Takatoshi, 1986, "Capital Controls and Covered Interest Parity," NBER working paper no. 1187, and *Economic Studies Quarterly 37*, 223-241.

Ito, Takatoshi, 1988, "Use of (Time-Domain) Vector Autoregressions to Test Uncovered Interest Parity," *Review of Economics and Statistics 70*, pp. 296–305.

Ito, Takatoshi, 1989, "Japan's Structural Adjustment: The Land/Housing Problem and External Balance," International Monetary Fund (revised Feb., NBER Summer Institute).

Ito, Takatoshi, 1990, "Foreign Exchange Rate Expectations: Micro Survey Data," *American Economic Review 80*, no. 3 (June 1990), pp. 434–49.

Iwata, Kazumasa, and Atsushi Yoshida, 1987, "Capital Cost of Business Investment in Japan and the United States under Tax Reform," Kennedy School of Government, Harvard University. In Dale Jorgenson and Ralph Landau (eds.), *International Comparisons of the Cost of Capital*, Washington, DC: Brookings Institution (Spring 1992).

Iwata, Kazumasa, and Atsushi Yoshida, 1990, "Capital Cost of Business Investment in Japan and the United States under Tax Reform: The Case of an Open Economy," *Japan and the World Economy 2*.

Jensen and Meckling, 1976, "Theory of the Firm: Managerial Behavior, Agency Costs and Ownership Structure," *Journal of Financial Economics*, pp. 305–60.

Jorgenson, Dale, 1971, "Econometric Studies of Investment Behavior: A Review," *Journal of Economic Literature 9*, pp. 1111–47.

Kaplan, Steven, 1992, "Top Executive Rewards and Firm Performance: A Comparison of Japan and the U.S.," paper presented at conference on Corporate Governance: New Problems and New Solutions, Center for Economic Policy Research, Stanford, CA., May 1-2.

Kester, W. Carl, and Timothy Luehrman, 1989, "Real Interest Rates and the Cost of Capital: A Comparison of the United States and Japan," *Japan and the World Economy 1*, pp. 199–232.

Kester, W. Carl, and Timothy Luehrman, 1991, "The Price of Risk in the United States and Japan," *Japan and the World Economy 3*, pp. 223–42.

Kester, W. Carl, and Timothy Luehrman, 1992, "Cross-Country Differences in the Cost of Capital: A Survey and Evaluation of Recent Empirical Studies," Working Paper 92-011, Harvard Business School. Forthcoming in *Time Horizons of American Management*, Harvard Business School and the American Council on Competitiveness.

Kikutani, Tatsuya, and Toshiaki Tachibanaki, 1990, "Taxation of Income from Capital in Japan: Historical Perspectives and Policy Simulations," in Charles Hulten (ed.), *Productivity Growth in Japan and the United States*, NBER Studies in Income and Wealth Vol. 53, Chicago: University of Chicago Press, pp. 267–93.

Kim, Sun Bae, 1992, "Corporate Financing through a Shareholder Bank: Lessons from Japan," *Pacific Basin Working Paper Series No. PB92-03*, Federal Resrve Bank of San Francisco.

Kyuno, Masao, 1989, "A Glimpse of the Financial Revolution in Japan," *Journal of International Economic Studies 3*, pp. 1–24.

Lawler, Patrick, Bonnie Loopesko, and Marc Dudey, 1988, "An Analysis of Some Aspects of the Japanese Stock Market," Nov. 10 ["not to circulate or be quoted without permission of authors"].

Lee, Hiro, 1988, "Imperfect Competition, Industrial Policy, and Japanese International Competitiveness," University of California Ph.D. dissertation, Berkeley (September).

Lincoln, Edward, 1988, *Japan: Facing Economic Maturity*, Brookings Institution, Washington, D.C.

Lippens, Robert, 1991, "The Cost of Capital: A Summary of Results for the U.S. and Japan in the 1980s," *Business Economics 26*, no.2 (April), pp. 19–25.

Mayer, Colin, 1988, "New Issues in Corporate Finance," *European Economic Review 32*, no. 5 (June), pp. 1167–89.

McCauley, Robert and Stephen Zimmer, 1989, "Explaining Differences in the Cost of Capital," *Federal Reserve Bank of New York Quarterly Review* (Summer), pp. 7–28.

McKinnon, Ronald, and David Robinson, 1989, "Dollar Devaluation, Interest Rate Volatility, and the Duration of Investment," CEPR Conference on Economic Growth and the Commercialization of New Technologies, Stanford, CA, September 11-12.

Meerschwam, David, 1989, "The Japanese Financial System and the Cost of Capital," National Bureau of Economic Research. Forthcoming in Paul Krugman (ed.), *The US and Japan in the '90s*, Chicago: University of Chicago Press.

Meerschwam, David, 1990, "The United States and Japan's Dangerous Liaison and the Irrelevance of the Cost of Capital," Harvard Business School.

Morita, Akio, 1992, "A Turning Point for Japanese Managers?" *Bungei Shunju* (January 10); translated to English in *International Economic Insights* (May/June), pp. 2–10.

Myers, Stewart, and N. Majluf, 1984, "Corporate Financing and Investment Decisions When Firms Have Information that Investors Do Not Have," *Journal of Financial Economics*, pp. 187–221.

Noguchi, Yukio, 1985, "Tax Structure and Saving-Investment Balance," U.S.-Japan Consultative Group on International Monetary Affairs, Hakone, Japan, March.

Otani, Ichiro, 1983, "Exchange Rate Instability and Capital Controls: The Japanese Experience 1978–81," in: D. Bigman and T. Taya (eds.), *Exchange Rate and Trade Instability: Causes, Consequences and Remedies*, Cambridge, MA: Ballinger.

Otani, Ichiro, and Siddath Tiwari, 1981, "Capital Controls and Interest Rate Parity: The Japanese Experience 1978-81," *International Monetary Fund Staff Papers 28*, no.4 (December), pp. 793–815.

Poterba, James, 1991, "Comparing the Cost of Capital in the United States and Japan: A Survey of Methods," *Federal Reserve Bank of New York Quarterly Review* (Winter), pp. 20–32.

Prowse, Stephen David, 1989, "Firm Financial Behavior in the US and Japan: The Role of Agency Relationships," National Bureau of Economic Research, August 11.

Rosenbluth, Frances McCall, 1989, *Financial Politics in Contemporary Japan,*

Ithaca: Cornell University Press.

Sachs, Jeffrey and Peter Boone, 1988, "Japanese Structural Adjustment and the Balance of Payments," NBER Working Paper no. 2614 (June); and *Journal of the Japanese and International Economies*, September 2–3, pp. 286–327.

Sakakibara, Eisuke and Akira Kondoh, 1984. *Study on the Internationalization of Tokyo's Money Markets*, Tokyo: Japan Center for International Finance, Study Series, no. 1 (June).

Semiconductor Industry Association, 1980, "U.S. and Japanese Semiconductor Industries: A Financial Comparison," Report prepared by Chase Financial Policy, June.

Shiller, Robert, Fumiko Kon-ya and Yoshiro Tsutsui, 1991a, "Investor Behavior in the October 1987 Stock Market Crash: The Case of Japan," *Journal of the Japanese and International Economies 5,* no. 1 (March), pp. 1–13.

Shiller, Robert, Fumiko Kon-ya and Yoshiro Tsutsui, 1991b, "Speculative Behavior in the Stock Markets: Evidence from the United States and Japan," NBER Working Paper No. 3613, Feb.

Shinkai, Yoichi, 1988, "The Internationalization of Finance in Japan," in T. Inoguchi and D.I. Okimoto (eds.), *The Political Economy of Japan, Volume 2: The Changing International Context*, Stanford, CA: Stanford University Press, pp. 249–71.

Shoven, John, 1989, "The Japanese Tax Reform and the Effective Rate of Tax on Japanese Corporate Investments," NBER Working Paper no. 2791; in L.Summers (ed.), *Tax Policy and the Economy*, M.I.T. Press: Cambridge, MA.

Shoven, John and Toshiaki Tachibanaki, 1988, "The Taxation of Income from Capital in Japan," Center for Economic Policy Research Publication No. 60; in J. Shoven (ed.), *Government Policy Towards Industry in the United States and Japan,* Cambridge, UK: Cambridge University Press.

Stein, Jeremy, 1989, "Efficient Capital Markets, Inefficient Firms: A Model of Myopic Corporate Behavior," *Quarterly Journal of Economics.*

Suzuki, Yoshio, 1987, *The Japanese Financial System*, Oxford, UK: Clarendon Press.

Suzuki, Yoshio, 1991, "Japan in the World Economic Scene," Nomura Research Institute, June.

Takagi, Shinji, 1988, "Recent Developments in Japan's Bond and Money Markets," *Journal of the Japanese and International Economies* 2, no. 1 (March), pp. 63–91.

Takagi, Shinji, 1989, "The Japanese Equity Market: Past and Present," *Journal of Banking and Finance 13* (March), pp. 537–70.

Takenaka, Heizo, 1986, "Economic Incentives for Industrial Investment: Japanese Experience," Institute for Fiscal and Monetary Policy, Ministry of Finance, Japan (February).

Ueda, Kazuo, 1990, "Are Japanese Stock Prices Too High?", *Journal of the*

Japanese and International Economies 3, no. 4 (December), pp. 351–70.

Wells, Robin, and Jeffrey Frankel, 1993, "Monitoring, Investment, and the Transition to Public Debt Markets," Stanford University Business School working paper (January).

Zielinski, Robert and Nigel Holloway, 1991, *Unequal Equities: Power and Risk in Japan's Stock Market*, Tokyo and New York: Kodansha International.

Ziemba, William, 1991, "The Chicken or the Egg: Land and Stock Prices in Japan," in W. T. Ziemba, W. Bailey, and Y. Hamao (eds.), *Japanese Financial Market Research*, Amsterdam: North-Holland, pp. 45–68.

Zysman, John, 1983, *Governments, Markets and Growth*, Ithaca, NY: Cornell University Press.

CHAPTER 10

COST OF CAPITAL IN THE BANKING INDUSTRY IN JAPAN AND A COMPARISON WITH U.S. BANKS

Toshiaki Tachibanaki

I. INTRODUCTION

The purpose of this chapter is to estimate the cost of capital in the banking industry in Japan and to compare the empirical results with related data about U.S cost of capital. The financial sector in Japan has become quite important: the ratio of financial assets to GNP has been increasing drastically, and changes in financial and monetary policies have affected strongly the real economy. Incidentally, the majority of the largest ten banks in the world based on assets are Japanese banks. Internationalization, globalization and liberalization in the financial sector are recent phenomena in the world as well as Japan. The investigation of the cost of capital is useful in understanding these phenomena for both Japan and the U.S.

This chapter has several specific purposes. First, it examines time-series data, from 1971 to current for Japan and from 1976 to current for the U.S. This enables us to understand the historical change in cost of capital, and thus to investigate its role in the banking industries historically. Second,

The author is most grateful to Kazuto Ikeo, Kiyoshi Mitsui, and Hiroshi Kitagawa for their useful suggestions and comments as well as to Mamoru Tanaka for his excellent research assistance.

we estimate the cost of capital separately for each category of bank that is permitted under Japanese law: city banks, regional banks, long-term credit banks and community banks. It is interesting to investigate the differences among them with respect to their ability to accumulate financial resources and management. Third, we estimate the cost of capital for several representative individual banks. This complements the empirical result of the second point since the cost of capital differs not only from one category of bank to the other but also among individual banks within the same category. Fourth, we examine the effect of unrealized capital gains, which are accrued from holding securities, on cost of capital for several large city banks. Banks in Japan are allowed to hold shares of other corporations unlike banks in the U.S. This has significant influence on the management and financial activities of banks, as Tachibanaki, Mitsui, and Kitagawa (1991), and Tachibanaki and Taki (1991) propose. Fifth, this chapter examines the effect of various regulations on the difference in the cost of capital across classes or categories of banks, and thus the working of the capital market. The financial sector in Japan has been heavily regulated, although deregulation is under way currently. We look into two representative examples of such regulation: regulated interest rates and separations of financial industries into various discrete business areas. Finally, we estimate the cost of capital of banks in the U.S. in order to compare the aggregate banking industries in Japan and the U.S. A separate study would be required to compare individual banks as well as each category of banks between the two countries. As noted previously, integration of world capital markets is now under way. Capital mobility between Japan and the U.S. is very high, and it has brought about a close integration of capital between them. This study sheds light on this issue by examining banks' cost of capital in Japan and comparing it to that of the U.S.

The remaining part of this chapter is organized as follows. Section II presents the theoretical basis for determining the cost of capital in the banking sector and the estimation procedure. Section III gives the empirical result in Japan in three parts: by category of banks, by several representative individual banks, and for several large city banks in order to investigate the effect of unrealized capital gains. Section IV gives the empirical result estimated for the U.S. banks and compares it with the Japanese result. Finally, Section V presents concluding remarks.

II. ESTIMATION PROCEDURE

Cost of capital is defined as follows: the minimum required before-tax rate of return, when one unit of investment is made by a firm. In other words, a firm or a shareholder would not perform an investment project if the return to this project were lower than cost of capital.

Although the definition is fairly straight-forward, empirical estimations are not so simple because there are considerable variations in measurements. We have to be careful to take into account various characteristics peculiar to the different measurement methods when we interpret the estimated result. In particular, it is important to understand the difference between nonfinancial industries (i.e., largely manufacturing industries) and financial industries because of their different financing methods.

We follow the tradition of King (1977), and King and Fullerton (1984) as the basis for our analysis. It is necessary, however, to reformulate the estimation procedure for the banking sector since the previous estimation method was used in search of the manufacturing sector.

Let p be cost of capital and a function of the real interest rate r,

$$p = c(r) \tag{10.1}$$

where c indicates the influence of tax and other factors.

Suppose a firm provides one unit of investment. The net rate of return to one unit of investment is given by equation (10.2),

$$p = MMR - \delta \tag{10.2}$$

where MRR is the gross rate of return, and δ is the rate of depreciation.

Denoting the corporate tax rate by τ, and the nominal discount rate by ρ, the after-tax discounted profit V is given by equation (10.3),

$$\begin{aligned} V &= \int_0^{\infty} (1-\tau)\, MMR \exp[-(\rho+\delta-\pi)\, u]\, du \\ &= \frac{(1-\tau)\, MRR}{\rho+\delta-\pi} \end{aligned} \tag{10.3}$$

where π is the rate of inflation. The nominal discount rate is determined endogenously and dependent upon the real interest rate and the method of financing.

Suppose A is the reduction of tax by preferential treatment or other institutional arrangements. The unit cost is given by equation (10.4).

$$c = 1 - A \tag{10.4}$$

For an investor to find this investment attractive, the investment must produce a gross rate of return (*MRR*) that equates V and c under the given value of discount rate. In other words, the after-tax rate of interest, which enables an investor to finance, is ρ that equates V and c under the given rate of return to the investment (*MRR*). Equation (10.5) is obtained by equating V and c,

$$\mathrm{P} = \frac{(1-A)}{(1-\tau)}(\rho + \delta - \pi) - \delta \tag{10.5}$$

The above is a standard formulation of the cost of capital for many industries.

We now consider how the banking industry differs from the manufacturing industry, when we evaluate the method of financing for investment. Similar to a manufacturing firm a bank normally has three methods of financing: borrowing, issuance of new shares, and retained earnings. The difference between manufacturing firms and banks appears with respect to borrowing: While a manufacturing firm borrows funds from a bank, a bank borrows funds from both banks and consumers (or savers). The latter is a normal banking business in any country, namely collecting funds from savers in the form of demand deposits, time deposits, and other savings. We refer to all such funds as deposits for convenience. The former is a practice that is fairly common in Japan. The Japanese banks commit to interbank loans, and the share of funds collected by this method has increased considerably. We call such funds interbank loans for convenience.

The above discussion suggests that there are four methods of financing (or collecting funds) for banks in Japan: deposits, interbank loans, new shares, and retained earnings. As is true in many countries, the share of new shares is very marginal as a method of financing in the Japanese banking industries. Although banks in Japan have recently used equity financing by new share issues to satisfy the BIS capital adequacy rule and it may be somewhat unrealistic to ignore new shares in the present analysis, the role of new shares is still minor in comparison with other methods of financing. Consequently, we ignore new shares in this chapter and consider only the other three methods, namely (i) deposits, (ii) interbank loans, and (iii) retained earnings.

We now derive the nominal discount rate for each method of financing. For deposits, let i be the market rate of interest (or the economic rate of interest), x be the nonmonetary benefit (or the implicit rate of interest), i_d be the effective rate of interest to deposit, and m be the marginal tax rate on deposit. The arbitrage with respect to interest gives the following equation.

$$i\,(l-m)=i_d(l-m)+x \qquad (10.6)$$

Since a tax is levied on the nominal interest income, and a payment of nominal interest is tax-deductible, the nominal discount rate ρ_d is equal to the after-tax rate of interest. Therefore, equation (10.7) is obtained.

$$\rho D=\{i-m(i-i^d)\}(k-\tau) \qquad (10.7)$$

The possibility for arbitrage between i and i_d, since domestic markets may be sufficiently segmented—particularly in the field of business territories—by past regulations. Competition among banks, however, both within the common category of banks, and across banks outside of this category, has been fairly strong both in the deposit market and in the lending market. Therefore, markets were probably not sufficiently segmented to create opportunites for arbitrage.

Next, the nominal discount rate for interbank loan is considered. This loan is called a "call-loan" in Japan and is used as short-term lending and borrowing among banks in order to adjust for temporary shortages in fund. Since this is virtually equivalent to the usual lending and borrowing between a bank and a firm, the nominal discount rate ρ_M is given by the following equation,

$$\rho_M=i\,(l-\tau) \qquad (10.8)$$

Finally, the nominal discount rate for retained earnings ρ_R is considered. (As noted previously, we ignore new share issuance in this chapter.) If we could assume that it is equal to the discount rate for new shares, we could easily derive the discount rate for retained earnings. Unlike the U.S., Japan does not allow repurchasing of shares; this means that the "trapped equity hypothesis" must be kept. Therefore, unlike Bernheim and Shoven (1986), we have to derive the discount rate for retained earnings separately. King and Fullerton (1984) derived it for a firm, and we can apply it for a bank.

$$\rho_R = i \left(\frac{l-m}{l-z} \right) \tag{10.9}$$

where z is the effective tax rate on unrealized capital gains. Equation (10.9) is derived under the condition that $\rho_R(l-z) = i\,(l-m)$ holds. The merit of retained earnings for investors is a lower tax rate on capital gains than on dividend income.

Equations (10.7), (10.8), and (10.9) are the formulations of the nominal discount rate for each source of finance for banks. Since the weight of each source differs not only among categories of banks but also from bank to bank, it is necessary to consider the weighted average of the three components given by equation (10.10),

$$\rho = \sum_i \omega_i \, \rho_i \, , i = D, M, R \tag{10.10}$$

where ω_i is a weight given by the bank's balance sheet.

The final form of the cost of capital is easily obtained by plugging equation (10.10) into equation (10.5). So far we have not discussed the cost saving factor (A) and the depreciation rate δ, which have been important subjects in the estimation of the effect of taxation on investment.

Let us consider these points now. There exists a great difference between manufacturing firms and banks with respect to assets. The largest assets in a bank are loans and securities, while in the case of a manufacturing firm they are machines. If we are concerned with real assets, the share of buildings and land is also important to bank. This is especially true, when we examine the component of investment. Since depreciation for buildings is very slow, we can safely assume $\delta = 0$ for the banking industry. (If the share of machines were higher, as in the case of a manufacturing firm, the above assumption would be unrealistic.) There remains one problem: investment in computers by banks. Recently the amount of investment in computers is fairly significant, and it is very likely that depreciation is rapid. A future work will have to consider the effect of depreciation of computers.

Since tax law in Japan does not allow a large amount of tax allowances for the banking industry in comparison to those granted to the manufacturing industry, it is possible to assume $A = 0$. The one tax allowance that might be considered is allowance for bad debts. It is possible to guess that banks enjoy tax deduction by this allowance. Unfortunately, the banks' financial statements currently do not disclose the information that would enable us to calculate the cost saving associated with this tax allowance. Thus, we are obliged to assume $A = 0$. Tachibanaki and Kimura (1992) take up this matter.

Finally, I include a note about the treatment of inflation. As is obvious from its formulation, this chapter adopts the real basis rather than the nominal one with respect to the contribution of inflation. Although some economists prefer the latter, we adopt the usage of King and Fullerton, who prefer the former. A result that we will see later is that the cost of capital figures reveal considerable year-to-year variations.

III. EMPIRICAL RESULTS OF COST OF CAPITAL AT BANKS IN JAPAN

Data Source

We shall briefly describe the data source for estimating cost of capital at banks in Japan. The main data source is the Annual Report of Financial Statements for Banks published by the Federation of Banking Association in Japan. The report gives the annual and semi-annual figures of banks' financial conditions, not only in the aggregate, but also individual bank's figures. Some aggregations were attempted in order to calculate the figures of each category of banks such as city banks, regional banks, long-term credit banks and mutual banks. We use the published figures for our estimation. Estimates of unrealized capital gains were obtained through another source, which will be explained later.

Interest rates were calculated using the *effective* basis rather than the *nominal* basis reported in the statistics of the Bank of Japan. Concretely speaking, the effective rate of interest is calculated by the ratio of interest paid over the amount of deposits reported in the financial statements of banks. The nonmonetary interest is calculated in a similar way. One of the most important reasons for applying the effective basis rather than the nominal basis is that it clearly differentiates the rates of interest of an individual bank from the various categories of banks. One of our purposes of this chapter is to examine the performance of not only an individual bank, but also of each category of banks. Although there is some merit in adopting the nominal basis rather than the effective basis, a full explication of the relative advantage between these two methods is outside of the scope of the present chapter.

The figures for the U.S. banks were obtained from the "Federal Reserve Bulletin." This data source gives only the aggregate figures of all banks. Thus, a comparison between Japan and the U.S. is made only based upon the aggregate figures of all banks in Japan and the U.S. Although the financial statements of individual banks are available in the U.S., a comparison of individual banks is a difficult task. A study comparing individual banks, however, would be useful and could be undertaken in the future.

Time-Series Study for Each Category of Banks

There are various categories of banks in Japan. We investigate four categories of banks, namely (i) city banks, (ii) regional banks, (iii) mutual banks and (iv) long-term credit banks. The following is a brief description of each category. City banks conduct their business all over Japan. Their asset values are far bigger than the other banks, and thus they represent the major banks in Japan. Regional banks restrict their businesses within particular prefectures and lend their funds mainly to medium-sized and small firms. Mutual banks are smaller in terms of assets than regional banks, and their business territories are more restricted. Long-term credit banks are very special because they collect their funds largely by issuing long-term bonds and lend their funds to larger firms. There are only three long-term credit banks, but the role of their financial activities is important. It should be emphasized that fairly strong regulations of the banking industry are responsible for the existence of various categories of banks in Japan.

Figure 10–1, taken from data in Tables 10–1 and 10–2, shows how the cost of capital for each category of banks has varied historically since 1971. Broadly speaking, there is not so much difference in the estimated cost of capital among the categories of banks. Moreover, their variations are generally parallel each other. Several reasons might seem to explain this observation. First, it is unlikely that there would exist much difference in the cost of capital among banks under a strictly regulated banking sector. The most

FIGURE 10–1
Time-Series Change in the Cost of Capital in the Banking Sector by Category

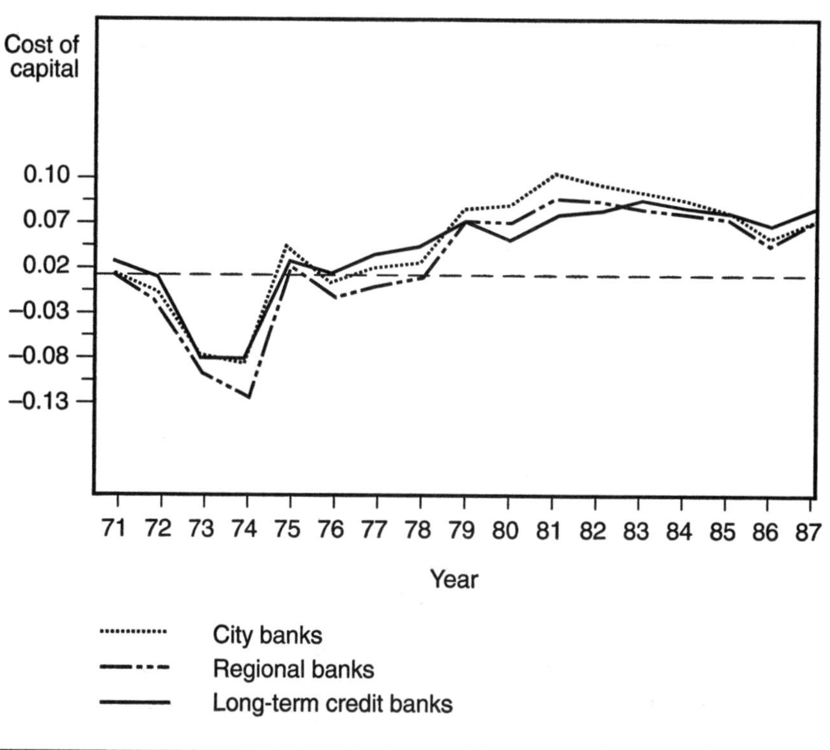

effective regulation for bringing about the same level of the cost of capital for banks is a regulation on interest rates so that an individual bank is prohibited from setting up its own interest rate. The interest rate for deposits has been determined largely by the Ministry of Finance and/or the Bank of Japan, and followed by all banks. Thus, there has been no difference in the rate of interest among banks, although there has been a considerable degree of difference in the implicit rate of interest among banks. One may plausibly infer that banks have attempted to diversify their services to customers by using the implicit rate of interest since the formal nominal rate of interest was common to all banks by regulation. Another reason for the parallel movements of the cost of capital among all categories of banks is that the

TABLE 10-1
Cost of Capital and Related Statistics (All Banks)

	XI	*XID*	*RHOD*	*WD*	*RHOM*	*WM*	*RHOR*	*WR*	*RHO*	*PI*	*TAU*	*P*	*X*	*Y*
1971	0.0628	0.0415	0.0535	0.8040	0.0554	0.1550	0.0708	0.0410	0.0545	0.0490	0.1179	0.0062	0.0191	0.0107
1972	0.0624	0.0407	0.0539	0.8111	0.0559	0.1487	0.0703	0.0402	0.0538	0.0670	0.1042	–0.0136	0.0194	0.0097
1973	0.0791	0.0443	0.0693	0.7919	0.0726	0.1692	0.0891	0.0388	0.0706	0.1570	0.0823	–0.0941	0.0312	0.0104
1974	0.0990	0.0553	0.0864	0.7815	0.0905	0.1804	0.1115	0.0381	0.0881	0.1890	0.0853	–0.1103	0.0392	0.0121
1975	0.0859	0.0553	0.0773	0.7890	0.0802	0.1733	0.0968	0.0377	0.0785	0.0610	0.0655	0.0188	0.0274	0.0130
1976	0.0747	0.0507	0.0675	0.7928	0.0698	0.1698	0.0842	0.0374	0.0685	0.0750	0.0664	–0.0070	0.0218	0.0132
1977	0.0671	0.0453	0.0605	0.7926	0.0626	0.1703	0.0756	0.0371	0.0614	0.0540	0.0666	0.0080	0.0195	0.0130
1978	0.0623	0.0380	0.0558	0.7982	0.0582	0.1661	0.0702	0.0357	0.0567	0.0440	0.0659	0.0136	0.0217	0.0122
1979	0.0801	0.0451	0.0732	0.7861	0.0766	0.1805	0.0903	0.0333	0.0744	0.0260	0.0437	0.0506	0.0314	0.0116
1980	0.0982	0.0630	0.0908	0.7880	0.0947	0.1802	0.1093	0.0318	0.0921	0.0460	0.0352	0.0478	0.0312	0.0115
1981	0.1031	0.0742	0.0962	0.7826	0.0994	0.1851	0.1148	0.0323	0.0974	0.0250	0.0362	0.0751	0.0256	0.0116
1982	0.0902	0.0606	0.0825	0.7852	0.0857	0.1856	0.1004	0.0293	0.0836	0.0160	0.0501	0.0712	0.0262	0.0105
1983	0.0789	0.0548	0.0720	0.7753	0.0746	0.1958	0.0878	0.0289	0.0730	0.0060	0.0544	0.0708	0.0213	0.0101
1984	0.0825	0.0585	0.0761	0.7718	0.0787	0.2008	0.0918	0.0274	0.0771	0.0150	0.0455	0.0651	0.0212	0.0093
1985	0.0710	0.0521	0.0655	0.7676	0.0675	0.2044	0.0790	0.0280	0.0663	0.0150	0.0490	0.0539	0.0168	0.0091
1986	0.0559	0.0429	0.0508	0.7611	0.0522	0.2113	0.0622	0.0276	0.0515	0.0150	0.0651	0.0390	0.0115	0.0086
1987	0.0520	0.0399	0.0468	0.7667	0.0481	0.2052	0.0579	0.0280	0.0474	–0.0010	0.0759	0.0523	0.0108	0.0080

Notes

XI = nonmonetary benefit (implicit rate of interest)
XID = effective rate of interest
RHOD = discount rate by deposit
WD = its weight
RHOM = discount rate by interbank loan
WM = its weight
RHOR = discount rate by retained earnings
WR = its weight
PI = inflation rate
TAU = effective corporate tax rate
P = cost of capital
X = service of noninterest
Y = unit cost of deposit

TABLE 10–2
Cost of Capital by Categories of Banks

	City Banks				*Regional Banks*				*Long-Term Credit Banks*				*Mutual Banks*			
	RHOD	*RHOM*	*RHOR*	*P*	*RHOD*	*RHOM*	*THOR*	*P*	*RHOD*	*RHOM*	*RHOR*	*P*	*RHOD*	*RHOM*	*RHOR*	*P*
1971	0.0520	0.0536	0.0683	0.0043	0.0473	0.0487	0.0649	–0.0008	0.0571	0.0603	0.0727	0.0121	0.0501	0.0514	0.0649	0.0016
1972	0.0462	0.0472	0.0589	–0.0224	0.0420	0.0428	0.0561	–0.0281	0.0621	0.0655	0.0785	–0.0017	0.0431	0.0439	0.0561	–0.0266
1973	0.0782	0.0822	0.0989	–0.0827	0.0701	0.0740	0.0963	–0.0988	0.0653	0.0681	0.0793	–0.0920	0.0705	0.0743	0.0963	–0.0985
1974	0.1056	0.1113	0.1335	–0.0867	0.0843	0.0890	0.1189	–0.1219	0.0713	0.0732	0.0857	–0.1202	0.0870	0.0917	0.1189	–0.1161
1975	0.0846	0.0881	0.1052	0.0263	0.0662	0.0682	0.0850	0.0069	0.0727	0.0753	0.0885	0.0148	0.0682	0.0700	0.0850	0.0084
1976	0.0652	0.0671	0.0804	–0.0096	0.0553	0.0564	0.0698	–0.0207	0.0712	0.0743	0.0881	–0.0010	0.0565	0.0574	0.0698	–0.0195
1977	0.0539	0.0550	0.0654	0.0005	0.0441	0.0445	0.0556	–0.0103	0.0678	0.0711	0.0850	0.0179	0.0453	0.0456	0.0556	–0.0090
1978	0.0487	0.0499	0.0596	0.0056	0.0419	0.0431	0.0535	–0.0017	0.0646	0.0675	0.0795	0.0244	0.0426	0.0436	0.0535	–0.0012
1979	0.0803	0.0839	0.0975	0.0572	0.0723	0.0765	0.0937	0.0514	0.0702	0.0714	0.0828	0.0468	0.0731	0.0773	0.0937	0.0513
1980	0.1075	0.1126	0.1288	0.0647	0.0924	0.0977	0.1154	0.0505	0.0779	0.0776	0.0883	0.0327	0.0935	0.0986	0.1154	0.0506
1981	0.1160	0.1209	0.1386	0.0952	0.0932	0.0987	0.1166	0.0736	0.0809	0.0782	0.0897	0.0558	0.0941	0.0995	0.1166	0.0741
1982	0.0941	0.0976	0.1133	0.0826	0.0754	0.0794	0.0958	0.0654	0.0752	0.0742	0.0861	0.0612	0.0761	0.0801	0.0958	0.0652
1983	0.0761	0.0785	0.0916	0.0745	0.0630	0.0656	0.0797	0.0631	0.0725	0.0729	0.0841	0.0695	0.0642	0.0667	0.0797	0.0630
1984	0.0819	0.0843	0.0978	0.0706	0.0655	0.0684	0.0820	0.0553	0.0759	0.0751	0.0859	0.0622	0.0664	0.0691	0.0820	0.0552
1985	0.0676	0.0694	0.0807	0.0557	0.0589	0.0610	0.0730	0.0479	0.0673	0.0676	0.0778	0.0545	0.0594	0.0613	0.0730	0.0479
1986	0.0493	0.0501	0.0594	0.0369	0.0431	0.0442	0.0538	0.0314	0.0573	0.0579	0.0672	0.0448	0.0432	0.0440	0.0536	0.0313
1987	0.0455	0.0463	0.0560	0.0510	0.0440	0.0456	0.0550	0.0494	0.0518	0.0518	0.0608	0.0559	0.0438	0.0452	0.0550	0.0494

Notes

RHOD = discount rate by deposit
RHOM = discount rate by interbank loan
RHOR =discount rate by retained earnings
P = cost of capital

estimation of the cost of capital is influenced strongly by inflation. The impact of the first oil-crisis is particularly impressive because it induced the negative cost of capital for all categories of banks. This negative cost of capital may be regarded as a subsidy to banks; a subsidy borne by consumers and savers.

From 1977 to 1982, significant fluctuation occurred with respect to the estimated cost of capital among bank categories. The highest cost of capital was at long-term credit banks during the first half of this period, followed by city banks, and regional banks. The ranking from the highest to the lowest during the second half of this period was city banks, regional banks, and long-term credit banks. Results, obtained for 1986 and 1987 suggest the same ranking as the one during the first half—i.e., long-term credit banks, city banks and regional banks—although the degree of the difference in the estimated cost of capital declined.

Reasons for the difference in the cost of capital by categories of banks are important. Here are several explanations for the recent result.

First, when we compare city banks with regional banks, the cost of interest payments in city banks is higher. This is especially apparent with respect to interbank loans. Since city banks have greater lending potential and better portfolio management capability, they are eager to collect higher amounts of funds. The easiest way is to borrow funds from other banks, usually smaller banks, even if the interest rate is higher. This is one of the reasons for the higher cost of capital at city banks.

Second, a similar explanation applies to interest payment on deposits. Namely, city banks pay higher costs of interest—both the economic interest rate and the implicit interest rate—to depositors than regional banks do. At first glance it is surprising to observe the different rates under the regulated interest rates. One of the reasons for the different rates between city banks and regional banks is the time lag; higher interest rates may have to be tolerated for two or three years by city banks because of the longer duration of deposits, i.e., two years after the deposit contract with a fixed rate of interest is settled. This is less likely to be the case at regional banks. Another reason for the difference is that city banks introduced deregulated interest rates, which resulted in higher costs earlier than regional banks.

Third, since long-term credit banks do not specialize in the deposit business, the cost of collecting deposits for them is significantly higher than for city and regional banks. The share of deposits to total funds of city and regional banks is about 80–90 percent, while the share of interbank loans for long-term credit banks is over 70 percent. The majority of long-term credit banks obtain capital through bond issuance, which some would argue are "interbank loans" while other says are a variant of deposits. In any case, the cost of collecting funds for long-term credit banks has risen.

Individual Banks

The previous section presented the aggregated results of the estimated cost of capital for each category of banks. In this section we shall focus on the performance of individual banks. Since there are so many banks, we present results only for selected banks and recent years. We included the largest five city banks, several smaller city banks, and randomly selected regional and mutual banks for years between 1985 and 1987. We do not take into account the contribution of unrealized capital gains. The measurement of the interest rate for each bank is made on the basis of the simple average of the figures at the beginning and at the end of each accounting period.

Table 10–3 provides the estimated cost of capital for individual banks. Since we have so many individual banks, we include only a few remarks in Table 10–3. Detailed evaluation should be the task of a management specialist. Such an evaluation requires a significant amount of knowledge on the performances of individual banks and goes beyond the scope of economic analysis.

First, it is quite natural that the results based on Table 10–3 reveal more strongly the findings based on Tables 10–1 and 10–2. Second, the variance of the cost of capital for regional banks is much larger than that for city banks. This suggests that the method of collecting funds and their performance are more diversified in regional banks than in city banks. In other words, city banks are not so different from each other in quality and management, while regional banks vary considerably. Third, several banks that are reported to perform very well report relatively lower cost of capital. This supports a finding that the cost of capital is one of the indicators of management abilities.

Unrealized Capital Gains

We noted earlier that Japanese banks hold large amounts of shares of other corporations and enjoy unrealized capital gains (or face unrealized capital loss) according to the fluctuation of share prices. This affects the business behaviour of banks as pointed out by Tachibanaki, Mitsui and Kitagawa (1991), and Tachibanaki and Taki (1991). In this section we will examine

TABLE 10–3
Cost of Capital by Individual Banks

	1985				*1986*				*1987*			
	RHOD	*RHOM*	*RHOR*	*P*	*RHOD*	*RHOM*	*RHOR*	*P*	*RHOD*	*RHOM*	*THOR*	*P*
DKB	0.0602	0.0680	0.0788	0.0488	0.0455	0.0523	0.0621	0.0342	0.0464	0.0433	0.0533	0.0522
Sumitomo	0.0615	0.0652	0.0762	0.0500	0.0542	0.0484	0.0563	0.0398	0.0507	0.0447	0.0545	0.0555
Fuji	0.0596	0.0663	0.0777	0.0488	0.0504	0.0474	0.0571	0.0329	0.0470	0.0462	0.0562	0.0526
Mitsubishi	0.0583	0.0668	0.0773	0.0473	0.0499	0.0505	0.0603	0.0379	0.0481	0.0491	0.0598	0.0543
Sanwa	0.0605	0.0683	0.0794	0.0494	0.0505	0.0488	0.0579	0.0376	0.0475	0.0434	0.0522	0.0518
CB5-T	0.0600	0.0669	0.0779	0.0489	0.0499	0.0495	0.0587	0.0374	0.0479	0.0454	0.0553	0.0533
Kyowa	0.0570	0.0692	0.0808	0.0464	0.0487	0.0492	0.0584	0.0362	0.0452	0.0455	0.0543	0.0497
Saitama	0.0593	0.0646	0.0750	0.0474	0.0474	0.0537	0.0638	0.0359	0.0473	0.0576	0.0675	0.0529
Hokutaku	0.0633	0.0739	0.0846	0.0519	0.0546	0.0542	0.0628	0.0413	0.0528	0.0498	0.0578	0.0556
Hiroshima	0.0514	0.0868	0.1034	0.0428	0.0443	0.0628	0.0762	0.0341	0.0404	0.0569	0.0682	0.0464
Shikoku	0.0584	0.0597	0.0705	0.0466	0.0516	0.0375	0.0445	0.0379	0.0466	0.0388	0.0460	0.0502
Musashino	0.0501	0.1183	0.1426	0.0420	0.0445	0.0874	0.1059	0.0348	0.0394	0.0456	0.0552	0.0446
Ohsaka	0.0543	0.0540	0.0662	0.0437	0.0492	0.0374	0.0446	0.0355	0.0454	0.0473	0.0553	0.0492
Shonai	0.0594	0.0532	0.0640	0.0480	0.0528	0.0345	0.0414	0.0400	0.0454	0.0136	0.0166	0.0492
IBJ	0.0710	0.0674	0.0773	0.0553	0.0530	0.0581	0.0676	0.0437	0.0632	0.0511	0.0605	0.0598
Chogin	0.0761	0.0662	0.0765	0.0558	0.0592	0.0591	0.0690	0.0465	0.0633	0.0538	0.0631	0.0602
Nissaigin	0.0670	0.0706	0.0808	0.0565	0.0644	0.0625	0.0716	0.0495	0.0597	0.0556	0.0641	0.0597
Fukuoka-S	0.0527	0.0581	0.0700	0.0421	0.0443	0.0429	0.0539	0.0333	0.0423	0.0314	0.0390	0.0471
Kohchi-S	0.0593	0.0371	0.0441	0.0462	0.0531	0.0296	0.0361	0.0403	0.0496	0.0651	0.0790	0.0569
Kokumin-S	0.0564	0.0497	0.0591	0.0442	0.0446	0.0323	0.0415	0.0335	0.0388	0.0210	0.0273	0.0447
Akita-S	0.0595	0.0177	0.0205	0.0445	0.0539	0.0201	0.0233	0.0387	0.0477	0.0340	0.0403	0.0510

Notes
RHOD = discount rate by deposit
RHOM = discount rate by interbank loan
CB5-T = largest five city banks
RHOR =discount rate by retained earnings
P = cost of capital

whether unrealized capital gains have an influence on the cost of capital. The calculation of unrealized capital gains in this chapter is more crude than the one performed in Tachibanaki, Mitsui and Kitagawa (1991), and uses a rough estimate released by two economic journals, "Toyo-keizai" and "Diamond," for the five largest city banks. The asset value of shares held by a bank is transformed from the book value level to the current (i.e., market) value level, but the debt value is kept unchanged. In sum, the research strategy and method of this section is fairly simple, and the result should be understood as preliminary.

Table 10–4 shows the estimated cost of capital for the five largest city banks. We again avoid detailed interpretations of the results for each bank, but give only a general observation. A general conclusion is that, with few exceptions, the estimated cost of capital that takes account of unrealized capital gains will be somewhat higher than the one that does not. We suggest two factors that interact to explain this. First, the weight of retained earnings in comparison with deposits and interbank loans increases when we consider unrealized capital gains. Second, the nominal discount rate for retained earnings is higher than that for deposits or interbank loans, generally speaking.

IV. COMPARISON WITH THE UNITED STATES

Performing an international comparative study is not an easy task. With respect to the banking sector there are several obstacles such as the differences in institutional backgrounds, accounting procedures, legal arrangements, and others. The current chapter does not attempt the arduous task of obtaining strictly comparable data but rather uses only existing data. Also, the comparison is attempted only for the aggregated figures of all banks.

It would be useful to mention the motivation for such a comparative study of the banking sectors between Japan and the United States. Deregulation, internationalization, and globalization are three key words that symbolize the current trend of the banking industries in both Japan and the United States, although the liberalization of U.S. banking has advanced further. Capital markets are highly integrated across the Pacific Ocean and competition between these two countries have become very severe. If the cost of capital in a home country is lower, the bank would be at a competitive advantage in a foreign country: the funds it collected relatively cheaply at home could be used efficiently in a foreign country through international

TABLE 10–4
Cost of Capital and Related Statistics for Five City Banks in Which Unrealized Capital Gains Are Taken into Account

	1985				*1986*				*1987*			
	RHOD	*RHOM*	*RHOR*	*P*	*RHOD*	*RHOM*	*RHOR*	*P*	*RHOD*	*RHOM*	*THOR*	*P*
DKB	0.0670	0.0688	0.0788	0.0549	0.0522	0.0537	0.0621	0.0399	0.0439	0.0442	0.0533	0.0499
Sumitomo	0.0648	0.0659	0.0762	0.0530	0.0491	0.0492	0.0563	0.0359	0.0456	0.0456	0.0545	0.0511
Fuji	0.0656	0.0672	0.0777	0.0540	0.0486	0.0490	0.0571	0.0362	0.0466	0.0472	0.0562	0.0522
Mitsubishi	0.0659	0.0677	0.0773	0.0537	0.0514	0.0522	0.0603	0.0391	0.0492	0.0499	0.0598	0.0556
Sanwa	0.0674	0.0690	0.0794	0.0554	0.0496	0.0501	0.0579	0.0369	0.0441	0.0443	0.0522	0.0488
CB5-T	0.0661	0.0677	0.0779	0.0542	0.0501	0.0508	0.0587	0.0375	0.0459	0.0463	0.0553	0.0516

Notes
RHOD = discount rate by deposit
RHOM = discount rate by interbank loan
CB5-T = largest five city banks
RHOR =discount rate by retained earnings
P = cost of capital

capital mobility. In other words, it is possible to predict fairly well competitiveness in the international banking business by examining the cost of capital.

An examination of banking in Japan and the United States is useful in view of Japanese and U.S. power in international banking and the high degree of capital mobility between the two countries. Although there are a few studies that conduct international comparisons of the cost of capital in the banking industry—including Aliber (1984), Goldberg and Saunders (1980), and Porzencanski (1981)—these studies do not necessarily concentrate on Japan and the United States.

Let us examine briefly past comparative studies dealing with the cost of capital in Japan and the United States not only for the banking industries but also for the manufacturing industries. Abstracting the two countries' banking sectors from the previously mentioned studies, it seems that there is a consensus that U.S. banks have a higher cost of capital than Japanese banks. Umene (1986) is one exception, arguing that the cost of capital is essentially the same. It should be emphasized, however, that the method of the estimation differs from study to study.

What is the result of studies of the nonfinancial industries? We can find a large number of investigations: Baldwin (1986), Ando and Auerback (1988a, 1988b), Bernnheim and Shoven (1986), Hatsopoulos and Brooks (1987), Friend and Tokutsu (1986), Shoven and Tachibanaki (1988), Kikutani and Tachibanaki (1990). Many studies suggest that competition between Japan and the United States in the manufacturing sector is very severe, and considerable interest has been shown regarding the effect of taxation on the cost of capital.

It is important to point out that the method of estimation and coverage of industries and firms vary from study to study. It is risky to propose a strict conclusion, but a consensus suggests that the cost of capital is higher for U.S. nonfinancial firms than for Japanese firms. The exception is Baldwin (1986), who argues that the U.S. cost of capital is lower.

In summary, almost all the studies reviewed suggest that the cost of capital is higher in the United States for both the manufacturing and the banking industries.

The findings of this study are set forth below. Note that Table 10–5 shows the aggregate result for U.S. banks, which may be compared with Table 10–1 and Figure 10–2 shows a graph.

First, the movements in time-series are roughly parallel for the two countries. This reflects the fact that the estimated cost of capital is influ-

TABLE 10-5
Cost of Capital and Related Statistics for the U.S. Banks (Total)

	XI	*XID*	*RHOD*	*WD*	*RHOM*	*WM*	*RHOR*	*WR*	*RHO*	*PI*	*TAU*	*P*	*X*	*Y*
1976	0.0593	0.0281	0.0479	0.5875	0.0563	0.3494	0.0494	0.0632	0.0509	0.0640	0.0504	−0.0137	0.0223	0.0160
1977	0.0590	0.0298	0.0481	0.5944	0.0559	0.3434	0.0491	0.0622	0.0508	0.0670	0.0522	−0.0171	0.0209	0.0157
1978	0.0761	0.0297	0.0596	0.5725	0.0721	0.3664	0.0633	0.0611	0.0644	0.0740	0.0529	−0.0102	0.0332	0.0156
1979	0.1089	0.0341	0.0840	0.5452	0.1044	0.3942	0.0907	0.0606	0.0925	0.0880	0.0416	0.0046	0.0535	0.0161
1980	0.1319	0.0427	0.1031	0.5345	0.1276	0.4048	0.1098	0.0607	0.1134	0.0910	0.0325	0.0232	0.0639	0.0170
1981	0.1653	0.0576	0.1320	0.5136	0.1619	0.4253	0.1376	0.0612	0.1450	0.0960	0.0206	0.0501	0.0771	0.0180
1982	0.1383	0.0632	0.1151	0.5019	0.1361	0.4361	0.1151	0.0620	0.1242	0.0650	0.0159	0.0602	0.0537	0.0189
1983	0.0978	0.0615	0.0853	0.5391	0.0953	0.3979	0.0814	0.0630	0.0890	0.0390	0.0251	0.0513	0.0260	0.0186
1984	0.1159	0.0608	0.0978	0.5597	0.1130	0.3762	0.0965	0.0642	0.1034	0.0370	0.0249	0.0681	0.0395	0.0183
1985	0.0896	0.0541	0.0771	0.5624	0.0868	0.3718	0.0746	0.0657	0.0805	0.0290	0.0311	0.0532	0.0254	0.0185
1986	0.0737	0.0470	0.0631	0.5706	0.0715	0.3636	0.0615	0.0658	0.0666	0.0270	0.0326	0.0409	0.0192	0.0184
1987	0.0725	0.0366	0.0601	0.5727	0.0700	0.3628	0.0604	0.0645	0.0637	0.0330	0.0355	0.0318	0.0257	0.0184

Notes

XI = nonmonetary benefit (implicit rate of interest)
XID = effective rate of interest
RHOD = discount rate by deposit
WD = its weight
RHOM = discount rate by interbank loan
WM = its weight
RHOR = discount rate by retained earnings
WR = its weight
PI = inflation rate
TAU = effective corporate tax rate
P = cost of capital
X = service of noninterest
Y = unit cost of deposit

FIGURE 10–2
Times-Series Change in the Banking Industry in Japan and the United States

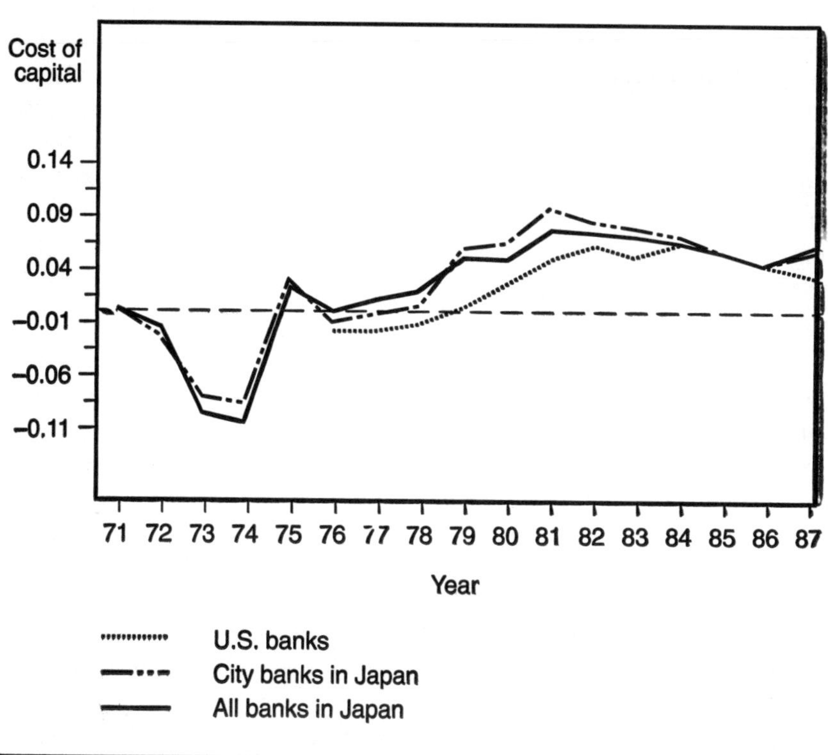

enced by the rate of inflation, and both countries have experienced fairly similar changes in their actual inflation rates.

Second, despite the limited degree of the parallel movements, the estimated cost of capital in the two countries was different from 1977 to 1983. Specifically, U.S. banks had a lower cost of capital than Japanese banks. This is a somewhat unexpected outcome in view of the general observation described above.

Third, the cost of capital in Japan and the U.S. has converged in recent years. In particular, the levels evened out in 1984 because of the increase in the cost of capital at U.S. banks. This probably reflects higher interest rates in the U.S. relative to other countries. After 1984 the two countries show a common declining trend, staying at roughly equal levels. The result for 1987 is an exception.

These observations compel explanation. Before going to these issues, we briefly summarize several distinctive features of the banking industries in Japan and the United States on the basis of Tables 10–1 and 10–5. First, for many years both the implicit and the effective rates of interest in the United States are higher than in Japan. Also, the fluctuation of these rates is greater in the U.S. than in Japan. Second, deposits are far more important (about 80 percent) as a source of funds in the Japanese banks, while they are less important in the U.S. banks (about 50–60 percent). Incidentally, interbank loans show a smaller share, but are as important (about 40 percent) as deposits in the United States. Both countries show very low shares of retained earnings. Third, the Japanese effective corporate tax rates are higher than in the U.S. in nearly all years.

Next we compare the estimated discount rate for each source of funds. First, the nominal discount rate for deposits fluctuated more strongly in the United States than in Japan. This is a reflection of the first comparative result set out above. Also, with the exceptions of 1976, 1977, and 1985, the discount rate in the United States is higher than in Japan. This suggests that the cost of capital in the United States would be higher than that in Japan if the other conditions were the same. Second, the nominal discount rate for interbank loans in American banks has been higher than in Japanese banks over many years with the exception of 1976 and 1977. This also suggests that the U.S. cost of capital would otherwise have been higher in many years.

Let us go back to the comparison of the estimated cost of capital. We can suggest several reasons for the lower cost of capital in the United States than in Japan in the early years of the observation period. First, the exceptions described above have some influence. Second, the higher rate of inflation in the United States contributed to the lowering of the cost of capital. As the tables suggest, the U.S. inflation rates were in general higher than Japan's during the observation period. Third, as noted previously, the effective corporate tax rates for the banking sectors were higher in Japan than in the United States. This raised the estimated cost of capital in Japan and lowered it in the United States. These three effects are regarded as the main reasons for the higher cost of capital in Japanese banks than in U.S. banks during the early years of the observation period.

What happened in recent years? The two countries have the nearly the same levels of estimated cost of capital. Since the discount rates for both deposits and interbank loans were higher in U.S. banks than in the Japanese banks, the U.S. cost of capital would have to be higher. The actual story does not support this in recent years. Two reasons are suggested. First, the effect of inflation is currently fairly minor because the difference in the rates of inflation between Japan and the U.S. is not large. Second, the tax rates are now about the same so they have little effect on the comparable costs of capital. Finally, internationalization and globalization of banking activities through international capital mobility, in particular between Japan and the United States, could be contributing to the equalizing of the cost of capital between the two countries. Another work is necessary to confirm or reject this speculation.

V. CONCLUDING REMARKS

This chapter offered a method for estimating the cost of capital in the banking sector in which the method of collecting funds and financing is significantly different from that used by the manufacturing sector. The estimated cost of capital in the Japanese banking industry was presented and compared with that of U.S. banks. Emphasis was placed upon the difference in the estimated cost of capital among various categories of banks in Japan such as city banks, regional banks, mutual banks, and long-term credit banks as well as among individual banks. The contribution of unrealized capital gains caused by Japanese banks' holding of other corporations' shares was examined very briefly.

The findings of this study are summarized briefly below. Although the fluctuation of the cost of capital between various categories of banks in Japan is roughly parallel historically, differences exist in the cost of capital among various categories of banks and among individual banks. This suggests that each category of bank adopts a different business strategy to cope with the problem of collecting funds in a system that strictly regulates interest rates. Additionally, efficiency or management ability differs from bank to bank to a certain extent. Unrealized capital gains, however, contributed only marginally to this variation. Finally, our comparison of Japanese cost of capital with the U.S. cost of capital indicates that the two countries have recently maintained similar levels of estimated cost of capital, although Japan had a higher cost of capital than the U.S. during the period 1977–1983. The examination of the cost of capital in the financial sector is very important because a greater degree of international capital mobility, in particular between Japan and the U.S., is now common. The author hopes that this study may serve as a starting point for future research in this area.

Finally, the study identified considerable year-to-year variations in the cost of capital. This may cause some confusion regarding the differences in the cost of capital among various categories of banks and among individual banks. As emphasized in the main text, the adjustment for the rate of inflation is largely responsible for year-to-year variations in both Japan and the United States. A comparison on a nominal basis would reduce the ambiguity of our result; this would test whether the hypothesis of equality across all categories of banks holds. Accordingly, the conclusions of this chapter with respect to year-to-year variations should be understood as being preliminary.

REFERENCES

Aliber, R. Z. (1984), "International Banking: A Survey," *Journal of Money, Credit and Banking,* vol. XVI. No. 4. November, pp. 661–77.

Ando, A., and A. J. Auerback (1988a), "The Corporate Cost of Capital in Japan and the U.S.: A Comparison," in John B. Shoven (ed.), *Government Policy Towards Industry in the U.S.A. and Japan,* Cambridge University Press, pp. 21–50.

Ando, A., and A. J. Auerback (1988b), "The Cost of Capital in the United States and Japan: A Comparison," *Journal of Japanese and International Economies,* vol. 2, No. 2, pp. 134–58.

Baldwin, C. Y. (1986), "The Capital Factor: Competing for Capital in a Global Environment, " in M. E. Porter (ed), *Competition in Global Industries,* Boston, Harvard University Press, pp. 185–223.

Bernheim, D.B., and John B. Shoven (1986), "Taxation and the Cost of Capital: An International Comparison," Center for Economic Policy Research discussion paper no. 90.

Friend, I., and I. Tokutsu (1986), "The Cost of Capital to Corporations in Japan and the U.S.A.," Rodney L. White Center for Financial Research, Wharton School, University of Pennsylvania.

Goldberg, L. G., and A. Saunders (1981), "The Determinants of Foreign Banking Activity in the United States, " *Journal of Banking and Finance,* vol. 5 (March), pp. 17–32.

Hatsopoulos, G. N., and S. H. Brooks (1987), "The Cost of Capital in the U.S. and Japan," *International Conference on the Cost of Capital,* Harvard University.

King, M. (1977), *Public Policy and the Corporation,* Cambridge Studies in Applied Econometrics No. 3, Chapman and Hall Ltd.

King, M., and D. Fullerton (1984), *The Taxation of Income from Capital,* The University of Chicago Press.

Kikutani, T., and T. Tachibanaki (1990), "The Taxation of Income from Capital in Japan: Historical Perspectives and Policy Simulations," in C. Hulten (ed.), *Productivity Growth in Japan and the United States,* University of Chicago Press.

Porzencanski, A. C. (1981), "The International Financial Role of U.S. Banks, Past and Future," *Journal of Banking and Finance,* vol. 5, March, pp. 5–16.

Shoven, J. B., and T. Tachibanaki, (1988), "The Taxation of Income from Capital in Japan," in John B. Shoven (ed.), *Government Policy Towards Industry in the U.S.A. and Japan,* Cambridge University Press, pp. 51–96.

Tachibanaki, T., and A. Taki (1991), "Shareholding and Lending Activity of Financial Institutions in Japan," *Bank of Japan Monetary and Economic Studies,* vol. 9, no. 1, March, pp. 23–60.

Tachibanaki, T., K. Mitsui, and H. Kitagawa (1991), "Economies of Scope and Intercorporate Share Ownership in the Japanese Banking Industries," *Journal of Japanese and International Economies,* Vol. 5, pp. 261–81.

Tachibanaki, T., and T. Kimura, "The Cost of Capital in Financial Institutions in Japan: City Banks, Regional Banks, Long-Term Credit Banks, Trust Banks, and Life Insurance Companies," Kyoto Institute of Economic Research discussion paper no. 361.

Umene, T. (1986), "Cost of Capital Comparison Empirical Results: Japanese Banks and U.S. Banks," University of Chicago Business School mimeo.

CHAPTER 11

A CONTRARY VIEW OF JAPAN'S COST OF CAPITAL ADVANTAGE

Timothy A. Luehrman

For many years managers have been encouraged, partly by academic financial economists, to think of capital as a commodity traded in world markets. In this view, getting a "good deal" is difficult, but sometimes possible for companies that are large, sophisticated, frequent issuers, and alert to special opportunities for tax and regulatory arbitrage. Consequently, many companies have come to regard minimizing the cost of capital as a highly specialized sourcing problem, to be addressed with external solutions. The financial officer in charge of this process in a large multinational corporation may behave more like a grain buyer than a financial manager. However, unlike grain, capital will be expensive regardless of where it is sourced if it is expected to be used inefficiently. Recent advances in corporate finance theory suggest that corporations need to be efficient and informative *users* of capital, and that efficiency depends on several factors besides operations. A corporation's capital, ownership, governance, and compensation structures also affect how efficiently capital will be used to the extent that they affect how *future* investment, financing, and payout decisions will be made. In this view, minimizing the cost of capital is also a managerial problem, with internal solutions.

This distinction between internal and external determinants of the cost

I am grateful to Ken Froot and Carl Kester for helpful discussions. Any errors are solely the author's responsibility.

of capital is important for assessing differences in capital costs across firms and, *a fortiori*, across countries. Many academic studies have attempted to measure and compare the average cost of capital in Japan and the United States. Most, though not all, report that capital was consistently and significantly less expensive in Japan during the 1970s and 1980s. With few exceptions, such studies are designed to discover differences in capital costs that originate externally, in the capital markets, rather than internally, in the firms. In this chapter the distinction between internal and external phenomena is combined with a critical evaluation of previous studies' methodologies to produce a contrary view of Japan's cost of capital advantage, which may be summarized in three specific observations.

First, the statistical evidence of a persistent Japanese cost-of-capital advantage is unconvincing. The formal studies reporting lower capital costs in Japan have serious methodological problems and limitations. In fact, presently available statistical evidence cannot reject the hypothesis that external capital markets supplied funds to the U.S. and Japanese manufacturing sectors on substantially similar terms, on average, for the past twenty years. This fact is entirely compatible with, indeed it is suggested by, the view that capital is a commodity traded in global markets. It does not support the view that government restrictions on either investors or issuers have succeeded in lowering the average cost of capital.

Second, however, some Japanese corporations may indeed have been more efficient users of capital during the past two decades than their U.S. counterparts, due to certain features of the Japanese systems of industrial organization and corporate governance. If such an "efficiency gap" existed, it would indeed constitute a sustainable cost-of-capital advantage, and it could help explain differences in U.S. and Japanese corporate investment behavior. But it is *not* the external cost gap that most studies are designed to detect and many claim to have found. Nor is it certain that it existed, or if it did, how significant it was. Indeed, it was more likely isolated and transient rather than pervasive and persistent.

Third, as the Japanese economy continues to evolve and as managerial practices change, Japan's present systems of corporate organization and governance could produce a moderate cost-of-capital *dis*advantage in the future. Some of the necessary ingredients are now present in Japan for an erosion of the relatively high degree of trust, consensus, and cooperation that has characterized Japanese financial relationships in the past and fostered the efficient use of capital.

This chapter is organized in three sections corresponding to these observations. The first examines the limitations of existing statistical comparisons of Japanese and U.S. capital costs. The second sketches linkages between the internal corporate decision-making apparatus and the cost of capital. It briefly compares some of the stylized facts about U.S. and Japanese systems and summarizes the scarce empirical evidence on this topic. The third section concludes by speculating about the prospects for a future Japanese cost-of-capital disadvantage, rooted in environmental, institutional and managerial changes.

PRESENT STATISTICAL EVIDENCE

In the early 1980s several studies were published in the United States that reported startling differences in the cost of capital between the United States and Japan.[1] The earliest studies were conceptually flawed, but they spawned many subsequent investigations which also reported significantly lower costs of capital in Japan than in the United States. The latter include, for example, Hatsopoulos and Brooks (1986), Bernheim and Shoven (1987), Friend and Tokutsu (1987), Ando and Auerbach (1988a, 1988b, 1990) and McCauley and Zimmer (1989).[2] Most of these researchers offer several differently constructed estimates of the gap between the two countries. The preponderance of the estimates favor Japan, by anywhere from 0% to 7% per year on average, over sample periods dating back to the early 1960s.

The Weighted Average Cost of Capital

The methodology employed by most such studies is to compute a weighted average cost of capital (WACC) for both countries, and then compare them. The WACC is the average of the after-corporate tax cost of debt and the cost of equity, each weighted by its proportion of the capital structure:

$$\text{WACC} = [D/(D+E)]\, k_d[1-t_c] + [E/(D+E)]k_e,$$

where D and E are the debt and equity in the capital structure, respectively; k_d and k_e are the costs of debt and equity, respectively; and t_c is the corporate tax rate. Under some circumstances, the WACC is an appropriate estimate of the opportunity cost of capital a firm should use in deciding whether to undertake an investment. This is by no means universally so, and even if it were, it is extremely difficult to estimate a WACC for entire countries. Such comparisons have at least four serious drawbacks.[3]

Violations of MM Proposition 1.

Researchers construct estimates of each country's WACC from separate estimates of national average capital structures, and national average costs of debt and equity. However, the costs of debt and equity *depend* on the capital structure, and estimating each component separately is highly unlikely to properly reflect this dependence. For example, some studies have noted historically higher leverage in Japan, and pointed out that, all else equal, more debt and less equity results in a significantly lower WACC.[4] But all else is *not* equal when capital structure changes. The costs of debt and equity are *both* higher for a more highly levered firm, and failure to recognize this leads to gross errors in the estimation of the WACC.

Similarly, many researchers have gone to great pains to adjust corporàte financial accounting data to compute national average debt and equity ratios. But then they combine the ratios with inappropriate debt and equity costs. For example, Hatsopoulos and Brooks (1986) use yields on AAA-rated corporate bonds as the cost of debt for both Japan and the United States.[5] This is inappropriate because the national average capital structure is not AAA-quality in either country. The same error results when researchers carefully match data sources across countries to make sure, for example, that they use a AAA bond from each. Such matching is indisputably wrong unless average leverage is the same in both countries, yet the researchers themselves typically assert that it is not.

Finally, most studies do not properly treat large changes over time in national average leverage ratios. Most agree that leverage has changed in both Japan and the United States. Poterba (1990), for example, estimates that Japanese debt-equity ratios fell from 1.33 to 0.55 from 1985 to 1989, a period in which U.S. leverage was rising. Researchers accordingly change the debt and equity ratios in their WACC computation for each year, but they fail to change the benchmark bond yield or lending rate, even though credit quality has clearly changed. The resulting estimate of WACC can hardly fail to be wrong more often than right.

Each of the problems just outlined is a violation of Modigliani and Miller's (1958) Proposition 1. The problems afflict the estimated WACC for each country at any point in time; they afflict each estimate differently at different times; and they afflict each country differently. Unfortunately, there is no reason to believe the errors in existing WACC comparisons are small; on the contrary, simple numerical examples show that they can be quite large [see Kester and Luehrman (1991b)]. Nor is there any reason to expect that they tend to cancel one another. Further, every cross-country comparison of WACCs published so far is afflicted with this shortcoming. The only sure way to overcome it is to *jointly estimate* leverage ratios and debt and equity costs for each firm, and *then* compare the cross-sectional distribution of WACCs for each country. No study has yet attempted this difficult project.

Inadequate Controls For Risk

Different businesses should have different costs of capital if one is riskier than the other. The same is true of countries. A difference in capital costs that is attributable to differences in risk should not be regarded as a true cost advantage or disadvantage. Formal cross-country comparisons need to be controlled for differences in risk, yet most are not. Of those that do control for risk, none report significant differences between the countries.[6]

Because risk is difficult to measure, it is difficult to control for it. Researchers must either select samples according to a risk-based criterion, or measure risk and adjust the data for it. Neither approach is perfect and both introduce errors that could obscure a true cost of capital gap. Nonetheless, given manifestly different manufacturing bases, manufacturing practices, and investment opportunity sets in the United States and Japan over the last thirty years, it seems unlikely that risk was the same in both countries over that time.

Country-level Measurement Errors

National differences in the extent to which corporate financial accounts accurately reflect reality are an unavoidable source of measurement error in WACC comparisons. To the extent such errors are *systematic* rather than random, estimates of the cost of capital will be *biased* rather than simply inefficient. Some measurement errors arise simply from differences in accounting rules and adjustments can be made for many of these.[7] Other problems are more difficult to handle with simple adjustments because the necessary data are unavailable. For example, hidden assets, such as land on Japanese corporate balance sheets, may be hard to identify and value correctly.[8]

Even if both countries' accounts could be stated using the same rules, country level measurement error still remains a problem to the extent that the gap between book and market values differs systematically across countries. Simple examples are differences in the average age of plant and equipment, or in the rate of change in the value of land carried at historical cost. Another example is differences in the extent to which price-earnings ratios (even after accounting adjustments) approximate the cost of equity.

None of the published comparisons of the cost of capital make all the indicated adjustments because for some, the necessary data are unavailable. This is a serious problem because most of the widely recognized biases run the same direction; they make Japanese capital costs appear lower than they really are. Furthermore, measurement errors in the individual components of the cost of capital are compounded when the WACC is computed. The resulting bias is likely to be significant, even compared to the WACC; it is still more significant compared to the *difference* in WACCs for each country.

Noise and Heteroscedasticity

Even if estimates of the cost of capital were unbiased, a comparison of means across countries has very little power to reject the hypothesis that the cost of capital is the same for both countries. Most studies do not report standard errors or confidence intervals for their estimates of the gap, but these must be very large compared to the reported gap. This is because key components of the WACC have large standard errors, particularly leverage ratios and costs of equity.[9] The process of combining components in the WACC formula, and subtracting one country's WACC from the other's does not reduce the standard errors much, if at all. The large standard errors originate in part from noise and heteroscedasticity in the data, especially stock market data that generate the price-earnings ratios and/or realized equity returns that are most often used to estimate the cost of equity. Econometric sophistication helps only very little; what is needed instead is substantially more data, which do not yet exist.

In short, even ignoring all the previously-mentioned problems, the cost-of-capital gap reported by most studies is quite unlikely to be statistically significant. Nor is the statistical significance of the gap much enhanced by regarding all the results of all the studies together. Because so many studies use similar methodologies and data, the estimates they report should not be regarded as independent. In other words, the fact that so many studies reach qualitatively similar conclusions should *not* raise our overall confidence in the result itself.

Alternatives to the Weighted Average Cost of Capital

The four problems described above make cross-country comparisons of the weighted average cost of capital unreliable. Fortunately, there are alternative ways to compare Japanese and U.S. costs of capital. Though each of these has limitations of its own, they generally do not corroborate the large gaps reported in WACC comparison studies.

The first alternative is to compare real interest rates in Japan and the United States. Such comparisons omit the risk premium associated with equity investments, but they consequently avoid some of the problems just outlined, particularly violations of MM Proposition 1 and measurement error due to accounting differences.

Differences between U.S. and Japanese long term real interest rates are hard to measure because reliable data are scarce, but the differences do not appear to have been large. Bernheim and Shoven (1987) estimate a differential of 0.30% (U.S. minus Japan) during 1971–82. French and Poterba (1991) report a difference of 0.58% during 1986–88. Even these estimates are likely to overstate the gap because the available historical data on long term Japanese interest rates (from banks and government and corporate bond markets) clearly understate actual borrowing costs. Until fairly recently, long term Japanese government bonds were issued, at inflated prices, solely to certain Japanese institutions that were prevented from actively trading them. Posted bank lending rates similarly understate Japanese corporate borrowing costs because they do not reflect compensating balances, nor the web of commercial and financial relationships and transactions that tie together Japanese banks and their corporate customers.[10] Finally, until quite recently, the public corporate bond market in Japan was too small, illiquid, and unrepresentative to supply data on borrowing costs for the manufacturing sector as a whole.

The data for short term instruments, such as Gensaki, are more prevalent and reliable, though obviously less indicative of long term corporate capital costs. Using these data and realized inflation, Kester and Luehrman (1989) found that real riskless rates differed substantially at many different points during 1977–85, but that the differences favored neither country overall. The mean difference in 90-day ex post real rates was essentially zero during that period.

It is important to note that if the gap between real interest rates truly is small, maybe even non-existent, it is difficult to explain, even theoretically, a large gap in WACCs—these two results are incompatible in all but a few circumstances. The most promising possibilities for reconciling these positions are: differences in interest tax shields; differences in riskiness; and differences in the price of risk.

The first of these, tax shields, is attributed to relatively greater use in Japan of tax-advantaged debt financing.[11] However, it is implausible that this accounts for a large difference in capital costs as measured by WACCs. When MM Proposition 1 is properly observed, the difference between the WACC for a levered versus an unlevered firm is simply not that large. Cross-country differences in leverage would have to be *huge* in order for interest tax shields alone to account for even a modest difference in WACCs. The empirical evidence shows that they were not huge in the 1970s and early 1980s (see Michel and Shaked (1985) and Kester (1986)). They certainly are not huge now, or if they are, it is not the Japanese companies that are more highly levered (see, for example, Poterba (1990) and Ando and Auerbach (1988b, 1990).[12]

Riskiness, measured by the variance of expected returns on the market portfolio in each country, does not appear to differ significantly across countries (see Kester and Luehrman (1991a)). However, the data are not good enough for drawing strong inferences about market-wide risk characteristics. Moreover, risk could differ significantly across matched industry samples, even without significant aggregate differences. In any event, even a well-documented risk gap would not constitute a cost-of-capital gap. It would only underscore the importance of controlling WACC estimates for differences in risk.

Differences in the price of risk could explain a cost of capital gap, and these are not picked up in comparisons of real interest rates. The price of risk is defined as the slope of the capital market line, that is, the increase in the required expected return associated with a marginal unit of risk. Gultekin, Gultekin, and Penati (1989) and Kester and Luehrman (1991a), tested for differences in the price of risk in Japan and the United States using data from the 1980s and somewhat different methodologies. Neither study found significant differences in the price of risk.[13]

ON USING CAPITAL EFFICIENTLY—THE MICRO-STRUCTURE OF THE FIRM

The isolation of Japan's capital markets during the thirty years following World War II should have made capital more rather than less expensive compared to countries such as the United States with better diversification opportunities for investors. Some Japanese companies or industries may indeed have been granted preferential access to funds, perhaps at low rates, but this occurred at the expense of other parts of the economy. Japan as a whole experienced a scarcity of capital that was acute at times. Some good projects failed to attract financing because capital was, in effect, rationed. For such projects the cost of capital was infinite. This makes it difficult to measure an "average" cost of capital for Japan during this period.

More recently, a sustained cost of capital advantage for any one nation seems inconsistent with the global mobility of capital and the profusion of new instruments, issuers, and management techniques that now characterize the capital markets. Indeed, the statistical evidence discussed above does not demonstrate the existence of any such sustained national advantage. In what sense then, might Japanese capital be less expensive than U.S. capital?

It may help to think of competitive capital markets as a perceptive and prudent person who sits on a stool behind a window, who understands nearly everything you say, but who cannot speak except in rates. When you need capital, you go to the window and explain what you plan to do and how you are organized to do it. Then you request an amount, a currency, and a maturity and you are told a rate. That rate is your cost of capital. We assume that this is the only capital window in the world, so you and all your competitors have to use it.

Now suppose you go to the window but you *do not* explain what you are going to do or how you are organized to do it. You just request an amount, a currency, and a maturity. You will still be told a rate, and you can still get the capital you need. But the rate is going to be higher. It has to be, just in case you have in mind a risky plan or one that you are not well-equipped to execute. You are going to have a higher cost of capital, *not* because of the market, but because of you. Further, you might be charged a higher rate than your competitors even if you *do* tell the person in the window everything about your plans. Your plans may be riskier than theirs, or less efficient. Or perhaps your organization does not fit well with your plans, or is more prone to unproductive haggling among different types of claimants.

This cartoon is a very different depiction of the way the world works than one in which every country has its own little capital window, which is manipulated behind the scenes by the local government, and to which only local firms have access. In the former, note that whether the cost of capital is *generally* high or low is largely determined by the person in the window, i.e., the global capital market. But whether capital costs are *relatively* high or low across particular firms is largely determined by the firms. It is these latter firm-specific, organizationally-driven differences in capital costs that can be translated into competitive advantages. It is possible, of course, that some such differences arise solely from differences in the currencies and maturities that companies select. More likely, they are produced by differences in the market's perception of each company's plans and capabilities.

What would a researcher studying this system observe? In a very large sample of companies and their costs of capital, probably not much. By construction, the market is rational, and the mean difference for entire countries would be small. It is the *tails* of the distribution of differences that would be interesting. A careful comparison of particular industries or even individual competitors would probably reveal that some are charged less than others. To the extent that firms' opportunities, plans, and organizational capabilities are correlated with their national identities, such a gap would look like gap across countries. But any competitive advantage should be attributed to the firms themselves and not to capital markets.

In the real world the outstanding organizational difference between U.S. and Japanese companies is in their ownership and governance structures. Ownership of the typical large Japanese company is concentrated in the hands of large financial institutions which are clustered around the main bank, and other, often commercially affiliated, manufacturing concerns. Ownership of the typical large U.S. company is much more dispersed. Institutional investors such as pension funds and mutual funds might collectively hold a majority of its shares, but they are basically passive, nearly as much so as small private investors.

The contrast is important because for Japanese companies historically, the person behind the capital window was the main bank. The main bank owned a large block of stock in addition to its outstanding loans to the company. It had extensive, reliable information about the firm's prospects and performance, including some of its own former officers in key positions inside the company. It also had the capacity to become quickly and actively involved in the management of the company when problems arose. In the event of a crisis, the main bank's leadership within the group of lenders, owners, and affiliates that surrounded the company was unquestioned, and it was heavily relied upon. These relationships made it safer to provide capital, not only for the main bank, but for other lenders as well. In principle at least, this made it possible to charge less for capital.[14]

Of course, the network of relationships among Japanese industrial companies and their banks is much broader and more complex than just described. It has been documented and studied in greater detail elsewhere; for example, in Abbeglen and Stalk (1985) and Kester (1991a, 1991b). These defining relationships among Japanese firms have been durable partly because they are reciprocal. For example, when the bank needs to go to the capital window (as many have since the adoption of new BIS capital requirements), the person sitting there is its familiar corporate client, who owns a significant block of equity in the bank, and who is expected to take up a pro rata share in new stock offerings.

In contrast, company-bank relationships in the United States have deteriorated steadily over the past thirty years. U.S. banks are prohibited from owning large blocks of equity in their customers. When problems arise, they are potentially liable to shareholders if they become too closely involved in the management of the company. In most cases, they lack practical knowledge about the borrower's business. In the event of a crisis, leadership may arrive late and from unpredictable quarters. Indeed, it may not arrive at all and a leaderless band of claimants may assemble instead in bankruptcy court, where rules and prevailing customs do not particularly favor lenders.

When comparing the stylized Japanese firm and its stylized American competitor, *any* supplier of capital might deem the Japanese company the more desirable credit and lend at an accordingly lower expected rate of return. It may or may not be the case that the *likelihood* of distress is lower for the Japanese firm; the *cost* of distress, given that it occurs, is lower. In a traditional static tradeoff model of optimal capital structure, the Japanese firm will have a higher optimal debt ratio and realize more value from interest tax shields. In effect, it has a lower WACC.[15]

Other models of optimal capital structure explicitly incorporate costs associated with agency and information problems.[16] These models suggest even more strongly that organizational structures that attenuate conflict between agents and principals or that overcome certain information asymmetries should favorably affect the terms on which capital is made available to a company. Such theories are typically illustrated with examples in which a firm's endowment of investment opportunities (great or small), or the nature of its assets (tangible or intangible) determines the severity of the agency or information problem it confronts. But they apply as well to examples in which all firms confront the same basic agency or information problem, but are differently constrained in their organizational responses to it. Hodder (1991), for example, presents a specific version of this general argument in his discussion of the role of Japanese main banks in reducing agency costs through their monitoring activities.

No new theory is required to extend agency and information-based models of capital structure from endowment and asset characteristics to organizational characteristics. But admitting the latter into consideration immediately suggests the relevance of many managerial concerns. In financial economists' jargon, the "micro-structure" of the firm is another determinant of its cost of capital. The micro-structure includes those features of its organization used in making individual decisions and executing individual transactions, e.g., reporting relationships, formal and informal information channels, cash flow channels, budgeting rules, performance measures, incentive and reward schemes, and dozens of personal relationships inside and outside the company. In absolute terms, the effect of the micro-structure on the cost of capital is probably quite small. But in *relative* terms it may be significant. That is, it may explain a significant fraction of those cross-sectional differences in the cost of capital that are competitively important.

Differences in the cost of capital that result from organizational design seem unlikely to show up in gross comparisons of national averages. This is partly because they may not be large enough *on average* to be extracted from the noise that characterizes large samples. More important, it is because they are not due to national factors alone, but also to many firm-level factors. Nevertheless, there is evidence that they exist, even within a single country.

Hoshi, Kashyap, and Scharfstein (1990a) divided a large sample of Japanese industrial companies into groups according to the simple criterion of whether the company had a close affiliation with a main bank. They found that for firms with strong ties to banks, investment was insensitive to corporate liquidity. In contrast, investment by firms without such ties was quite sensitive to internal liquidity. The authors observed that "While international cost-of-capital comparisons are generally quite difficult to make, the evidence here documents that Japanese institutions may circumvent certain capital-market imperfections [e.g., information asymmetries]. To the extent that the U.S. capital market has no analogous institutional arrangement, U.S. firms may be operating at a disadvantage."[17] In a related study, Hoshi, Kashyap and Scharfstein (1990c), the same authors exploit a similar research design to show how the relationship of a Japanese firm with its main bank reduces the apparent cost of financial distress. The results of the Hoshi, Kashyap, and Scharfstein studies are notable because they do not rely on (flawed) estimates of the cost of capital but on observations of investment behavior. Further, the documented differences all arise *within* Japan, across firms that are differently organized.[18]

A small number of other studies provide additional, indirect empirical support for the notion that organizational design affects the cost of capital. Dodd and Millar (1986) and Prowse (1989) adopt the premise that they way firms are organized, in addition to the types of assets and opportunities they possess, affects their value. Each of these studies presents evidence that links proxies for agency costs to specific elements of corporate financial structures in Japan and the United States. Their results support the hypothesis, though they do not test it directly, that agency costs under the Japanese systems of corporate organization and governance are lower than under the U.S. model.

RECENT CHANGES IN JAPANESE FINANCING PRACTICES

Capital is no longer scarce in Japan, for several reasons. Good new investment opportunities are less prevalent; prior investments in certain product markets are now supplying more cash than they consume; and capital markets are less isolated. On the face of it, these developments would seem to suggest that capital is or will soon become even less expensive. However, at the same time, and for some of the same reasons, the relationships between suppliers and users of capital that have traditionally fostered efficient use of capital have been eroding.

This is most evident in the rapid decline in corporate leverage that began in the mid-1980s.[19] Some companies used their abundant operating cash flow to pay down debt. Others simply invested the cash in securities, but the effect on leverage was the same. Japanese companies also moved quickly to raise funds outside Japan when the Foreign Exchange Control Law was relaxed in 1980. Total funds raised outside Japan jumped from an average of ¥560 billion per year in 1975–79 to ¥1.4 trillion in 1981. By 1985 nearly 50% of all securities issues by Japanese companies took place overseas, compared to less than 20% prior to 1980. Most of the proceeds of these foreign issues went to repay domestic bank borrowings and notes payable.

Data in Kester (1991) offer an illuminating glimpse at what has happened in Japan's 250 largest non-financial corporations. During 1985–87, fully 44% of their increase in total assets was comprised of cash and securities, and another 38% of "other long term investments." Meanwhile, on the other side of the balance sheet, increases in bonds, debentures, accruals, and equity equalled *190%* of the increase in total assets. In other words, bank credit, trade credit, and reserves, the traditional mainstays of Japanese corporate financing, *dropped* by 90% of the increase in assets. By 1987, cash and marketable securities exceeded total debt for these 250 large companies as a group; in effect, their leverage was negative.[20]

Such changes have strained the traditional relationships between companies and their banks. Both sides feel that they benefit less from the relationship than previously. Company managers are less dependent on banks for new capital and do not wish to have their stewardship of the company subjected to the close scrutiny it received in the past. Banks are unable to make profitable loans to the top tier of Japanese corporations, and feel obliged to turn to fee-generating, transaction-oriented services and middle-market loans to sustain profitability. Parties on both sides see less reason to own each other's equity. Banks receive low dividend yields on their holdings, and at the same time are under pressure to either sell assets or increase capital. Major corporations have little need to raise external equity, and they chafe at the idea of purchasing large new equity issues from banks. Not surprisingly, some banks and some companies have begun selling shares held for many years under implicit cross-shareholding agreements.

One of the puzzles these changes present is why, if the existing system was so effective, is it being abandoned in favor of what Frankel (1991) calls "market finance"? One possibility is that Japanese firms now have the best of both worlds: traditional relationships and access to markets, and each time they raise funds they will choose the cheaper source. It is unclear, though, why one source would dominate sometimes but not always, and it is doubtful that traditional relationships can survive this arrangement. Another possibility is that traditional Japanese financing practices were never best for all firms, but only recently were binding restrictions sufficiently eased for those who preferred to opt out to do so. The problem with this argument is that the firms that have reduced their leverage most, and participated most actively in external capital markets are the same large, highly visible firms that many observers thought were so well served by the traditional system.

Another possibility is suggested by examining the same companies' investment decisions. As a group, these companies have been criticized recently for investing too much in mature businesses (e.g., tires); for making large investments in unrelated businesses (e.g., Nippon Steel's well-publicized diversification moves); for speculating in securities markets; and for generally paying too high a price for too many recently acquired assets. The hypothesis this suggests is that managers have begun to use capital inefficiently at the margin, judged from the perspective of a capital supplier. Companies' moves to distance themselves from their lenders is itself a manifestation of this behavior. Their investment decisions are another.

Similar behavior in the United States is often criticized as self-interested opportunism on the part of managers (see, for example, Jensen (1986)). The same criticism may apply in Japan. However, Kester (1991) proposes a variation on this theme in the case of Japan. He argues that the implicit contracting among stakeholders that is vital to large Japanese enterprises is much more difficult to sustain in the absence of high growth. The faster the pie is growing, the easier it is for everyone to agree to cooperate and share it. Without high growth, some implicit long term contracts (e.g., those made with employees) cannot be honored easily. Managers who feel bound to honor these contracts and to keep stakeholder relationships intact may view large investments in unrelated businesses as their only hope of doing so. Clearly though, if these activities continue for a long period, implicit contracts and traditional relationships with *other* stakeholders, namely shareholders and lenders, will be damaged.

This presents a dilemma for Japanese corporate managers that is not easily escaped. If all stakeholders adopt the assumption that high growth is over, sharp disagreements will emerge concerning how best to exploit a company's strongest market positions and what to do with resources that are not required in the core business. The Japanese system is designed to bring into the firm and efficiently deploy a scarce resource, namely capital. It is less well-suited to harvesting cash and getting it safely back outside the firm. The basic mechanisms for getting cash out, dividends and share repurchases, are not well-developed in Japanese corporations. Share repurchases are illegal, and dividend yields are extremely low. Dividend payout ratios are less than half the level that prevails outside Japan.

Cash trapped inside a firm that lacks attractive investment opportunities will be the subject of many disagreements. Stakeholders that formerly cooperated to create the cash now being generated in product markets, will begin to assert conflicting claims on the harvest. It remains unclear how the tremendous wealth created by Japan's industrial success ultimately will be distributed. Labor will press a claim for higher wages and shorter hours. Shareholders will press for higher dividends. Managers will assert greater independence and may choose to compensate themselves better. They also may wish to retain and reinvest earnings in new businesses, which implies a great deal of unrelated diversification. Finally, not least, the government may wish to tax companies and make social investments.

It is not, of course, a bad thing to have lots of wealth to argue over. The point here is that the arguing itself is not conducive to the efficient use of capital. Some capital inevitably will be wasted and the marginal cost of capital may be higher as a result. The typical Japanese firm's existing microstructure has not yet had to confront this particular dispute. No doubt it will adapt, but this will be costly and take time. None of the "easy" solutions appear to be so on closer inspection. For example, higher dividend payouts have been suggested as a way to get cash out of companies and reward investors who made success possible. But managers, who also made success possible, will likely oppose this unless the dividends their company receives from all its shareholdings is substantially equal to what it pays out. Managers will regard a fundamental shift in dividend policy as a de facto wealth transfer. As such, it has net "winners" and "losers"; indeed, if this were not so, the basic problem of how to get cash out would remain.[21] Other stakeholders might similarly resist such a solution, and exert their influence to stop it or tax it or both.

A more likely development in the short run is that managers will find ways to continue investing internal cash flow. Some of these investments will no doubt be good and prudent, but more than in the past, many will not. Nevertheless, the investing will continue because, as a class, professional managers in Japan have voting control of the Japanese corporate sector, through cross-shareholdings in other companies. This will only change if shares now held by financial institutions are either sold or managed actively, sometimes in opposition to incumbent managers.

It is not the purpose of this chapter to predict how these events will unfold. It is rather to observe that all of the more likely possible paths seem to imply greater friction, less efficient use of capital, and at the margin, a somewhat higher cost of capital in Japan than previously. Of course, what this means for the cost of capital in Japan relative to the United States and Europe is impossible to say without speculating about their futures as well.

In conclusion, I do not believe that Japan ever had a cost of capital advantage vis-à-vis the United States as large as popularly supposed. It is theoretically questionable, in the context of modern portfolio theory and manifest capital mobility. It is empirically doubtful, given the multiple serious problems with widely-cited comparisons and the lack of a gap associated with less flawed methodologies. Last, it does not make practical sense—if the *mean* difference over a long period really was 7%, imagine what differences would be in the *tails* of the distribution!

Nevertheless, the salient features of traditional Japanese systems of corporate organization and governance do appear to lend themselves to the attenuation of common agency and information problems, which may promote more efficient internal use of capital. It is possible that some Japanese companies enjoyed slightly lower capital costs than their American competitors as a result. But the reverse is also true, and by the same reasoning, some Japanese companies have lower costs of capital than other Japanese companies, and likewise for the United States and comparisons of American companies.

The traditional Japanese systems of organization and governance have come under considerable stress. Almost all the recent developments one can name, from large cash inflows, to changes in demographics, to changes in market rules and access, to changes in bank capital requirements, to the sharp drop in the Tokyo stock market, appear to stress rather than reinforce the system's basic structure. If so, the system can no longer be relied upon to help keep capital costs low. Instead, it may cause costs to go up somewhat. This is by no means a dire prediction, for Japanese companies and institutions will undoubtedly adapt to changing circumstances, as they have in the past. If the prediction is useful at all, it will be because the underlying hypotheses about internal determinants of the cost of capital help managers adapt more speedily to change.

NOTES

1. See Hatsopoulos (1983, 1984), Chase Financial Policy (1980), and U.S. Department of Commerce (1983).
2. For a more complete bibliography of related research, see Frankel (1991) and Kester and Luehrman (1991a, 1991b).
3. This presentation of the problems with WACC estimates draws heavily on Kester and Luehrman (1991b and 1992).
4. See for example, Hatsopoulos (1983) and Ellsworth (1985).
5. McCauley and Zimmer (1989) do essentially the same thing, but with a hybridized AA credit.
6. Abuaf and Carmody (1990) do adjust for risk and still report a difference between Japan and the United States. However, this study has other serious design problems and, in any event, the reported cross-country difference of 1.5 percentage points is almost surely not significant, though the authors report no standard errors. To see the importance of controlling for risk, see Baldwin (1986) or compare Ando and Auerbach's (1988a) with their (1988b).
7. For a discussion of many of the accounting differences between Japan and the Untied States, see Kester (1986), Aron (1987), or Ando and Auerbach (1988a).

8. Ando and Auerbach (1990) is one of the few studies that adjusts for accounting differences, for the value of land, and for crossholdings of equities by Japanese companies. After making all these adjustments they find very little difference between the two countries.
9. See Kester (1986) on the distribution of debt ratios in each country, and Kester and Luehrman (1991a, 1991b) on difficulties of comparing costs of equity.
10. For example, Morgan Guaranty Trust's *World Financial Markets* reports an average of twelve Japanese city banks' posted lending rates. This average is often below yields on government bonds, sometimes by as much as 100 basis points.
11. Friend and Tokutsu (1987) and Hatsopoulos, Krugman, and Summers (1988), and many others make this suggestion.
12. A differences in interest tax shields is just one of the ways in which the amount and structure of taxation could produce a cost of capital gap. However, more general comparisons of systems and rates also fail to show a large sustained advantage for one country over the other. See Baldwin (1986), Bernheim and Shoven (1987), Shoven and Tachibanaki (1988), and Shoven (1989). See also Frankel's (1991) discussion of these papers.
13. Gultekin, Gultekin and Penati (1989) also investigated the late 1970s, using various tests. Their results for this period are inconclusive, with some tests rejecting equality of risk premia for certain portfolios in each country. This result is difficult to interpret, however. The portfolios compared are unlikely to have equal risk, so the fact that they have unequal risk premia cannot be unequivocally attributed to different prices of risk. For further discussion, see Kester and Luehrman (1991b).
14. In this vein, it is interesting to note that corporations typically pay their main banks a premium of about 25 basis points over what other banks are paid. Whether this still represents a bargain to the borrower is less interesting than the fact that borrower and lender alike explicitly acknowledge some value in the role played by the main bank.
15. See Brealey and Myers (1991), pp. 421–55, for an overview and comparison of capital structure theories.
16. See, for example, Jensen and Meckling (1976), Myers (1977), and Myers and Majluf (1984).
17. Hoshi, Kashyap, and Scharfstein (1990a), p. 23. See also Hoshi, Kashyap, and Scharfstein (1990b) for corroborating evidence that shifts in Japanese banking relationships have been accompanied by shifts in investment behavior by Japanese industrial companies.
18. In the same vein, Kester and Luehrman (1992) argue that within the United States also, some firms manage capital better than others and have lower costs of capital as a result.
19. Several authors have made the observation that traditionally strong relationships have been loosened. See, for example, Kester (1991), Hoshi, Kashyap and Scharfstein (1990b), and Frankel (1991) for a catalog of specific environmental and regulatory changes, and for some descriptive statistics of changes in financing and investment behavior.
20. Kester (1991), pp. 192–3.
21. The same argument applies to share repurchases, which, for purposes of this discussion, are the same as dividends. Legalizing repurchases would be unlikely to flush a great deal of cash out of the Japanese corporate sector.

REFERENCES

Abegglen, J., and G. Stalk, *Kaisha, The Japanese Corporation*. New York: Basic Books, 1985.

Abuaf, N., and K. Carmody, "The Cost of Capital in Japan and the Unied States: A Tale of Two Markets," Salomon Brothers, Financial Strategy Group mimeo, July 1990.

Ando, A., and A. Auberbach, "The Cost of Capital in Japan and the U.S.: A Comparison," in: J.B. Shoven (ed.), *Governmen Policy Towards Industry in the United States and Japan*. New York: Cambridge University Press, 1988a.

Ando, A., and A. Auberbach, "The Cost of Capital in the United States and Japan: A Comparison," *Journal of the Japanese and International Economies 2* (1988b), pp. 134–58.

Ando, A., and A. Auberbach, "The Cost of Capital in Japan: Recent Evidence and Further Results," *Journal of the Japanese and International Economies 4*, (1990), pp. 323–50.

Aron, Paul, "Japanese Price Earnings Multiples: Updated as of Aug. 31, 1987," Paul Aron report no. 31. New York: Daiwa Securities America, 1987.

Baldwin, Carliss, "The Capital Factor: Competing for Capital in a Global Environment," in: Michael E. Porter (ed.), *Competition in Global Industries*. Boston: Harvard Business School Press (1986), pp. 185–223.

Bernheim, B. Douglas, and John B. Shoven, "Taxation and the Cost of Capital: An International Comparison," in Walker and Bloomfield (eds.), *The Consumption Tax: A Better Alternative?* Cambridge, MA: Ballinger (1987), pp. 61–86.

Brealey, R., and S. Myers, *Principles of Corporate Finance*, 4th ed. (1991), New York: McGraw Hill.

Chase Financial Policy (a Division of the Chase Manhattan Bank, N.A.), "U.S. and Japanese Semiconductors Industries: A Financial Comparison," report prepared for the Semiconductor Industry Association, 1980.

Dodd, M., and J. Millar, "Financial Structure in Japanese and American Firms: An Indirect Test of Agency Relationships," Georgetown University working paper, October 1986.

Ellsworth, R., "Capital Markets and Competitive Decline," *Harvard Business Review*, September-October 1985.

Frankel, J., "The Japanese Cost of Finance: A Survey," *Financial Management 20*, no. 1 (1990), pp. 95–127.

French, K., and J. Poterba, "Are Japanese Stock Prices Too High?" Cambridge, MA: National Bureau of Economic Research working paper (1991), (forthcoming in *Journal of Financial Economics*).

Friend, Irwin and Ichiro Tokutsu, "The Cost of Capital to Corporations in Japan and the U.S.A.," *Journal of Banking and Finance* 11, no. 2 (1987), pp. 313–27.

Gultekin, Mustafa N., N. Bulent Gultekin, and Alessandro Penati, "Capital Controls and International Capital Market Segmentations: The Evidence from the Japanese and American Stock Markets," *Journal of Finance 44*, no. 4 (September 1989), pp. 849–69.

Hatsopolous, George N., "High Cost of Capital: Handicap of American Industry," Waltham, MA: Thermo Electron Corporation, 1983.

Hatsopolous, George N., "Memorandum to the Presidential Commission on Industrial Competitiveness, Update of the Study 'High Cost of Capital: Handicap of American Industry.'" Waltham, MA: American Business Conference and the Thermo Electron Corporation, 1984.

Hatsopoulos, George N., and Stephen H. Brooks, "The Gap in the Cost of Capital: Causes, Effects, and Remedies," in R. Landau and D. Jorgensen (eds.), *Technology and Economic Policy*. Cambridge, MA: Ballinger (1986), pp. 221–80.

Hatsopoulos, George N., Paul Krugman, and Lawrence Summers, "U.S. Competitiveness: Beyond the Trade Deficit," *Science*)July 1988), pp. 299–307.

Hodder, J., "Is the Cost of Capital Lower In Japan?", *Journal of the Japanese and International Economies*, vol. 5, no. 1 (March 1991), pp. 86–100.

Hoshi, T., A. Kashyap, and D. Scharfstein, "Corporate Structure, Liquidity, and Investment: Evidence From Japanese Panel Data," *Quarterly Journal of Economics* (1990a), 106.

Hoshi, T., A. Kashyap, and D. Scharfstein, "Bank Monitoring and Investment: Evidence From the Changing Structure of Japanese Corporate Banking Relationships," in R. G. Hubbard (ed.), *Asymmetric Information, Corporate Finance and Investment*. Chicago: University of Chicago Press (1990b), pp. 105–26.

Hoshi, T., A. Kashyap, and D. Scharfstein, "The Role of Banks in Reducing the Costs of Financial Distress in Japan," *Journal of Financial Economics* 27, no. 1 (September 1990c), pp. 67–88.

Jensen, M., "Agency Costs of Free Cash Flow, Corporate Finance, and Takeovers," *American Economic Review*, vol. 76 (May 1986), pp. 323–29.

Jensen, M., and J. Meckling, "Theory of the Firm: Managerial Behavior, Agency Costs, and Ownership Structure," *Journal of Financial Economics*, vol.1, no. 2 (1976), pp. 305–60.

Kester, W. Carl, "Capital and Ownership Structure: A Comparison of United States and Japanese Manufacturing Corporations," *Financial Management* (Spring 1986), pp. 5–16.

Kester, W. Carl, "Contractual Governance and Investment Time Horizons,"*Time Horizons of American Management*, Harvard University and the U.S. Council on Competitiveness, 1991a.

Kester, W. Carl, *Japanese Takeovers: The Global Contest For Corporate Control.* Boston: Harvard Business School Press, 1991b.

Kester, W. Carl, and Timothy A. Luehrman, "Real Interest Rates and the Cost of

Capital: A Comparison of the United States and Japan," *Japan and the World Economy 1* (1989), pp. 279–301.

Kester, W. Carl, and Timothy A. Luehrman, "The Price of Risk in the United States and Japan,"*Japan and the World Economy 3*, no. 3 (1991a), pp. 223–42.

Kester, W. Carl, and Timothy A. Luehrman, "Cross-Country Differences in the Cost of Capital: A Survey and Evaluation of Recent Empirical Studies," HBS Working paper #92-011, prepared for *Time Horizons of American Management*, Harvard University and the U.S. Council on Competitiveness, 1991b.

Kester, W. Carl, and Timothy A. Luehrman, "The Myth of Japan's Low-Cost Capital," *Harvard Business Review*, May-June 1992.

McCauley, Robert N., and Steven A. Zimmer, "Explaining International Differences in the Cost of Capital," *Federal Reserve Bank of New York Quarterly Review* (Summer 1989), pp. 7–28.

Modigliani, F., and M. Miller, "The Cost of Capital, Corporation Finance and the Theory of Investment," *American Economic Review 48* (June 1958), pp. 261–97.

Michel, A., and I. Shaked, "Japanese Leverage: Myth or Reality?", *Financial Analysts Journal*, July–August 1985.

Myers, S., "Determinants of Corporate Borrowing," *Journal of Financial Economics*, vol. 5 (1977), pp. 147–75.

Myers, S., and N. Majluf, "Corproate Financing and Investment Decisions When Firms Have Information that Investors Do Not Have," *Journal of Financial Economics,* vol. 13 (1984), pp. 187–222.

Poterba, J., "International Comparisons of the Cost of Capital: A Survey of Methods, with Reference to the U.S. and Japan," Massachusetts Institute of Technology and NBER working paper (December 1990).

Prowse, S., "Institutional Investment Patterns and Corporate Financial Behavior in the U.S. and Japan," Washington, DC: Board of Governors, Federal Reserve System, Division of Research and Statistics (November 1989).

Shoven, J., "The Japanese Tax Reform and the Effective Rate of Tax on Japanese Corporate Investments," National Bureau of Economic Research working paper no. 2791 (December 1988).

Shoven, J., and T. Tachibanaki, "The Taxation of Income From Capital in Japan," in J. Shoven (ed.), *Governemnt Policy Towards Industry in the United States and Japan* . Cambridge, U.K.: Cambridge University Press (1988).

U.S. Department of Commerce, International Trade Administration, "A Historical Comparison of the Cost of Financial Capital in France, the Federal Republic of Germany, Japan, and the United States." Washington, DC: U.S. Government Printing Office (1983).

PART FOUR

ISSUES OF CONDUCT AND CORPORATE GOVERNANCE

CHAPTER 12

ETHICS AND MARKETS

Clifford W. Smith, Jr.

INTRODUCTION

There appears to be an unprecedented focus on ethics in the business community: articles in the financial press regularly decry unethical business behavior, professional organizations are reviewing their codes of conduct, many business schools are initiating ethics courses. Although much of this attention focuses on moral principles and details legal/regulatory requirements, I want to discuss a complementary set of issues. The evidence indicates that markets impose substantial costs on institutions and individuals that engage in unethical behavior; thus, market forces provide private incentives for ethical behavior.

In the second section, I identify the nature of these market forces in more detail, how they help to enforce contracts, and transactions where they are most likely to be effective. In the third section, I examine the Salomon Brothers treasury bond bidding scandal as an example of the effectiveness of market forces in imposing costs on parties to unethical conduct. In final section, I summarize my conclusions.

COSTS OF UNETHICAL BEHAVIOR

Ethical issues arise in a broad range of business problems. This entire range cannot be addressed here. To focus my discussion, I consider a transaction for the delivery of a product of a specified quality. I examine incentives to reduce costs by lowering quality, rather than supplying products of the promised quality.

The effectiveness of market forces in enforcing contract varies across transactions. Important transaction characteristics include: (1) the cost of ascertaining product quality prior to purchase, (2) likelihood that the transaction will be repeated, (3) the asset/cost structure of the seller, and (4) the specific terms of the transaction.

Costs of Determining Quality For products where quality can be determined at low cost prior to purchase, markets easily solve this problem. If buyers can cheaply monitor quality, they have strong incentives to do so. In such cases, the product will only sell for a price that reflects actual quality, not promised quality. For example, if a buyer for Kodak is negotiating a purchase of silver, quality can be accurately and inexpensively ascertained prior to purchase by assay.

However for some products, quality is impossible be determine prior to purchase. For example, the quality of an airplane ticket can only be known after the plane has landed, parked at the gate, and the passengers have retrieved their luggage. If quality is expensive to measure, sellers have incentives to cheat on quality. Yet a rational seller will provide products of lower than promised quality only if the expected gains exceed the expected costs.

Several market forces can be important mechanisms that impose substantial costs on suppliers that cheat on quality thereby constraining them from cheating. The potential for future sales provides powerful incentives for contract compliance (see Telser (1980)). So long as the costs of expected future lost sales exceed the gains from opportunistic behavior, supplying, products of lower than promised quality will not be profitable.

The costs of cheating on quality are higher if the information about such activities are more rapidly and widely distributed to potential future customers. Hence, a business transaction that is expected to be repeated between the same parties faces a lower probability of cheating. For example, in markets like the diamond trade in New York, cheating on quality is very rare. This market is dominated by a close-knit community of Hasidic Jews; thus, information about unethical behavior is rapidly distributed throughout the market.

In other broader markets, specialized information services that monitor the market help insure contract performance. For example, *Consumer Reports* evaluates products from toasters to automobiles, the *Investment Deal-*

ers Digest reports on activities of investment bankers, and *Business Week* ranks MBA programs. By lowering the costs for potential customers to determine quality, these information sources increase the costs of cheating.

Where quality is difficult to ascertain prior to purchase, buyers will discount their demand prices to reflect the uncertainty they face. Thus, sellers have incentives to provide credible assurance to potential customers that they will not cheat in order to reduce the compensation for bearing this risk demanded by customers. For example, given that a firm has established a brand name, entry into related product markets can be less costly. For example, given IBM's position in the mainframe computer industry, they face lower costs of credibly supplying high quality IBM branded personal computers. Subjecting both revenue streams to the adverse reputation consequence of cheating faces the firm with stronger incentives for contract compliance. This implies that this mechanism will be more effective when (1) the products are more closely related and (2) the linkage is more prominently emphasized.

If future corporate existence is more uncertain, so are the expected costs of foregone future sales. This helps to explain the deterioration in the records for flight cancellations by Piedmont and Pacific Southwest Airlines prior to their mergers into the USAir system.

Moreover, firms in financial distress are more likely to cheat on quality than financially heathy firms. Thus firms can adopt financial policies that helps to bond product quality. Since financial distress is more costly for firms that market products where quality is difficult to ascertain, such firms have incentives to adopt financing policies that imply a lower probability of financial distress. Therefore, such firms should have lower leverage, fewer leases, and engage in more hedging.

In credit markets specialized credit-information services like Moody's and Dun and Bradstreet perform both a monitoring and an information dissemination function [see Wakeman (1981) and Mian/Smith (1992)]. Fama/Jensen (1985) suggest that the existence of such intermediaries provides an opportunity for the firm to guarantee quality. Firms pay Moody's to have their debt rated over the life of the bond issue. By issuing rated public debt a firm lowers the cost to other potential corporate claimholders (including potential customers) to ascertain the firm's financial condition. Moreover, James (1987) argues that banks have a comparative advantage in monitoring the financial condition of borrowers; thus, the use of bank credit also helps control these incentive problems.

The structure of the market also can be important in determining quality. Grieve (1984) examines prices in two wholesale used car markets. One requires more complete disclosure about the condition of the automobile than the other. She finds that prices in the market with more required disclosure are higher. Thus the ability to precommit to disclose information reduces the potential information disparity between buyer and seller and reduces the discount buyers apply to their demand prices.

Seller Asset/Cost Structure Klein/Leffler (1981) note that the higher the expected future steam of quasi-rents, the less likely is the firm to cheat on quality. Thus, a firm with an established market position and substantial franchise value faces higher costs of cheating and hence are less likely to do so.

Firm's can bond quality by investing in firm-specific assets whose value is neglible if the company fails. For example, Coca Cola's advertising budget represents an investment in brand-name capital that would depreciate substantially if the company were to cheat on quality. This also helps to explain "image" advertising (for example by Xerox or IBM) where there is no discussion of the company's products. Similarly, by choosing a distinctive architectural design for its outlets. a firm more effectively bonds product quality. For example, if Taco Bell outlets would have limited alternate uses if the enterprise fails; hence, if it developed a reputation for cheating on promised quality, the company would suffer even greater losses than it would have if a more generic structure had been erected.

As the Continental Bank was restructuring, there was substantial uncertainty about whether it would successfully re-emerge as a major force in corporate banking. If the management team had better information than the market and they concluded that the probability of success was high, their decision to underwrite the *Journal of Applied Corporate Finance* would to be a strategy that should provide a credible signal. If the bank's reorganization is successful, the *Journal* would be a valuable marketing tool that would help to build franchise value. If they are unsuccessful, the venture would be of negative value. Thus, underwriting projects that are valuable only if the firm is successful is a valuable signaling mechanism.

Organizational Structure Incentives to provide high quality products vary across ownership structures. Individual proprietorships and partnerships impose unlimited liability on the principals and thus offer stronger incentives for contract compliance than the limited liability provided through the corporate form. This is one reason why professional service firms like law firms, accounting firms and investment banking firms are frequently set up as partnerships.

Fast food firms must decide whether to franchise or own particular outlets. Outlets located at expressway interchanges will receive fewer repeat sales than other locations. Brickley/Dark (1987) argue that these outlets are less likely to be franchised because their managers incur fewer costs of lower sales if quality is lowered. They not only predict these locations will be owned, they should be subjected to more intense monitoring from corporate headquarters, as well.

The hierarchical management structure that corporations employ is an important mechanism to guarantee quality (see Fama 1980)). In this structure top managers have strong incentives to monitor their subordinates. Moreover, competition among managers for these top jobs provides incentives for lower managers to monitor upper managers, as well. This mutual monitoring imposes constraints on an individual manager's ability to cheat on quality.

Oversight of the firm's manager is the responsibility of the board of directors. Board structure can provide valuable monitoring of the internal management team—especially the monitoring by outside board members. This perspective helps explain why many Fortune 500 companies have academics or religious leaders on their boards. In board meetings proprietary information is discussed and hence the meeting must be closed to protect the value of this information. Yet closed meetings provide an opportunity for the management team and board to collude and adopt a set of policies that would reduce the value of the firm, but make themselves personally better off. By including an individual whose career choices indicate that maximizing income is not that individual's most important goal, the firm makes a believable promise to focus on value maximizing policies when the board meets behind closed doors.

Mayers/Shivdasani/Smith (1992) offer evidence that mutual life insurance companies employ more outside board members than similar stock life insurers. In a mutual the ownership claims are inalienable; thus, hostile takeovers are impossible in a mutual (Mayers/Smith (1981). Facing less effective discipline from the market for corporate control, mutuals more extensively employ substitute control mechanisms like outside board members. Their evidence indicates that 80% of their sample of mutuals have outside members comprising more than 50% of the board, while 80% of their stocks have less than 50% outside board members.

Transaction Structure There are ways to structure the transaction that reduce the likelihood of cheating. One is to provide a product warranty. To understand where warranties will be most extensively employed, it is useful to subdivide product failures into three classes: (1) failures that result from factors that are under the firm's control (such as manufacturing tolerances), (2) failures that result from factors that are under the customers' control (such as product use), and (3) failures that result from uncontrollable factors. When failures are due primarily to factors that are under the firm's control, warranties will be most useful. In this case warranties directly impose the cost of failure on the parties who have the most input into their control. However when failures are due to primarily to factors that are under the customers' control, the moral-hazard problem will be greater and warranties are less useful as a quality-assurance mechanism.

As Smith (1987) and Mian/Smith (1992) note, providing trade credit so that payment is required only after the product is received can provide important incentives not to cheat on product quality. For example, when B.Altman's filed for Bankruptcy, suppliers demanded payment in advance rather than offering merchandise on standard terms. *The Wall Street Journal* (1/30/90) reported that "In the weeks that separated B. Altman's orders from its payments, many vendors sold the Altman goods to other retailers. Then, rather than return the checks, they would send Altman what they had in the warehouse." Sellers have stronger incentives to resolve problems with disputed orders if they have not been paid.

THE SALOMON BIDDING SCANDAL

The costs imposed on the firm for an ethical breech depends on the market's judgement of the behavior. The more serious the offense and the greater the consensus, the higher the costs imposed. I now focus on the Salomon Brothers treasury bond bidding scandal because their illegal bids are such a clear case of an ethical conduct violation. [See also Smith (1992)].

Case Background In auctioning Treasury bonds, the U.S. Treasury awards bonds first to the highest bidder at their quoted prices, then they move to the next highest bidder. This process continues until the issue is exhausted. If the Treasury receives multiple bids at the price that exhausts the issue, it allocates bonds in proportion to the size of the bid. The Treasury limits the size of bids to no more than 35% of the issue.

In December 1990, the head of Salomon's Government-bond trading desk, Paul W. Mozer, submitted bids for 35 percent of an $8.57 billion auction of four-year notes. He also submitted another bid for $1 billion under the name of a customer, but without the customer's authorization. The two bids represented 46 percent of the issue. This tactic was repeated in February at a $9.04 billion auction for five-year notes, in April at a $9.06 billion auction for five-year notes, and in May at a $12.26 billion auction of two-year notes.

In April Mr. Mozer informed Salomon Chairman John H. Gutfreund, President Thomas W. Strauss, Vice Chairman John W. Meriwether, and General Counsel Donald M. Feuerstein an February illegal bid in the February auction. No immediate action was taken. In June the Securities Exchange Commission and Justice Department issued subpoenas to Salomon and some of its clients for records involving auctions. Salomon initiated a review of its government-bond operations and in August disclosed its illegal bids in the period between December and May.

Legal penalties On 18 August 1991, the Treasury Department barred Salomon from bidding in government securities auctions for customer accounts; however it allowed the firm to continue bidding for its own account. In February 1992, lawyers for Salomon began negotiations with the SEC to determine sanctions and penalties the firm would face. On 20 May 1992, Salomon settled with the SEC and other government agencies. They agreed to pay $122 million to the Treasury to settle charges that it violated securities laws and $68 million for claims made by the Justice Department. The firm also established a $100 million restitution fund for payments of private damage claims that might result from approximately 50 civil lawsuits stemming from the scandal that the firm still faces. (Unclaimed amounts in this fund revert to the Treasury, not Salomon). Salomon announced that they would take a second quarter charge off of $185 million in addition to the $200 million reserve for potential liabilities from the scandal that it had already established. The Federal Reserve Bank of New York also announced that it had decided to retain Salomon's designation as a primary dealer, but that their authority to trade with the Bank would be suspended for June 1st through August 3rd. This suspension could cost Salomon approximately $4 billion in trading volume, but also bars the firm's traders from the information derived from the intelligence derived from daily contact with the Fed's Open Market Desk.

While these legal/regulatory penalties are substantial, I want to focus on the costs imposed by private mechanisms on events that occurred in the nine-month period between public disclosure of the illegal bids in August 1991 and this settlement in May 1992 to provide a clearer understanding of the market forces that impose sanctions on parties to unethical behavior.

Financial Markets Coverage by the financial press is quite sophisticated; financial transactions are among the most closely scrutinized of any market. In the week that Salomon disclosed the illegal bids, this was the lead story in the financial press. For example, *The Wall Street Journal* carried seven different stories about the scandal on 19 August 1991. Thus, information about this event was rapidly and widely distributed after the initial disclosure.

In that week, Salomon Brothers stock prices dropped by one third. This indicates that the market expected Salomon to bear significant costs from these actions. This $1.5 billion fall in market value seems much too large to simply reflect fines and other expected legal/regulatory sanctions.

Consistent with the hypothesis that bond-rating agencies perform valuable monitoring and information dissemination functions in the market, before the end of August 1991, Moody's Investor Service downgraded Salomon's debt rating on their $7 billion long-term debt and $6.6 billion commercial paper issues. Moreover, major banks indicated that they were reexamining the terms of their loans to Salomon.

Obviously the stock price change and the debt reaction were not independent events—anything that lowers the company's value by one third would make the debt riskier; moreover, less favorable credit terms would lower the value of the equity. The more important point is that there was a consistent reaction across the financial community.

Labor Markets The individual at the center of the scandal, Paul Mozer, was suspended from his Salomon duties in August. Not only does he face potential criminal penalties for his actions, he has also been named as a defendant in lawsuits filed by Salomon customers. He probably has ruined his career, could lose much of his accumulated wealth, and could spend a substantial amount of time in prison.

Consistent with the mutual monitoring hypothesis, Salomon Chairman Gutfreund, President Strauss, Vice-Chairman Meriwether, and General Counsel Feuerstein were asked by the Board to resign. While the requested resignations largely reflect their inaction following the April meeting, these gentlemen also were the senior managers most responsible for monitoring the activities of subordinates to insure such illegal actions do not occur.

In response to the scandal, Salomon has lost many valued employees. To help keep others, Salomon took the unusual step of guaranteeing that the 1992 pay pool for its stock-research group would be at least 20 percent higher than the 1991 pool. While this input is motivated as an effort to shelter a group from adverse results that were outside their control, it also is another reflection of a change in reservation wages by employees. Building coordinated teams of employees throughout the organization is a time-consuming task that takes years to accomplish. These personnel losses that are in response to the scandal will affect Salomon's productivity and competitiveness for years to come.

Product Markets Different aspects of Salomon's business are affected by the scandal in different ways. I suggested that in markets where quality is more difficult to measure, seller reputation will be more important. In the new-issue market, firms generally employ investment bankers who participate regularly and thus have more reputational capital at stake [see Booth/Smith (1987) and Smith (1987)]. The illegal bids severely reduced the value of Salomon's reputational capital and thus significantly reduced its competitiveness as an underwriter. For example, *The Wall Street Journal* (5/7/92) reports: "Salomon continues to be shunned by many corporate clients in receiving lead-management mandates for stock underwriting, even amid a record volume of new stock and bond issues."

Major customers, including the World Bank and the State of California, suspended trading with Salomon. The illegal bids must raise potential questions among customers about the effectiveness of their representation if they continued to employ Salomon as a broker.

In order to reassure potential customers after the scandal became public, Salomon instituted several important steps:

1. In addition to removing employees implicated in the scandal, the firm forced the resignation of Salomon's outside counsel, Wachtell, Lipton, Rosen and Katz. The law firm had conducted the internal investigation into the scandal beginning in early July, but they did not approach the government until a month later.

2. The board appointed Warren Buffett as interim chairman. By moving quickly to appoint a respected outside boardmember like Mr. Buffett as interim Chairman, the Salomon board sends a strong message to the market that this behavior is unlikely to be repeated.

3. They appointed Deryck Maughan as new Chief Operating Officer. Since Mr. Maughan had just transferred from Tokyo to New York, his appointment helped assure that the new senior management team would not be implicated in the scandal and thus would not be diverted from dealing with containing the costs imposed on the firm by the scandal.

4. They beefed up the firm's internal controls by forming a compliance committee and by hiring Coopers and Lybrand to institute a compliance review of its securities operations. This is consistent with the Watts/Zimmerman (1986) argument that a public accounting firm's value ultimately depends on maintaining a reputation for competence and independence.

The area of Salomon's business least likely to be directly affected by the scandal is Salomon's proprietary trading activities. But even this part of their business was indirectly affected. Because of the liquidity problems that resulted form the downgrading of their commercial paper and less favorable terms with banks, Salomon liquidated almost one third of its asset portfolio. This reduced substantially the firm's trading capacity. Similarly, the reduction in Salomon's credit rating disqualified the firm as an acceptable counterparty for certain swap and other derivative securities transactions. This limited Salomon's ability to offer customers certain structured transactions.

The scandal changed the margin with respect to other risks the firm decided were acceptable. For example, Salomon's Philbro Energy unit was instructed to sever all ties with a major client, Marc Rich and Co. Salomon management evidently concluded that the firm could not risk another scandal involving transactions with a customer whose head had been a fugitive from the US since 1983.

In late October 1991, Salomon announced that it had settled a class-action lawsuit stemming from the buyout of Revco Drug Stores, Inc. Salomon agreed to pay nearly $30 million to security holders in Revco's $1.25 billion buy-out. The bidding scandal could have produced a less favorable settlement in at least two ways: (1) It might consume so much management attention that Salomon would settle to eliminate the distraction. (2) The firm's bargaining position is impaired because Salomon's credibility at trial is reduced due to the scandal.

CONCLUSIONS

The central thesis in this discussion has been that private markets impose potentially significant costs on individuals and firms that engage in unethical behavior. Although I do not believe that market incentives alone are sufficient to ensure ethical behavior, this analysis of these costs helps explain why ethical behavior is so widely observed in markets: ethical behavior is generally profitable. This is especially important in financial services, where business depends as much on reputation as on performance. I believe that more widespread understanding of these consequences would result in fewer ethical-conduct violations.

Some argue that if competitors have adopted low ethical standards, it would be unprofitable for a firm to adopt high standards. My analysis suggests this is incorrect. Potential customers discount their demand prices where there is uncertainty about the quality of the product to be supplied. By credibly promising to act ethically, a firm can differentiate their product and increase their demand substantially.

My analysis suggests that a board concerned with the ethical conduct of the firm's employees should spend less time exhorting the human resource manager to search (like Diogenes) for an honest man; but rather should spend more resources to focus on potential incentive problems between the firm and its customers, creditors, and employees. Once identified, attention can be focused on the constructive resolution of the incentive problems.

This brings me to my final point. The Treasury has chosen a set of bidding procedures that create incentives to cheat. By employing a discriminatory auction and charging bidders their announced reservation prices, the structure of the auction provides incentives for bidders to collude, as well as providing incentives to seek ways around the announced bidding limits. These incentives would be eliminated if they employed a single-price auction where the entire block of securities is allocated to the high bidders at the market-clearing bid. Such a rule change would eliminate the winner's curse faced by potential bidders under the current system. Auction theory suggests that potential bidders would employ a different bidding strategy with the different rules. Moreover the available evidence suggests the total funding cost to the Treasury would be reduced [see Milgrom/Webber (1982) and Milgrom (1989)]. These gains would be in addition to the reduced monitoring costs incurred by the government from reducing incentives to cheat. If the Treasury had spent more time worrying about the incentives to cheat that their bidding procedures introduced, this entire unfortunate set of events might never have occurred.

REFERENCES

Booth, James R. and Richard L. Smith, II (1986), "Capital Raising, Underwriting and the Certification Hypothesis," *Journal of Financial Economics*, Vol. 15 pp. 261–81.

Brickley, James A., and F. H. Dark (1987), "The Choice of Organizational Form: The Case of Franchising," *Journal of Financial Economics,* Vol 18, p. 401.

Fama, Eugene F. (1980), "Agency Problems and the Theory of the Firm," *Journal of Political Economy,* Vol. 88, No 2. pp. 288–307.

Fama, Eugene F., and Michael C. Jensen (1985), "Organizational Forms and Investment Decisions," *Journal of Financial Economics,* Vol. 14, pp. 101–19.

Fama, Eugene F., and Michael C. Jensen (1983), "Agency Problems and Residual Claims," *Journal of Law and Economics,* Vol. 26 pp. 327–49.

Grieve, Helen (1984), "Quality Certification in a "Lemons' Market: An Empirical Test of Certification in Wholesale Leased Car Auctions," University of Rochester unpublished working paper.

James, Christopher M. (1987), "Some Evidence on the Uniqueness of Bank Loans," *Journal of Financial Economics*, Vol 19, pp. 217–35.

Mayers, David, Anil Shivdasani, and Clifford W. Smith, Jr. (1992), "Board of Director Composition in the Life Insurance Industry," University of Rochester unpublished manuscript.

Klein, Benjamin, and Keith B. Leffler (1981), "The Role of Market Forces in Assuring Contract Performance," *Journal of Political Economy*, Vol 89, pp. 615–41.

Mian, Shehzad, and Clifford W. Smith, Jr. (1992), "Accounts Receivable Management Policy: Theory and Evidence," *Journal of Finance*, Vol. 67, pp. 169–200..

Milgrom, Paul R. (1989) "Auctions and Bidding: A Primer," *Journal of Economics Perspectives*, vol. 3, pp. 3–22.

Milgrom, Paul R and Robert J. Webber (1982), " A Theory of Auctions and Competitive Building," *Econometrics*, Vol. 50 pp. 105–14.

Smith, Clifford W., Jr. (1992), "Economics and Ethics," *Journal of Applied Corporate Finance*, Vol. 5, No. 2, pp. 23–28.

Smith, Clifford W., Jr. (1986), "Investment Banking and the Capital Acquisition Process," *Journal of Financial Economics*, Vol. 15, pp. 3–29.

Smith, Janet K. (1987), "Trade Credit and Informational Asymmetry," *Journal of Finance*, Vol 62, pp. 863–71.

Telser, Lester G. (1980), "A Theory of Self-enforcing Agreements," *Journal of Business*, Vol. 53, No. 1, pp. 27–44.

Wakeman, Lee J. (1981), "The Real Function of Bond Rating Agencies," *Chase Financial Quarterly*, Vol. 1, pp. 18–25.

Watts, Ross, and Jerold L. Zimmerman, (1986). *Positive Accounting Theory*, Prentice Hall: Englewood Cliffs, NJ.

CHAPTER 13

NONPRICE COMPETITION AMONG JAPANESE BROKERAGE COMPANIES: A GAME THEORETIC APPROACH TO EXPLAIN LOSS COMPENSATION

Young S. Park

I. INTRODUCTION

In 1976 the Tokyo Stock Exchange (TSE) finally allowed non-Japanese brokerage companies to become members. This reflected the Japanese government's various policies for internationalization of domestic markets as well as foreign investor's interest in what, for a time, was the world's largest stock market in terms of capitalization. For a long time, foreign brokerage companies struggled to break into the Japanese markets. However, many foreign brokerage companies in Tokyo complained about the lack of transparency and equity in Japanese financial markets. Therefore, they were pleased with the exposure of the 1991 scandal with the expectation that it would gear up the deregulation of financial markets and the removal of obstacles to market access.

The author is grateful to Mr. T. Yamashita at Daiwa Security Co. for helpful discussions, Prof. T. Hiraki at IUJ and Ms. F. Konya at Japan Security Research Institute for data, and the International Management Research Institute (IMRI) and International University of Japan (IUJ) for research support. The author remains solely responsible for the contents.

The financial scandals in the summer of 1991 uncovered how unhealthy the Japanese financial system was. The Japan Security Dealers Association (JSDA) announced that the Big-Four and 13 second tier brokerage companies paid ¥171.9 billion ($1.3 billion) in loss compensation to 608 corporate clients and 9 individuals. These payments by brokerage companies were believed to violate the Security and Exchange Law, which prohibits security firms from attracting customers by promising compensation for possible losses on their investments or from paying compensation without promising it beforehand.

Several factors contributed to the generation of loss compensation. During the second half of the 1980s, corporate Japan was overflowing with excess liquidity mainly caused by the then record high trade surplus. The excess money was channelled into both the stock market and the real estate market and rapidly changed hands within those markets. Due to the high speed of transactions caused by excess liquidity, the prices of stock and real estate went up tremendously. Taking advantage of this opportunity to raise low cost money, Japanese industrial corporations raised a huge amount of money through capital markets. However, a sizable amount of this money was not invested into real sectors for production. Instead, it was reinvested in the stock market and real estate market through the so-called *Zaiteck*. Therefore, industrial corporations occupied the position of being extremely important double income sources to the brokerage companies: they provided significant commissions through both brokerage and underwriting activities. Therefore, industrial corporation investors became increasingly important customers to brokerage firms because of the growth in the ratio of operation related to corporate investors.

The Japanese security industry is under strong government regulation. The Japanese government introduced a barrier to entry through the license system. Also, brokerage and underwriting commissions are fixed. Therefore, the brokerage companies cannot use the price mechanism when they compete with each other. In Japanese brokerage companies, there is no "Chinese Wall" between brokerage and underwriting functions. This facilitates smooth behind-the-scenes teamwork, through which the maximum level of firm profitability can be pursued. The big security companies wanted to maintain a stable trading with major customers and made frantic efforts to keep leading underwriter status. It was in this context that loss compensation was delivered as a way to compete using nonprice instruments.

Another major factor that played a pivotal role in the generation of the loss compensation was the unique preference structures of the fund managers at industrial corporations. Under current Japanese corporate culture, demonstrated by life-time employment and the seniority system, the fund managers at industrial corporations have no incentive to set higher return and higher risk goals. As a result, fund managers show a high degree of aversion toward risk and behave extremely conservatively, one of the important underlying factors behind loss compensation. They also show strong interest in investment opportunities where they could be guaranteed a certain level of minimum return. However, at the same time, they are not concerned about loosing excess returns when the market exceeds the guaranteed level. Therefore, loss compensation itself could be another potential source of profit to the brokerage companies when the guaranteed return is below the real return from the investment.

To satisfy the needs of fund managers at industrial corporations and desires of brokerage companies to keep market shares, *eigyo-tokkin* accounts were mainly employed as a vehicle for the loss compensation. Different from ordinary *tokkin* (specified money in trust) contracts, where fund trustor or investment advisory companies advise trust banks how to invest funds, brokerage companies directly manage funds under *eigyo-tokkin* accounts.[1] Under such discretionary accounts, the security companies guaranteed minimum return while enjoying potential brokerage fees through unnecessary transactions by drawing off excess return above the guaranteed level.

The purpose of this chapter is to present a game theoretical framework that analyzes what the underlying factors behind the popularity of loss compensation in the Japanese brokerage industry are. Based on this analysis, we can provide the answer to the question, "Can we prevent loss compensation by the liberalization of brokerage commissions?" To provide an initial perspective, this chapter starts with an overview of the brokerage industry in Japan. Following this section, loss compensation is analyzed under the game theoretic approach to explain why it was so popular in the Japanese brokerage industry. Finally, a brief conclusion and suggestion end the chapter.

II. AN OVERVIEW

Japan emerged as one of the world's economically strong countries after overcoming the rubble of World War II. Although Japanese management style played a significant role, a lower cost of capital was also an important element behind the scene. The Japanese government deployed financial intermediaries as levers for providing cheap money to provide competitiveness to Japanese corporations. The estimation of cost of capital in Japan and U.S. vary widely, but most studies agree that cost of capital was much cheaper in Japan for most of the period after the World War II.[2] Low cost capital can encourage more risk-taking and more innovation, and maybe increased productivity. Also, the difference in cost of capital strongly affects investment decision, especially for long-term projects.

Financial markets perform one of the most important economic functions, channeling funds from those who have saved surplus funds to those who are in shortage. In direct finance, borrowers borrow funds directly from lenders in financial market by selling them securities that are claims on the borrower's future income or assets. On the other hand, financial intermediaries play an important role in case of indirect financing.

Compared to direct financing, where borrowers and lenders meet face to face without employing intermediaries, indirect financing permitted the Japanese government ample space and freedom to play a role as a controller and distributor of the capital. According to Bank of Japan statistics, bank borrowing accounted for more than 80% of corporate financing during the period of 1965–1985. Reflecting the substantial increase in stock prices of TSE during 1987–1989, it went down to 60.5% in 1988. However, Japanese banks continue to play an important role in corporate financing compared to that in the U.S.

In this section, we will enumerate the current characteristics of TSE and its participants related to the creation of loss compensation.

A. Government Regulated Brokerage Industry

In Japan, the Securities Bureau of the Ministry of Finance (MOF), which corresponds to the US Securities and Exchange Commission (SEC), supervises and administers the security industry under the Security and Exchange Law and other laws. It is in charge of licensing and supervision of securities industry including all security related organizations, designation and supervision of central depository agencies, inspection of security companies, and supervision of securities-related nonprofit organizations. It administers planning and drafting of policies related to the securities in general. Also, it administers policy planning and coordination for the primary market and the secondary market by ensuring the formation of fair prices, and by examining securities reports and the certified public accountant system.

Article 65 of the Securities and Exchange Act of 1948 is the Japanese version of the 1933 U.S. Glass-Steagall Act. The Glass-Steagall Act created a barrier between commercial banks and brokerage companies by means of functional separation. In Japan, Article 65 is protects the brokerage industry from the traditionally superior power of the banking industry.
Brokerage fees in Japan are based upon a commission scale that is nonnegotiable and relatively inflexible. One of the basic economic principles posits that, under price regulation, firms resort to nonprice tools to compete. For example, the U.S. moved from fixed brokerage commission to negotiated brokerage commission in May 1975. Under fixed commission, investment banks on Wall Street competed with each other using informal negotiation (i.e., rebate) to attract institutional investors.

B. Oligopolistic Brokerage Industry Dominated by the Big Four

In 1965, the Japanese government introduced the license system in the brokerage industry by replacing the registration system. Under the license system, only security companies licensed by the MOF can engage in the security business. The ministry examines the applicant corporation for the license and grants it if the applicant satisfies the following criteria: (1) soundness in financial resources; (2) appropriateness of personnel; and (3) adequacy in engaging in the security business from the viewpoint of the business environment in the region in which the applicants wants to do business.

The security business is classified into four categories and a license is issued separately for each. The first category is called the dealing business, or trading securities on their own accounts; the second is the brokerage business, or trading securities based on orders from customers; the third is the underwriting business, or underwriting new securities or making public offerings of outstanding securities; the fourth is the selling business, or engaging in a retail distribution of securities offered publicly.[3]

As is shown in Figure 13–1, the number of security companies in Japan has been reduced from the peak of 601 in 1962 to 272 in 1990 including 52 foreign securities companies. During the period of 1970–1990, the number of security companies did not change much. However, the security industry has grown 20 times in terms of aggregated net income and 24 times in terms of total amount of brokerage sales during the same period.[4] Through the license system, the Japanese government has introduced an entry barrier in the brokerage industry, thereby making control of the industry easier.

FIGURE 13–1
Number of Securities Companies in Japan

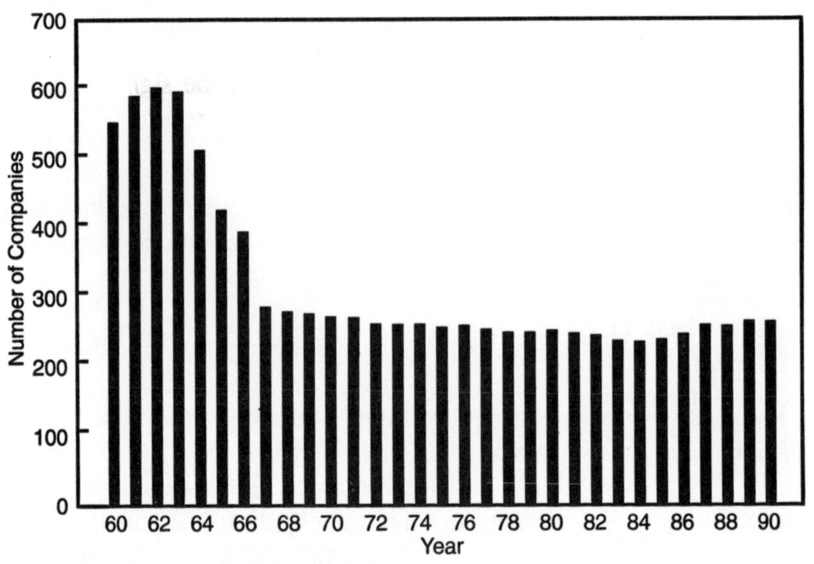

Source: Japan Securities Dealers Association

Brokerage companies in Japan can be classified into three tiers. The first consists of the "Big Four" securities companies of Nomura, Daiwa, Nikko and Yamaichi. The Big Four dominate the market heavily: Together they account for almost half of the trading of TSE and two thirds of all convertible bond dealings. This dominant position of the Big Four makes them leaders in an industry that is characterized as an oligopoly within Japan. The second-tier security companies include ten smaller companies and third-tier security companies are an agglomeration of all the remaining companies in the industry. Actually, many of the second and third-tier securities companies are affiliates of the Big Four.

Another pillar of the Big Four business strength is underwriting, an area in which all four hold an extremely high share. In the past, this sector was entirely monopolized by the Big Four; now their share runs about 80% for stock and 70% for corporate bond issues.[5] Because of their dominant market control, newly listed companies have no choice but to turn to the Big Four. In almost all underwriting cases, one of the Big Four serves as the "lead underwriting manager" with the other participants as "co-managers."[6]

As shown in Figure 13–2, Japanese industrial corporations financed a huge amount of money through capital markets during the second half of the 1980s. Therefore, the weight of underwriting activity in the business of brokerage companies multiplied during that period. At the same time, as is shown in Table 13–1, a sizable sum of financed money was not invested into real sectors for production. This has highlighted the significance of industrial corporations as an important double income sources to the brokerage companies.

C. Decline of Importance of Individual Investors in the Stock Market

It is said that stock investors in U.S. are pursuing either monetary return (through dividends and/or capital gains) or control. However in Japan, share ownership serves an additional function; there is a peculiar group of investors who are pursuing neither monetary returns or control. They are corporate shareholders who do not hold stocks to sell. They hold each other's

FIGURE 13–2
Amount of Equity and Bond Financing[a]

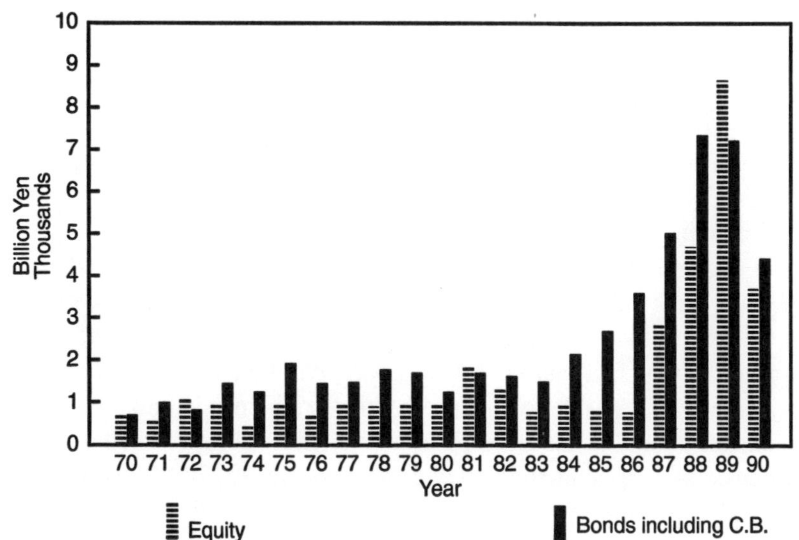

[a] Equity is including issues in foreign countries and bonds excluding issues in foreign countries.

Source: Tokyo Stock Exchange Fact Book, 1991

TABLE 13–1
Sources and Uses of Funds for Japanese Corporations (in billions of yen)

Year	*Change in Cash and Savings*[a, c]	*Direct Financing from Capital Market*[b]	*Balance of Tokkin and Fund Trust*[b]	*Cash Flow*[c]	*Invest-ment in Facility*[c]
1983	2,480	2,814	1,430	8.570	9,800
1984	1,890	3,996	2,190	9,710	10,236
1985	1,161	4,517	8,810	10,253	11,409
1986	5,299	5,781	20,430	10,093	11,704
1987	7,532	16,812	29,980	10,997	11,613
1988	9,323	17,557	35,210	12,425	13,618
1989	11,104	24,816	42,660	13,667	16,063
1990	–	10,496	36,730	–	–

[a] Includes short-term security investment.
[b] Based on all industry.
[c] Based on all industry, except financial institutions.

Source: Nihon Keizai Shimbun, July 5, 1991

stocks for strategic reason. This cross holding, *Mochiai*, keeps the company from worrying about takeovers.

The pattern of Japanese corporate cross-holding reflects the unique structures of post-war Keiretsu. The Japanese stock market crash of 1965 contributed significantly to the development of the cross-holding system. Facing depressed share prices and continuous liberalization of the Tokyo market, business corporations and financial institutions feared takeovers. They responded to this perceived threat by substantially increasing their mutual holdings with friendly firms.

As shown in Figure 13–3, stock holdings of individuals as a percentage of the total outstanding shares have declined consistently since the war and dropped to a postwar low of 22.4 at the end of fiscal year 1989. The decline is attributed to the fact that the share of corporate holdings has risen significantly in recent years due to an increase in interlocking shareholders among business firms, and to an increase in institutional investors such as banks, trust banks, and pension funds. Other reasons are: (1) In 1950s and early 1960s, individual investors kept on selling part of their shares when companies issued new shares below market value under a right offering.[7] (2) It is getting harder for individual investors to put money directly into equity since stock prices are soaring and the minimum order is 1,000 shares.

FIGURE 13–3
Shareownership by Types of Investors[a]

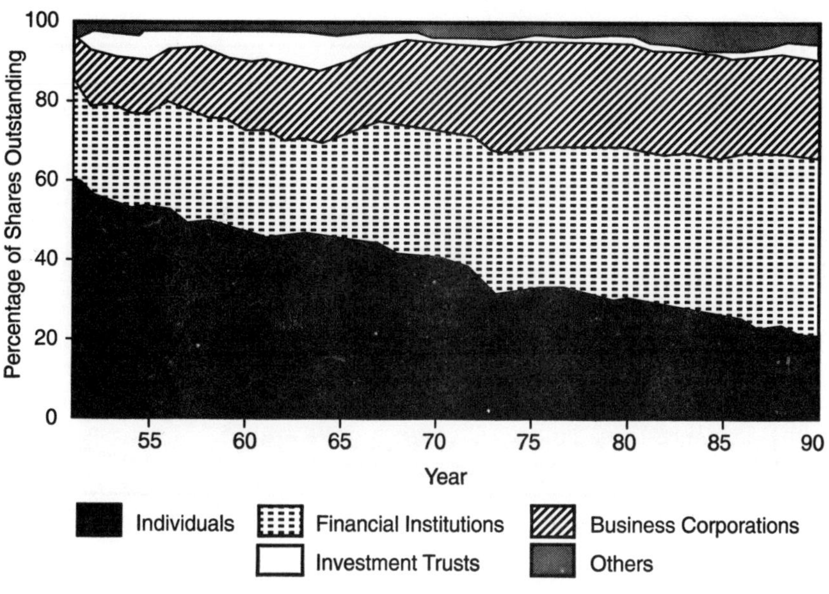

[a] Based on all listed corporations

Source: Tokyo Stock Exchange Fact Book, 1991

According to Figure 13–4, the percentage of total stock transactions by individual investors amounted to 58% in 1975 and dropped to 23.3% in 1990. On the other hand, the share by banks has grown rapidly from 1984 when the balance of tokkin account started to grow, peaking at 20.2% in 1989 due to the fact that brokerage companies can generate brokerage commissions through unnecessary transactions when the return on investment is higher than guaranteed return.

D. Lack of Incentive for Fund Managers at Industrial Corporation to Take Risks

In the U.S., evaluating portfolio performance is important to the investor in several respects. First, it enables the investor to appraise how well the fund trustee has done in achieving desired return targets and how well risk has been controlled in the process. Second, it enables the investor to assess how well the trustee has achieved these targets in comparison with other manag-

FIGURE 13–4
Stock Transactions by Investment Sectors

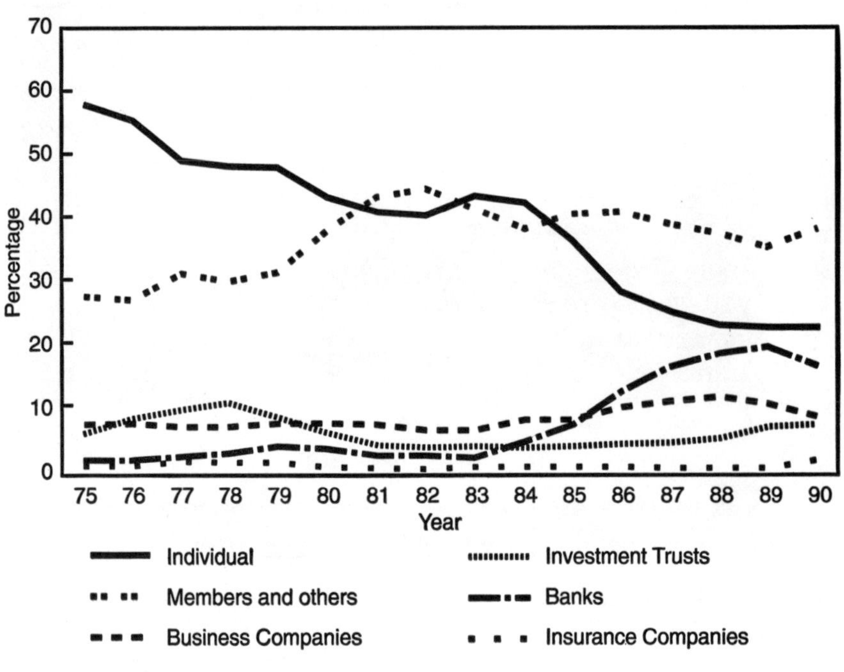

Source: Tokyo Stock Exchange Fact Book 1991

ers. Moreover, the trustee is constantly subject to monitoring by impartial rating agencies .

Viner (1988) argues that fund consignors in Japan are not evaluated by their performance and fund managers in the industrial corporations are neither rewarded for good performance results nor fired for consistently poor results. Under current Japanese corporate culture, which is well demonstrated by life-time employment and the seniority system, the fund managers at industrial corporations have no incentives to set the goal at higher return with higher risk. They show a high degree of aversion toward risk and behave extremely conservatively. This played a pivotal function in giving birth to loss compensation. Fund managers showed a great interest in investment opportunities where they could be guaranteed a certain level of minimum return. However, at the same time, they did not care for loosing excess return above the guaranteed level. Therefore, loss compensation itself could be another potential source of profit to the brokerage companies when the guaranteed return is below the real return from the investment.

III. THE GAME AMONG THE JAPANESE BROKERAGE COMPANIES

One of the most active and exciting areas of economic and financial research over the last decade has been the use of noncooperative games of incomplete information to model industrial competition. In the standard industrial competition, firms can use various instruments to compete in the market. Usually, price, cost structure and product characteristics are the main instruments that a firm can adjust easily and effectively.

Under fixed commission, Japanese brokerage companies cannot control the price of providing brokerage service. We can expect that under the strong competition, brokerage companies are likely to turn to nonprice or quality variables in order to compete for business. For example, they could take the forms of free gifts for opening account, providing better information through sophisticated market research, and supplying other extra conveniences.

According to a basic principle in fiance, there is always a trade off between expected return and risk, i.e., investors are compensated with higher expected return when they take more risk. The trade off ratio between risk and return depends on individual's preference structure. Investors with high risk tolerance will choose a risky portfolio with high expected return. On the other hand, investors with low risk tolerance would choose a portfolio with low risk and low expected return.

In section 2, we found that the Japanese brokerage industry is characterized by: (1) a government regulated market under entry barriers and fixed commissions; (2) oligopolistic competition; (3) decline of importance of individual investors; and (4) lack of incentive for fund managers at industrial corporations to take risk.

In the mid-1980s, soaring stock prices and Japanese companies' desire for easy equity sparked massive growth at the major security companies. Japanese listed companies raised about ¥70 trillion (more than $510 billion) in the financial markets from 1987 and 1990. This included some cases of finance for which no real capital requirement existed. When they invested excess low-cost funds in securities, they needed a system that could make it possible to distinguish it from *Mochiai*. *Tokkin* accounts were set up for that purpose. At the same time, large corporations were important sources of revenue through underwriting. This was another factor that made the competition much stronger.

Unlike ordinary *tokkin* contracts, in which institutional investors advise trust banks on how to invest funds, brokerage companies directly manage funds in *eigyo tokkin* accounts. Such discretionary accounts enabled the securities companies to easily move in and out of big clients' accounts. By late 1989, at their peak, ¥5 trillion was invested in *eigyo tokkin* accounts according to industry estimate.

Using a game theoretic approach, we will analyze the nonprice competition among Japanese brokerage companies to attract industrial corporate investors.

a. Problem Formulation

Consider a pair of identical brokerage companies 1 and 2 engaged in a game of duopoly.[8] Under fixed brokerage commission, they are competing with each other using nonprice competition strategies. The total market demand for brokerage service from institutional investors is D. If they do not employ nonprice competition, they will divide the market equally. There are two different tools they can employ under nonprice competition: (1) the guarantee of loss compensation; and (2) the provision of commission kick backs.[9]

Fund managers from large corporations have a preference structure that is quite different from that of individual investors. Fund managers are very concerned about the possibility of realizing an investment return that is below the money market interest rate plus some positive markup.

$$\underset{i=1,2}{\text{Min}}\ Pr[\,F_i\,(r_i\,) < (r_f + \alpha)] \tag{13.1}$$

where Pr = probability
$F_i(\,)$ = transformation of r_i through the package of brokerage company i under competition
r_i = net return of a portfolio managed by i and $r_i \sim N(\mu,\sigma^2)$
r_f = risk free rate available from money market
α = a positive markup above r_f

For example, when the brokerage company i guarantees minimum return, $(r_f + \alpha)$, $F_i\,(r_i\,)$ would be expressed $r_f + a$.[10] In this case, the probability of $F_i\,(r_i\,) < (r_f + \alpha)$ is equal to 0. If the brokerage company can provide kick backs of commissions, it can transform the distribution of r_i to reduce the probability of $F_i(r_i) < (r_f + \alpha)$. For example, when $F_i(r_i) = r_i + a$ (where $a > 0$), then the probability of $F_i(r_i) < (r_f + \alpha)$ would be less than the probability of $r_i < (r_f + \alpha)$,where no additional services are provided.

Under the preference of equation (13.1), we can see that a security company will try to minimize the probability of $F_i(r_i) < (r_f + \alpha)$ through various methods to attract cash rich corporations. At the same time, fund managers in cash rich corporations would search for the brokerage company that provides the best package based on criteria of equation (13.1).

When choosing from three, the Japanese corporate fund manager would rank loss compensation as first, kick back of commissions as second, and no package as last place.

The profit function of brokerage firm i is as follows:

$$\pi^i = [(c - v) + u - p(k)]{*}D_i - F$$

where D_i = D when i provides a superior package
$D/2$ when i and j provide the same package
0 when i provides an inferior package

c = brokerage commission per unit
v = variable cost per unit
u = underwriting fee per each brokerage activity
F = fixed cost
$P(k)$ = net cost of providing package k when
with no package $k = 1$ $p(1) = 0$
kick back $k = 2$, $p(2) > 0$
loss compensation $k = 3$, $p(3)$ <(>)0

Therefore, π^i would take the forms of

$\pi_1 = [(c - v) + u]{*}(D/2) - F$ when $i = j = 1$
$\pi_2 = -F$ when $i < j$
$\pi_3 = [(c - v) + u - p(2)]{*}D - F$ when $i = 2$ and $j = 1$
$\pi_4 = [(c - v) + u - p(2)]{*}(D/2) - F$ when $i = 2$ and $j = 2$
$\pi_5 = [(c - v) + u - p(3)]{*}D - F$ when $i = 3$ and $j \neq 3$
$\pi_6 = [(c - v) + u - p(3)]{*}(D/2) - F$ when $i = j = 3$

Letting T_1 and T_2 denote the respective packages of firms 1 and 2, we can summarize the profit opportunities described above in tabular form.

P2\P1	1	2	3
1	(π_1, π_1)	(π_3, π_2)	(π_5, π_2)
2	(π_2, π_3)	(π_4, π_4)	(π_5, π_2)
3	(π_2, π_5)	(π_2, π_5)	(π_6, π_6)

The following assumptions describe the relative magnitudes of profit.

Assumption 1. $\pi_j > 0 \; \forall j \in \{1,3,4,5,6\}$ and $\pi_2 < 0$

Assumption 2. $p(3) < 0$

Assumption 3. $\pi_3 > \pi_6$

Assumption 1 states that competing firms can make positive profits as long as they do not provide an inferior package. When firm *i* provides an inferior package, firm *i* would end up with the negative return π_2. Assumption 2 indicates that α is small enough to make $\mu - (r_f + \alpha) > 0$. This assumption sounds feasible especially in the context of the Japanese stock market in the late 1980s when μ is much higher than r_f. Under assumption 2, we can compare the relative size of πs as follows: $\pi_5 > \pi_3$ and $\pi_6 > \pi_1 > \pi_4$.

Assumption 3 indicates that keeping the whole market share would be more profitable than enjoying extra profit by offering loss compensation in a shared market. Additionally, if we consider the large profits that the brokerage company is deriving from the same institutional investors under underwriting activity (i.e., high u), the assumption sounds much more reliable. Under assumption 2 and 3, we can rank πs as follows: $\pi_5 > \pi_3 > \pi_6 > \pi_1 > \pi_4 > \pi_2$.

b. Nash Equilibrium in Pure Strategies

The problem set in section a can be modeled and solved in a game theoretic framework.

Definition 1. The strategy space for player *i* is $S_i = \{1,2,3\}$. A pure strategy for *i* is a $T_i \in S_i$.

Letting T_1 and T_2 denote the strategies of firms 1 and 2, the firms' payoffs are given in Definition 2 below.

Definition 2. The payoff to firm 1 is

$$V^1(T_1, T_2) \equiv \begin{cases} \pi_1 & \text{if } T_1 = T_2 = 1 \\ \pi_2 & \text{if } T_1 < T_2 \\ \pi^i_3 & \text{if } T_1 = 2, T_2 = 1 \\ \pi^i_4 & \text{if } T_1 = T_2 = 2 \\ \pi^i_5 & \text{if } T_1 = 3, T_2 \neq 3 \\ \pi^i_6 & \text{if } T_1 = T_2 = 3 \end{cases}$$

The payoff to firm 2 is simply $V^2(T_1,T_2) \equiv V^1(T_2, T_1)$.

Definition 3. The set of best responses for i to T_j is

$$\phi_i(T_j) = \{T_i \in S_i \mid V_i(T_i, T_j) \geq V_i(T, T_j) \; \forall \, T'_i \in S_i\}$$

Definition 4. $T_i \in S_i$ is a dominated strategy for player i if

$$V_i(T, T_j) \geq V_i(T_i, T_j) \; \exists \mathrm{T} \in S_i \text{ and } \forall T_j \in S_j.$$

Definition 5. $T_i \in S_i$ is a dominant strategy for player i if

$$V_i(T_i, T_j) \geq V_i(T, T_j) \; \forall \mathrm{T} \in S_i \text{ and } \forall T_j \in S_j.$$

Definition 6. A strategy pair (T^N_1, T^N_2) is a Nash Equilibrium for the game $G = (V^1, V^2, S^1, S^2)$ if

(a) $T^N_i \in Si, i = 1,2$
(b) $V^1(T^N_1, T^N_2) \geq V^1(T_1, T^N_2) \; \forall \mathrm{T}_1 \in S_1$; and
(c) $V^2(T^N_1, T^N_2) \geq V^2(T^N_1, T_2) \; \forall \mathrm{T}_2 \in S_2$.

Alternatively, (T^N_1, T_2) is a Nash Equilibrium if $T^N_1 \in \phi_i(T^N_2)$ and $T^N_2 \in \phi_2(T^N_1)$; that is, each strategy is a best response to the other.

Theorem 1. For player i, $T_i = 1$ is a dominated strategy.
Proof For player 1,
$V^1(3,1) = \pi_5 \geq \pi_1 = V^1(1,1)$ by assumption 2 and 3;
$V^1(3,2) = \pi_5 \geq \pi_2 = V^1(1,2)$ by assumption 1; and
$V^1(3,3) = \pi_6 \geq \pi_2 = V^1(1,3)$ by assumption 1.

For player 2,
$V^2(1,3) = \pi_5 \geq \pi_1 = V^2(1,1)$ by assumption 2 and 3;
$V^2(2,3) = \pi_5 \geq \pi_2 = V^2(2,1)$ by assumption 1; and
$V^2(3,3) = \pi_6 \geq \pi_2 = V^2(3,1)$ by assumption 1. ||

Theorem 2. There exists a unique *Nash Equilibrium* in pure strategy $(T_i^N, T_2^N) = (3,3)$.

Proof Using the results of Theorem 1, we can delete strategy 1 from S_1 and S_2. Under the reduced game, strategy 3 is a dominant strategy for each firm because for 1 and 2;
$V^1(3,2) = \pi_5 \geq \pi_4 = V^1(2,2)$ by assumption 2 and 3;
$V^1(3,3) = \pi_6 \geq \pi_2 = V^1(2,3)$ by assumption 1;
$V^2(2,3) = \pi_5 \geq \pi_4 = V^2(2,2)$ by assumption 2 and 3; and
$V^2(3,3) = \pi_6 \geq \pi_2 = V^2(3,2)$ by assumption 1. ||

From this analysis, we can find that under the current Japanese financial system, brokerage companies are employing loss compensation as the dominant strategy to capture market shares in brokerage and underwriting activities with the industrial corporations. In the Nash Equilibrium, security companies provided loss compensation to the fund managers at industrial corporations. As shown in the previous analysis, the peculiar preference structure of investors from industrial corporations as well as the lack of distinction between brokerage activity and underwriting are very important factors behind the loss compensation. We can also argue that even if brokerage fees are liberalized there will remain a strong motivation for brokerage companies to resort to loss compensation rather than the price mechanism.

V. CONCLUSION

The characteristics of the current Japanese brokerage industry are summarized by (1) strong government regulations with a license system and fixed brokerage commissions, (2) oligopolistic brokerage industry dominated by the Big Four, (3) decline of the importance of individual investors in the stock market, and (4) lack of incentive for fund managers at industrial corporations to take high risk with high return.

Under these circumstances, major brokerage companies in Japan competed to keep important market shares in brokerage and underwriting businesses with corporate customers. In Japan, there is no clear distinction between brokerage and underwriting functions, which facilitated smooth behind-the-scenes teamwork. Therefore, it became possible for brokerage companies to make such a manipulation for the sake of maintaining strategic position.

With excess funds raised through security markets, Japanese corporations reinvested in the security market. They needed a system that could make it possible to distinguish them from *Mochiai. Tokkin* accounts were set up for that purpose. Unlike ordinary *tokkin* contracts in which investor or designated advisory companies instruct trust banks on how to invest funds, brokerage companies directly manage funds in *eigyo-tokkin* accounts. Such discretionary accounts enabled the security companies to easily move in and out of big clients' accounts. In return for guaranteeing minimum return, brokerage companies could turn the excess returns (i.e., return above guaranteed return) from *eigyo-tokkin* accounts into brokerage commissions through unnecessary transactions.

This chapter presented a game theoretical analysis which shows that providing loss compensation to fund managers from industrial corporations is the dominant strategy for the Japanese brokerage companies under nonprice competition. Using different preference structures, we showed that the liberalization of brokerage commissions alone would not solve the loss compensation problem. As a preventive measure, providing incentives to the fund managers at large corporations to set goals at higher returns should be accompanied by liberalization of brokerage commissions.

NOTES

1. See Yamashita (1989) for detailed information about *tokkin* accounts.
2. See Frankel (1991) for detailed information.
3. A security company that has been granted the license of the four category business with capital stock of ¥ 3 billion or more is called the "integrated" security company.
4. Source is *Security Statistics 1991* by Japan Security Dealers Association.
5. Source: "The Securities Bureau Annual Report," *MOF Year Book,* various years.
6. The role of "lead underwriting manager" in direct financing is equivalent to that of "main bank" in indirect financing. Japanese companies have a very special long-term relationship with brokerage companies in the area of financing and investment.
7. In the case of a right offering with discount, investors with no additional money to invest sell a part of their holdings to subscribe. Therefore, the percentage of holdings by individual investors declines after a right offering.
8. Without generating further implications, this analysis can be analyzed in the case of oligopoly that is close to the Japanese brokerage industry.

9. In the same way, we can interpret any kind of strategy which can change the expected return and variance of portfolio return through the brokerage company.
10. a is a positive constant and does not depend on the level of risk.

REFERENCES

Frankel, Jeffrey A., 1991, "The Japanese Cost of Finance: A Survey," *Financial Management 20,* 95–127.

Japanese Ministry of Finance, Okura-Sho Shoken Kyoku Nempo (*Annual Report of the Securities Bureau*), Tokyo: Kinyu Zaisei Jijo Kenkyukai, various years.

Japan Security Dealers Association, 1991, *Security Statistics,* (JSDA, 1991).

Tokyo Stock Exchange, 1991 Tokyo, *Stock Exchange Fact Book* (TSE, 1991).

Viner, Aron, 1988, *Inside Japanese Financial Markets.* Homewood, IL: Dow Jones-Irwin.

Yamashita, Takeji, 1989, *Japan's Securities Markets: A Practitioner's Guide,* Singapore: Butterworth.

Zielinski, Robert, and Nigel Holloway, 1991, *Unequal Equities: Power and Risk in Japan's Stock Market,* Kodansha International, Japan.

CHAPTER 14

CORPORATE DISCLOSURE POLICY IN AN ASYMMETRIC WORLD

Frederick D.S. Choi

In 1887, Dr. L. L. Zamenhof, a Russian physician, invented Esperanto, an artificial language he hoped would be adopted as a uniform means of communication by all peoples of the world. As we all know, that attempt, although a noble one, proved unsuccessful.

Today, we are witnessing an attempt similar to Zamenhof's in the world of commerce and finance. Owing to the globalization of business and investment, significant resources are being expended to develop a set of international accounting and reporting standards that will serve as a common language for international business. This effort stems from the asymmetry that exists between international financial decisions on the one hand, and national accounting practices on the other. While financial decisions are becoming increasingly international in scope, financial statements of most business enterprises continue to be prepared in line with local rules, which are in turn, rooted in local business cultures. Far from being an international language, accounting remains a babble of heterogeneous dialects.

In this chapter, I marshal recent empirical evidence on the capital market effects of international accounting and reporting differences. The policy implications of these findings for market regulators and corporate issuers in Japan are then discussed.

INTERNATIONALIZATION OF FINANCIAL DECISIONS

When accounting measurements are communicated via published financial statements and used solely within the confines of a single country, problems of understanding and interpretation are less problematic. In these instances, the information communicated to a knowledgeable reader is usually based on a familiar set of measurement rules, language and currency of denomination. Problems arise when financial statements are read by decision makers who normally base their decisions on financial statements generated by a different measurement framework. Unless the statement user is familiar with the preparer's measurement process, he can be easily misled as to underlying relations being reported on.

Whether this problem is extensive or not is an empirical question and I will have more to say about this later. However, there are a number of forces at work that are increasing the need for corporate financial managers, investors and market regulators to rely on foreign financial statements. So to the extent there is a problem, this problem is destined to grow. Most of the forces I will describe are closely interrelated making it difficult to order them sequentially or to gauge their relative importance. Hence, I discuss some of them in combination.

Global Competition A major force which is necessitating a global perspective on the part of managers, investors and market regulators is the phenomenon of global competition. Market and product interpenetration is being hastened by such forces as the continued reduction in national trade barriers, the emergence of Europe as a unified market, the convergence of consumer tastes and preferences, and a growing sophistication of business firms, large, medium and small, in penetrating foreign markets either directly or indirectly through strategic alliances, joint ventures and other cooperative arrangements. These developments mean that uninational approaches to the production and marketing of goods and services (and their financing) are no longer sufficient. (Bartlett and Ghoshal, 1989) The analysis of competitor strengths and weaknesses, in turn, are highly dependent on information gleaned from published financial reports. In instances where collaboration is warranted, partners to strategic alliances and joint venture arrangements need to understand each others financial characteristics. Trading partners likewise need to read and understand each others financial information as a basis for appraisals of credit worthiness and productive capacity.

Internationalization of Capital Markets Encouraged by recent advances in telecommunications and the gradual deregulation of national capital markets, domestic investors are expanding their purchases of foreign debt and equity. Motivating investor behavior are enhanced returns that are frequently available abroad as well as the opportunity to reduce portfolio risk by diversifying internationally. (Grubel 1968; Solnik 1988) In similar fashion, business enterprises interested in increasing the supply of investable funds, and reducing their capital costs, are increasingly sourcing their external capital needs abroad, both in terms of new issues and listings on foreign stock exchanges. (Eiteman and Stonehill, 1983) Communicating with foreign statement readers who are used to differing language, currency and financial reporting frameworks is a problem of no small proportion.

The International Market for Corporate Control Driven by financial market considerations and facilitated by new developments in corporate finance, corporate takeovers and restructurings are spreading rapidly from the U.S. to Europe and Asia, and increasingly involves cross-border commercial and financial elements. (Walter and Smith 1989) Shareholder value perspectives, which were often viewed as an American aberration among European corporations, are now becoming a driving force in their strategies as well. (Lessard 1989) Needless to say merger and acquisition activities require a sophisticated understanding of foreign accounting practices.

Advances in Financial Technology Underlying many of the driving forces just described are the many advances that are occurring in computer and telecommunications technology. Technological advances have accelerated transactions processing and settlement, increased the liquidity of financial markets around the world and facilitated around-the-clock trading in a variety of complex financial instruments. It is now possible to shift interest rate and currency risks via financial intermediaries to the shoulders of counterparts located in distant offshore locations. This places a greater burden of credit evaluations on a larger pool of international participants (Levich, 1989).

ACCOUNTING AND ITS ENVIRONMENT

Despite the increasing globalization of financial decisions, the measurement and disclosure principles underlying financial statement preparation have largely remained a nationalistic affair. Why is this the case? Just as accounting impacts its environment in terms of its effect on user decisions, accounting is, in turn, influenced and shaped by its social, economic and legal milieu. Some of the environmental factors that shape national patterns of accounting development are briefly described.

Legal Systems In Roman or code law countries (e.g., Germany, France, Italy) codification of accounting standards and procedures is common practice. Understandably, accounting reports in such environments tend to be oriented toward compliance with legal requirements (e.g., statutory depreciation guidelines). In environments where accounting policies are established through the efforts of private sector professional bodies (e.g., Australia, the United Kingdom, the United States), accounting tends to be geared more toward user needs. Here, depreciation schedules tend to be based on an asset's estimated "useful" life.

Political Systems In centrally planned economies where private ownership of the means of production does not exist, accounting generally serves more macroeconomic decision processes. Here the emphasis tends to be on cost-accounting systems which serve as the basis for "administered prices." This differs markedly from free market economies where accounting serves more microeconomic decisions and reported earnings are the basis upon which access to money capital or the cost of that capital is largely determined.

Nature of Business Ownership/Financing In countries where public participation in corporate securities is limited, or where the bulk of investable funds are provided by the banks or the State (e.g., Germany, Italy, Switzerland), disclosure tends to be minimal and financial reporting principles tend to be oriented toward creditor needs. Thus, the establishment of hidden reserves to understate assets and to minimize reported earnings (and hence, the dividend declaration or wage negotiation base) are viewed as acts of financial prudence that are consistent with creditor and internal user needs. Such practices are frowned upon in countries (e.g., Canada, the Netherlands, the United Kingdom) where public ownership of corporate equities is widespread and unbiased estimates of future events (e.g., earnings or cash flows) are valued.

Influence of Tax Law Tax legislation often requires the application of certain accounting principles. Examples of countries in which there exists a high degree of book and tax conformity are France, Germany and Japan. These countries' standards require companies to deduct for financial reporting purposes deductions such as reserves, write-offs, and accelerated depreciation, which are deducted for tax purposes. As a result, accounting earnings are much more conservative than if the book and tax conformity requirement did not exist.

INTERNATIONAL ACCOUNTING DIVERSITY

The environmental influences identified above are far from exhaustive. Nevertheless, they give rise to observed differences in national accounting practices. This is illustrated in Table 14–1.

Examination of Table 14–1 reveals that while the countries surveyed demonstrate some similarities in accounting treatments, the differences are extensive. Take the case of Japan. Using the United States as a benchmark, major differences in reporting practices relate to:

	United States	Japan
1.	*Consolidated financial statements*	
	Primary statements • full disclosure Parent GAAP required; i.e., local statements are restated U.S. GAAP prior to consolidation	Supplemental information • minimal disclosure Alternative GAAP permissible; i.e., foreign sub's can adhere to their local GAAP
2.	*Goodwill*	
	Goodwill amortized over a period not exceeding 40 years	Goodwill amortized over five years.
3.	*Depreciation*	
	Straight line method predominant	Declining balance method
4.	*Severance Indemnity*	
	Considered a pension under U.S. GAAP. Obligation based estimated future benefits and discounted at at market rates. Past service costs and other gains and losses spread over extended period.	Liability, payable in a lump sum at retirement (or when employee leaves if earlier), is not funded. Based on salaries and length of service at balance sheet date. Majority book 40% of liability which is amount allowable for tax. Expense equal to change in liability during year.

5. *Allowance for Bad Debts*	
Provide for estimated bad debts.	General provision allowable for tax based on percentage of receivables, including intercompany accounts. Specific provisions for bad debts also made.
6. *Inventories*	
Lower cost or market	Generally cost
7. *Foreign Currency Translation*	
Current exchange rate used to translate balance sheet when local currency is the functional currency; temporal method is used when U.S. dollar is the functional currency. Income statements translated at average rate.	Modified temporal method used. Major differences are: long-term receivables and payables translated at historic rates. Transaction gain or loss deferred as an asset or liability. Net income translated at current rates.
8. *Foreign Currency Transactions*	
Receivables and payables from foreign currency transactions translated at current rate. Unrealized exchange gains or losses recognized in income.	Long-term foreign currency receivables and payables translated at historic rates.
9. *Deferred Taxes*	
Required.	Not permitted in parent company statements; minority practice in consolidated statements.
10. Research and Development	
Expense immediately.	May either be expensed or capitalized and amortized.
11. Stock Dividends	
No accounting effect to recipient.	Income to recipient if issued from retained earnings.
12. Long-term Leases	
Lease capitalization required under specified circumstances.	Generally no-lease capitalization.

TABLE 14–1
Comparison of International Accounting Principles

Accounting Principles	*UK*	*USA*	*France*	*Germany*	*Netherlands*	*Sweden*	*Switzerland*	*Japan*
1. Consistency—accounting principles and methods are applied on the same basis from period to period	Yes	Yes	Yes	Yes	Yes	PP	PP	Yes
2. Realization—revenue is recognized when realization is reasonably assured	Yes	Yes	Yes	Yes	Yes	Yes	PP	Yes
3. Fair presentation of the financial statement is required	Yes	Yes	Yes	Yes	Yes	Yes	Yes	Yes
4. Historical cost convention—departures from the historical cost convention are disclosed	Yes	Yes	Yes	Yes	Yes	Yes	RF	Yes
5. Accounting policies—a change in accounting principles or methods without a change in circumstances is accounted for by a prior-year adjustment	Yes	No	Yes	MP	RF	MP	MP	No
6. Fixed assets—revaluations—in historical cost statements, fixed assets are stated at an amount in excess of cost which is determined at irregular intervals	MP	No	Yes	No	RF	PP	No	No

TABLE 14–1, continued

Accounting Principles	*UK*	*USA*	*France*	*Germany*	*Nether-lands*	*Sweden*	*Switzer-land*	*Japan*
7. Fixed assets—revaluations—when fixed assets are stated, in historical cost statements, at an amount in excess of cost, depreciation based on the revaluation amount is charged to income	Yes	No	Yes	No	Yes	Yes	No	No
8. Goodwill amortized	MP	Yes	Yes	Yes	M	Yes	MP	Yes
9. Finance leases capitalized	Yes	Yes	No	No	No	Yes	RF	No
10. Short-term marketable securities at the lower of cost or market value	Yes	Yes	Yes	Yes	Yes	Yes	Yes	Yes
11. Inventory—valued at the lower of cost or market value	Yes	Yes	Yes	Yes	Yes	Yes	Yes	Yes
12. Manufacturing overhead allocated to year-end inventory	Yes	Yes	Yes	Yes	Yes	Yes	Yes	Yes
13. Inventory costed using FIFO	PP	M	M	MM	M	PP	PP	M
14. Long-term debt includes maturities longer than one year	Yes	Yes	Yes	No[a]	Yes	Yes	Yes	Yes
15. Deferred tax recognized where accounting income and taxable income arise at different times	Yes	Yes	Yes[b]	No[c]	Yes	No	No	Yes

16. Total pension fund assets and liabilities excluded from a company's financial statements	Yes	Yes	Yes	No	Yes	Yes	Yes	Yes
17. Research and development expensed[d]	Yes	Yes	Yes	Yes	Yes	Yes	Yes	Yes
18. General purpose (purely discretionary) reserves allowed	No	No	Yes	Yes	Yes	Yes	Yes	Yes
19. Offsetting—assets and liabilities are offset against each other in the balance sheet only when a legal right of offset exists	Yes	Yes	Yes	Yes	Yes	Yes	PP	Yes
20. Unusual and extraordinary gains and losses are taken to the Income Statement	Yes	Yes	Yes	Yes	Yes	Yes	Yes	Yes
21. Closing rate method of foreign currency translation employed	Yes[e]	Yes[e]	Yes	Yes	Yes	No[f]	Yes	No
22. Currency translation gains or losses arising from trading are reflected in current income	Yes	Yes	MP	MP	MP	MP	MP	No
23. Excess depreciation permitted	Yes	No	Yes	Yes	Yes	Yes	Yes	Yes
24. Basic statements reflect a historical cost valuation (no price level adjustment)	Yes	Yes	Yes	Yes	M	Yes	Yes	Yes
25. Supplementary inflation—adjusted financial statements provided	MP	MP	No	No	MP	Yes	No	No

TABLE 14–1, concluded

Accounting Principles	*UK*	*USA*	*France*	*Germany*	*Netherlands*	*Sweden*	*Switzerland*	*Japan*
26. Accounting for long-term investments:								
(a) less than 20% ownership—cost method	Yes	Yes	Yes	Yes	No[g]	Yes	Yes[h]	Yes
(b) 20–50% ownership—equity method	Yes	Yes	Yes	No	Yes	MP	M	Yes
(c) More than 50% full consolidation	Yes	Yes	Yes	Yes	Yes	Yes	Yes	Yes
27. Both domestic and foreign subsidiaries consolidated	Yes	Yes	Yes	M	Yes	Yes	MP	Yes
28. Acquisitions accounted for under the purchase cost method	PP	PP	Yes	Yes	Yes	PP	Yes	Yes
29. Minority interest excluded from consolidated income	Yes	Yes	Yes	Yes	Yes	Yes	Yes	Yes
30. Minority interest excluded from consolidated owners' equity	Yes	Yes	Yes	Yes	Yes	Yes	Yes	Yes

Key: PP = Predominant practice MP = Minority practice M = Mixed practice RF = Rarely or not found

[a] Long-term debt includes maturities longer than four years.

[b] Deferred tax most commonly seen in conjunction with (1) *Provisions reglementées,* (2) *Amortissement exceptionnel,* (3) *Provisions pour payées congées.*

[c] Financial statements are oriented towards the tax calculations. To obtain the maximum benefit from tax allowances, the most favorable tax-oriented valuations have to be taken up in the financial statements.

[d] Under certain circumstances, research and development expenses can be capitalized.

[e] In certain cases the temporal method is acceptable.

[f] Monetary/nonmonetary method of foreign currency translation used.

[g] Proportional consolidation can also be used.

[h] Equity/net asset value method used.

FINANCIAL STATEMENT EFFECTS OF ACCOUNTING DIVERSITY

What then are the implications of this diversity for international users of corporate financial accounts? A direct implication is that it will be very difficult to compare accounting reports prepared in one country, say Japan, with those prepared in another; e.g., the United States. Differences in national accounting treatments can materially distort key financial statistics of interest to international investors, including reported earnings, shareholders' equity and even cash flow.[1]

Table 14–2 reports the results of a study that was undertaken by Prudential Bache Securities of the telecommunications industry. (Schieneman 1988) It contains a restatement of the accounts of 13 major non-U.S. telecommunications companies to a basis consistent with U.S. generally accepted accounting principles (GAAP).

As can be seen, differences in accounting practices had a very significant effect on financial statements of most of the non-U.S. companies in the study. U.S. GAAP adjustments caused reported net earnings to change anywhere from a negative 27 percent for the U.K.'s Standard Telephones & Cables to an increase in excess of 40 percent for Germany's Siemens. The effect on shareholders' equity was even larger. While minimal differences were noted for the Japanese companies in the sample, this was attributed to the fact that the companies surveyed had conformed their accounts to U.S. GAAP.

INTERNATIONAL ACCOUNTING STANDARDS AND ORGANIZATIONS

In the interest of reducing the diversity that exists in accounting principles and practices around the world, there is today renewed interest in achieving some form of global accounting harmony. While the quest for international accounting standards is not the province of any single organization, the International Accounting Standards Committee (IASC) has been the most active and respected player in the field.

Established in 1973, IASC is a private sector initiative that currently represents more than 100 accounting organizations from 70 countries around the world. Its stated objectives are to formulate a set of internationally-accepted standards and to promote their worldwide acceptance. Since

TABLE 14–2
Non-U.S. Telecommunications Equipment Companies—Local vs. U.S. GAAP Comparison, Fiscal 1986 (Local Currency Millions)

	Net Income			*Shareholders' Equity*		
Company	*Local*	*Adjusted*	*% Change*	*Local*	*Adjusted*	*% Change*
Canada						
Mitel	(81)	(75)	7.4	344	275	–20.1
Bell Canada Enterprises	1,024	867	–15.3	8,366	7,791	–6.9
Japan (billions of yen)						
NEC	15	15	([a])	514	514	([a])
NTT	186	186	([a])	3,587	3,587	([a])
Sumitomo Electric	17	16	–5.9	214	209[b]	–2.3
Germany						
Siemens	1,474	2,065	40.1	15,135	19,793[b]	30.7
The Netherlands						
Philips	10,015	903	–11.0	15,858	13,889	–12.4
Sweden						
Ericsson	563	654	16.2	7,299	8,605	17.9
U.K.						
British Telecom	1,313	1,508	14.9	7,057	4,767	–32.5
G.E.	435	431	–1.0	2,895	3,477	2.0
Plessey	116	113	–2.6	597	622	4.2
Racal	48	37	–19.6	450	677	50.4
Standard Telephones & Cables	103	75	–27.1	542	868	60.1

[a] Local financial statements are based on U.S. GAAP.
[b] Balance sheet adjustments are incomplete

its inception it has issued some 31 international accounting standards (IASs) the titles of which are reproduced in Table 14–3.

To date most of the IASC's standards have been broad in nature and have often permitted alternative accounting treatments as acceptable. Recognizing that this posture is no longer acceptable, the IASC has recently developed a conceptual framework to guide it in developing standards that are coherent and internally consistent. It has also embarked on a program to

TABLE 14–3
Current Status of IASC Statements

International Accounting Standards	
IAS 1	Disclosure of Accounting Policies
IAS 2	Valuation and Presentation of Inventories in the Context of the Historical Cost System
IAS 4	Depreciation Accounting
IAS 5	Information to be Disclosed in Financial Statements
IAS 7	Statement of Changes in Financial Position
IAS 8	Unusual and Prior Period Items and Changes in Accounting Policies
IAS 9	Accounting for Research and Development Activities
IAS 10	Contingencies and Events Occurring After the Balance Sheet Date
IAS 11	Accounting for Construction Contracts
IAS 12	Accounting for Taxes on Income
IAS 13	Presentation of Current Assets and Current Liabilities
IAS 14	Reporting Financial Information by Segment
IAS 15	Information Reflecting the Effects of Changing Prices
IAS 16	Accounting for Property, Plant and Equipment
IAS 17	Accounting for Leases
IAS 18	Revenue Recognition
IAS 19	Accounting for Retirment Benefits in the Financial Statements of Employees
IAS 20	Accounting for Government Grants and Disclosure of Government Assistance
IAS 21	Accounting for the Effects of Changes in Foreign Exchange Rates
IAS 22	Accounting for Business Combinations
IAS 23	Capitalization of Borrowing Costs
IAS 24	Related Party Disclosures
IAS 25	Accounting for Investments
IAS 26	Accounting and Reporting by Retirement Benefit Plans
IAS 27	Consolidated Financial Statements and Accounting for Investments in Subsidiaries
IAS 28	Accounting for Investment in Associates
IAS 29	Financial Reporting in Hyperinflationary Economies
IAS 30	Disclosures in the Financial Statements of Banks and Similar Financial Institutions
IAS 31	Financial Reporting of Interests in Joint Ventures
Framework	
	Framework for the Preparation and Presentation of Financial Statements
Statement of Intent	
	Comparability of Financial Statements
Exposure Drafts	
E33	Accounting for Taxes on Income
E36	Cash Flow Statements
E37	Research and Development Activities
E38	Inventories
E39	Capitalization of Borrowing Costs
E40	Financial Instruments
E41	Revenue Recognition (revised IAS 18)
E42	Construction Contracts (revised IAS 11)
E43	Property, Plant and Equipment (revised IAS 4 and IAS 16)
E44	Effects of Changes in Foreign Exchange Rates (revised IAS 21)
E45	Business Combinations (revised IAS 22)

tighten its standards by eliminating as many alternatives as possible and offering more detailed guidance. Known as its comparability project, the IASC has targeted early 1993 as the completion date for this important undertaking.

In a recent show of support, the International Organization of Securities Commissions (IOSCO), issued the following statement(IASC 1989):

> The technical Committee of IOSCO supports the initiatives by the IASC to revise and expand international accounting standards. A primary impediment to international offerings of securities is that different countries have different accounting standards. Mutually acceptable international accounting standards are a critical goal because they will reduce the unnecessary regulatory burdens resulting from current disparities between the various national accounting standards, while protecting investors through adequate disclosure in financial statements.

The IASC is not the only organization interested in harmonizing accounting standards, however. Intergovernmental organizations such as European Community (EC), Organization for Economic Cooperation and Development (OECD), the United Nations (UN) and IOSCO, previously mentioned, are also active participants.

Policy Issues for Japanese Issuers and Regulators

With more and more capital markets opening their doors to foreign investors and issuers, market participants must cope with a greater variety of accounting issues. While market participants include investors, rating agencies, investment underwriters, corporate issuers and market regulators, we narrow our focus to corporate issuers and market regulators.

Japanese Issuers Firms in Japan face a relatively inelastic supply of capital if limited to sourcing in their own domestic markets. Freer access to foreign capital markets enables Japanese corporate issuers to lower their financing costs by increasing the elasticity of supply of money capital. However, the ability to issue or list securities outside of the home market also brings with it certain reporting obligations. Firms trading their securities abroad must attempt to communicate with a wider audience of foreign readers. They must also comply with capital market requirements that mandate alternate accounting and disclosure practices. In this regard, corporate treasurers face a trade-off. While investors may respond favorably to additional disclosure or conformity to alternate accounting standards, these activities are not costless. Designing accounting systems to provide new accounting data can be administratively expensive. An even greater cost is the value of such information to competitors, as well as other reporting constituencies such as tax authorities and labor unions.

Thus, in attempting to minimize their capital costs, Japanese treasurers must think about cost of capital in a broad manner. The total cost of raising funds abroad includes (1) the financial cost, (2) information preparation costs, and (3) competitive costs. Japanese financial managers must produce that level of information that optimizes the trade-off between lowering a firm's financing costs and raising its preparation and competitive costs.

In accessing off-shore capital markets, Japanese financial managers can adopt several courses of action. One alternative is to insist on providing reports based on Japanese accounting and reporting practices. This strategy of maintaining the status quo can be supplemented by other non-accounting coping mechanisms. To begin, Japanese firms can elect to seek funds in markets that do not demand additional accounting information or disclosures. Raising funds in the Eurobond market or accessing the U.S. private placement market under rule 144A[2] are examples in this regard. Alternatively, a Japanese issuer could maintain its local accounting practices and host analysts meetings or go on road shows to provide analysts with supplementary information or interpretations of local accounting numbers. Yet another tack would be for a Japanese firm to encourage foreign institutional investors to "come to them;" i.e., invite foreign investors to purchase its existing shares or new issues directly in the Japanese market. This strategy is appealing if large institutional investors are viewed as "long-term" in their orientation. Foreign public offerings often attract short-term investors.[3]

Another course of action for Japanese financial managers would be to conform their accounting and disclosure practices to the reporting requirements of the host country. Complying with the reporting requirements of the U.S. SEC, which are undoubtedly the most stringent in the world, could have benefits in the form of improved access to other national capital markets whose accounting and reporting requirements are not as extensive as those of the United States but which exceed those of Japan. A variant of this approach would be to provide supplementary (secondary) financial statements that have been prepared according to some internationally-accepted reporting norm. These standards could embrace, but are not limited to, the reporting standards of the International Accounting Standards Committee.

Market Regulators in Japan Securities market regulators are usually concerned with investor protection, maintaining a level playing field for corporate issuers, and promoting an efficient and stable trading system. How to deal with these concerns in the case of foreign issuers is no small problem. Moreover, accounting diversity is related to each of these concerns.

One option for Japanese regulators would be embrace the practices of market regulators in the United States. Concerned with investor protection issues, the U.S. Securities and Exchange Commission requires foreign issuers who are making an original offering or listing their shares on a major exchange to comply with accounting disclosures that are comparable to those required of U.S. firms. The policy intent is to assure comparability across financial statements and to assure that investors are provided ample information on which to base their investment decisions. Owing to differing economic situations, however, identical accounting treatments do not necessarily make accounting reports of two firms comparable, Indeed, if markets are segmented and dominated by local investors, it could be argued that U.S. investors would be better served by reading the same accounting reports available to the dominant foreign investors.

Owing to developments in computer and telecommunications technology, security transactions are no longer confined to any single market. As a consequence, regulators of domestic securities markets currently find themselves in direct competition with foreign markets. At issue is whether the choice of accounting principles and disclosure requirements is a factor in attracting foreign issuers to the Japanese versus some other particular market (Biddle and Saudagaran, 1989). The United States is perhaps alone in requiring non-U.S. firms with publicly traded securities to reconcile their national accounting principles to U.S. GAAP. While this policy is designed to assure a level playing field, it clearly imposes costs on non-U.S, issuers. That few Japanese issuers have chosen to float their equity issues in the United States is evidence that the U.S. markets may be experiencing a competitive disadvantage because of accounting diversity.

Another policy option would be for Japan to continue its policy of reciprocity in accepting accounting and reporting requirements of the home country. Japanese regulators may cope with the accounting diversity entailed by this policy in several ways. They may place greater reliance on sponsoring banks or other institutions to support the application of a foreign firm. They may also feel less inclined to protect small private investors.

Alternatively, market regulators in Japan may consider requiring foreign issuers or listers to subscribe to some uniform minimum standard that is internationally acceptable. International accounting standards being promulgated by the IASC would be a possibility.

Behavioral Effects of GAAP Differences

While harmonized accounting and reporting standards are increasingly being promoted as a promising solution to reporting problems associated with international accounting diversity, acceptance of international standards by Japan's financial executives and market regulators as a solution guide is likely to be slow in the absence of any empirical evidence as to whether or not international accounting differences actually matters, in the sense that it actually impacts market behavior.

To date empirical evidence on the relationship between international accounting diversity and capital market decisions has been limited. There is, however, a vast literature on the subject of stock market data and accounting information that indirectly bears on the question at hand. This literature can be divided into three categories. First are studies that test to see if accounting information is indeed impounded by market prices. If favorable accounting results are correlated with favorable stock market or economic performance, then this suggests that accounting measures, however generated, provide useful information. The evidence thus far supports the conclusion that earnings announcements (current, quarterly and annual) are associated with changes in the distribution of stock prices (Ball and Brown, 1968; Patell, 1976; Gonedes, 1974; Brown and Kennely, 1972; Firth, 1976; Deakin, Norwood and Smith, 1974; Ooghe, Begin and Verbaere, 1981; Korhonen, 1975; Coenenberg and Brandi, 1976; and Forsgardh and Hertzen, 1975) This, in turn, is consistent with the contention that earnings announcements (including those generated under U.S. GAAP, U.K. GAAP, Australian GAAP, Swedish GAAP, and so forth) provide timely and relevant information to the marketplace. These results, however, beg the question of whether some other accounting system would provide still more useful information.

The second strand of research examines whether differences in discretionary accounting techniques have an impact on investors, managers and firms. If discretionary changes do not impact market decisions, this would suggest that markets are able to "see through" the diverse accounting information being presented and set share prices fairly. Studies of cross-sectional differences in accounting practices seem to suggest that investors are not fooled by accounting changes; yet some anomalies have been reported. Evidence also suggests that investors have some ability to discern nonsubstantive accounting changes; but here too, the evidence is not without surprises. On the whole, the evidence is consistent with a variety of hypotheses, none of which can be ruled out at this stage of our knowledge (Lev and Ohlson, 1982). Moreover, the evidence on this aspect of accounting diversity does not address the question of how costly it is for investors to process diverse accounting information, and of whether, based on their analyses, foreign investors are confident enough to participate in international markets to the extent required to hold well-diversified portfolios.

The third strand considers how capital markets respond to increases in (deviations from) a standard reporting level. If capital markets respond favorably to an increase in information, this suggests that accounting information has value and that firms must decide on the optimal amount and type of information to release. Choi (1973a) has adapted this argument to the case of firms operating in global capital markets. He describes the case for more standardized and complete disclosure as follows:

> Increased firm disclosure tends to improve the subjective probability distributions of a security's expected return streams in the mind of an individual investor by reducing the uncertainty associated with the return stream. For firms which generally outperform the industry average, it is also argued that improved financial disclosure will tend to increase the relative weighting which an investor will place on favorable firm statistics relative to other information vectors which he utilizes in making judgments with respect to the firm. Both of the foregoing effects will entice an individual to pay a larger amount for a given security than otherwise, thus lowering a firm's cost of capital.

The hypothesis that a firm would tailor its provision of accounting information in order to achieve a financial objective can be subjected to empirical testing. In a study of European firms, mostly multinationals, that were preparing to issue bonds on the Eurobond market, Choi (1973b) concluded that the majority of firms preceded their offering by an increase in the volume and quality of their financial disclosures. The results suggest that these actions were taken to lower the cost of funds and increase the chances for a successful offering. And during the study period, the Eurobond market was indeed the low cost source for corporate funding.

A recent study by Meek and Gray (1989) reaches much the same conclusion but in the context of the equity market. Meek and Gray examine 28 Continental European firms with shares listed on the London Stock Exchange. The authors find that the companies have exceeded Exchange requirements through a wide range of voluntary disclosures. In some cases, the authors conclude, the additional voluntary disclosures were "substantial." These results suggest that firms have found it in their interest to provide additional accounting disclosures in the hope of improving their share prices, reducing their cost of funds, and competing with other firms for capital in the international market.

Market Responses to International Accounting Differences

While the foregoing research is relevant in assessing the market effects of accounting differences, most have examined the effects of accounting diversity within the context of a single country. From a policy standpoint, the evidence marshaled to date begs the question of whether diverse national accounting systems act as a non-tariff barrier affecting the capital market decisions of investors and issuers, and whether a common harmonized accounting system would provide more useful information to market participants than the diverse systems now in place.

I now report on two recent investigations in which I participated. After summarizing their findings, I discuss the policy implications of these studies for corporate issuers and market regulators in Japan.

Capital Markets Survey The first study, conducted with R. Levich, was designed to find out directly from market participants whether, and to what extent, differences in accounting principles, financial disclosure and auditing practices affect the measurement of their decision variables and, ultimately, their financial decisions. Interviews were conducted with 52 institutional investors, corporate issuers, investment underwriters and market regulators in Germany, Japan, Switzerland, the United Kingdom and the United States.[4]

Those interviewed had to have direct decision responsibility; i.e., actually make international investment, funding, underwriting, regulatory and rating decisions. The findings are summarized in Table 14–4.

Overall, half of those interviewed state that their capital market decisions are affected by accounting diversity.[5] This finding understates the proportion of respondents who feel that accounting differences matter as it ignores second order behavioral effects; e.g., users who changed the way in which they analyze investments in foreign markets. For those whose decisions are affected by accounting differences, diversity is often associated with capital market effects including the geographic location of market activity, the types of companies invested in, types of securities issued, security valuation or expected returns and, and to a lesser extent, information processing costs.

As can be seen in Table 14–4, response patterns were not uniform among respondent categories. More than one-half of the institutional inves-

TABLE 14–4
Summary Findings for Investors, Issuers, Underwriters, Regulators and Others

Key Question: "Does accounting diversity affect your capital market decisions?"

	Yes	*No*	*N.A.*	*Total*
Investors	9	7	1	17
Issuers	6	9		15
Underwriters	7	1		8
Regulators	0	8		
Raters & Others	2	1		3
Total	24	26	1	51[a]

[a] An organization interested in promulgating international accounting standards was interviewed but their answers are not included here.

tors interviewed felt that accounting differences hinder the measurement of their decision variables and ultimately affected their investment decisions. Comparisons between Japanese and non-Japanese companies were cited as especially difficult.

A significant number of investors cope with accounting diversity by restating foreign accounting numbers to the reporting principles of the investor's country-of-domicile or to a set of internationally-recognized standards. Restatement, however, did not appear sufficient to remove the problem of accounting diversity. This suggests that existing restatement algorithms may not be optimal, are not being applied effectively, or are incapable of producing meaningful information.

Some investors coped by developing a multiple principles capability (MPC), relying on foreign financial statements in their original form, together with an intimate knowledge of foreign accounting practices and financial market conditions. While small in number, these investors reported no decision problems or capital market effects associated with accounting differences.

Investors were evenly divided as to the necessity or utility of international accounting standards. Those in favor felt that harmonization would not only make analyst's lives easier but would enlarge investor interest in international markets.

Most corporate issuers did not feel that differences in accounting measurement rules affect their decisions. Reasons for the non-effect include company funding strategies that insulate a company from reporting to foreign investors (e.g., reliance o internal funding, bank borrowing and private placements), management's focus on economic fundamentals, management's confidence in investors' abilities to deal with accounting differences, the value of name recognition, and various coping strategies that have proved effective. On the other hand, financial disclosure differences did impact their funding decisions, especially for issuers domiciled in Japan and Germany, suggesting that accounting diversity and regulatory diversity are closely related issues.

Size and nationality had a bearing on issuer responses. Large firms, especially those from the United States and the United Kingdom, whose standards of accounting and financial disclosure tend to be relatively high, appear to have greater flexibility in accessing international capital markets. In contrast, German, Japanese and Swiss firms appear to have less flexibility.

Corporate issuers who said that accounting differences did affect their behavior attempted to cope with such differences. In some cases accounting coping takes the form of GAAP restatements. In others it takes the form of road shows or hosting meetings with analyst groups. All coped in a financial sense; i.e., all avoided raising funds in the United States by either (1) bypassing the U.S. market for the Eurobond market, (2) relying on domestic bank financing, (3) encouraging foreign investors to come to their financial market to buy their shares, (4) offering sponsored but unlisted ADRs in the United States, and (5) undertaking a private placement.

Demand for international standards was not voiced unanimously by the corporate sector. In view of the multiple constituencies with which a company must cope, compliance with international standards would impose an added variable to the decision calculus of financial managers.

Surprisingly, none of the eight regulatory bodies interviewed reported being hindered by accounting principle differences when attempting to measure their decision variables. Owing to the nature of their organizations, most regulators cope with disclosure differences by simply requesting additional information. While accounting measurement differences did impose additional information processing costs, this cost was not considered significant. Two regulators, however, indicated that disclosure differences had some adverse effect on the volume of foreign issuing or listing activities conducted in their national jurisdictions. One acknowledged the loss of foreign issuers or listers to markets requiring less extensive disclosure practices. On the other hand, the other expressed concern that excessive disclosure leniency produced similar capital market effects by reducing investor confidence in its market.

Accounting Diversity and Merger Premia When asked which accounting measurement differences proved troublesome, the foregoing respondents identified the list appearing in Table 14–5. Of this list, the accounting principle mentioned most frequently was accounting for goodwill, particularly the difference in accounting treatments between the United Kingdom and United States.

In an acquisition accounted for as a purchase, any difference between the purchase price and the fair value (generally market value) of the net assets that are acquired is usually recognized as an intangible asset, goodwill. In the United States, this merger premium must be capitalized and amortized to expense over a period not to exceed 40 years. While a similar methodology can also be employed in the United Kingdom, the accounting treatment preferred by U.K. managers is to write off goodwill immediately against reserves. This allows British companies to report higher earnings than would be the case if U.S. GAAP were used. (Gray and Weetman, 1990) In effect, the present value of performance-based management compensation is increased by accounting procedures that shift reported earnings from future periods to the present.

Conventional wisdom says that differences in accounting treatment for goodwill provide an incentive for British companies to offer more than U.S. acquirers for a U.S. target because future earnings need not be reduced by the higher price paid. Except for reasons associated with management compensation, the notion that merger premia are affected by an accounting measure is unsupported. Goodwill is not deductible for tax purposes in the United Kingdom and the United States. Hence, differences in the treatment of goodwill do not appear likely to be economically substantive in their effect. Furthermore, even if differing goodwill treatments give U.K.

TABLE 14–5
GAAP Items Most Frequently Mentioned As Troublesome

Multinational consolidations	Discretionary reserves
Valuation of fixed assets	Foreign currency transactions
Deferred taxes	Goodwill
Marketable securities	Leases
LT construction contracts	Depreciation
Provisions	Inventory valuation

acquirers a bidding advantage, they need not pass on these benefits to target shareholders in the absence of competition from other non-U.S. bidders.

To ascertain whether conventional wisdom is supported empirically, we sought answers to the following questions:

1. Do U.K. acquirers pay higher premiums on average than their U.S. counterparts when bidding for U.S. targets?
2. Are premium differentials paid by U.K. acquirers associated with not having to amortize goodwill to earnings?

To answer these questions, we first compared average premiums paid by U.S. acquirers with those paid by U.K. acquirers of U.S. target companies.[6] We then performed regression analyses to see whether goodwill, in addition to other variables identified in the literature, explained cross-sectional variations in merger premia offered by U.K. acquirers. To control for other variables found to be associated with merger premia, such as type of acquisition, mode of payment, foreign exchange rates, tender offers, hostile bids, and industry of the acquired company, we matched U.K. with U.S. acquirers based on explanatory variables identified in the previous regression. For each matched pair, we then regressed observed premium differences against goodwill differences and a proxy variable for the effect of differing national accounting treatments for goodwill.

We defined merger premia as the difference between the total offering price announced on the deal announcement date and the market value of the net assets acquired prior to the announcement date. While the preferred measure of goodwill is the difference between the purchase price actually paid and the fair market value of the net assets acquired, we used as a proxy the difference between the market value and the book value of the net assets acquired. This was necessitated by considerations of data availability and objectivity.

What did we find? We find that merger premia associated with U.K. acquisitions are consistently higher, on average, than those for U.S. acquisitions (see Table 14–6). Moreover, premiums paid by U.K. acquirers are associated with goodwill and higher premiums paid by U.K. acquirers do appear to be associated with not having to amortize good will to earnings (see Table 14–7).

This finding suggests that national differences in accounting do impact managerial behavior in the market for corporate control.

As German and Japanese companies have also been active acquirers of U.S. companies, we recently replicated our goodwill study to include Japanese and German acquirers of U.S. targets with one difference. Whereas

TABLE 14–6
Mean Premiums paid per Dollar of Equity Purchased (Comparison of US and UK Acquisitions)

Acquirer	*N*	*PREM1D*[a]	*PREM1W*[a]	*PREM1M*[a]	*PREM2M*[a]
UK	104	0.9329	1.0595	1.1283	1.4109
USA	1056	0.3876	0.4555	0.5135	0.5423
Difference:		0.5453	0.6040	0.6148	0.8686
Mean Difference:					
Prob > ITI[b]		.0133	.0147	.0113	.0249

[a] These premium values are calculated as follows:
PREM1D = Total premium (Calculated one day prior to announcement) divided by purchased equity.
PREM1W = Total premium (calculated one week prior to announcement) divided by purchased equity.
PREM1M = Total premium (calculated one month prior to announcement) divided by purchased equity.
PREM2M = Total premium (calculated two months prior to announcement) divided by purchased equity.

[b] These *t*-test *p* values are based on the results of the F-test of equal variance.

goodwill is not deductible for taxes in either the U.S. or U.K., it is deductible for taxes in Germany and Japan.

We find that merger premia offered by German and Japanese acquirers, who enjoy advantageous accounting or tax treatments relative to U.S. acquirers, to be higher, on average, than those offered by U.S. acquirers. Premia offered by German companies are the highest. Regression analyses again show that goodwill accounting does explain merger premia. The higher regression coefficient on our goodwill measure for German acquisitions, relative to Japanese acquisitions, indicates that merger premia are associated with accounting diversity among countries in the sense that, while tax benefits are available in both Japan and Germany, more favorable accounting treatments are operative in Japan (see Table 14–8).

In addition to providing additional evidence on the market effects of international accounting differences, a major implication of our findings is that while international accounting standards are increasingly viewed as a necessary ingredient for the creation of a level merger and acquisition playing field, they may not be sufficient in a world characterized by international tax differences.

TABLE 14–7
Regression Results—Matched Pair[a] Comparisons (N = 104)

PANEL D: $PRMDF_i = a_0 + b_1 GWDF_i + b_2 XRP_i + b_3 GWCO_i + e_i$

Variable	*PRMDF1D*	*PRMDF1W*	*PRMDF1M*	*PRMDF2M*
R^2	.8311	.8411	.8377	.7273
Intercept	-0.2349	-0.2771	-0.1971	-0.4928
	(-2.212)	(-2.310)	(-1.769)	(-2.640)
GWDF	0.4604	0.5437	0.5255	1.0192
	(31.595)	(14.358)	(16.166)	(5.250)
XRP	0.7752	0.8592	0.9593	-0.5806
	(1.637)	(1.583)	(1.891)	(0.462)
GWCO	0.2785	0.3350	0.2309	0.9191
	(4.291)	(4.244)	(2.635)	(3.515)
Model Specification[b]:				
Prob>c²	.0308	.3329	.1127	.4102

Note: The numbers presented in parentheses are *t* statistics adjusted for heteroscedasticity, based on White's (1980) Chi-square statistics.

Variable Descriptions:

PRMDF = Differences in premium values between UK and US acquisitions, computed using the target company's stock prices on one day (PRMDF1D), one week (PRMDF1W), one month (PRMDF1M), and two months (PRMDF2M) prior to announcement, respectively.

GWDF = Goodwill differences per dollar of purchased equity between UK and US acquisitions. These values are computed at four discrete time points: one day, one week, one month, and two months prior to announcement.

XRP = Exchange rate parity calculated as dollar per pound exchange rate at the UK acquisition announcement date divided by the dollar per pound exchange rate at the US acquisition announcement date minus one. The exchange rates are retrieved from CITIBASE.

GWCO = The portion of goodwill per dollar of purchased equity that is common to both UK and US acquisitions. This variable is used as a proxy for the possible benefits enjoyed by UK acquirers due to their advantageous goodwill accounting treatment relative to US acquirers.

[a] Matching is based on the following priorities: industry relationships based on SIC code groupings of both target and acquiring companies, type of deal, whether the deal involves a public tender offer to shareholders, whether the target's attitude toward the bid is hostile, and mode of payment.

[b] This is based on White (1980)'s model specification tests.

TABLE 14–8

PANEL C: $PRMDF_i = a_0 + b_1GWDF_i + b_2GWCO_i + b_3DFCO_i + b_4XRP_i + e_i$

Variable	*PRMDF1D*	*PRMDF1W*	*PRMDF1M*	*PRMDF2M*
R^2	.2422	.1223	.0428	.0819
Intercept	-0.0383	0.0021	0.1815	0.2473
	(-0.180)	(0.009)	(0.672)	(0.924)
GWDF	0.3298	0.2855	0.1845	0.2224
	(3.854)	(2.907)	(1.667)	(1.912)
GWCO	0.2851	0.1456	0.0308	-0.0029
	(2.109)	(0.865)	(0.166)	(-0.015)
DFCO	0.5185	0.3974	0.3335	0.1262
	(2.191)	(1.227)	(0.863)	(0.321)
XRP	0.7390	0.7586	1.1885	1.3446
	(1.280)	(1.147)	(1.594)	(1.831)
Model Specification[b]: Prob>c^2	.7121	.4721	.8325	.5732

Note: The numbers presented in parentheses are *t* statistics.

Variable Descriptions:

PRMDF = Differences in premium values between foreign and US acquisitions, computed using the target company's stock prices on one day (PRMDF1D), one week (PRMDF1W), one month (PRMDF1M), and two months (PRMDF2M) prior to announcement, respectively.

GWDF = Goodwill differences per dollar of purchased equity between foreign and US acquisitions. These values are computed at four discrete time points: one day, one week, one month, and two months prior to announcement.

GWCO = The portion of goodwill per dollar of purchased equity that is common to both foreign and U.S. acquisitions. This variable is used as a proxy for the possible benefits enjoyed by foreign acquirers due to their advantageous goodwill accounting treatment relative to U.S. acquirers.

DFCO = D*GWCO, where D is 1 for German acquisitions and 0 for Japanese acquisitions.

XRP = Exchange rate parity calculated as dollar per pound exchange rate at the foreign acquisition announcement date divided by the dollar per pound exchange rate at the US acquisition announcement date minus one. The exchange rates are retrieved from CITIBASE.

[a] Matching is based on the following priorities: industry relationships based on SIC code groupings of both target and acquiring companies, type of deal, whether the deal involves a public tender offer to shareholders, whether the target's attitude toward the bid is hostile, and mode of payment.

[b] This is based on White (1980)'s model specification tests.

CONCLUSIONS AND POLICY IMPLICATIONS

The studies I just described suggests that accounting differences are important and affect the capital market decisions of a significant number of market participants. What then are the implications of these findings for Japanese financial corporate financial managers and regulators?

Issuers One implication is that Japanese firms face the choice of how much they wish to accommodate the information needs of foreign readers. In communicating with an investor population whose tolerance for accounting diversity varies, firms have several options from which to choose.

They can restate their accounting numbers to the accounting framework of the reader's home country. However, in doing so, firms must be careful to avoid losing something in the translation. Supplementary disclosures that enable investors to understand the company and its operating environment seem called for; e.g., explaining the reason for high debt ratios in Japan or why consolidated numbers do not give an accurate reflection of the nature of Japanese groups.

Alternatively, Japanese issuers can provide foreign investors with their original financial statements. To avoid the risk of misunderstanding by readers who are not familiar with the reporting firm's accounting procedures, periodic road shows in which management meets with analysts to resolve accounting and other questions may be useful.

A third option is for Japanese issuers to actively court sophisticated investors who understand their companies and can deal with accounting differences. Given the size of institutional investors, it is just as economic for sophisticated investors to visit quality issuers as it is for issuers to travel to foreign markets.

Corporate issuers from the United States and, in some cases, the United Kingdom appear to have greater flexibility in accessing international capital markets than issuers from Japan. While this may be partially due to the fact that many capital markets outside the U.S. practice reciprocity while the U.S. practices national treatment, it appears that corporate transparency is an important ingredient in affording Japanese firms access to certain capital markets. Corporate size, as well as nationality, has a bearing on funding flexibility. Large well-known companies, such as Canon, Hitachi or Toyota, appear to have greater flexibility than less large firms in terms of their capital market access. Accordingly, they do not have to cater as much to non-MPCers and are less concerned with accounting considerations.

It was observed that investors who make the effort to familiarize themselves with local environmental norms and develop skills in interpreting foreign accounts in their original form(the MPC approach) are least likely to encounter problems caused by accounting differences. If an investor's optimal coping mechanism is to be an MPCer, then the issuer's best coping mechanism may be to help the investor to implement an MPC approach.

Market Regulators The finding that accounting diversity affects the location of market activity raises a dilemma for Japanese regulators. Requirements that are too stringent discourage firms from issuing or listing their shares in Japan. On the other hand, requirements that are too lenient discourage international investors from participating in the Japanese markets. Then too, requirements for foreign issuers that are more lenient than those required of Japanese corporations is discriminatory.

Market regulators around the world are now aware of the problems caused by accounting and disclosure systems that vary from country to country. Most seemed committed to finding a system that minimizes regulatory impediments to international securities offerings without reducing investor protection. In this regard, one option being considered by market regulators, such as the U.S. SEC, is the reciprocal approach in which disclosure documents prepared in accordance with the standards of one country would be automatically accepted as meeting the disclosure requirements of another. A problem with the reciprocal approach in its pure form is that the costs of reciprocity would fall on those countries whose regulatory requirements were most at variance with other nations. The disclosure practices of a country like Zonolia (fictitious name) might not meet the standards of Japan. In this sense Japanese issuers or listers would be held to a higher standard than Zonolia's placing Japanese issuers at a competitive disadvantage.

Another option being considered is the common prospectus approach in which participating regulators would agree to a common set of disclosure standards that could be simultaneously filed with the regulator of each country in which a securities offering was made. In its pure form, the common prospectus notion would be based on a system of international standards. The cost of this approach is a set of standardized accounting rules that are out of synchronization with the underlying environmental conditions facing the firm and its managers. How for example will a harmonized standard be applied in countries that do not distinguish between tax versus external accounting? If managers base their decisions on tax or other figures rather than the harmonized figures, will the harmonized numbers be useful to investors?

What seems called for is a compromise position; namely, reciprocity above some *minimum threshold.* Based on comments I have heard during our interviews with capital market participants, U.S. financial reporting and disclosure norms do not necessarily constitute the ideal threshold. Standards being issued by the IASC are also viewed as "second-best."

What then are some promising alternatives? One option is to consider the harmonized disclosure standards and listing requirements that are being formulated by the European Community. This initiative is designed to achieve the completion of a single internal European capital market by the end of 1992, or soon thereafter. Then, there is the market-based benchmark offered by the Eurobond market. This market with its distinctive features of international syndication techniques, flexible currency options, and relative freedom from rigid regulation has thrived. Disclosure standards in this market have evolved in response to investor demands. Finally, there is the new Rule 144A market in the United States in which private placements by foreign issuers can be resold without SEC registration and without any holding period if they are sold to "qualified institutional buyers." The SEC permits the market to determine what information in the way of a prospectus or offering circular is necessary for buyers to make an informed decision. Japan's regulators would do well to look to these international markets for guidance.

NOTES

1. While many have advocated the use of cash flow measures as a means of circumventing the international diversity issue, this has not been the case in practice. Analysts frequently adopt short-cut methods of computing cash flow in which certain non-cash expenses such as depreciation and amortization of intangibles are added back to reported income. To the extent accounting differences affect the reported earnings number, cash flow is also affected.
2. Essentially, Rule 144A exempts resale of private placements to large institutional investors from the registration requirements for the distribution of publicly offered securities under the Securities Act of 1933.
3. Small investors often sell their shares after an initial public offering. In the absence of foreign buyers, arbitrage will cause the shares to flow back to the home market, thus defeating the purpose of the foreign floatation.
4. See the Appendix B for a list of organizations interviewed. This survey was funded by a research grant to the Stern School of Business from Arthur Andersen & Co. and Salomon Brothers, Inc. The fuller study from which these findings are excerpted is entitled *The Capital Market Effects of International Accounting Diversity* (Chicago:

Dow Jones-Irwin Publishing Company, 1990).

5. A more detailed breakdown of responses is contained in Appendix B.
6. Our sample consisted of 1,160 deals in which the target is a U.S. company and the acquirer either a U.S. or U.K. company as reported by Automatic Data Processing, Inc., a fee-based M&A data base. It includes 1,056 U.S. and 104 U.K. deals announced between 1985 and 1989.

BIBLIOGRAPHY

Ball, R. J., and P. Brown. "An Empirical Evaluation of Accounting Income Numbers," *Journal of Accounting Research* (Autumn 1968), pp. 159-78.

Ball, R. J. "Changes in Accounting Techniques and Stock Prices," *Empirical Research in Accounting: Selected Studies, 1972.* Supplement to *Journal of Accounting Research, 10* (Spring 1972), pp. 159–78.

Bartlett, C., and S. Ghoshal. *Managing Across Borders: The Transnational Solution* (Boston: Harvard Business School Press, 1989).

Beaver, W. H., and R. E. Dukes. "Delta-Depreciation Methods: Some Empirical Results," *The Accounting Review* (July 1973), pp. 549–59.

Beaver, W. H., P. Kettler and M. Scholes. "The Association Between Market Determined and Accounting Determined Risk Measures," *The Accounting Review* (October 1970), pp. 654–82.

Benston, G. J. "Public (U.S.) Compared to Private (U.K.) Regulation of Corporate Financial Disclosure," *The Accounting Review* (July 1976), pp. 483–98.

Biddle, G., and S. Saudagaran. "The Effects of Financial Disclosure Levels on Firm's Choices Among Alternative Foreign Stock Exchange Listings," *Journal of International Financial Management and Accounting* (Spring 1989), pp. 55–87.

Brown, P., and J. W. Kennelly. "The Informational Content of Quarterly Earnings: An Extension and Some Further Evidence," *Journal of Business* (July 1972), pp. 403–15.

Choi, F. D. S. "Financial Disclosure in Relation to a Firm's Capital Costs," *Accounting and Business Research* (Autumn 1973a), pp. 282–92.

Choi, F. D. S. "Financial Disclosure and Entry to the European Capital Market," *Journal of Accounting Research* (Autumn 1973b), pp. 159–75.

Choi, F. D. S., and S. B. Hong. "The Decision Utility of Restating Accounting Information Sets: Korea," in Raj Aggarwal (ed.), *Advances in Financial Planning and Forecasting*. (Connecticut: JAI Press, forthcoming).

Choi, F. D. S., and R. L. Levich. *The Capital Market Effects of International Accounting Diversity* (Homewood, Illinois: Dow Jones-Irwin, 1990).

Choi, F. D. S., and C. W. Lee, "Merger Premia and National Differences in Accounting for Goodwill," *Journal of International Financial Management and Accounting*, forthcoming.

Choi, F. D. S., and C. W. Lee, "Effects of Alternative Goodwill Treatments on Merger Premia: Further Empirical Evidence," New York University Salomon Center working paper, 1992.

Choi, F., and G. Mueller. *International Accounting*, 2nd edition (Englewood Cliffs, NJ: Prentice-Hall, Inc., 1992).

Collins, D. W. "SEC Product-Line Reporting and Market Efficiency," *Journal of Financial Economics* (June 1975), pp. 125–64.

Conenberg, A., and E. Brandi. "The Information Content of Annual Accounting Income Numbers of German Corporations: A Review of German Accounting Standards and Some Preliminary Empirical Results," *Internationale Arbeitsberichte zur Betriebswirtschaftslehre der Universitat Augsburg* (No. 7, 1976).

Deakin, E. B., G. R. Norwood, and C. H. Smith. "The Effect of Published Earnings Information on Tokyo Stock Exchange Trading," *International Journal of Accounting* (Fall 1974), pp. 124–36.

Eiteman, D., and A. Stonehill. *Multinational Business Finance*, 4th edition (Reading, MA: Addison-Wesley Publishing Company, 1986).

Eskew, R. K. "An Examination of the Association Between Accounting and Share Price Data in the Extractive Petroleum Industry," *The Accounting Review* (April 1975),pp. 316–24.

Firth, M. "The Impact of Earnings Announcements on the Share Price Behavior of Similar Type Firms," *Economic Journal* (June 1976), pp. 296–306.

Forsgardh, L-E., and K. Hertzen. "The Adjustment of Stock Prices to New Earnings Information: A Study of the Efficiency of the Swedish Stock Market," in E. Elton and M. Gruber (eds.), *International Capital Markets* (Amsterdam: North-Holland Publishing Company, 1975).

Foster, G. "Quarterly Accounting Data: Time Series Properties and Predictive-Ability Results," *The Accounting Review* (January 1977), pp. 1–21.

Gonedes, N. J. "Capital Market Equilibrium and Annual Accounting Numbers: Empirical Evidence," *Journal of Accounting Research* (Spring 1974), pp. 26–62.

Grubel, H. G. "International Diversified Portfolios: Welfare Gains and Capital Flows," *American Economic Review 58* (1968), pp. 1299–1314.

Gurwitz, Aaron S. "SEC Rule 144A and Regulation S: Impact on Global Fixed Income Markets," *Fixed Income Research Series* (New York: Goldman Sachs, September 1989).

Kaplan, R. S., and R. Roll. "Investor Evaluation of Accounting Information: Some Empirical Evidence," *Journal of Business* (April 1972), pp. 225–57.

Korhonen, A. "Accounting Income Numbers, Information and Stock Prices: A Test of Market Efficiency," *The Finnish Journal of Business Economics* (Vol. 24, 1975), pp. 306–22.

Lessard, D. "Corporate Finance in the 1990's—Implications of a Changing Competitive and Financial Context," *Journal of International Financial Management and Accounting* (Autumn 1989), pp. 209–31.

Lev, B., and J. A. Ohlson. "Market-Based Empirical Research in Accounting: A Review, Interpretation, and Extension," *Empirical Research in Accounting: Selected Studies, 1982.* Supplement to *Journal of Accounting Research 20*, pp. 249–322.

Levich, R., "Recent International Financial Innovations: Implications for Financial Management," *Journal of International Financial Management and Accounting* (Spring 1989), pp. 1–14.

Meek, G. K., and S. J. Gray. "Globalization of Stock Markets and Foreign Listing Requirements: Voluntary Disclosures by Continental European Companies Listed on the London Stock Exchange," *Journal of International Business Studies* (Summer 1989), pp. 315–36.

Ooghe, H., P. Beghin, and V. Verbaere. "The Efficiency of Capital Markets: A Semi-Strong Form Test," *Tijdschriftvoor Economie en Management* (Vol. 26, 1981), pp. 421–40.

Patell, J. M. "Corporate Forecasts of Earnings Per Share and Stock Price Behavior: Empirical Tests," *Journal of Accounting Research* (Autumn 1976), pp. 246–76.

Schieneman, G., The Effect of Accounting Differences on Cross Border Comparisons," *International Accounting and Investment Review* (April 29, 1988), pp. 1–14.

Solnik, B. *International Investments* (Reading, MA: Addison-Wesley Publishing, 1988).

Stonehill, Arthur, and Kare Dullum. *Internationalizing the Cost of Capital* (New York: John Wiley, 1982).

Walter, I., and R. C. Smith. *Investment Banking in Europe* (Oxford: Basil Blackwell, 1989).

Watts, R. L., and J. L. Zimmerman. *Positive Accounting Theory* (Englewood Cliffs NJ: Prentice Hall, 1986).

Weetman, P., and S. J. Gray, "International Financial Analysis and Comparative Corporate Performance: The Impact of UK versus US Accounting Principles on Earnings," *Journal of International Financial Management and Accounting* (Summer & Autumn 1990), pp. 111–30.

CHAPTER 15

CAPITAL STRUCTURE AND CORPORATE GOVERNANCE IN JAPAN

Watanabe Shinichi

1. INTRODUCTION

Two observations seem to be particularly interesting among many changes in the sources of finance of the Japanese corporate sector since the 1960s: (1) the fraction of funds financed from internal resources increased significantly (from 31.2%, during 1960–1974 to 62.8% during 1975–1988) among major corporations; (2) large size firms reduced the fraction of their bank borrowing (from 32.9% during 1960–1974 to 1.7% during 1975–88) as a source of external finance and turned to security markets to raise their funds, while small- and medium-sized firms increased the fraction of their bank borrowing (from 8.8% to 23.8% during the same periods) and reduced a fraction of borrowing from their trade partners.[1]

The first observation has been explained by the sharp decline in the potential growth rate of the Japanese economy in the mid-1970s. This account seems to be quite plausible, given the fact that dividend payments were kept at the minimum and all profits were reinvested to support the growth of a firm. The second observation is believed to reflect the emergence of "reputation" effects built on the growth of a firm. This is also plausible because a firm can tap new sources of finance by using its reputation. However, these accounts, given separately, are not quite satisfactory as an explanation of the two observations. They cannot tell whether a relationship between the two observations is necessary. Is it a mere coincidence that the transitions took place simultaneously since the mid-1970s? This chapter answers this question by analyzing the roles of a financial intermediary in an economic environment in which the growth potential of the economy and reputation effects are embedded as key ingredients.

The model of this chapter is built upon the work of Boyd and Prescott (1986) which analyses the roles of financial institutions in an economic environment with adverse selection and evaluation technology. They have shown how a financial intermediary emerges endogenously at an equilibrium as an arrangement to overcome the problem of adverse selection. This chapter is an extension of their work in the sense that it analyses a change in financial arrangements in the economy with private information. However, the characteristics of the economic environment studied in this chapter is different from theirs in three important aspects. First, although it is the basic rationale for the existence of financial intermediary in Boyd and Prescott, no evaluation technology is present in this chapter. A financial intermediary comes into existence in this chapter by different forces which is not present in Boyd and Prescott, that is, a moral hazard problem and the need of monitoring entrepreneurial activities. This is related to the second point. In this chapter, individuals are not endowed with investment opportunities, but must find them by using their own resources. This modification enables us to model an interesting interaction between an incentive compatibility problem and a moral hazard problem, the latter of which not being present in Boyd and Prescott. A financial intermediary emerges at an equilibrium as an arrangement of corporate governance as well as financial intermediation. Thirdly, the economy of this chapter has a more complicated dynamic structure than Boyd and Prescott in order to model reputation effects. The economy lasts three periods. When the parameters take on values in a certain range, the equilibrium of a dominant player game (a bank being a dominant player) is found to be an equilibrium arrangement that supports a core allocation. The time consistency problem that arises in a dynamic dominant player game is resolved by commitments by both the bank and entrepreneurs not to raise the loan interest rate and not to seek the fund outside the coalition, respectively.

The chapter is organized as follows. Section 2 describes an economic environment studied in this chapter. Section 3 finds core allocations that are not blocked by any other incentive compatible coalitions in the given environment. Section 4 finds an equilibrium arrangement and explores the implications of the change in one of the key parameters for a financial arrangement that supports the core allocation. Section 5 discusses the relevance of the theoretical results obtained in the previous section in interpreting the observations noted at the beginning. Section 6 concludes the chapter.

2. ECONOMY

This section describes the elements of the economic environment studied in this chapter.

Investment Opportunities

There are infinitely many projects. A project is characterized by its type i and the conditional probabilities $\pi(r \mid i)$ of the rate of return r of an investment in that project. A rate of return r takes on either g or b, $g>b$. There are two types of projects and in order to simplify notations we index a type i either by $i = g$ (a good type) or $i = b$ (a bad type). Type i contains information on the return of investment and we assume that

$$1 > \pi(r=g \mid i=g) > \pi(r=g \mid i=b) > 0.$$

We also assume that the type of a project remains the same for two periods.[2] There is an upper limit to the amount of resources each project can absorb each period. We denote the upper limits for each period by X_1 and X_2.

Endowment

There are countably infinitely many agents who live three periods. Each agent is endowed with one unit of time in period 1. Each agent can use its time for only one of the following three purposes: (1) searching for an investment opportunity (referred to as a project hereafter); (2) monitoring search activities; and (3) producing one unit of investment good that may be invested in the project found by a searcher. There is no endowment in the second and third periods. For simplicity we assume that time is indivisible.

Search Technology

Every searcher finds one investment opportunity by using its time. The probability of finding a project of type i is given by $\pi(i)$, $i \in \{g,b\}$. The type of a project is a private knowledge of a searcher who finds it. As noted above, the realization of its return cannot tell whether $i = g$ or b and a searcher may falsely claim that the project it has found is of a good type without being detected. We also assume that a bad project is so abundant that a searcher can always find a project of a bad type without using its time.

Monitoring Technology

Monitoring technology is described by the linear cost function with a parameter m: the number of monitors is m times the number of searchers.

Storage Technology

The rate of return of storage is assumed to be the same as that of a bad-type project.

Preference

The preference of an agent is given by the expected consumption in the third and final period: $E\{c\}$.

Sequence of Events

At the beginning of period 1, an agent who chooses to be a searcher invests its time to find a project, which is of a good type with probability $\pi(g)$. Some agents monitor search activities. The rest of the agents produce investment goods that are invested in projects found by searchers. The value of the rate of return of an investment is observed at the beginning of period 2.

The output produced in period 1 is reinvested in period 2 in projects some or all of which are found in period 1. The rate of return of each project is observed at the beginning of period 3. The only economic activity in period 3 is consumption.

An Allocation

The state of the economy is specified by a set of variables that describes a resource allocation among different economic activities in period 1 and 2 and a consumption allocation in period 3. Let

z_s = the fraction of searchers in period 1
z_m = the fraction of monitors in period 1
z_v = per capita investment in period 1
z_{v12} = per capita investment in period 2 in the projects found in period 1
z_{v2} = per capita investment in bad projects in period 2
x_1 = an amount invested in period 1 in a good project found in period 1
x_{12} = an amount invested in period 2 in a good project found in period 1
x_{b1} = an amount invested in a bad project found in period 1
x_{b12} = an amount invested in period 2 in a bad project found in period 1
Y_t = per capita output at the beginning of period $t + 1$ ($t = 1,2$).

A resource allocation is specified by $(z,x) = (z_s, z_m, z_v, z_{v12}, z_{v2}, x_1, x_{b1}, x_{12}, x_{b12})$. A resource allocation is feasible when it satisfies

(period 1)

$$z_s + z_m + z_v \leq 1$$

$$z_m = mz_s \text{ (if monitoring exists), } = 0 \text{ (otherwise)} \tag{15.1}$$

$$z_v = x_1 \pi(i = g)z_s + x_{b1} \pi(i = b)z_s$$

(period 2)

$$z_{v12} + z_{v2} \leq Y_1$$

$$z_{v12} = x_{12} \pi(i = g)z_s + x_{b12} \pi(i = b)z_s \tag{15.2}$$

$$Y_1 = x_1 \pi(i = g)z_s E\{r \mid i = g\} + x_{b1} \pi(i = b)z_s E\{r \mid i = b\}$$

We assume that

$$\text{(A)} \qquad \frac{X_1 \, \pi(i=g)}{X_1 \, \pi(i=g)+1+m} E(r \mid i=g) > E(r \mid i=b)\,.$$

The left hand side is the value of Y_1 when $z_s + z_m + z_v = 1$ and $x_1 = X_1$ and $x_{b1} = 0$. The equality $z_s + z_m + z_v = 1$ holds when a project is not funded unless it is found by a search. The assumption (A) implies that the return of a search for the society is higher than that of a bad project even in the short run. The case when this condition is violated will be discussed briefly in Section 5.

A consumption allocation is a set of individual consumptions that depend upon the roles and performances of individual agents in producing output. The consumption of a monitor and an investor is not random because the size of a coalition is large. But the consumption of a searcher is random and depends on the outcomes of search and the project it has found. We describe a consumption allocation by $(c_{sirr'}, c_m, c_v)$, where

$c_{sirr'}$ = consumption of a searcher who finds type i project in period 1, which turns out to have rates of return r and r' in period 1 and period 2, respectively
c_m = consumption of a monitor
c_v = consumption of an investor

A consumption allocation $(c_{sirr'}, c_m, c_v)$ is feasible when

(Consumption good constraint)

$$\sum_{i,r,r'} z_s \pi(i, r, r') c_{sirr'} + c_m z_m + c_v z_v \le Y_2 \qquad (15.3)$$

where

$$\begin{aligned} Y_2 = {} & x_{12}\, \pi(i=g) z_s E\{r' \mid i=g\} \\ & + x_{b12}\, \pi(i=b) z_s E\{r' \mid i=b\} + z_{v2} E\{r' \mid i=b\}. \end{aligned} \qquad (15.4)$$

3. A CORE ALLOCATION

In order to find out the utility allocation attainable in the economic environment specified above, we first consider a cooperative game and its core allocation. In Section 4 we will search for an institutional arrangement whose equilibrium supports the core allocation. If an arrangement exists that supports the core allocation, then we can claim that the arrangement is stable.

A coalition in a cooperative game is a group of agents who agree to a set of rules that specify appropriate actions of individuals, a structure of rewards paid to individuals and a model of information exchange. We require that an allocation of a coalition satisfy incentive compatibility conditions in addition to the feasibility conditions. In general, the incentive compatibility and feasibility conditions for a coalition are different from those for the economy as a whole. But, since agents are identical ex ante in the present environment, every coalition is also identical and subject to the same conditions. Thus, the feasibility conditions of a coalition is given by (1) and (2) described in Section 2. The incentive compatibility conditions of a coalition are given by a truth-telling condition for a searcher:

$$\begin{aligned}\sum_{r,r'} \pi(r, r' \mid i = g)c_{sgrr'} &\geq \sum_{r,r'} \pi(r, r' \mid i = g)c_{sbrr'} \\ \sum_{r,r'} \pi(r, r' \mid i = b)c_{sbrr'} &\geq \sum_{r,r'} \pi(r, r' \mid i = b)c_{sgrr'}\end{aligned} \tag{15.5}$$

the conditions of individual rationality:

$$\begin{aligned}\sum_{i,r,r'} \pi(i, r, r')c_{sirr'} &\geq \sum_{r,r'} \pi(r, r' \mid i = b)r\,r' \\ c_n &\geq \sum_{r,r'} \pi(r, r' \mid i = b)r\,r',\ n = m, v.\end{aligned} \tag{15.6}$$

and the equality of expected utilities of searchers, monitors and investors, that is:

$$\sum_{i,r,r'} \pi(i, r, r')c_{sirr'} = c_m = c_v = Y_2. \tag{15.7}$$

The last condition follows directly from the assumption that agents are identical *ex ante*.

A core allocation is defined as follows.

Definition A core allocation (z^*, x^*, c^*) is an allocation that is not blocked by any coalition that satisfies feasibility and incentive compatibility constraints, (15.1)~(15.6).

In general, it is difficult to show the existence of a core allocation, but it is straightforward to find it in the present economic environment. Since all coalitions are identical, an allocation is in a core if it is not Pareto-dominated by any other allocation that satisfies constraints (15.1)~(15.6). So it is sufficient to find a Pareto-efficient allocation subject to the conditions (15.1)~(15.6).

From (15.6) the expected utility is common to all agents and is highest when Y_2 is maximized. So we first find an allocation (z, x) that maximizes Y_2 for each of the cases with and without monitoring. Since $c_m = c_v = Y_2$, what remains is to find a consumption allocation for a searcher. We will find the consumption allocation that maximizes the expected utility of a searcher who finds a good project. We will also specify the necessary conditions on the parameter values for monitoring to exist.

Consider the maximization problem

$$\max_{z,x} Y_2$$

subject to the feasibility constraints (15.1)~(15.2). We take note of the following facts in finding the solution (z^*, x^*). First, from the assumption (A), a search is always better than an investment in a bad project in terms of the expected per capita output for a coalition when a good project is fully funded and no bad project is undertaken. It follows immediately that

$$\begin{aligned} x_1^* &= X_1, \\ x_{b1}^* &= x_{b12}^* = 0, \\ z_s^* &= 1/[X_1\ \pi(i = g) + 1 + m], \\ z_m^* &= mz_s^*, \\ z_v^* &= X_1\ \pi(i = g) z_s^*. \end{aligned}$$

Clearly the monitoring is wasteful and reduces the amount of search or investment. The optimal allocation in the second period depends crucially on the potential growth rate of a project. That is, when $X_2/X_1 > E\{r \mid i = g\}$,

$$
\begin{aligned}
x_{12}^* &= X_1 E\{r \mid i=g\} = kX_2, \ (k = X_1 E\{r \mid i=g\}/X_2 < 1) \\
z_{r'12}^* &= X_1 E\{r \mid i=g\} \ \pi(i=g) z_s^* \\
z_{r'2}^* &= 0
\end{aligned}
$$

and, when $X_2/X_1 \leq E\{r \mid i=g\}$,

$$
\begin{aligned}
x_{12}^* &= X_2 \\
z_{r'12}^* &= X_2 \ \pi(i=g) z_s^* \\
z_{r'2}^* &= [X_1 E\{r \mid i=g\} - X_2] \ \pi(i=g) z_s^*.
\end{aligned}
$$

When the potential growth rate is high, the fund is rationed among the good projects $\pi(i = g)z_s^*$. An excess demand exists for funds by $(X_2 - X_1 E\{r \mid i=g\})\ \pi(i=g)z_s^*$ when the cost of fund is less than $E\{r \mid i=g\}$. On the other hand, when the potential growth rate is low, the good projects are fully funded and the excess funds are allocated for investment in bad projects, which are readily available.

Now consider maximizing the expected utility of a searcher who has found a good project

$$
\max_{(c_{sgrr'})} \quad \sum_{r,r'} \pi(r, r' \mid i=g) c_{sgrr'}
$$

subject to the constraints (15.4) and (15.6). Note that $c_{sgrr'}^* = 0$ unless $(r, r') = (g, g)$. If not, the key incentive constraint (15.4) for $i = b$ can be made nonbinding without affecting the objective function, which implies that the value of the objective function could be increased. The consumption allocation for $i = b$ is determined uniquely up to its expected value, c_b^*, that is,

$$
c_b^* = \sum_{r,\, r'} \pi(r, r' \mid i=b) c_{sbrr'} = \pi(r=g, r'=g \mid i=b) c_{sggg}^*. \qquad (15.8)
$$

Let $c_g^* = c_{sggg}^*$. Then, from (15.6) and (15.8), c_g^* satisfies

$$
c_g^* = Y_2^*/[\pi(i=g, r=g, r'=g) + \pi(i=b, r=g, r'=g)]. \qquad (15.9)
$$

One important characteristic of the optimal consumption allocation is that a searcher who fails to find a good project receives a positive compensation. But the existence of the positive compensation for a failure to find a good project creates an incentive for a searcher to spend its time in its backyard to produce output for its own consumption and still to claim the compensation for finding a bad project, which is found without cost. In fact it is necessary to monitor whether or not a searcher is engaged in a search activity if the expected return of a search is smaller than the sum of the compensation and the expected return from an investment in the backyard.

We assume that the parameter values are such that monitoring is necessary. Let Y_2^0, $c_g^{\,o}$, and $c_b^{\,o}$ be the optimal values when $m = 0$. Then the restriction on the parameter values is given by the inequality

$$Y_2^0 < c_b^{\,o} + E\{r\,r' \mid i = b\},$$

which can be rewritten as

(B) $$\pi(i=g)\,[\pi(r=g, r'=g \mid i=g) - \pi(r=g, r'=g \mid i=b)]\,c_g^{\,o} < E\{r\,r' \mid i=b\}.$$

Hereafter we will assume that the parameter values are such that the inequality (B) is satisfied. Such an assumption requires that the probability of finding a good project is small and the difference in the probabilities of getting a good return is small between a good type and a bad one.

4. EQUILIBRIUM

Now we find an arrangement (or a noncooperative game) in which the core allocation found in the previous section is supported by its equilibrium. Such an arrangement, if it exists, is stable in the sense that its equilibrium allocation is in a core and cannot be blocked by any other arrangement once it comes into existence.

We define an equilibrium as follows.

Definition Equilibrium is defined by an arrangement and an allocation (z^e, x^e, c^e) such that

(i) (z^e, x^e, c^e) is feasible and solves the decision problems of agents defined under the given arrangement; and

(ii) $(z^e, x^e, c^e) = (z^*, x^*, c^*)$.

The first condition is a standard requirement for equilibrium choices for a given noncooperative game. The second one is a requirement that the assumed noncooperative game is stable.

Consider a noncooperative game between a bank and an entrepreneur, a bank being a dominant player. A bank is a group of monitors and chooses the interest rates for deposits and loans. Further, it offers a compensation scheme for an entrepreneur who searches for a good project. An entrepreneur searches for a good project and finances its project by obtaining external funds. An investor places its investment good in the bank or lends it directly to an entrepreneur.

In finding an appropriate arrangement among the economic agents it is important to consider the credit market condition in period 2 explicitly. When $X_2/X_1 > E\{r \mid i = g\}$, there will be excess demand for credits as long as the loan interest rate is less than $E\{r' \mid i = g\}$. Therefore, without some commitment by the bank, an entrepreneur with a good project would not be able to get any quasi-rent for finding a good project in period 2 and the core consumption allocation $\{c_{sirr'}^*\}$ would be impossible to support for an entrepreneur in a dominant player game. This problem is related to the time consistency problem in a dominant player game and we need an arrangement in which the bank commits itself to a loan-compensation policy over three periods in order to establish the credibility of its policy in period 1. On the other hand, when $X_2/X_1 \leq E\{r \mid i = g\}$, the credit market condition is loose and the cost of external funds will drop to $E\{r \mid i = b\}$ in a competitive market. An entrepreneur with a good project will be able to realize its quasi-rent fully for finding a good project under such credit market conditions and needs no arrangement with a commitment by the bank to support the core consumption allocation c^*. An entrepreneur would be better off severing its tie with a bank even when it obtained the loan in period 1 at a relatively low interest rate under the assumption that it would continue to borrow from the bank at the stable interest rate.[3]

Therefore, we consider two different arrangements depending on the inequality $X_2/X_1 \gtreqless E\{r \mid i = g\}$.

Case I $\qquad X_2/X_1 > E\{r \mid i = g\}$

Let R be the one-period loan interest rate and d the one-period deposit interest rate both of which remain constant over two periods. We will find a long-term contractual arrangement between an entrepreneur and the bank.

An entrepreneur maximizes its income by choosing (1) whether or not to search, (2) whether or not to report the outcome of its search truthfully, and (3) how much to borrow to finance its project and from which source, given the loan rate R and the arrangement with the bank when it fails to find a good project or when the realization of its project turns out to be bad.

The bank maximizes its income by choosing (1) the deposit rate d, (2) the loan rate R and the amount of a loan it extends to an entrepreneur, (3) the compensation it pays to an entrepreneur when an entrepreneur fails to find a good project, and (4) the arrangement when the return of the project turns out to be bad and an entrepreneur cannot repay the loan.

Let w be the compensation paid to an entrepreneur at the beginning of period 3 who fails to find a good project, L_1 the first period loan and L_{2r} ($r = g,b$) the second period loan for the project whose return in period 1 is r. Let

$$d^* = Y_2^{*1/2}$$
$$w^* = c_b^*$$
$$L_1^* = X_1$$

and R^*, L_{2g}^* and L_{2b}^* be the solutions of

$$L_{2g} = X_1 E\{r \mid i = g\} - X_1(g - R)$$

$$L_{2b}^* = X_1 E\{r \mid i = g\} - X_1(b - R)$$

$$X_1 E\{r \mid i = g\}g - RL_{2g} = c_g^*. \tag{15.11}$$

Since c_g^* is a per capita value, R^* exists if X_1 is sufficiently large. Now let us verify that $\{d^*, w^*, R^*, L_1^*, L_{2g}^*, L_{2b}^*\}$ is an equilibrium contract combined with an arrangement that: (1) the ownership of a project is transferred to the bank and an entrepreneur receives no compensation whenever the entrepreneur fails to repay the loan; and (2) an entrepreneur with $r = g$ borrows in period 2 from the same bank as it borrowed from in period 1. The second condition is necessary to support the commitment of the bank. If an entrepreneur tried to borrow from other banks or directly from investors by offering a higher interest rate than R in period 2, it could do so because it had already established a good reputation to having a good project whose expected return was $E\{r \mid i = g\}$. But, if that happened, the bank would lose its depositors and entrepreneurs would end up paying higher interest rates and consequently lose their quasi-rents for good projects. Therefore the access of an entrepreneur to various sources of credits must be restricted, including the direct finance in the security market.

The left side of the equation (15.11) is an expected profit of an entrepreneur with $i = g$ and $r = g$. An entrepreneur can increase its profit by borrowing more in period 2, but L_{2g}^* is the maximum credit offered by the bank and it cannot borrow from others by the contract. In period 1, an entrepreneur with a good project raises the maximum fund, X_1, that a project can absorb. An entrepreneur with a bad project will be contented to receive the compensation w^* by reporting its result truthfully to the bank. Thus, an entrepreneur is maximizing its expected utility, which is equal to Y_2^* at equilibrium.

The bank is also maximizing its profits. It cannot lower d^* nor raise R^*. If it did, it would lose depositors or borrowers altogether and all agents would become bankers, which would be impossible. The expected utility of a banker is Y_2^*. Thus it follows that no agent has an incentive to switch its function among a depositor, an entrepreneur and a banker.

Summarizing the equilibrium contract,

(1) A bank and entrepreneurs make a multiperiod contract in the first period under which each entrepreneur promises to use its time to search for a good project and, if it succeeds, it receives the fund X_1 and $[X_1 E\{r \mid i = g\} - X_1 (g - R^*)]$ from the bank in the first and second periods to finance the project. If it fails, it receives a compensation w^* at the beginning of the third period. The bank monitors search activities of entrepreneurs. Whenever the rate of return of the project financed by a loan from the bank turns out to be bad, the entrepreneur receives no compensation. Only when the rates of return are good for two consecutive periods does the entrepreneur receive the compensation c_g^* at the beginning of period 3. The bank charges the interest rate R^* and entrepreneurs are prohibited from raising their funds outside the bank. Note that a project with $r = b$ continues to be funded and receives $X_1 E\{r \mid i = g\}$ plus $X_1(R^* - b)$ in the second period.

(2) An investor who deposits one unit of good at a bank in the first period receives Y_2^* at the beginning of the third period. The implicit one period gross interest rate is d^*.

(3) Agents who form a bank and monitor search activities in the first period share profits equally among themselves at the beginning of

the third period. The profit per one agent is Y_2^* under the given condition.

The bank under this equilibrium contract seems to share some of the important features of the roles of a main bank in Japan. That is, (1) a bank is involved in a search process of good projects rather than merely funding projects already discovered, (2) a bank pays compensation to an entrepreneur who fails to find a good project, that is, a bank shares the risk of searching good projects, (3) a bank provides a fund necessary for interest payments when the result of a project is bad in period 1 and the project with $r = b$ continues to be funded, (4) the bank rations its limited amount of funds among entrepreneurs with good projects rather than raising its interest rate in the period when excess demand for funds exists, and (5) banks honor the long term relationships between other banks and entrepreneurs and do not compete with each other to get entrepreneurs who have earned good reputations from others. Furthermore, it is possible to interpret various restrictions imposed by the government on direct finance in securities markets as a part of an arrangement described above, which restricts the access of entrepreneurs to the fund outside the existing long-term contract with the "main" bank.[4]

Case II $\qquad X_2/X_1 \leq E\{r \mid i = g\}$

In this case the credit market condition is loosened in period 2 in the sense that excess supply exists in the credit market if $R_2 > E\{r \mid i = b\}$. Therefore, both interest rates for deposits and loans will drop to $E\{r \mid i = b\}$ in period 2. Entrepreneurs who have established a reputation to have good projects in the first period can raise funds at $E\{r \mid i = b\}$, the lowest possible cost, directly from the investors without using a bank loan. A long-term arrangement is not necessary for entrepreneurs with a good reputation. Thus, the arrangement among entrepreneurs, a bank and investors is based on a one-period short term contract. Let $\{d_1, w, R_1, L_1\}$ be a first period contract and $\{d_2, R_2, L_{2g}\}$ a second period contract between a bank and other agents. Let S_{2g} be the number of securities issued in period 2 by an entrepreneur with a good project whose rate of return was found to be equal to g at the beginning of period 2. The security promises to pay the gross interest rate r_2 when $r' = g$ and the rate b when $r' = b$.

Now let r_2^* satisfy

$$\pi(r = g \mid i = g)r_2^* + \pi(r = b \mid i = g)b = E\{r \mid i = b\}$$

and the loan interest rates R_1^* and R_{2g}^* satisfy the equalities

$$\pi(r=g \mid i=g)R_2^* + \pi(r=b \mid i=g)b = E\{r \mid i=b\}.$$
$$gX_2 - R_2^*[X_2 - X_1(g - R_1^*)] = c_g^*.$$ [5]

Also let

$$d_1^* = Y_2^*/E\{r \mid i=b\}$$
$$w^* = c_b^*$$
$$L_1^* = X_1$$
$$d_2^* = E\{r \mid i=b\}$$
$$L_{2g}^* + S_{2g}^* = X_2 - X_1(g - R_1^*)$$
$$L_{2b}^* = X_2 - X_1(b - R_1^*)$$

By an argument similar to the one developed for the case when $X_2/X_1 \leq E\{r \mid i=g\}$, we can show that the contracts $\{d_1^*, w^*, R_1^*, L_1^*\}$ for period 1 and $\{d_2^*, R_2^*, L_{2g}^*, L_{2b}^*\}$ for period 2 are equilibrium contracts between the bank, depositors and entrepreneurs, combined with the requirement that the ownership of a project is transferred to the bank when an entrepreneur fails to repay its loan. Furthermore $\{r_2^*, S_{2g}^*\}$ is an equilibrium in the security market in period 2.

Let the parameters take on the following values:

$$\pi(i=g) = .01$$
$$\pi(r=g \mid i=g) = .50$$
$$\pi(r=g \mid i=b) = .05$$
$$r_g = 2$$
$$r_b = 1$$
$$X_1 = 300$$
$$m = .1.$$

This implies that $E\{r \mid i=g\} = 1.5$ and $E\{r \mid i=b\} = 1.05$. These parameter values satisfy the assumption (A). The core allocation of agents (or time) in period 1 is given by

$$z_s^* = .244$$
$$z_m^* = .024$$
$$z_v^* = .732.$$

When $X_2 > X_1 E\{r \mid i = g\} = 450$, the core allocation in period 2 and 3 is given by

$$Y_1^* = 1.098$$
$$x_{12}^* = 450.000$$
$$z_{v12}^* = Y_1^*$$
$$Y_2^* = 1.646$$
$$c_g^* = 330.923$$
$$c_b^* = .827\,.$$

The equilibrium values of the interest rates and credits are

$$d^* = 1.283$$
$$w^* = .827$$
$$R^* = 1.650$$
$$L_1^* = 300.000$$
$$L_{2g}^* = 344.940$$
$$L_{2b}^* = 644.940\,.$$

When $X_2 = 330 < X_1 E\{r \mid i = g\} = 450$, the core allocation in periods 2 and 3 is given by

$$Y_1^* = 1.098$$
$$x_{12}^* = 330.000$$
$$z_{v12}^* = .805$$
$$z_{v2}^* = .293$$
$$Y_2^* = 1.519$$
$$c_g^* = 305.324$$
$$c_b^* = .763$$

The equilibrium values of interest rates and credits are

$$d_1^* = 1.447$$
$$w^* = .763$$

$$
\begin{aligned}
L_1^* &= 300.000 \\
R_1^* &= 1.975 \\
d_2^* &= 1.050 \\
L_{2b}^* &= 622.431 \\
R_2^* &= 1.100 \\
\mathrm{r}_2^* &= 1.100 \\
L_{2g}^* + S_{2g}^* &= 322.431
\end{aligned}
$$

It is easy to verify that $c_g^{\,o} = 339.196$ for the case when $m = 0$. It satisfies the condition (B) of the existence of the moral hazard problem. Note that R_1^* is slightly smaller than g, allowing entrepreneurs to earn positive profits when $r = g$.

5. DISCUSSION

The analysis given above suggests that some elements of the financial system developed in Japan after World War II have been outdated: various restrictions imposed on the development of security markets which served to support an efficient allocation of resources have not been necessary since the mid-1970s. The crucial hypothesis in this argument is that a change took place in potential profit opportunities for many Japanese firms around mid-1970s. That is, the binding constraint for the growth of a firm shifted from the availability of funds to that of investment opportunities. This assumption is consistent with a broad range of facts observed in different fields. For example, the position of Japanese firms in developing their products has shifted to an earlier stage of a product life cycle, that is, from standardized products based on imported technology to non-standardized products based on the technology developed by its own R&D investments. Further, this change is accompanied by the need to satisfy an ever increasingly diversified demand for their products. It is also worth noting that a chronic surplus in the trade balance of Japan has brought upon various restrictions on its exports.[6]

The equilibrium arrangement is found to possess some important functions of the main bank system observed in Japan after the World War II, such as monitoring and "risk sharing." It supports and monitors entrepreneurial activities in the search for good projects as well as finances them when they are discovered. But there is also an important difference. In the main bank system a project is co-financed by many banks, while in our model financing and monitoring are not separable and a project is financed exclusively by the "main" bank. This discrepancy, however, does not invalidate the argument of this chapter. It will be possible to extend the present model to an economic environment in which project risks cannot be canceled out within one bank and which would allow banks to share default risks among themselves. We will be able to get the main bank system as a solution to the problem of minimizing monitoring costs for the banks as a whole by allowing banks to delegate the function of monitoring to a particular bank under a certain condition on the monitoring technology. But such an extension does not change the main message of this chapter: Monitoring and financing are tightly connected, especially when the main bank finances the fund necessary to repay the loans to other banks when a firm is unable to repay the loans.[7]

6. CONCLUDING REMARKS

This chapter has applied the method of analysis developed by Boyd and Prescott to explain the change in the corporate finance as well as the transition of a financial system in Japan since the middle of 1970s. It has shown in an abstract environment that, when the growth potential of a project is high and a binding factor is the availability of the fund to finance investments, a core allocation is supported by a financial arrangement that is centered around an intermediary institution similar to the "main" bank that possesses the various functions such as monitoring and risk sharing. The arrangement is also accompanied by restrictions on the use of security markets. When the growth potential of a project is low, an entrepreneur with a reputation to have good projects raises funds directly in a security market. The results are consistent with the stylized facts observed in Japan over the past thirty years.

NOTES

1. *Analysis of Management of Major Enterprises*, Bank of Japan, various issues. Another way to characterize the changes is to observe that financing has become increasingly independent of particular economic relationships. In the case of small-scale firms, the

course of credit shifted from their trade partners to financial institutions and, in the case of large-scale firms, from financial institutions to investors in general. Financing has become less "transaction-specific." Clearly there has been a change in the structure of monitoring costs.

2. Alternatively, the type may follow a Markov chain. The result will not change as long as the type is persistent.
3. This is the time consistency problem pointed out by Mayer (1988), which emphasizes the central importance of the time consistency problem for the theory of corporate finance.
4. Mayer (1988) observes also that "The Japanese banking system has been instrumental in preserving corporate structures and, through its equity participation, protecting firms from the detrimental effects of excess competition in financial markets."
5. When $c_g^* - (g - R_2^*)X_2 < 0$, then $R_1^* > g$. That is, even an entrepreneur with a good return cannot repay the loan in period 1. This is not implausible in the present model since an entrepreneur can raise funds necessary to cover the loss and the second period investment. It is possible to avoid such a case by restricting the parameter values further.
6. Kinugasa (1979) argues the need for Japanese firms to redesign their corporate strategies in a new economic environment in which: (1) it is increasingly difficult to import tehcnology; and (2) severe restrictions are imposed by foreign governments on the Japanese exports of standardized products.
7. The cofinancing arrangement among banks may be important, however, in answering the question this paper does not address: that is, who monitors the bank which monitors entrepreneurs. If the activity of a banker is not observable without costs, a moral hazard problem may arise. The main bank system obliges the main bank to guarantee debt contracts with other banks and creates a mechanism in which banks monitor monitoring-activities each other. It may be interesting to examine whether or not such an arrangement can avoid a free rider problem.

REFERENCES

J. Boyd and E. Prescott (1986), "Financial Intermediary Coalitions," *Journal of Economic Theory 38*, pp. 211–32.

C. Mayer (1988), "New Issues in Corporate Finance," *European Economic Review 32*, pp. 1167–89.

CHAPTER 16

JAPANESE CORPORATE GOVERNANCE: SOURCE OF EFFICIENCY OR RESTRAINT OF TRADE?

W. Carl Kester

"...putting a stockholder whom the American courts had labeled a greenmailer on our board would be highly irresponsible. Greenmailers — Japanese or American —are not welcome on Koito's board."

—Takao Matsuura, *The Wall Street Journal*,
April 18, 1990, p. A22

"All I've asked for is representation. ...Give me a chance. Is that an unusual request for someone who has bought a substantial part of a company?"

–T. Boone Pickens, Jr., *The Japan Economic Journal*, June 28, 1990, p. 2

The occasion prompting the above statements was the widely observed publicity battle between T. Boone Pickens, a well known American corporate raider and, in the eyes of many, a champion of shareholder rights, and the management of Koito Manufacturing, Ltd., a traditional Japanese autoparts manufacturer and a member of the Toyota group. They were made during Mr. Pickens's 1990 attempt to obtain a seat on Koito's board of directors. Both the incident and these personal points of view epitomize the sharp divergence of opinion in Japan and America concerning the constitution of good corporate governance and the desirability of an active (and often hostile) market for corporate control.

Of course, many Americans—particularly American managers—despise the adversarial role frequently played by Mr. Pickens and similar corporate raiders. Doubtlessly too, many Japanese business people are resentful of the long-term commercial relationships existing within some of Japan's largest keiretsu, which make it more difficult for new competitors to establish themselves and flourish. But by and large, the tendency within both nations is to view the corporate governance institutions and practices of the other with suspicion and even, at times, philosophic disdain.

Japanese observers tend to view the American system of corporate governance as ineffectual and prone to short-term biases. The highly active American market for corporate control is also frequently seen as inefficient at best, if not actually brutalizing and destructive of sound business practices. For their part, Americans tend to view Japanese practices as blatant attempts to restrain trade and entrench corporate management. The lack of an active market for corporate control within Japan, and the virtual impossibility of a successful hostile takeover, is accepted as prima-facie evidence that corporate governance in Japan is self-serving and contrary to the best interests of shareholders and consumers alike. Along with American concepts of fair trade, it is this interpretation of the Japanese system of corporate governance that has provided the intellectual, if not also the moral, underpinnings of the U.S. Justice Department's recently declared policy of extending its anti-trust enforcement activities to foreign corporations whose business practices *abroad* harm U.S. exporters. Although the Justice Department claims the policy is not aimed at any particular company, earlier remarks by the U.S. Attorney General conveyed the distinct impression that Japanese keiretsu were primary targets for this new policy.[1]

To some extent, both sides of this debate have valid points, and both are guilty of errors borne of parochialism. Nonetheless, the position presented here is that the Japanese system of corporate governance is, in fact, a source of substantial business efficiencies and not one of chiefly welfare-reducing restraint of trade. Further, it is argued that the absence of an active market for corporate control in Japan is more adequately explained by the diminution of motives to corporate takeover and does not, therefore, constitute satisfactory evidence that there is an undesirable failure of market discipline in Japan as far as corporate control is concerned. This diminution stems from the success of the Japanese system of corporate governance in reducing self-interestedly opportunistic behavior by corporate managers and by companies operating in a close trading relationship with each other. By attenuating such behavior, the Japanese system of corporate governance diminishes the need to employ corporate takeovers as a means of imposing discipline on wayward corporate managers, or for companies to integrate vertically in order to ensure the reliability of upstream suppliers or downstream customers.

Removed from the narrow context of U.S.-Japanese trade frictions, a global perspective on corporate governance and the market for corporate control reveals that the various systems of corporate governance used in Anglo-American economies, while sharing much in common with each other, are quite unlike those employed in many other developed industrial nations. Like Japan, the governance systems found in much of western Europe, Scandinavia, and other parts of Asia are predicated upon the construction and preservation of long-term vertical business relationships among transacting companies, and characterized by cross-shareholdings, concentrated ownership, and selective intervention by major stakeholders when circumstances warrant. Indeed, even sectors of the U.S. economy are moving toward this model. Before charging others with unfairly cooperative arrangements at home and seeking to destroy them, American policy makers would do better to appreciate the economic purposes served by such arrangements, and to examine critically the relative efficacy of existing U.S. governance institutions in comparison to those found in other nations.

For their part, Japanese policy makers should be cautious in responding to external (or even internal) demands to dismantle the keiretsu system of corporate ownership and governance. There are some deficiencies to be found in this system, not least of which is the ease with which illegal securities and other transactions can be carried out. Recent scandals involving high-level corporate executives and government officials are widely viewed inside as well as outside Japan as contrary to healthy, ethical business practices, and for good reason: they corrode the basis of trust among corporate stakeholders upon which much of successful corporate governance and, indeed, business itself in Japan depends. But in attempting to address these problems, Japanese policy makers should also seek first to understand why the Japanese system works as well as it does, and the economic purposes served by the various commercial, financial, ownership, and information-sharing relationships found among Japanese companies. Only then can they make intelligent, discriminating choices about which practices should be proscribed, which retained, and which adjusted to bring about desired performance improvements.

FACTORS SHAPING U.S. PRACTICE AND PERSPECTIVE

Predicated upon the ideal of shareholder democracy and the perceived need to prevent abuse of corporate power, the American corporate governance system is a product of constantly evolving American legislation and jurisprudence.[2] It seeks to promote allocative efficiency through securities, banking, tax, and antitrust laws. These laws separate the interests of numerous stakeholders, keep them in atomistic competition with one another, and seek to maintain the accountability of corporate managers to corporate owners through the board of directors and the proxy-voting mechanism.

Consider, for example, the laws that determine the role that commercial banks and insurance companies may play in corporate ownership and governance. The *Glass-Steagall Act of 1933* prohibits banks themselves from owning stock in other companies directly or indirectly through affiliations with investment banks. The *Bank Holding Company Act of 1956* prohibits banks from owning more than 5% of the voting stock in any nonbank company or from otherwise controlling an industrial firm. Additionally, the U.S. tax code encourages diversification of bank-managed trust holdings so that no more than 10% of a bank's trust funds can be invested in any one corporation. Finally, lenders that exert actual or effective control over a company could be subject to "equitable subordination" of their loans in the event of a bankruptcy proceeding, and might even be subject to other liabilities, up to and including penalties under the *Racketeer Influence and Corrupt Organizations Law* (RICO)! American insurance companies, which are regulated primarily by state laws, must abide by the most restrictive of these state laws if they wish to operate nationwide; the strictest of these prohibit insurance companies from putting more than 2% of their assets into a single company, and from owning more than 5% of the voting stock of any one corporation.

Although pension funds control two-thirds of institutionally owned U.S. equities, they have virtually no representation on corporate boards as a result of laws that limit their voting power and discourage their active involvement in corporate governance. If it wishes to receive favorable tax treatment as a diversified fund, a pension fund must not hold more than 10% of any one company's stock. Other laws discourage pension funds from becoming too involved in management issues. The *Employee Retirement Income Security Act of 1974* established a prudent standard for fiduciaries: managers of pension funds must be "prudent experts" in the business they undertake. Hence, if pension fund managers were to become active on the boards of business corporations in which their funds invest, they could become liable to meet higher standards of care in their investments. Although funds might attempt to coordinate themselves by initiating shareholder resolutions and voting in blocks on issues of mutual concern, they must first obtain approval from the Securities and Exchange Commission (SEC) if they wish to influence the voting of more than ten stockholders.

Like pension funds, mutual funds tend to refrain from exercising large shareholder rights in order to receive favorable tax treatment. If a mutual fund is not diversified, its income is taxed first at the corporate tax rate and then again when it is distributed to the fund's shareholders. To be considered diversified under the tax code and the *Investment Company Act of 1940*, a fund must have at least half its investments in companies that constitute 5% or less of its portfolio, and cannot own more than 10% of any company's stock. Even if a fund owned 5% of a company's stock, the portfolio company would become a statutory affiliate of the mutual fund and its principal underwriter. If the fund wished to exercise control with another affiliate, it would need SEC approval.

Finally, judicial interpretation of U.S. anti-trust legislation has had a chilling effect on the ability of American companies to develop close *vertical* as well as horizontal relationships. Today, nearly any action or agreement that binds companies together more closely than would otherwise transpire in arm's-length contracts struck in competitive markets tends to be viewed as inherently anti-competitive and, therefore, subject to legal scrutiny.

Although many other countries have individual rules that resemble some of the above (e.g., limitations on corporate equity ownership by banks and insurance companies, proxy-voting restrictions, antitrust limitations on cooperative agreements among companies, and so forth), few, if any, outside the Anglo-American family of nations have anything like the same overall pattern that has come to shape American corporate governance. As a result, certain building blocks of corporate governance that were once employed in American industrial enterprises, but later cast aside in the wake of American antitrust, banking, and securities legislation, have been preserved in the systems of other nations such as Germany and Japan.

Consider some common Japanese business practices such as cross-shareholdings, reciprocal trade agreements, presidents clubs (within major keiretsu), and lifetime employment, to name but a few. For the most part, these are viewed by many Americans with suspicion or are actually scorned as being inimical to principles of fair competition and shareholder democracy. Long-term reciprocal trade agreements with negotiated (versus bid) pricing, for instance, are seen largely as blatant attempts to erect barriers to entry by new competitors. Their financial counterpart, cross-shareholding arrangements, are likewise seen as supporting this anticompetitive behavior and entrenching management, which is viewed as inherently contrary to the long-run best interests of shareholders. Exclusively "inside" boards of executive or managing directors, weak proxy regulations, and perfunctory shareholders meetings lasting approximately thirty minutes are also interpreted as furthering the likelihood of realizing this adverse outcome. Informal information sharing among corporate chief executives through institutions such as the presidents councils of the large keiretsu are also viewed as a source of potential abuse by insiders of outside minority shareholders and non-keiretsu competitors. Although not himself a universally popular figure in the United States, the inability of T. Boone Pickens to have any serious and lasting impact on the management of Koito Manufacturing is taken by many Americans as evidence that the Japanese system of corporate governance is closed to outsiders, especially foreigners, and is not susceptible to change through legitimate, legally sanctioned means and mechanisms.

In short, Americans tend to view Japanese corporate governance as mostly an insider's game with decisions made in "smoke-filled back rooms" by powerful parties reaping private gains at the expense of others. Other differences from Anglo-American corporate governance not attributed to insider entrenchment and restraint of trade tend to be viewed as mere cultural artifacts that are unique to Japan and not transferrable elsewhere.

AN ALTERNATIVE PERSPECTIVE

A different interpretation of Japanese corporate governance is presented here. Specifically, it is argued that many of the practices viewed with the greatest suspicion from an Anglo-American perspective are, in fact, part of a coherent set of incentives, safeguards, and dispute resolution processes that function primarily to foster substantial transactional efficiencies. They do so by making it easier to build and maintain long-term trading relationships among companies doing business with each other. Whatever original intentions (which may, indeed, have been self-serving) may have first motivated the emergence of these practices, they have evolved into a set of economically rational responses to the ubiquitous hazards posed by efficient, but risky, relationship-specific investments. Moreover, because they can be found in one form or another in many capitalist economies outside Japan (e.g., Italy, Korea, Germany, Sweden, and Switzerland, to name but several), these responses appear not to be culture bound. As in Germany and elsewhere, they evolved in Japan because they worked and were found to be economically efficient. For the same reason, they may even be found to be gaining ground in the United States as American companies reduce their degree of vertical integration, adopt preferential supplier and customer relationships, and experiment with alternative ownership structures and governance mechanisms such as those found in leveraged-buyout (LBO) associations.[3]

Contracting, Investment, and Corporate Governance

In Anglo-American economies, with their generally wide separation of corporate ownership from control, the central problem addressed by systems of corporate governance is the resolution of problems associated with this separation—problems, in short, of properly monitoring and controlling professional managers through a board of directors so as to safeguard shareholder interests. But in Japan, corporate governance has much wider scope than this. Because the major shareholders of large Japanese companies are often those companies' major lenders, customers, suppliers, and so forth, the governance of Japanese companies is heavily intertwined with the management of their long-term business relationships. Indeed, Japanese corporate governance might be more accurately described as a process of continuously building and sustaining long-term business relationships among companies by balancing the needs and priorities of a coalition of equity-owning stakeholders, the majority of which generally possess other significant claims against the corporation in question (e.g., commercial loans, bonds, trade credit, purchase or supply agreements, service contracts, etc.) besides simply equity. Consequently one cannot separate the study of corporate governance in Japan from that of the network of commercial transactions in which companies participate and the investments made in support of those transactions. Corporate governance, *contractual* governance, and corporate investment are interdependent processes.

Large natural resource projects provide common examples of this interdependence outside of Japan.[4] Besides specifying the terms and amounts of financing to be provided, most "project financings" structured for such investments involve completion guarantees from sponsors, construction contractors, or both; firm supply contracts; marketing agreements; take-or-pay contracts from major customers; government commitments to undertake infrastructure development; and so on. Many even have explicit dispute resolution processes (e.g., arbitration arrangements) specified in the final agreement to provide predetermined means of handling frictions among the various parties involved.

The reason all these contracts, and a reliable means for governing their execution, are preconditions to the provision of capital is the substantial risk incurred by investors once capital is committed. Many of the assets associated with, say, large mining projects are things like railroad spurs, waterways, worker villages, and, of course, the mines themselves. These are all highly location-specific assets; that is, their value depends critically on the existence and continuity of agreements with specific customers, suppliers, or other owners of assets supporting the mine's operation. As attractive as some large new mining project may appear, investors will naturally be reluctant to commit capital if they fear the possibility that one or more of the other stakeholders on which the success of the mine depends are likely to behave opportunistically by defecting from the project or changing the conditions of their continued participation *after* investors have made substantial and largely irreversible investments. If the project seems valuable enough, investors will find it worth their while to expend resources in the careful customizing of agreements and the structuring of a formal system of incentives, safeguards, and dispute resolution processes designed to ensure that the project's various stakeholders remain committed to the project even as market conditions change.

Similar hazards of self-interested opportunism are also present in less complex investments by industrial companies whenever the assets involved are of a specialized nature; that is, whenever the assets have physical, locational, or functional attributes that make them difficult to redeploy. Such assets are often quite attractive to acquire because of the value-creating efficiencies that they provide; but they also expose their owners to exploitation. For example, an auto manufacturer may find it economical to build an assembly plant in a location that has attractive labor costs but is remote from other centers of production. Auto parts suppliers will then be faced with potentially attractive investment opportunities: locating plants of their own near the assembler to permit low-cost, just-in-time delivery of parts. They face the risk, however, that changes in model design, model cancellations, or even a decision by the assembler to integrate backwards into the production of certain parts and subassemblies could make their distant plants, or customer-specific equipment used within those plants, superfluous. They risk being stuck with some customer-specific assets that have little value in other uses. Once their investment is made, the bargaining advantage passes into the hands of the assembler, making the suppliers potential targets for abuse.

In summary, whereas owners of truly general purpose assets can respond to opportunism simply by seeking new business elsewhere, owners of specialized assets cannot do so easily. They must bear potentially large reductions in value if the stream of transactions being supported by those assets is suddenly reduced or eliminated due to opportunistic behavior by a major trading partner.

When such potential losses are high relative to the expected efficiency benefits, several outcomes are possible. At one extreme, potential investors may avoid investing altogether. Alternatively, they may elect to invest in general purpose assets which, while less efficient than specialized assets in the same application, at least reduce the expected costs of defection or attempted expropriation of returns by trading partners.

At the other extreme, the hazards of investment in specialized assets may be obviated by extending hierarchical control over those companies whose behavior is uncertain; in other words, to integrate vertically. Integrating ownership, however, may have problems of its own, particularly if it is done on a large scale. Internal suppliers, customers, or subcontractors tend to be insulated from direct exposure to high-powered market incentives, often resulting in less efficient management of the assets in question (more specifically, the incurrence of agency costs). In addition, other bureaucratic disabilities may emerge.

The operating efficiencies foregone due to a failure to invest in specialized assets or to a choice of general purpose assets, and the sometimes excessive costs associated with integration, suggest that there may be gains to the construction of customized agreements and governance systems designed to restrict opportunistic behavior by parties in a long-term trading relationship. Such contracts and systems can also span a continuum bounded at one end by the writing of highly explicit, detailed contracts, which may then be enforced in courts of law in the event of attempted breach of contract. At the other end is reliance on implicit contracting founded on trust relationships and reinforced by primarily non-legalistic mechanisms structured to encourage compliance with informal agreements. Broadly speaking, Anglo-American economies have gravitated to contracting and governance mechanisms at the legalistic, explicit-contracting end of this continuum;

Japan, Germany, and several other countries, in contrast, have gravitated to the less legalistic, largely implicit-contracting end.[5]

The Governance Structure of Japanese Corporations

One of the most important and enduring characteristics of Japanese business is the tendency of Japanese companies to engage in tight, long-term commercial relationships. These are made most manifest in keiretsu—complex groups of companies federated around a major bank, trading company, or large industrial manufacturer. The aforementioned Koito Manufacturing, Ltd., for example, is a well known member of the Toyota group; indeed, with the exception of Honda Motors, virtually all important Japanese automotive companies may be identified with specific industrial groups.[6] Not all keiretsu are alike, as suggested by the rough taxonomy provided in Table 16–1. Some are modern descendants of former zaibatsu, others are centered around newly-prominent banks, and still others have sprung up around newly-evolved major manufacturers. But all are broadly characterized by a great deal of stability in group affiliation and loyalty as far as the favored status group members give each other in their business dealings.[7]

It is critical to recognize, however, that this stability and loyalty to the group is not simply a cultural artifact that can be safely counted upon to yield high levels of performance. The same sort of hazards associated with self-interested opportunism and the ownership of specialized assets that exist elsewhere in the world reside within keiretsu as well. Steady, long-term business relationships might lead to slothfulness and loss of efficiency, for example, if a group member begins to take its business with others for granted.[8]

Thus it is that, in Japan as elsewhere, we have observed the evolution of a governance structure designed to attenuate these hazards. This structure is comprised of six major building blocks, which are themselves made up of numerous individual elements (see Table 16–2). At the pinnacle of the structure is the building and maintenance of long-term business relationships, the distinctive competence of the Japanese corporate governance system and the chief means by which transactional efficiencies and value maximization are sought in the Japanese business culture. Because of their widespread reliance on flexible, implicit contracting, these relationships are heavily dependent on the existence of trust and forbearance from self-interested opportunism. Trustworthy behavior is fostered by frequent, extended

TABLE 16–1
Major Japanese Industrial Groups

Former Zaibatsu	*New Bank-Centered Groups*	*New Manufacturer-Centered Groups*
Mitsubishi	DKB	Nippon Steel
Mitsui	Sanwa	Hitachi
Sumitomo	IBJ	Nissan
Fuyo	Tokai	Toyota
		Matsushita
		Toshiba-IHI
		Tokyu
		Seibu

interaction among mangers of vertically cooperative companies and very long-term ("lifetime") employment for those managers.

Networks of "alumni" officers, presidents councils within some keiretsu, and other types of business associations also contribute to the building of trust relationships. More importantly, however, they function to narrow information asymmetries among key stakeholders. Reciprocal equity ownership and concentrated ownership among financial institutions, commercial banks in particular, serve to align stakeholder priorities regarding the objectives and policies of the corporation, thereby mitigating stakeholder conflicts. The widespread expectation that share-owning stakeholders will intervene in the affairs of an underperforming company (selective intervention) to correct problems empowers them to become truly active investors who can and will occasionally supplant managerial autonomy with (usually temporary) tight control by them. Finally vigorous horizontal rivalry in most product markets is the linchpin ensuring that extensive vertical cooperation does not devolve into mere restraint of trade characterized by insulation from market incentives, managerial sloth, and a general loss of welfare. Each of these functions are discussed separately in greater detail below.

Implicit Contracting One of the key features of Japanese corporate governance that supports the preservation of long-term business relationships is the tendency of companies to engage in highly informal, implicit contracts. The typical "basic agreement" between a Japanese auto assembler and one of its suppliers, for example, is little more than legal "boilerplate" stipulating that the supplier and assembler will operate on a basis of mutual

TABLE 16–2
Building Blocks of the Japanese Corporate Governance Structure

Sustain Vertical Long-Term Relationships

- Implicit contracting

Build Trust and Forbearance from Opportunism

- Extensive managerial interaction
- Lifetime employment
- Reputation effects

Reduce Information Asymmetries

- Presidents clubs and business associations
- Managerial interaction
- "Alumni" executive networks

Align Stakeholder Priorities

- Cross-shareholdings
- Equity ownership by lenders
- Comingling of claims

Allow Investor Activism

- Selective intervention by major stakeholders

Preserve High-Powered Market Incentives

- Multiple preferred relationships
- Group members dependent on nongroup sales
- Vigorous horizontal rivalry

respect for each other's autonomy and maintain an atmosphere of mutual trust in their business dealings.[9]

Because implicit contracts are easier to adapt to changed circumstances, they are particularly valuable when long-term continuity in a trading relationship is desired. Assuming a foundation of mutual trust and shared expectations, implicit contracting among individual managers better enables companies to make rapid, informal, and highly refined adjustments in the terms of trade to preserve the spirit and substance of a business agreement rather than merely the letter of a written contract. Their inherent flexibility allows implicit contracts to withstand greater stress and promotes the longevity of the commercial relationship.[10]

This approach to contracting and relationship management represents a fundamental difference with Anglo-American business practices. Anglo-American contracting tends to be highly discrete in that the scope of the agreement is carefully defined as are exact terms of exchange, performance specifications, specific duties under relevant future contingencies, and even, at times, formal procedures to be followed (e.g., third-party arbitration) to settle disputes arising from unforeseen circumstances. At all points during the life of the agreement, whether it be in its execution, adjustment, or in the adjudication of a dispute, the point of reference is the formal contract itself. For most Japanese companies, however, the reference point for all future discussions regarding a commercial agreement tends to be the ongoing business relationship in its entirety, not merely the formal contract. As one Japanese senior executive put it:

> In America, you have many rules [to govern business transactions]. Here in Japan, everything is very fluid. There may be rules, but they are constantly changing to suit the environment. ... *The overall benefits of an ongoing relationship is what really matters* [in Japan], more so than, say, the occasional leakage of some of our technology to a competitor through one of our suppliers. [Emphasis added].

In short, the execution and adaptation of business agreements in Japan are made primarily by reference to an internal set of norms and expectations built up over a long history of transacting. Good managers in Japan are those who understand the interests and priorities of stakeholder groups, are alert to the network of implicit contracts binding the company to these groups, and can be trusted to uphold them over time through changing circumstances.

Trust and Forbearance from Opportunism As suggested by the above discussion, trust and forbearance from self-interestedly opportunistic behavior is of critical importance to the viability of implicit contracts and, therefore, to the preservation of long-term business relationships. Japanese ethnic and cultural homogeneity help create the trust needed to support implicit contracting. Well defined and widely adhered to social and religious norms regarding one's obligations to others make it easier to form reliable expectations about the behavior of counterparts in an exchange relationship. Some keiretsu may also have evolved their own subcultures within the broader Japanese culture that further enhances the formation of trust relationships within the group.

But widespread trust and forbearance are not exclusively, nor even primarily, cultural phenomena. A considerable investment is made by Japanese companies in the building of trust relationships through the careful hiring, development, and *entrenchment* of managers. Most Japanese managers are hired directly after graduating from college; undergo years of training and development in which they are rotated among various functional areas of the corporation, thereby receiving exposure to a wide array of the company's internal and external constituencies; and are discouraged from separating by a reward system that makes it unattractive to leave the company.[11] It is also not uncommon for a Japanese manager to be temporarily seconded to key customers, suppliers, or subcontractors to work on a collaborative project or to help solve performance problems.

Whatever other purpose these rotations and transfers may serve, they inevitably result in the creation of an extensive network of enduring personal relationships among individual managers inside and outside the company. These are crucial to the efficacy of implicit contracting in Japan, for the terms of such agreements are held more between individual managers interacting at the trading interface than between the companies per se. It is at this individual managerial level that mutual obligations are formed and bonds of trust are forged.

Once created, the Japanese practice of lifetime employment serves to preserve these personal relationships for many years. It also raises the cost to individual managers of untrustworthy, opportunistic behavior. Consider the following observation by another senior Japanese executive:[12]

> It's especially important in Japan for both sides [in a business relationship] to be forthcoming. The reason is that we have lifetime employment. If you treat someone badly either inside or outside the company by taking advantage of them to profit for the moment, it will not soon be forgotten. This is because people remain with the same company throughout their entire careers.

In short, a Japanese manager's effectiveness depends quite heavily on his reputation for trustworthiness and his ability to contract implicitly with counterparts in other companies. This gives the individual manager a personal stake in ongoing transacting relationships. In doing so, the individual is given an incentive to act prophylactically against whatever broader organizational impulses may exist to take advantage of implicit agreements through opportunistic behavior.[13]

Reducing Information Asymmetries As important as trust is to the success of implicit contracting and the preservation of long-term business relationships, it is by no means relied upon exclusively. Reinforcing trust are other key components of the Japanese corporate governance system that serve to reduce the incentive, scope, and ability to behave opportunistically. A particularly important group of these serve the purpose of reducing information asymmetries among stakeholders cooperating in long-term transacting relationships.

One of the essential functions of any system of governance is to reduce the scope for engineering welfare transfers through hidden action or the exploitation of hidden information. To this end, the job of monitoring and controlling corporations is delegated to a board of directors, which is elected by shareholders to act on their behalf. However, its limited effectiveness as a shareholder safeguard has prompted virtually all countries to require periodic public disclosure of material information about performance to investors. The United States has been especially diligent in this regard, generally requiring as much, if not more, formal public disclosure of financial information than any other major industrialized nation. In addition to such public disclosures, limited information about one or another aspect of performance may also be disclosed to lenders, trade creditors, rating agencies, and so forth.

In Japan, formal public disclosure of financial performance information is augmented by private, informal information sharing among companies engaged in long-term business relationships with each other. Though informal, some of this information sharing is virtually institutionalized through the various business-interest associations, councils, committees, and clubs in which a large company's senior management will actively participate. Among the major keiretsu are at least six presidential councils that are composed of presidents of prominent companies within the group, and which meet monthly. The best known of these are the *Fuyo-kai* of the Fuyo group, the *Hakusui-kai* of the Sumitomo group, the *Kinyo-kai* of the Mitsubishi group, and the *Nimoku-kai* of the Mitsui group.[14] Although a core company of its own group, Toyota Motor is a member of the *Wakabu-kai* of the Tokai group and has "observer" status in the Mitsui group's *Nimoku-kai*. Toyota's 175 primary suppliers are also organized into a group known as the *Kyoho-kai*. Nissan's 162 primary suppliers are organized into the *Takara-kai*; and Mitsubishi Motors's, into the *Kashiwa-kai*.[15]

The resolutions of these councils are not binding on members, and they resist fiercely the image of being a group-level management body. But even so, their activities have extended to the level of coordinating group public relations, controlling the use of group trademarks, managing group joint ventures in research and production, and even discussing top personnel appointments in group members. In short, whatever the overt purpose of these councils, the collection and dissemination of information about members' experience with each other or, in the case of supplier groups, with a common purchaser are inevitable by-products of the association. The existence of hidden information is diminished and the scope for hidden action is narrowed.

Augmenting these institutional associations as information-gathering tentacles are networks of executive "alumni" from main banks and other core group companies that have formally retired from lifelong careers at their original employers and been placed in "second careers" as senior officers and directors of client companies. The aforementioned practice of transferring mid-career managers and engineers among manufacturing companies linked in a vertical chain of production also contributes to this ability to gather vital information in a timely manner.

Aligning Stakeholder Priorities Reciprocal equity ownership generally also links Japanese companies with important business relationships with each other. Cross shareholdings usually involve only minority equity positions with no more than a few percent of outstanding shares being exchanged on a bilateral basis (see Table 16–3 for an example involving core companies in the Mitsubishi group). In the aggregate, however, about 25% of the stock of member companies in an industrial group is owned under cross-shareholding arrangements within the group itself (see Table 16–4). Substantial numbers of shares are also typically owned by corporations and financial institutions with important business ties to companies within a group, even if they are not themselves part of that group. Indeed, as shown in Table 16–5, 70% of the outstanding equity of publicly-listed Japanese companies are owned by financial institutions and other corporations. Accompanying many (though not all)

TABLE 16–3
Selected Cross-Shareholdings in the Mitsubishi Group, 1990 (in percentage)

	Mitsubishi Bank	*Mitsubishi Corp.*	*Mitsubishi Heavy Industries*
Mitsubishi Bank	-	5.0	3.6
Mitsubishi Corp.	1.7	-	1.6
Mitsubishi Heavy Industries	3.0	3.2	-
Total owned by Mitsubishi Group	18.1	25.5	17.2

Source: *Industrial Groupings in Japan, 1990–1991* (9th ed.), Tokyo: Dodwell Marketing Consultants (1990), pp. 284–323.

TABLE 16–4
Percentage of Reciprocally Owned Shares in Japanese Industrial Groups, 1987

Group	*Percent*
Mitsui	18.0
Mitsubishi	25.3
Sumitomo	24.5
Fuyo	18.2
DKB	14.6
Sanwa	10.9

Source: Industrial Bank of Japan

of these holdings by the financial and corporate sectors are implicit but widely understood and rigorously observed agreements not to sell shares held in connection with on-going business relationships.

As noted by many western observers, two effects of these stable shareholdings are to create a potentially formidable barrier to takeover and, thus, to entrench management. But these are neither the only nor even the more important results. A subtle but ultimately more important effect of cross-shareholding arrangements among transacting companies is to commingle the types of claims against a company held by its various stakeholders. This is clearest in the case of lender-borrower relationships, for a Japanese company's major lenders usually also rank among its major shareholders.

TABLE 16–5
Ownership Structure of Listed Japanese Corporations, 1989

	Percentage	
Government	0.7	
Financial institutions	45.6	
All banks		22.1
Investment trusts		3.1
Annuity trusts		1.0
Life insurance companies		13.1
Nonlife insurance companies		4.2
Other financial institutions		2.1
Nonfinancial business corporations	24.8	
Securities companies	2.5	
Private households and others	22.4	
Foreigners	4.0	
Total	100.0	

Source: Tokyo Stock Exchange *Fact Book*, 1990.

Consider Nissan Motor, whose top ten shareholders in 1990 are listed in Table 16–6. Of those seven whose lending positions were known at the end of fiscal year 1990, six accounted for ¥192.1 billion of Nissan's then total outstanding borrowings of ¥579.5 billion; these same six held shares in Nissan worth approximately ¥558 billion. These financial institutions were neither pure debt nor pure equity holders. Their investment in Nissan was akin to owning a strip of Nissan's capital base.[16] To the extent that, say, a major supplier of an industrial company simultaneously had a supply agreement with a customer, provided the customer with trade credit, and owned equity in the customer, the co-mingling of claims becomes even more pronounced.

A benefit derived from this tendency to hold a portfolio of different financial and other contractual claims against a company is a reduction in the frictions that might normally arise among various stakeholder groups if each owned a separate and distinct claim. The incentive to breach contracts with suppliers and customers in the interest of transferring value to shareholders, or to borrow money and then take extraordinary risks that might benefit shareholders at the expense of lenders, are reduced when the injured stakeholders are themselves the company's principal shareholders. Helping troubled companies work out temporary financial problems will also be easier when the principal providers of capital hold roughly comparable bundles of claims against the company; conflicts of interest and free-riding problems will be minimized.

TABLE 16–6
Debt and Equity Ownership in Nissan Motor Corp., Top Ten Shareholders, 1990

	Equity Ownership		*Debt Ownership*	
Shareholder	*¥ billion*	*Percent*	*¥ billion*	*Percent*
Dai-Ichi Mutual Life Insurance	150.2	5.6	na	na
Industrial Bank of Japan	123.3	4.6	57.3	9.9
Fuji Bank	123.3	4.6	56.5	9.8
Nippon Life Insurance	112.6	4.2	9.0	1.6
Sumitomo Bank	69.7	2.6	38.4	6.6
Yasuda Trust & Banking	69.7	2.6	25.9	4.5
Kyowa Bank	64.4	2.4	n.a.	n.a.
Sumitomo Life Insurance	59.0	2.2	5.0	0.9
Mitsubishi Trust & Banking	56.3	2.1	0.0	0.0
Nissan Fire & Marine Insurance	53.6	2.0	n.a.	n.a.
Total, top ten	882.1	32.9	192.1	33.3
Grand total	2681.5	100.0	579.5	100.0

Source: *Industrial Groupings in Japan* (9th ed.), 1990-1991 (Tokyo: Dodwell Marketing Consultants, 1990) p. 496.

The common assertion by Japanese managers that shareholder interests rank comparatively low on their list of priorities can be explained, at least in part, by the fact that a substantial number of a large company's shareholders typically are its major creditors, customers, and suppliers. For most of these shareholders, their commercial trading or lending relationship with the company is as important, if not more so, than their equity investment per se. Not surprisingly, therefore, Japanese managers will tend to view their proximate task as being the preservation and enhancement of these complex relationships rather than an immediate, direct pursuit of any one stakeholder's interests such as that of exclusive equity owners.

Selective Intervention[17] Perhaps the most powerful safeguard in the Japanese corporate governance system is the ability of one or more equity-owning stakeholders it intervene from time to time directly and explicitly in the affairs of another company when necessary to correct a problem. This is by no means a routine or highly frequent occurrence, but it is common—indeed, expected—under certain circumstances. Typically, such intervention is led by a company's main bank, usually to remedy nonperformance in the face of impending financial distress. This "responsibility" generally falls to the troubled company's main bank because it usually is the largest single supplier of capital and has quicker access to more information than most other equity-owning stakeholders. It also typically holds both debt and equity claims against companies for which it acts as main bank. Whereas fear of triggering equitable subordination of their loans keeps most American lenders on the sidelines until a loan agreement is formally breached, and even then restrains the degree of intervention, Japanese main banks effectively assume such subordination from the outset and take far-reaching, early steps to limit the damage.

Intervention is by no means limited to banks, however. Although less common, major industrial stakeholders will take quick, decisive steps to supplant an important supplier's or customer's autonomy with temporary de facto administrative control when nonperformance becomes imminent. Mitsubishi Electric, for instance, played a leading role in the restructuring of Akai Electric, a major supplier and purchaser of electronic parts and equipment within the Mitsubishi group. In 1990, Nissan Motor also assumed cffective operating control of Fuji Heavy Industrics, the maker of Subaru automobiles. Although Nissan owned only 4% of Fuji Heavy Industries' stock at the time, it consistently sent executives to become directors of Fuji, relied on Fuji to produce Nissan brand passenger cars until 1986, and collaborated with Fuji in the manufacture of aerospace and marine products. The de facto "takeover" occurred without the restructuring of any debt or a single share of stock changing hands among Fuji's major equity-owning stakeholders.

Horizontal Rivalry Finally, the very bedrock of Japanese corporate governance is vigorous rivalry within product markets among large, efficient-scale competitors. However cooperative Japanese groups may be vertically, major Japanese manufacturers normally compete extremely aggressively with each other for market share. In many instances, Japanese industrial activity can be described as intense *horizontal* rivalry among *vertically* cooperative groups.

The automotive industry in Japan presents a classic example of this cooperation-competition duality. Though having a smaller domestic market for cars and trucks than that of the United States, Japan nonetheless has fifteen assemblers of cars and trucks compared to only six domestically owned assemblers for the United States. Admittedly, some of these Japanese producers are heavily dependent upon alliances with larger assemblers (e.g., Fuji Heavy Industries and Nissan Motors; Hino Motors and Toyota). But even after adjusting for these alliances, at least nine major independent auto assemblers remain.

A similar story can be told of the steel industries in Japan and the

United States. Though smaller in size domestically, Japan's steel industry today contains more than fifteen major independent domestic rivals with annual sales of $1 billion or more; the number of rivals of similar size in the United States has shrunk to only 8. Although the Japanese steel industry has been well known for engaging in horizontally cooperative cartels under government auspices during periods of overcapacity, these have been notoriously difficult to maintain. More often than not, efforts at price maintenance during the 1960s collapsed in the face of dissent of one or more of the major producers (usually the independently minded Sumitomo Metal Industries). Even when pricing discipline was maintained, producers continued to compete for future market position through investment in productive capacity, which more than quadrupled between 1960 and 1970 despite only a doubling of domestic demand.[18]

Even within groups, a healthy respect for, and preservation of, high-powered market incentives arising from horizontal product-market rivalry is in evidence. Intragroup commercial relationships are never exclusive. Notice, for example, that intragroup sales and procurement shown in Table 16–7 varies between 8% and 30%, indicating extensive dependence on nongroup business as well.

Where vigorous horizontal competition among efficient-scale rivals is lacking in Japan, so too is good industry performance. McCraw and O'Brien contrast the efficiency of the Japanese distribution sector with that of the Japanese steel industry and with the distribution sectors of other nations.[19] They observe that the restoration in 1956 of the previously repealed *Department Store Act* (which slowed the spread of chain branches of large department stores), its 1976 extension to manufacturers' direct retailing outlets through the *Special Act for the Adjustment of Retailing*, and the *Large-Scale Retail Store Act* of 1973 have all been used in Japan to protect small shopkeepers by limiting the competitive advantage of larger chains. The result, they conclude, has been a proliferation of small-scale wholesalers and retailers, and a complex, multilayered system of distribution in Japan in which superfluous middlemen add to the cost of bringing products to market without creating offsetting efficiencies.

Summary

In short, for all its subtleties and apparent idiosyncracies, corporate governance in Japan can be viewed as a rational attempt to secure the best of two worlds. By tying themselves to one another in stable groups, yet avoiding

TABLE 16–7
Intragroup Sales and Procurement in Major Japanese Keiretsu, 1981

	Six Major Keiretsu	*Original Zaibatsu Groups* [a]	*Modern Groups* [b]
Average Intragroup Sales [c]			
Presidents Council Members	10.8%	13.4%	8.6%
All Group Industrial Companies	20.4	29.0	14.9
Average Intragroup Procurement [c]			
Presidents Council Members	11.7%	14.8%	9.1%
All Group Industrial Companies	12.4	18.6	8.2

a The Mitsubishi, Mitsui, and Sumitomo groups.
b The Fuyo, DKB, and Sanwa groups.
c Statistics are exclusive of group financial institutions.

Source: Kigyo Shudan no Jittai ni tsuite (June 21, 1983).

outright majority ownership and control, Japanese corporations have been able to exploit high-powered market incentives that derive from independent asset ownership. At the same time, extensive information sharing, close monitoring, and selective intervention by key stakeholders allows them to adapt terms of trade as needed in response to changing circumstances. In place of arm's-length transactions among many strictly autonomous market participants, or extensive integration of asset ownership under large administrative hierarchies, Japanese corporations transact on a middle ground characterized by implicit contracting, close personal-trust relationships among managers, and extensive information sharing. Abuse of such business relationships is mitigated, and their longevity fostered, by the spreading of large *minority* equity claims among major stakeholders such as key lenders, customers, suppliers, subcontractors, and so forth. By enhancing adverse reputation effects associated with opportunistic behavior, lifetime employment also contributes to the mitigation of moral hazards and the preservation of long-term business relationships.

AN INTERNATIONAL PERSPECTIVE

America's preoccupation with Japan's industrial groups and their apparently exclusionary business practices is understandable in light of the tremendous Japanese competitive onslaught endured by many American companies in the last couple decades. But, distinctive as keiretsu may be, to view Japanese corporate governance as singular in the world (which in and of itself invites the presumption of abnormality about the system) is clearly erroneous. In point of fact, many differences in fine points notwithstanding, the Japanese system of corporate governance is more nearly like governance systems observed elsewhere in the rest of the industrialized world than is the Anglo-American system.

Consider the German system of corporate governance. The two-tiered board structure of large German corporations is perhaps the major distinguishing feature of that system. In most other major respects, however, the German system is highly similar to the Japanese. Major corporations generally have close, stable, long-term relationships with *Hausbanken* (main banks), which also own equity in their borrowing corporate clients. Large, publicly owned German companies appear to be at least as extensively owned by each other as are Japanese companies (see Table 16–8), and many of them have also been identified as belonging to distinct spheres of influence led by major companies such as Allianz, Deutsche Bank, Daimler-Benz, and Thyssen to name but several (see Table 16–9).[20]

Similarly, cross-shareholdings, traditional house-bank relationships, group-dominated ownership structures, and preferred customer and supplier relationships within groups are also common business practices in other European countries such as Italy, Switzerland, and the Scandinavian countries. Sweden, for example, has most of its publicly listed manufacturing corporations confederated into 20 industrial groups centered around family-controlled holding companies, major banks (although Swedish banks must exert their control indirectly through pension funds and other investment companies), and industrial corporations (see Table 16–10).

Such arrangements were once observable even in the United States in the late nineteenth and early twentieth centuries.[21] Although the United States did not evolve giant zaibatsu, large American banks owned equity in, as well as provided loans to, and underwrote the bonds of, their major industrial clients. The fortunes of these financial institutions became intimately linked to those of their major customers, resulting in close monitoring and coordination of their activities. Reciprocal trading agreements among companies were common, as were various forms of discriminatory pricing and subsidization among companies having trad-

TABLE 16–8
German Corporate Ownership Structure, 1989 (Percentage of Market Value)

	Amount (DM billions)		*%*	
Government	61.1		6.8	
Financial Institutions	215.2		19.5	
Banks		98.5		8.9
Insurance Companies		116.7		10.6
Business Corporations	433.4		39.2	
Private Households and Others	185.4		16.8	
Foreigners	160.3		17.7	
Total	1055.4		100.0	

Source: Deutsche Bundesbank, internal report (May 1990).

TABLE 16–9
Major German Industrial Groups

Bank-Centered Groups	*Industrial-Centered Groups*	*Family-Centered Groups*
Deutsche Bank	BASF	Flick
Genossenschaftsbank	Daimler Benz	Krupp
Hamburger Landesbank	Gutehoffnungshütte	
West LB	Höchst	
	Mannesmann	
	Thyssen	*Other*
		Aachen und Münchener[a]
		Allianz[a]
		Bank für Gemeinwirtschaft[b]
		Gerling[a]
		VEBA[c]

[a] Insurance company
[b] Hausbank for a cluster of companies owned by labor unions
[c] State-owned holding company

Source: Rolf Ziegler, Donald Bender, and Hermann Biehler, "Industry and Banking in the German Corporate Network," in *Networks of Corporate Power: A Comparative Analysis of Ten Countries* (Cambridge, U.K., Polity Press, 1985), pp. 94–97.

TABLE 16–10
Major Swedish Industrial Groups

Industrial-Centered Groups	*Bank-Centered Groups*	*Family-Centered Groups*	*Other Groups*
Volvo och Skanska	SHB	Bonnier	"Lastbilsägar"
	Sparbanks	Dunker	Mäklar
	Peter Gyllenhammar	Samhälls	
	Gustavsson		
	Lundberg		
	Mobilia		
	Norberg-Olsson		
	Nordstjernan		
	Penser		
	Stenbeck		
	Søderberg		
	Wall		
	Wallenberg		
	Weil		

Source: Sevn-Ivan Sundqvist, *Owners Status and Power in Sweden's Listed Companies* (Stockholm: Dagens Nyheter, 1990), pp. 21–40.

ing relationships and common suppliers of capital. Vertical contractual restrictions were present in lieu of vertical integration.

As such relationships and contractual restrictions became more prevalent in the modern industrial firm, the two nations evidently studied the arrangements through different lenses. Japan chose the lens of transactional efficiency, magnifying the role of these arrangements as elements of an effective system of corporate and contractual governance. The United States, in contrast, tended to view similar arrangements through the lens of anti-trust. Market-power and restraint-of-trade effects were magnified relative to others. Where Japan saw efficiency and sought to preserve it, the United States saw abuse and sought to remedy it. American anti-trust legislation, originally targeted towards monopoly power created by large horizontal mergers or trade agreements, was gradually interpreted as applying to *any* type of non-standard contractual restraints, vertical as well as horizontal, notwithstanding transactional efficiencies that may have been fostered by long-term relationships.[22] Meanwhile, banking and securities legislation and tax laws such as those described earlier evolved to constrain the degree to which banks and other large "inside" investors could involve themselves in corporate supervision.

A consequence of this U.S. public policy posture towards restrictive contractual relationships among firms was that many of the building blocks of corporate and contractual governance that were considered so vital in Japan and other nations for joining together the interests of diverse stakeholder groups were cast aside in the United States. In place of the ownership of commingled claims by long-term stakeholders, the United States saw the proliferation of separate and narrowly focused claimants that interacted more like special interests within the corporate body. Their claims became more explicit, more sharply differentiated from one another, and less customized in ways designed to preserve the continuity of long-term trading relationships.

Dispersed and separated from management and other stakeholders, equity investors retained only weak, indirect control over the companies they owned through their election of directors. In place of selective intervention by equity-owning banks such as evolved in Japan, the United States, with its bias for market-ordered solutions to trading hazards, developed an active market for corporate control as a mechanism for exerting control over specialized assets to remove the hazards of investment, and for effecting substantial change when shareholder interests become subject to abuse.

Given the attributes of the Anglo-American system of corporate governance, an active and occasionally hostile market for corporate control may be both necessary and desirable as a response to inadequate safeguards of shareholder interests within the system of governance itself. But it is not necessarily a good thing in and of itself, nor should the absence of an active market for corporate control be interpreted as a sign of deficiency or failure to protect shareholder interests in other environments. Countries such as Japan and Germany have not had active markets for corporate control largely because they have not needed them, not because they did not want or could not tolerate them. They have not needed active takeover markets because of the efficiency with which their traditional contractual governance systems have dealt with hazards associated with information asymmetries, investment in specialized assets, and the agency problems of large organizations. This efficiency has reduced the need to integrate vertically in order to secure upstream sources of supply or downstream markets. It has also blunted the need to exercise outright voting control in order to effect change in corporate strategies and policies detrimental to the welfare of the company's owners.

MALFUNCTIONS OF JAPANESE CORPORATE GOVERNANCE

This chapter's exposition of the merits of the Japanese corporate governance system should not obscure the fact that the system also embodies deficiencies and faces threats that, paradoxically, have sprung from its very success. Dominance in many product markets around the world, the retention of much of their cash flow, and fewer good investment opportunities in core businesses have resulted in considerable financial slack building up on the balance sheets of many Japanese corporations.[23] In conjunction with freer access to global capital markets, this has led to a recent distancing of Japanese industrial groups from their owner-lender banks, a widening of managerial discretion with respect to the allocation of resources, and a drive to escape dependence on a single industry. The resulting freedom from product and capital market discipline is prompting some Japanese managers to deploy cash in ways more likely to benefit themselves and other employees of the corporation by preserving jobs than to benefit other stakeholders, suppliers of capital in particular. The risky, probably uneconomic use of excess cash to speculate in financial markets and plunge into strategies of unrelated diversification are two major deployments of this nature.[24]

Widespread reliance on implicit contracting also gives rise to abuses. Extensive information sharing coupled with dealings on the basis of unwritten and even unspoken agreements with well known and routinely relied upon counterparties provides conditions amenable to illegal bribery, kickbacks, price fixing, and insider trading. The financial scandals that have rocked Japan's public and private sectors in recent years serve as unhappy reminders that the Japanese system can and is being abused.

Finally, as noted in the above discussion of the Japanese distribution sector (see the "Horizontal Rivalry" section of this chapter) it must be acknowledged that not all sectors of Japanese business are equal beneficiaries of the corporate governance system analyzed here. Predictably, when one of the major building blocks of Japanese corporate governance is missing—vigorous horizontal competition among efficient-scale rivals (in the case of the distribution sector)—efficiency is lacking, restraint of trade is in greater evidence, and overall sector performance is weak. Indeed, the common American view that many Japanese business practices are predicated upon restraint of trade, not transactional efficiency, is founded to a large extent upon experience with Japan's labyrinthine wholesale and retail distribution sectors, for they are the first and most costly impediments to the penetration of Japanese markets faced by most foreign competitors. Inaccurate generalizations about *all* of Japanese business tend to be predicated upon narrow experience with this one highly visible (to foreigners) sector.

REFORMING CORPORATE GOVERNANCE

As the world's capital and product markets integrate, and as companies domiciled in different nations engage in various cross-border investments and transactions (e.g., joint ventures, minority equity purchases, cross-border acquisitions), different national systems of corporate governance are increasingly coming into direct contact and, sometimes, conflict with one another. As they do so, the advantages and limitations of each are tested and become more clearly exposed. Given inequalities in the effectiveness of one system or another in addressing common hazards surrounding asset ownership and control, it is inevitable that a kind of Darwinistic competition among systems of governance will emerge. The economic institutions of capitalism are not static, and it is a good and healthy thing that they should adapt and evolve through exposure to competing systems.

The analysis of the Japanese system of corporate governance presented here suggests that, the efforts of T. Boone Pickens notwithstanding, there may be good reason to anticipate the eventual dominance of a system of corporate governance more nearly like what is observed in Japan, Germany, and other parts of western Europe than in the Anglo-American family of nations. Accordingly, recommendations to reform Japanese corporate governance practices in such a way as to reduce long-term dependence on preferred suppliers and customers should be viewed with healthy skepticism. Cross-shareholdings, reciprocal trade arrangements, presidents councils, and so forth, play legitimate roles in the process of good corporate governance and should not lightly be removed or weakened on grounds of restraint of trade.

A more enlightened role for government to take with respect to the reform of corporate governance in Japan would be to promulgate and vigorously enforce ethics laws designed to curtail abuses of private information or the illegal enrichment of individual stakeholders at the expense of others. It is abuses such as these that call the fairness of the Japanese system into question, and that corrode the critical basis of trust upon which the long-term success of the Japanese corporate governance system at large depends so critically. Japan should also seek to ensure that vigorous horizontal rivalry in product markets is achieved in those areas where it is presently deficient (e.g., wholesale and retail distribution), and maintained where it is already present and thriving.

In this latter regard, it should be noted that Japan has nothing to fear from opening itself further to foreign products and capital. Admittedly, doing so will expose some companies to unwanted attacks, as was the case with Koito Manufacturing, and will result in some casualties. But in the long run, given the efficacious effects of vigorous horizontal rivalry on corporate governance, Japan as a nation can only benefit from the presence of foreign investors and rivals.

NOTES

1. See Celia Hampton, "Long Arm of U.S. Antitrust Law," *Financial Times* (London: April 30, 1992), p. 12; and Donald I. Baker and Donald B. Ayer, "A Misguided Assault on Keiretsu, *The Sunday New York Times* (New York: March 22, 1992), p. F13.
2. For a more complete summary and further discussion of laws that shape American corporate governance, see Franklin R. Edwards and Robert A. Eisenbeis, "Financial Institutions and Corporate Myopia: An International Perspective," (unpublished working paper prepared in connection with the research project, *Capital Choices: Changing the Way America Invests in Industry,* jointly sponsored by the Council on Competitiveness and Harvard Business School's Division of Research; December 7, 1990), pp. 53–71; and Robert W. Lightfoot, "Note on Corporate Governance Systems: the United States, Japan, and Germany," (Harvard Business School Case No. 292-012). The discussion appearing in this section is based primarily upon these works.
3. For more on this last point, see Michael C. Jensen, "The Eclipse of the Public Corporation," *Harvard Business Review*, September-October 1989, pp. 61–74.
4. See Kester (July 1991) for further examples and discussion of investment in specialized assets.
5. W. Carl Kester, "Governance, Contracting, and Investment Time Horizons" (Harvard Business School working paper, 92-003), July 1991, pp. 9–14.
6. And even Honda can accurately be described as maintaining stable relationships with preferred suppliers, subcontractors, and financial intermediaries. Moreover, Honda's 1990 corporate reorganization of its car, motorcycle, and power products operations into three separate organizations could eventually pave the way for a spinning off of these units into separate but related companies that might one day be the core of a genuine Honda group.
7. W. Carl Kester, *Japanese Takeovers: The Global Contest for Corporate Control* (Boston: Harvard Business School Press, 1991), pp. 54–55.
8. Kester (July 1991), *Ibid.*, pp. 16–17.
9. See Kester (July 1991), pp. 18-21, for further discussion of contracting within the

Japanese automotive industry. Ballon and Tomita (1988, p. 54) claim more generally that a typical Japanese contract often does not even state definitely the transactions at stake so as not to restrict the flexibility considered necessary for good performance.

10. Kester, 1991. *Ibid.*, pp. 63–66.
11. Kester, 1991, *Ibid.*
12. Kester, July 1991, *Ibid.*, p. 23.
13. Kester, 1991, *Ibid.*, p. 63.
14. Dodwell Marketing Consultants, Industrial Groupings in Japan 1990/91, 9th ed. (Tokyo: Dodwell Marketing Consultants, 1990).
15. Dodwell Marketing Consultants, The Structure of the Japanese Auto Parts Industry, 4th ed. (Tokyo: Dodwell Marketing Consultants, 1990), p. 36.
16. Kester (July 1991), *Ibid.*, pp. 27–29.
17. Kester (July 1991), *Ibid.*, pp. 29–31.
18. Kester (1991), *Ibid.*, pp. 88–94.
19. Thomas K. McCraw and Patricia A. O'Brien, "Production and Distribution: Competition Policy and Industry Structure," in *American Versus Japan*, Thomas K. McCraw, ed. (Boston: Harvard Business School Press, 1986), pp. 77–116.
20. Ziegler, Rolf; Donald Bender, and Hermann Biehler. "Industry and Banking in the German Corporate Network," in *Networks of Corporate Power: A Comparative Analysis of Ten Countries.* Frans N. Stokman, Rolf Ziegler, and John Scott, eds. (Cambridge, U.K.: Polity Press, 1985), pp. 91–111.
21. Kester (July 1991), *Ibid.*, pp. 48–51.
22. For further discussion of this point, see Oliver E. Williamson, "Antitrust Enforcement: Where it has been; where it is going," in John Craven, ed., *Industrial Organization, Antitrust, and Public Policy*. (Boston: Kluwer-Nijhoff Publishing), pp. 41–68.
23. Kester (1991), *Ibid.*, pp. 189–93.
24. Kester (1991), *Ibid.*, pp. 219–35.

REFERENCES

Baker, Donald I., and Donald B. Ayer, "A Misguided Assault on Keiretsu." *The Sunday New York Times*. (March 22, 1992), p. F13.

Ballon, Robert J., and Iwao Tomita. *The Financial Behavior of Japanese Corporations*. Tokyo: Kodansha International (1988).

Dodwell Marketing Consultants. *Industrial Groupings in Japan, 1990-1991* (9th ed.), Tokyo: Dodwell Marketing Consultants (1990).

Dodwell Marketing Consultants. *The Structure of the Japanese Auto Parts Industry*. 4th ed. (Tokyo: Dodwell Marketing Consultants, 1990).

Edwards, Franklin R., and Robert A. Eisenbeis. "Financial Institutions and Corporate Myopia: An International Perspective." Columbia University, New York, and University of North Carolina, Chapel Hill, NC, working paper (December 7, 1990).

Hampton, Celia. "Long Arm of U.S. Antitrust Law." *Financial Times*. (April 30,

1992), p. 12.

Jensen, Michael C. "The Eclipse of the Public Corporation." *Harvard Business Review* (September-October 1989), pp. 61–74.

Kester, W. Carl. "Governance, Contracting, and Investment Time Horizons." Boston: Harvard Business School working paper 92-003 (July 1991).

Kester, W. Carl. *Japanese Takeovers: The Global Contest for Corporate Control.* Boston: Harvard Business School Press (1991).

Kigyo Shudan no Jittai ni tsuite (June 21, 1983).

Lightfoot, Robert W. "Note on Corporate Governance Systems: The United States, Japan, and Germany." Boston: Harvard Business School Case No. 292-012.

McCraw, Thomas K., and Patricia A. O'Brien. "Production and Distribution: Competition Policy and Distribution: Competition Policy and Industry Structure," in Thomas K. McCraw (ed.), *American Versus Japan*, Boston: Harvard Business School Press (1986), pp. 77–116.

Williamson, Oliver E. *The Economic Institutions of Capitalism: Firms, Markets, Relational Contracting*. New York: Free Press (1985).

Williamson, Oliver, "Antitrust Enforcement: Where it has been; where it is going." In John Craven (ed.), *Industrial Organization, Antitrust, and Public Policy.* Boston: Kluwer-Nijhoff Publishing (1990), pp. 41–68.

Ziegler, Rolf; Donald Bender, and Hermann Biehler. "Industry and Banking in the German Corporate Network," in Frans N. Stokman, Rolf Ziegler, and John Scott (eds.), *Networks of Corporate Power: A Comparative Analysis of Ten Countries*. Cambridge, U.K.: Polity Press (1985), pp. 91–111.

ABOUT THE AUTHORS

Yakov Amihud is Professor of Finance at the Stern School of Business, New York University.

Frederick D.S. Choi is Research Professor of Accounting and International Business at the Stern School of Business, New York University.

Jean Dermine is Professor of Finance at INSEAD, Fontainebleau, France.

Jeffrey A. Frankel is Professor of Economics, University of California, Berkeley.

Kevin Hebner is Assistant Professor, Faculty of Administrative Studies, York University and Visiting Professor, Institute of Economic Research, Kyoto University.

Takato Hiraki is Associate Professor of Finance at the Graduate School of International Management, International University of Japan.

W. Carl Kester is Professor of Business Administration at the Graduate School of Business Administration, Harvard University.

Yui Kimura is Associate Dean and Associate Professor of Business Administration at the Graduate School of International Management, International University of Japan.

Bevis Longstreth is a Partner at the law firm of Debevoise & Plimpton, New York City. Ivan P. Mattei and David P. Mason are Associates with the law firm of Debevoise & Plimpton in New York City.

Timothy A. Luehrman is Associate Professor at the Graduate School of Business Administration, Harvard University.

Haim Mendelson is Professor at the Graduate School of Business, Stanford University.

Young S. Park is Assistant Professor of Finance at the Graduate School of International Management, International University of Japan.

Thomas A. Pugel is Professor of Economics and International Business at the Stern School of Business, New York University.

Clifford W. Smith, Jr., is Clarey Professor of Finance at the William E. Simon Graduate School of Business Administration, University of Rochester.

Roy C. Smith is Professor of Finance at the Stern School of Business, New York University.

Toshiaki Tachibanaki is Professor of Economics, Institute of Economic Research, Kyoto University.

Shinji Takagi is Associate Professor of Economics, University of Osaka.

Ingo Walter is the Charles Simon Professor of Applied Financial Economics, Stern School of Business, New York University and Director, New York University Salomon Center, and Swiss Bank Corporation Professor of International Management at INSEAD, Fontainebleau, France.

Shinichi Watanabe is Associate Professor of Economics at the Graduate School of International Relations, International University of Japan.

INDEX

J

K

L